Using MPI-2

Scientific and Engineering Computation

Janusz Kowalik, editor

Using MPI-2
Advanced Features of the Message-Passing Interface

William Gropp
Ewing Lusk
Rajeev Thakur

The MIT Press
Cambridge, Massachusetts
London, England

This book was set in LaTeX by the authors and was printed and bound in the United States of America.

Library of Congress Cataloging-in-Publication Data
Gropp, William.
   Using MPI-2: advanced features of the message-passing interface /
   William Gropp, Ewing Lusk, Rajeev Thakur.
        p.   cm.—(Scientific and engineering computation)
   Includes bibliographical references and index.
   ISBN 0-262-057133-1 (pb.: alk. paper)
   1. Parallel programming (Computer science). 2. Parallel computers—
Programming. 3. Computer interfaces. I. Lusk, Ewing. II. Thakur,
Rajeev. III. Title. IV. Series.
QA76.642.G762   1999
005.2′75–dc21   99-042972
                                      CIP

To Christopher Gropp, Brigid Lusk, and Pratibha and Sharad Thakur

Contents

Series Foreword

The world of modern computing potentially offers many helpful methods and tools to scientists and engineers, but the fast pace of change in computer hardware, software, and algorithms often makes practical use of the newest computing technology difficult. The Scientific and Engineering Computation series focuses on rapid advances in computing technologies, with the aim of facilitating transfer of these technologies to applications in science and engineering. It will include books on theories, methods, and original applications in such areas as parallelism, large-scale simulations, time-critical computing, computer-aided design and engineering, use of computers in manufacturing, visualization of scientific data, and human-machine interface technology.

The series is intended to help scientists and engineers understand the current world of advanced computation and to anticipate future developments that will affect their computing environments and open up new capabilities and modes of computation.

This book describes how to use advanced features of the Message-Passing Interface (MPI), a communication library specification for both parallel computers and workstation networks. MPI has been developed as a community standard for message passing and related operations. Its adoption by both users and implementers has provided the parallel-programming community with the portability and features needed to develop application programs and parallel libraries that will tap the power of today's (and tomorrow's) high-performance computers.

Janusz S. Kowalik

Preface

MPI (Message-Passing Interface) is a standard library interface for writing parallel programs. MPI was developed in two phases by an open forum of parallel computer vendors, library writers, and application developers. The first phase took place in 1993–1994 and culminated in the first release of the MPI standard, which we call MPI-1. A number of important topics in parallel computing had been deliberately left out of MPI-1 in order to speed its release, and the MPI Forum began meeting again in 1995 to address these topics, as well as to make minor corrections and clarifications to MPI-1 that had been discovered to be necessary. The MPI-2 Standard was released in the summer of 1997. The official Standard documents for MPI-1 (the current version as updated by the MPI-2 forum is 1.2) and MPI-2 are available on the Web at `http://www.mpi-forum.org`. More polished versions of the standard documents are published by MIT Press in the two volumes of *MPI—The Complete Reference* [27, 79].

These official documents and the books that describe them are organized so that they will be useful as reference works. The structure of the presentation is according to the chapters of the standard, which in turn reflects the subcommittee structure of the MPI Forum.

In 1994, two of the present authors, together with Anthony Skjellum, wrote *Using MPI: Portable Programming with the Message-Passing Interface* [31], a quite differently structured book on MPI-1, taking a more tutorial approach to the material. A second edition [32] of that book has now appeared as a companion to this one, covering the most recent additions and clarifications to the material of MPI-1, and bringing it up to date in various other ways as well. This book takes the same tutorial, example-driven approach to its material that *Using MPI* does, applying it to the topics of MPI-2. These topics include parallel I/O, dynamic process management, remote memory operations, and external interfaces.

About This Book

Following the pattern set in *Using MPI*, we do not follow the order of chapters in the MPI-2 Standard, nor do we follow the order of material within a chapter as in the Standard. Instead, we have organized the material in each chapter according to the complexity of the programs we use as examples, starting with simple examples and moving to more complex ones. We do assume that the reader is familiar with at least the simpler aspects of MPI-1. It is not necessary to have read *Using MPI*, but it wouldn't hurt.

We begin in Chapter 1 with an overview of the current situation in parallel computing, many aspects of which have changed in the past five years. We summarize the new topics covered in MPI-2 and their relationship to the current and (what we see as) the near-future parallel computing environment.

MPI-2 is not "MPI-1, only more complicated." There are simple and useful parts of MPI-2, and in Chapter 2 we introduce them with simple examples of parallel I/O, dynamic process management, and remote memory operations.

In Chapter 3 we dig deeper into parallel I/O, perhaps the "missing feature" most requested by users of MPI-1. We describe the parallel I/O features of MPI, how to use them in a graduated series of examples, and how they can be used to get high performance, particularly on today's parallel/high-performance file systems.

In Chapter 4 we explore some of the issues of synchronization between senders and receivers of data. We examine in detail what happens (and what must happen) when data is moved between processes. This sets the stage for explaining the design of MPI's remote memory operations in the following chapters.

Chapters 5 and 6 cover MPI's approach to remote memory operations. This can be regarded as the MPI approach to shared memory, since shared-memory and remote-memory operations have much in common. At the same time they are different, since access to the remote memory is through MPI function calls, not some kind of language-supported construct (such as a global pointer or array). This difference arises because MPI is intended to be portable to distributed-memory machines, even heterogeneous clusters.

Because remote memory access operations are different in many ways from message passing, the discussion of remote memory access is divided into two chapters. Chapter 5 covers the basics of remote memory access and a simple synchronization model. Chapter 6 covers more general types of remote memory access and more complex synchronization models.

Chapter 7 covers MPI's relatively straightforward approach to dynamic process management, including both spawning new processes and dynamically connecting to running MPI programs.

The recent rise of the importance of small to medium-size SMPs (shared-memory multiprocessors) means that the interaction of MPI with threads is now far more important than at the time of MPI-1. MPI-2 does not define a standard interface to thread libraries because such an interface already exists, namely, the POSIX threads interface [42]. MPI instead provides a number of features designed to facilitate the use of multithreaded MPI programs. We describe these features in Chapter 8.

In Chapter 9 we describe some advanced features of MPI-2 that are particularly useful to library writers. These features include defining new file data representations, using MPI's external interface functions to build layered libraries, support for mixed-language programming, attribute caching, and error handling.

In Chapter 10 we summarize our journey through the new types of parallel programs enabled by MPI-2, comment on the current status of MPI-2 implementations, and speculate on future directions for MPI.

Appendix A contains the C, C++, and Fortran bindings for all the MPI-2 functions.

Appendix B describes how to obtain supplementary material for this book, including complete source code for the examples, and related MPI materials that are available via anonymous `ftp` and on the World Wide Web.

In Appendix C we discuss some of the surprises, questions, and problems in MPI, including what we view as some shortcomings in the MPI-2 Standard as it is now. We can't be too critical (because we shared in its creation!), but experience and reflection have caused us to reexamine certain topics.

Appendix D covers the MPI program launcher, `mpiexec`, which the MPI-2 Standard recommends that all implementations support. The availability of a standard interface for running MPI programs further increases the portability of MPI applications, and we hope that this material will encourage MPI users to expect and demand `mpiexec` from the suppliers of MPI implementations.

In addition to the normal subject index, there is an index for the usage examples and definitions of the MPI-2 functions, constants, and terms used in this book.

We try to be impartial in the use of C, Fortran, and C++ in the book's examples. The MPI Standard has tried to keep the syntax of its calls similar in C and Fortran; for C++ the differences are inevitably a little greater, although the MPI Forum adopted a conservative approach to the C++ bindings rather than a complete object library. When we need to refer to an MPI function without regard to language, we use the C version just because it is a little easier to read in running text.

This book is not a reference manual, in which MPI functions would be grouped according to functionality and completely defined. Instead we present MPI functions informally, in the context of example programs. Precise definitions are given in volume 2 of *MPI—The Complete Reference* [27] and in the MPI-2 Standard [59]. Nonetheless, to increase the usefulness of this book to someone working with MPI, we have provided the calling sequences in C, Fortran, and C++ for each MPI-2 function that we discuss. These listings can be found set off in boxes located near where the functions are introduced. C bindings are given in ANSI C style. Arguments that can be of several types (typically message buffers) are defined as `void*` in C. In the Fortran boxes, such arguments are marked as being of type `<type>`. This means that one of the appropriate Fortran data types should be used. To

find the "binding box" for a given MPI routine, one should use the appropriate
bold-face reference in the Function and Term Index: **C** for C, **f90** for Fortran, and
C++ for C++. Another place to find this information is in Appendix A, which
lists all MPI functions in alphabetical order for each language.

Acknowledgments

We thank all those who participated in the MPI-2 Forum. These are the people who
created MPI-2, discussed a wide variety of topics (many not included here) with
seriousness, intelligence, and wit, and thus shaped our ideas on these areas of par-
allel computing. The following people (besides ourselves) attended the MPI Forum
meetings at one time or another during the formulation of MPI-2: Greg Astfalk,
Robert Babb, Ed Benson, Rajesh Bordawekar, Pete Bradley, Peter Brennan, Ron
Brightwell, Maciej Brodowicz, Eric Brunner, Greg Burns, Margaret Cahir, Pang
Chen, Ying Chen, Albert Cheng, Yong Cho, Joel Clark, Lyndon Clarke, Laurie
Costello, Dennis Cottel, Jim Cownie, Zhenqian Cui, Suresh Damodaran-Kamal,
Raja Daoud, Judith Devaney, David DiNucci, Doug Doefler, Jack Dongarra, Terry
Dontje, Nathan Doss, Anne Elster, Mark Fallon, Karl Feind, Sam Fineberg, Craig
Fischberg, Stephen Fleischman, Ian Foster, Hubertus Franke, Richard Frost, Al
Geist, Robert George, David Greenberg, John Hagedorn, Kei Harada, Leslie Hart,
Shane Hebert, Rolf Hempel, Tom Henderson, Alex Ho, Hans-Christian Hoppe,
Steven Huss-Lederman, Joefon Jann, Terry Jones, Carl Kesselman, Koichi Kon-
ishi, Susan Kraus, Steve Kubica, Steve Landherr, Mario Lauria, Mark Law, Juan
Leon, Lloyd Lewins, Ziyang Lu, Andrew Lumsdaine, Bob Madahar, Peter Madams,
John May, Oliver McBryan, Brian McCandless, Tyce McLarty, Thom McMahon,
Harish Nag, Nick Nevin, Jarek Nieplocha, Bill Nitzberg, Ron Oldfield, Peter Os-
sadnik, Steve Otto, Peter Pacheco, Yoonho Park, Perry Partow, Pratap Pattnaik,
Elsie Pierce, Paul Pierce, Heidi Poxon, Jean-Pierre Prost, Boris Protopopov, James
Pruyve, Rolf Rabenseifner, Joe Rieken, Peter Rigsbee, Tom Robey, Anna Roun-
behler, Nobutoshi Sagawa, Arindam Saha, Eric Salo, Darren Sanders, William
Saphir, Eric Sharakan, Andrew Sherman, Fred Shirley, Lance Shuler, A. Gordon
Smith, Marc Snir, Ian Stockdale, David Taylor, Stephen Taylor, Greg Tensa, Mary-
dell Tholburn, Dick Treumann, Simon Tsang, Manuel Ujaldon, David Walker, Jer-
rell Watts, Klaus Wolf, Parkson Wong, and Dave Wright. We also acknowledge
the valuable input from many persons around the world who participated in MPI
Forum discussions via e-mail.

Our interactions with the many users of MPICH have been the source of ideas, examples, and code fragments. Other members of the MPICH group at Argonne have made critical contributions to MPICH and other MPI-related tools that we have used in the preparation of this book. Particular thanks go to Debbie Swider for her enthusiastic and insightful work on MPICH implementation and interaction with users, and to Omer Zaki and Anthony Chan for their work on Upshot and Jumpshot, the performance visualization tools we use with MPICH.

We thank PALLAS GmbH, particularly Hans-Christian Hoppe and Thomas Kentemich, for testing some of the MPI-2 code examples in this book on the Fujitsu MPI implementation.

Gail Pieper, technical writer in the Mathematics and Computer Science Division at Argonne, was our indispensable guide in matters of style and usage and vastly improved the readability of our prose.

Using MPI-2

1 Introduction

When the MPI Standard was first released in 1994, its ultimate significance was unknown. Although the Standard was the result of a consensus among parallel computer vendors, computer scientists, and application developers, no one knew to what extent implementations would appear or how many parallel applications would rely on it.

Now the situation has clarified. All parallel computing vendors supply their users with MPI implementations, and there are freely available implementations that both compete with vendor implementations on their platforms and supply MPI solutions for heterogeneous networks. Applications large and small have been ported to MPI, and new applications are being written. MPI's goal of stimulating the development of parallel libraries by enabling them to be portable has been realized, and an increasing number of applications become parallel purely through the use of parallel libraries.

This book is about how to use MPI-2, the collection of advanced features that were added to MPI by the second MPI Forum. In this chapter we review in more detail the origins of both MPI-1 and MPI-2. We give an overview of what new functionality has been added to MPI by the release of the MPI-2 Standard. We conclude with a summary of the goals of this book and its organization.

1.1 Background

We present here a brief history of MPI, since some aspects of MPI can be better understood in the context of its development. An excellent description of the history of MPI can also be found in [36].

1.1.1 Ancient History

In the early 1990s, high-performance computing was in the process of converting from the vector machines that had dominated scientific computing in the 1980s to massively parallel processors (MPPs) such as the IBM SP-1, the Thinking Machines CM-5, and the Intel Paragon. In addition, people were beginning to use networks of desktop workstations as parallel computers. Both the MPPs and the workstation networks shared the message-passing model of parallel computation, but programs were not portable. The MPP vendors competed with one another on the syntax of their message-passing libraries. Portable libraries, such as PVM [24], p4 [8], and TCGMSG [35], appeared from the research community and became widely used on workstation networks. Some of them allowed portability to MPPs as well, but there was no unified, common syntax that would enable a program to run in all the parallel environments that were suitable for it from the hardware point of view.

1.1.2 The MPI Forum

Starting with a workshop in 1992, the MPI Forum was formally organized at Supercomputing '92. MPI succeeded because the effort attracted a broad spectrum of the parallel computing community. Vendors sent their best technical people. The authors of portable libraries participated, and applications programmers were represented as well. The MPI Forum met every six weeks starting in January 1993 and released MPI in the summer of 1994.

To complete its work in a timely manner, the Forum strictly circumscribed its topics. It developed a standard for the strict message-passing model, in which all data transfer is a cooperative operation among participating processes. It was assumed that the number of processes was fixed and that processes were started by some (unspecified) mechanism external to MPI. I/O was ignored, and language bindings were limited to C and Fortran 77. Within these limits, however, the Forum delved deeply, producing a very full-featured message-passing library. In addition to creating a portable syntax for familiar message-passing functions, MPI introduced (or substantially extended the development of) a number of new concepts, such as derived datatypes, contexts, and communicators. MPI constituted a major advance over all existing message-passing libraries in terms of features, precise semantics, and the potential for highly optimized implementations.

In the year following its release, MPI was taken up enthusiastically by users, and a 1995 survey by the Ohio Supercomputer Center showed that even its more esoteric features found users. The MPICH portable implementation [30], layered on top of existing vendor systems, was available immediately, since it had evolved along with the standard. Other portable implementations appeared, particularly LAM [7], and then vendor implementations in short order, some of them leveraging MPICH. The first edition of *Using MPI* [31] appeared in the fall of 1994, and we like to think that it helped win users to the new Standard.

But the very success of MPI-1 drew attention to what was not there. PVM users missed dynamic process creation, and several users needed parallel I/O. The success of the Cray *shmem* library on the Cray T3D and the active-message library on the CM-5 made users aware of the advantages of "one-sided" operations in algorithm design. The MPI Forum would have to go back to work.

1.1.3   The MPI-2 Forum

The modern history of MPI begins in the spring of 1995, when the Forum resumed its meeting schedule, with both veterans of MPI-1 and about an equal number of new participants. In the previous three years, much had changed in parallel computing, and these changes would accelerate during the two years the MPI-2 Forum would meet.

On the hardware front, a consolidation of MPP vendors occurred, with Thinking Machines Corp., Meiko, and Intel all leaving the marketplace. New entries such as Convex (now absorbed into Hewlett-Packard) and SGI (now having absorbed Cray Research) championed a shared-memory model of parallel computation although they supported MPI (passing messages through shared memory), and many applications found that the message-passing model was still well suited for extracting peak performance on shared-memory (really NUMA) hardware. Small-scale shared-memory multiprocessors (SMPs) became available from workstation vendors and even PC manufacturers. Fast commodity-priced networks, driven by the PC marketplace, became so inexpensive that clusters of PCs combined with inexpensive networks, started to appear as "home-brew" parallel supercomputers. A new federal program, the Accelerated Strategic Computing Initiative (ASCI), funded the development of the largest parallel computers ever built, with thousands of processors. ASCI planned for its huge applications to use MPI.

On the software front, MPI, as represented by MPI-1, became ubiquitous as the application programming interface (API) for the message-passing model. The model itself remained healthy. Even on flat shared-memory and NUMA (nonuniform memory access) machines, users found the message-passing model a good way to control cache behavior and thus performance. The perceived complexity of programming with the message-passing model was alleviated by two developments. The first was the convenience of the MPI interface itself, once programmers became more comfortable with it as the result of both experience and tutorial presentations. The second was the appearance of libraries that hide much of the MPI-level complexity from the application programmer. Examples are PETSc [3], ScaLAPACK [12], and PLAPACK [94]. This second development is especially satisfying because it was an explicit design goal for the MPI Forum to encourage the development of libraries by including features that libraries particularly needed.

At the same time, non-message-passing models have been explored. Some of these may be beneficial if actually adopted as portable standards; others may still require interaction with MPI to achieve scalability. Here we briefly summarize two promising, but quite different approaches.

Explicit multithreading is the use of an API that manipulates threads (see [32] for definitions) within a single address space. This approach may be sufficient on systems that can devote a large number of CPUs to servicing a single process, but interprocess communication will still need to be used on scalable systems. The MPI API has been designed to be thread safe. However, not all implementations are thread safe. An MPI-2 feature is to allow applications to request and MPI implementations to report their level of thread safety (see Chapter 8).

In some cases the compiler generates the thread parallelism. In such cases the application or library uses only the MPI API, and additional parallelism is uncovered by the compiler and expressed in the code it generates. Some compilers do this unaided; others respond to directives in the form of specific comments in the code.

OpenMP is a proposed standard for compiler directives for expressing parallelism, with particular emphasis on loop-level parallelism. Both C [68] and Fortran [67] versions exist.

Thus the MPI-2 Forum met during time of great dynamism in parallel programming models. What did the Forum do, and what did it come up with?

1.2   What's New in MPI-2?

The MPI-2 Forum began meeting in March of 1995. Since the MPI-1 Forum was judged to have been a successful effort, the new Forum procedures were kept the same as for MPI-1. Anyone was welcome to attend the Forum meetings, which were held every six weeks. Minutes of the meetings were posted to the Forum mailing lists, and chapter drafts were circulated publicly for comments between meetings. At meetings, subcommittees for various chapters met and hammered out details, and the final version of the standard was the result of multiple votes by the entire Forum.

The first action of the Forum was to correct errors and clarify a number of issues that had caused misunderstandings in the original document of July 1994, which was retroactively labeled MPI-1.0. These minor modifications, encapsulated as MPI-1.1, were released in May 1995. Corrections and clarifications to MPI-1 topics continued during the next two years, and the MPI-2 document contains MPI-1.2 as a chapter (Chapter 3) of the MPI-2 release, which is the current version of the MPI standard. MPI-1.2 also contains a number of topics that belong in spirit to the MPI-1 discussion, although they were added by the MPI-2 Forum.

MPI-2 has three "large," completely new areas, which represent extensions of the MPI programming model substantially beyond the strict message-passing model represented by MPI-1. These areas are parallel I/O, remote memory operations, and dynamic process management. In addition, MPI-2 introduces a number of features designed to make all of MPI more robust and convenient to use, such as external interface specifications, C++ and Fortran-90 bindings, support for threads, and mixed-language programming.

1.2.1 Parallel I/O

The parallel I/O part of MPI-2, sometimes just called MPI-IO, originated independently of the Forum activities, as an effort within IBM to explore the analogy between input/output and message passing. After all, one can think of writing to a file as analogous to sending a message to the file system and reading from a file as receiving a message from it. Furthermore, any parallel I/O system is likely to need collective operations, ways of defining noncontiguous data layouts both in memory and in files, and nonblocking operations. In other words, it will need a number of concepts that have already been satisfactorily specified and implemented in MPI. The first study of the MPI-IO idea was carried out at IBM Research [71]. The effort was expanded to include a group at NASA Ames, and the resulting specification appeared in [15]. After that, an open e-mail discussion group was formed, and this group released a series of proposals, culminating in [90]. At that point the group merged with the MPI Forum, and I/O became a part of MPI-2. The I/O specification evolved further over the course of the Forum meetings, until MPI-2 was finalized in July 1997.

In general, I/O in MPI-2 can be thought of as Unix I/O plus quite a lot more. That is, MPI does include analogues of the basic operations of `open`, `close`, `seek`, `read`, and `write`. The arguments for these functions are similar to those of the corresponding Unix I/O operations, making an initial port of existing programs to MPI relatively straightforward. The purpose of parallel I/O in MPI, however, is to achieve much higher performance than the Unix API can deliver, and serious users of MPI must avail themselves of the more advanced features, which include

- noncontiguous access in both memory and file,
- collective I/O operations,
- use of explicit offsets to avoid separate `seek`s,
- both individual and shared file pointers,
- nonblocking I/O,
- portable and customized data representations, and

- hints for the implementation and file system.

We will explore in detail in Chapter 3 exactly how to exploit these features. We will find out there just how the I/O API defined by MPI enables optimizations that the Unix I/O API precludes.

1.2.2 Remote Memory Operations

The hallmark of the message-passing model is that data is moved from the address space of one process to that of another by means of a cooperative operation such as a `send`/`receive` pair. This restriction sharply distinguishes the message-passing model from the shared-memory model, in which processes have access to a common pool of memory and can simply perform ordinary memory operations (load from, store into) on some set of addresses.

In MPI-2, an API is defined that provides elements of the shared-memory model in an MPI environment. These are called MPI's "one-sided" or "remote memory" operations. Their design was governed by the need to

- balance efficiency and portability across several classes of architectures, including shared-memory multiprocessors (SMPs), nonuniform memory access (NUMA) machines, distributed-memory massively parallel processors (MPPs), SMP clusters, and even heterogeneous networks;
- retain the "look and feel" of MPI-1;
- deal with subtle memory behavior issues, such as cache coherence and sequential consistency; and
- separate synchronization from data movement to enhance performance.

The resulting design is based on the idea of remote memory access *windows*: portions of each process's address space that it explicitly exposes to remote memory operations by other processes defined by an MPI communicator. Then the one-sided operations *put*, *get*, and *accumulate* can store into, load from, and update, respectively, the windows exposed by other processes. All remote memory operations are nonblocking, and synchronization operations are necessary to ensure their completion. A variety of such synchronizations operations are provided, some for simplicity, some for precise control, and some for their analogy with shared-memory synchronization operations. In Chapter 4, we explore some of the issues of synchronization between senders and receivers of data. Chapters 5 and 6 describe the remote memory operations of MPI-2 in detail.

1.2.3   Dynamic Process Management

The third major departure from the programming model defined by MPI-1 is the ability of an MPI process to participate in the creation of new MPI processes or to establish communication with MPI processes that have been started separately. The main issues faced in designing an API for dynamic process management are

- maintaining simplicity and flexibility;
- interacting with the operating system, the resource manager, and the process manager in a complex system software environment; and
- avoiding race conditions that compromise correctness.

The key to correctness is to make the dynamic process management operations *collective*, both among the processes doing the creation of new processes and among the new processes being created. The resulting sets of processes are represented in an *intercommunicator*. Intercommunicators (communicators containing two groups of processes rather than one) are an esoteric feature of MPI-1, but are fundamental for the MPI-2 dynamic process operations. The two families of operations defined in MPI-2, both based on intercommunicators, are creating of new sets of processes, called *spawning*, and establishing communications with pre-existing MPI programs, called *connecting*. The latter capability allows applications to have parallel-client/parallel-server structures of processes. Details of the dynamic process management operations can be found in Chapter 7.

1.2.4   Odds and Ends

Besides the above "big three," the MPI-2 specification covers a number of issues that were not discussed in MPI-1.

Extended collective operations.   Extended collective operations in MPI-2 are analogous to the collective operations of MPI-1, but are defined for use on intercommunicators. (In MPI-1, collective operations are restricted to intracommunicators.) MPI-2 also extends the MPI-1 intracommunicator collective operations to allow an "in place" option, in which the send and receive buffers are the same.

C++ and Fortran 90.   In MPI-1, the only languages considered were C and Fortran, where Fortran was construed as Fortran 77. In MPI-2, all functions (including MPI-1 functions) have C++ bindings, and Fortran means Fortran 90 (or Fortran 95 [1]). For C++, the MPI-2 Forum chose a "minimal" approach in which the C++ versions of MPI functions are quite similar to the C versions, with classes defined for most of the MPI objects (such as `MPI::Request` for the C `MPI_Request`). Most MPI functions are member functions of MPI classes (easy to do because MPI has an object-oriented design), and others are in the MPI namespace.

MPI can't take advantage of some Fortran-90 features, such as array sections, and some MPI functions, particularly ones like `MPI_Send` that use a "choice" argument, can run afoul of Fortran's compile-time type checking for arguments to routines. This is usually harmless but can cause warning messages. However, the use of choice arguments does not match the letter of the Fortran standard; some Fortran compilers may require the use of a compiler option to relax this restriction in the Fortran language.[1] "Basic" and "extended" levels of support for Fortran 90 are provided in MPI-2. Essentially, basic support requires that `mpif.h` be valid in both fixed- and free-form format, and "extended" support includes an MPI module and some new functions that use parameterized types. Since these language extensions apply to all of MPI, not just MPI-2, they are covered in detail in the second edition of *Using MPI* [32] rather than in this book.

Language interoperability.   Language interoperability is a new feature in MPI-2. MPI-2 defines features, both by defining new functions and by specifying the behavior of implementations, that enable mixed-language programming, an area ignored by MPI-1.

External interfaces.   The external interfaces part of MPI makes it easy for libraries to extend MPI by accessing aspects of the implementation that are opaque in MPI-1. It aids in the construction of integrated tools, such as debuggers and performance analyzers, and is already being used in the early implementations of the MPI-2 I/O functionality [88].

Threads.   MPI-1, other than designing a thread-safe interface, ignored the issue of threads. In MPI-2, threads are recognized as a potential part of an MPI programming environment. Users can inquire of an implementation at run time what

---

[1] Because Fortran uses compile-time data-type matching rather than run-time data-type matching, it is invalid to make two calls to the same routine in which two different data types are used in the same argument position. This affects the "choice" arguments in the MPI Standard. For example, calling `MPI_Send` with a first argument of type `integer` and then with a first argument of type `real` is invalid in Fortran 77. In Fortran 90, when using the extended Fortran support, it is possible to allow arguments of different types by specifying the appropriate interfaces in the MPI module. However, this requires a different interface for each type and is not a practical approach for Fortran 90 derived types. MPI does provide for data-type checking, but does so at run time through a separate argument, the MPI datatype argument.

its level of thread-safety is. In cases where the implementation supports multiple levels of thread-safety, users can select the level that meets the application's needs while still providing the highest possible performance.

1.3 Reading This Book

This book is not a complete reference book for MPI-2. We leave that to the Standard itself [59] and to the two volumes of *MPI—The Complete Reference* [27, 79]. This book, like its companion *Using MPI* focusing on MPI-1, is organized around *using* the concepts of MPI-2 in application programs. Hence we take an iterative approach. In the preceding section we presented a very high level overview of the contents of MPI-2. In the next chapter we demonstrate the use of several of these concepts in simple example programs. Then in the following chapters we go into each of the major areas of MPI-2 in detail. We start with the parallel I/O capabilities of MPI in Chapter 3, since that has proven to be the single most desired part of MPI-2. In Chapter 4 we explore some of the issues of synchronization between senders and receivers of data. The complexity and importance of remote memory operations deserve two chapters, Chapters 5 and 6. The next chapter, Chapter 7, is on dynamic process management. We follow that with a chapter on MPI and threads, Chapter 8, since the mixture of multithreading and message passing is likely to become a widely used programming model. In Chapter 9 we consider some advanced features of MPI-2 that are particularly useful to library writers. We conclude in Chapter 10 with an assessment of possible future directions for MPI.

In each chapter we focus on example programs to illustrate MPI as it is actually used. Some miscellaneous minor topics will just appear where the example at hand seems to be a good fit for them. To find a discussion on a given topic, you can consult either the subject index or the function and term index, which is organized by MPI function name.

Finally, you may wish to consult the companion volume, *Using MPI: Portable Parallel Programming with the Message-passing Interface* [32]. Some topics considered by the MPI-2 Forum are small extensions to MPI-1 topics and are covered in the second edition (1999) of *Using MPI*. Although we have tried to make this volume self-contained, some of the examples have their origins in the examples of *Using MPI*.

Now, let's get started!

2 Getting Started with MPI-2

In this chapter we demonstrate what MPI-2 "looks like," while deferring the details to later chapters. We use relatively simple examples to give a flavor of the new capabilities provided by MPI-2. We focus on the main areas of parallel I/O, remote memory operations, and dynamic process management, but along the way demonstrate MPI in its new language bindings, C++ and Fortran 90, and touch on a few new features of MPI-2 as they come up.

2.1 Portable Process Startup

One small but useful new feature of MPI-2 is the recommendation of a standard method for starting MPI programs. The simplest version of this is

```
mpiexec -n 16 myprog
```

to run the program `myprog` with 16 processes.

Strictly speaking, how one starts MPI programs is outside the scope of the MPI specification, which says how to *write* MPI programs, not how to run them. MPI programs are expected to run in such a wide variety of computing environments, with different operating systems, job schedulers, process managers, and so forth, that standardizing on a multiple-process startup mechanism is impossible. Nonetheless, users who move their programs from one machine to another would like to be able to move their run scripts as well. Several current MPI implementations use `mpirun` to start MPI jobs. Since the `mpirun` programs are different from one implementation to another and expect different arguments, this has led to confusion, especially when multiple MPI implementations are installed on the same machine.

In light of all these considerations, the MPI Forum took the following approach, which appears in several other places in the MPI-2 Standard as well. It *recommended* to implementers that `mpiexec` be *one* of the methods for starting an MPI program, and then specified the formats of *some* of the arguments, which are *optional*. What it does say is that *if* an implementation supports startup of MPI jobs with `mpiexec` and uses the keywords for arguments that are described in the Standard, then the arguments must have the meanings specified in the Standard. That is,

```
mpiexec -n 32 myprog
```

should start 32 MPI processes with 32 as the size of MPI_COMM_WORLD, and not do something else. The name `mpiexec` was chosen so as to avoid conflict with the various currently established meanings of `mpirun`.

Besides the -n <numprocs> argument, mpiexec has a small number of other arguments whose behavior is specified by MPI. In each case, the format is a reserved keyword preceded by a hyphen and followed (after whitespace) by a value. The other keywords are -soft, -host, -arch, -wdir, -path, and -file. They are most simply explained by examples.

```
mpiexec -n 32 -soft 16 myprog
```

means that if 32 processes can't be started, because of scheduling constraints, for example, then start 16 instead. (The request for 32 processes is a "soft" request.)

```
mpiexec -n 4 -host denali -wdir /home/me/outfiles myprog
```

means to start 4 processes (by default, a request for a given number of processes is "hard") on the specified host machine ("denali" is presumed to be a machine name known to mpiexec) and have them start with their working directories set to /home/me/outfiles.

```
mpiexec -n 12 -soft 1:12 -arch sparc-solaris \
        -path /home/me/sunprogs myprog
```

says to try for 12 processes, but run any number up to 12 if 12 cannot be run, on a sparc-solaris machine, and look for myprog in the path /home/me/sunprogs, presumably the directory where the user compiles for that architecture. And finally,

```
mpiexec -file myfile
```

tells mpiexec to look in myfile for instructions on what to do. The format of myfile is left to the implementation. More details on mpiexec, including how to start multiple processes with different executables, can be found in Appendix D.

2.2   Parallel I/O

Parallel I/O in MPI starts with functions familiar to users of standard "language" I/O or libraries. MPI also has additional features necessary for performance and portability. In this section we focus on the MPI counterparts of opening and closing files and reading and writing contiguous blocks of data from/to them. At this level the main feature we show is how MPI can conveniently express parallelism in these operations. We give several variations of a simple example in which processes write a single array of integers to a file.

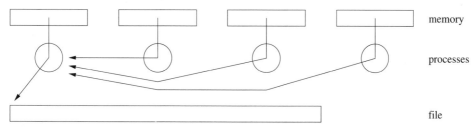

Figure 2.1
Sequential I/O from a parallel program

2.2.1 Non-Parallel I/O from an MPI Program

MPI-1 does not have any explicit support for parallel I/O. Therefore, MPI applications developed over the past few years have had to do their I/O by relying on the features provided by the underlying operating system, typically Unix. The most straightforward way of doing this is just to have one process do all I/O. Let us start our sequence of example programs in this section by illustrating this technique, diagrammed in Figure 2.1. We assume that the set of processes have a distributed array of integers to be written to a file. For simplicity, we assume that each process has 100 integers of the array, whose total length thus depends on how many processes there are. In the figure, the circles represent processes; the upper rectangles represent the block of 100 integers in each process's memory; and the lower rectangle represents the file to be written. A program to write such an array is shown in Figure 2.2. The program begins with each process initializing its portion of the array. All processes but process 0 send their section to process 0. Process 0 first writes its own section and then receives the contributions from the other processes *in turn* (the rank is specified in `MPI_Recv`) and writes them to the file.

This is often the first way I/O is done in a parallel program that has been converted from a sequential program, since no changes are made to the I/O part of the program. (Note that in Figure 2.2, if `numprocs` is 1, no MPI communication operations are performed.) There are a number of other reasons why I/O in a parallel program may be done this way.

• The parallel machine on which the program is running may support I/O only from one process.
• One can use sophisticated I/O libraries, perhaps written as part of a high-level data-management layer, that do not have parallel I/O capability.
• The resulting single file is convenient for handling outside the program (by `mv`, `cp`, or `ftp`, for example).

```c
/* example of sequential Unix write into a common file */
#include "mpi.h"
#include <stdio.h>
#define BUFSIZE 100

int main(int argc, char *argv[])
{
    int i, myrank, numprocs, buf[BUFSIZE];
    MPI_Status status;
    FILE *myfile;

    MPI_Init(&argc, &argv);
    MPI_Comm_rank(MPI_COMM_WORLD, &myrank);
    MPI_Comm_size(MPI_COMM_WORLD, &numprocs);
    for (i=0; i<BUFSIZE; i++)
        buf[i] = myrank * BUFSIZE + i;
    if (myrank != 0)
        MPI_Send(buf, BUFSIZE, MPI_INT, 0, 99, MPI_COMM_WORLD);
    else {
        myfile = fopen("testfile", "w");
        fwrite(buf, sizeof(int), BUFSIZE, myfile);
        for (i=1; i<numprocs; i++) {
            MPI_Recv(buf, BUFSIZE, MPI_INT, i, 99, MPI_COMM_WORLD,
                     &status);
            fwrite(buf, sizeof(int), BUFSIZE, myfile);
        }
        fclose(myfile);
    }
    MPI_Finalize();
    return 0;
}
```

Figure 2.2
Code for sequential I/O from a parallel program

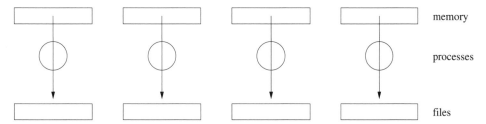

Figure 2.3
Parallel I/O to multiple files

• Performance may be enhanced because the process doing the I/O may be able to assemble large blocks of data. (In Figure 2.2, if process 0 had enough buffer space, it could have accumulated the data from other processes into a single buffer for one large write operation.)

The reason for not doing I/O this way is a single, but important one:

• The lack of parallelism limits performance and scalability, particularly if the underlying file system permits parallel physical I/O.

2.2.2 Non-MPI Parallel I/O from an MPI Program

In order to address the lack of parallelism, the next step in the migration of a sequential program to a parallel one is to have each process write to a separate file, thus enabling parallel data transfer, as shown in Figure 2.3. Such a program is shown in Figure 2.4. Here each process functions completely independently of the others with respect to I/O. Thus, each program is sequential with respect to I/O and can use language I/O. Each process opens its own file, writes to it, and closes it. We have ensured that the files are separate by appending each process's rank to the name of its output file.

The advantage of this approach is that the I/O operations can now take place in parallel and can still use sequential I/O libraries if that is desirable. The primary disadvantage is that the result of running the program is a set of files instead of a single file. This has multiple disadvantages:

• The files may have to be joined together before being used as input to another application.
• It may be required that the application that reads these files be a parallel program itself and be started with the exact same number of processes.
• It may be difficult to keep track of this set of files as a group, for moving them, copying them, or sending them across a network.

```
/* example of parallel Unix write into separate files */
#include "mpi.h"
#include <stdio.h>
#define BUFSIZE 100

int main(int argc, char *argv[])
{
    int i, myrank, buf[BUFSIZE];
    char filename[128];
    FILE *myfile;

    MPI_Init(&argc, &argv);
    MPI_Comm_rank(MPI_COMM_WORLD, &myrank);
    for (i=0; i<BUFSIZE; i++)
        buf[i] = myrank * BUFSIZE + i;
    sprintf(filename, "testfile.%d", myrank);
    myfile = fopen(filename, "w");
    fwrite(buf, sizeof(int), BUFSIZE, myfile);
    fclose(myfile);
    MPI_Finalize();
    return 0;
}
```

Figure 2.4
Non-MPI parallel I/O to multiple files

The performance may also suffer because individual processes may find their data to be in small contiguous chunks, causing many I/O operations with smaller data items. This may hurt performance more than can be compensated for by the parallelism. We will investigate this topic more deeply in Chapter 3.

2.2.3   MPI I/O to Separate Files

As our first MPI I/O program we will simply translate the program of Figure 2.4 so that all of the I/O operations are done with MPI. We do this to show how familiar I/O operations look in MPI. This program has the same advantages and disadvantages as the preceding version. Let us consider the differences between the programs shown in Figures 2.4 and 2.5 one by one; there are only four.

First, the declaration FILE has been replaced by MPI_File as the type of myfile. Note that myfile is now a variable of type MPI_File, rather than a pointer to an object of type FILE. The MPI function corresponding to fopen is (not surprisingly)

```
/* example of parallel MPI write into separate files */
#include "mpi.h"
#include <stdio.h>
#define BUFSIZE 100

int main(int argc, char *argv[])
{
    int i, myrank, buf[BUFSIZE];
    char filename[128];
    MPI_File myfile;

    MPI_Init(&argc, &argv);
    MPI_Comm_rank(MPI_COMM_WORLD, &myrank);
    for (i=0; i<BUFSIZE; i++)
        buf[i] = myrank * BUFSIZE + i;
    sprintf(filename, "testfile.%d", myrank);
    MPI_File_open(MPI_COMM_SELF, filename,
                  MPI_MODE_WRONLY | MPI_MODE_CREATE,
                  MPI_INFO_NULL, &myfile);
    MPI_File_write(myfile, buf, BUFSIZE, MPI_INT,
                   MPI_STATUS_IGNORE);
    MPI_File_close(&myfile);
    MPI_Finalize();
    return 0;
}
```

Figure 2.5
MPI I/O to separate files

called MPI_File_open. Let us consider the arguments in the call

```
    MPI_File_open(MPI_COMM_SELF, filename,
                  MPI_MODE_CREATE | MPI_MODE_WRONLY,
                  MPI_INFO_NULL, &myfile);
```

one by one. The first argument is a communicator. In a way, this is the most significant new component of I/O in MPI. Files in MPI are opened by a collection of processes identified by an MPI communicator. This ensures that those processes operating on a file together know which other processes are also operating on the file and can communicate with one another. Here, since each process is opening its own file for its own exclusive use, it uses the communicator MPI_COMM_SELF.

The second argument is a string representing the name of the file, as in `fopen`. The third argument is the mode in which the file is opened. Here it is being both created (or overwritten if it exists) and will only be written to by this program. The constants `MPI_MODE_CREATE` and `MPI_MODE_WRONLY` represent bit flags that are `or`'d together in C, much as they are in the Unix system call `open`.

The fourth argument, `MPI_INFO_NULL` here, is a predefined constant representing a dummy value for the `info` argument to `MPI_File_open`. We will describe the `MPI_Info` object later in this chapter in Section 2.5. In our program we don't need any of its capabilities; hence we pass `MPI_INFO_NULL` to `MPI_File_open`. As the last argument, we pass the address of the `MPI_File` variable, which the `MPI_File_open` will fill in for us. As with all MPI functions in C, `MPI_File_open` returns as the value of the function a return code, which we hope is `MPI_SUCCESS`. In our examples in this section, we do not check error codes, for simplicity.

The next function, which actually does the I/O in this program, is

```
MPI_File_write(myfile, buf, BUFSIZE, MPI_INT,
               MPI_STATUS_IGNORE);
```

Here we see the analogy between I/O and message passing that was alluded to in Chapter 1. The data to be written is described by the (address, count, datatype) method used to describe messages in MPI-1. This way of describing a buffer to be written (or read) gives the same two advantages as it does in message passing: it allows arbitrary distributions of noncontiguous data in memory to be written with a single call, and it expresses the datatype, rather than just the length, of the data to be written, so that meaningful transformations can be done on it as it is read or written, for heterogeneous environments. Here we just have a contiguous buffer of `BUFSIZE` integers, starting at address `buf`. The final argument to `MPI_File_write` is a "status" argument, of the same type as returned by `MPI_Recv`. We shall see its use below. In this case we choose to ignore its value. MPI-2 specifies that the special value `MPI_STATUS_IGNORE` can be passed to any MPI function in place of a status argument, to tell the MPI implementation not to bother filling in the status information because the user intends to ignore it. This technique can slightly improve performance when status information is not needed.

Finally, the function

```
MPI_File_close(&myfile);
```

closes the file. The address of `myfile` is passed rather than the variable itself because the MPI implementation will replace its value with the constant `MPI_-FILE_NULL`. Thus the user can detect invalid file objects.

```
/* example of parallel MPI write into a single file */
#include "mpi.h"
#include <stdio.h>
#define BUFSIZE 100

int main(int argc, char *argv[])
{
    int i, myrank, buf[BUFSIZE];
    MPI_File thefile;

    MPI_Init(&argc, &argv);
    MPI_Comm_rank(MPI_COMM_WORLD, &myrank);
    for (i=0; i<BUFSIZE; i++)
        buf[i] = myrank * BUFSIZE + i;
    MPI_File_open(MPI_COMM_WORLD, "testfile",
                  MPI_MODE_CREATE | MPI_MODE_WRONLY,
                  MPI_INFO_NULL, &thefile);
    MPI_File_set_view(thefile, myrank * BUFSIZE * sizeof(int),
                      MPI_INT, MPI_INT, "native", MPI_INFO_NULL);
    MPI_File_write(thefile, buf, BUFSIZE, MPI_INT,
                   MPI_STATUS_IGNORE);
    MPI_File_close(&thefile);
    MPI_Finalize();
    return 0;
}
```

Figure 2.6
MPI I/O to a single file

2.2.4 Parallel MPI I/O to a Single File

We now modify our example so that the processes share a single file instead of
writing to separate files, thus eliminating the disadvantages of having multiple files
while retaining the performance advantages of parallelism. We will still not be
doing anything that absolutely cannot be done through language or library I/O on
most file systems, but we will begin to see the "MPI way" of sharing a file among
processes. The new version of the program is shown in Figure 2.6.

The first difference between this program and that of Figure 2.5 is in the first
argument of the MPI_File_open statement. Here we specify MPI_COMM_WORLD instead
of MPI_COMM_SELF, to indicate that all the processes are opening a single file together.
This is a *collective* operation on the communicator, so all participating processes

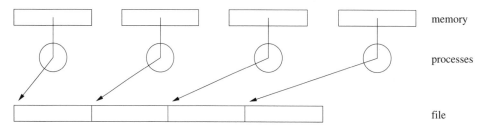

Figure 2.7
Parallel I/O to a single file

must make the MPI_File_open call, although only a single file is being opened.

Our plan for the way this file will be written is to give each process access to a part of it, as shown in Figure 2.7. The part of the file that is seen by a single process is called the file *view* and is set for each process by a call to MPI_File_set_view. In our example here, the call looks like

```
MPI_File_set_view(thefile, myrank * BUFSIZE * sizeof(int),
                  MPI_INT, MPI_INT, "native", MPI_INFO_NULL);
```

The first argument identifies the file. The second argument is the displacement (in bytes) into the file where the process's view of the file is to start. Here we multiply the size of the data to be written (BUFSIZE * sizeof(int)) by the rank of the process, so that each process's view starts at the appropriate place in the file. This argument is of a new type MPI_Offset, which on systems that support large files can be expected to be a 64-bit integer. See Section 2.2.6 for further discussion.

The next argument is called the *etype* of the view; it specifies the unit of data in the file. Here it is MPI_INT, since we will always be writing some number of MPI_INTs to this file. The next argument, called the *filetype*, is a very flexible way of describing noncontiguous views in the file. In our simple case here, where there are no noncontiguous units to be written, we can just use the etype, MPI_INT. In general, etype and filetype can be any MPI predefined or derived datatype. See Chapter 3 for details.

The next argument is a character string denoting the *data representation* to be used in the file. The native representation specifies that data is to be represented in the file exactly as it is in memory. This preserves precision and results in no performance loss from conversion overhead. Other representations are internal and external32, which enable various degrees of file portability across machines with different architectures and thus different data representations. The final argument

```
int MPI_File_open(MPI_Comm comm, char *filename, int amode, MPI_Info info,
        MPI_File *fh)

int MPI_File_set_view(MPI_File fh, MPI_Offset disp, MPI_Datatype etype,
        MPI_Datatype filetype, char *datarep, MPI_Info info)

int MPI_File_write(MPI_File fh, void *buf, int count, MPI_Datatype datatype,
        MPI_Status *status)

int MPI_File_close(MPI_File *fh)
```

Table 2.1
C bindings for the I/O functions used in Figure 2.6

is an `info` object as in `MPI_File_open`. Here again it is to be ignored, as dictated by specifying `MPI_INFO_NULL` for this argument.

Now that each process has its own view, the actual write operation

```
MPI_File_write(thefile, buf, BUFSIZE, MPI_INT,
            MPI_STATUS_IGNORE);
```

is exactly the same as in our previous version of this program. But because the `MPI_File_open` specified `MPI_COMM_WORLD` in its communicator argument, and the `MPI_File_set_view` gave each process a different view of the file, the write operations proceed in parallel and all go into the same file in the appropriate places.

Why did we not need a call to `MPI_File_set_view` in the previous example? The reason is that the default view is that of a linear byte stream, with displacement 0 and both etype and filetype set to `MPI_BYTE`. This is compatible with the way we used the file in our previous example.

C bindings for the I/O functions in MPI that we have used so far are given in Table 2.1.

2.2.5   Fortran 90 Version

Fortran now officially means Fortran 90 (or Fortran 95 [1]). This has some impact on the Fortran bindings for MPI functions. We defer the details to Chapter 9, but demonstrate here some of the differences by rewriting the program shown in Figure 2.6 in Fortran. The MPI-2 Standard identifies two levels of Fortran support: *basic* and *extended*. Here we illustrate programming with basic support, which merely requires that the `mpif.h` file included in Fortran programs be valid in both free-source and fixed-source format, in other words, that it contain valid syntax

```
MPI_FILE_OPEN(comm, filename, amode, info, fh, ierror)
            character*(*) filename
            integer comm, amode, info, fh, ierror

MPI_FILE_SET_VIEW(fh, disp, etype, filetype, datarep, info, ierror)
            integer fh, etype, filetype, info, ierror
            character*(*) datarep
            integer(kind=MPI_OFFSET_KIND) disp

MPI_FILE_WRITE(fh, buf, count, datatype, status, ierror)
            <type> buf(*)
            integer fh, count, datatype, status(MPI_STATUS_SIZE), ierror

MPI_FILE_CLOSE(fh, ierror)
            integer fh, ierror
```

Table 2.2
Fortran bindings for the I/O functions used in Figure 2.8

for Fortran-90 compilers as well as for Fortran-77 compilers. Extended support requires the use of an MPI "module," in which the line

```
include 'mpif.h'
```

is replaced by

```
use mpi
```

We also use "Fortran-90 style" comment indicators. The new program is shown Figure 2.8. Note that the type `MPI_Offset` in C is represented in Fortran by the type `INTEGER(kind=MPI_OFFSET_KIND)`. Fortran bindings for the I/O functions used in Figure 2.8 are given in Table 2.2.

2.2.6   Reading the File with a Different Number of Processes

One advantage of doing parallel I/O to a single file is that it is straightforward to read the file in parallel with a different number of processes. This is important in the case of scientific applications, for example, where a parallel program may write a restart file, which is then read at startup by the same program, but possibly utilizing a different number of processes. If we have written a single file with no internal structure reflecting the number of processes that wrote the file, then it is not necessary to restart the run with the same number of processes as before. In

```fortran
! example of parallel MPI write into a single file, in Fortran
PROGRAM main
    ! Fortran 90 users can (and should) use
    !     use mpi
    ! instead of include 'mpif.h' if their MPI implementation provides a
    ! mpi module.
    include 'mpif.h'

    integer ierr, i, myrank, BUFSIZE, thefile
    parameter (BUFSIZE=100)
    integer buf(BUFSIZE)
    integer(kind=MPI_OFFSET_KIND) disp

    call MPI_INIT(ierr)
    call MPI_COMM_RANK(MPI_COMM_WORLD, myrank, ierr)

    do i = 0, BUFSIZE
        buf(i) = myrank * BUFSIZE + i
    enddo
    call MPI_FILE_OPEN(MPI_COMM_WORLD, 'testfile', &
                       MPI_MODE_WRONLY + MPI_MODE_CREATE, &
                       MPI_INFO_NULL, thefile, ierr)
    ! assume 4-byte integers
    disp = myrank * BUFSIZE * 4
    call MPI_FILE_SET_VIEW(thefile, disp, MPI_INTEGER, &
                           MPI_INTEGER, 'native', &
                           MPI_INFO_NULL, ierr)
    call MPI_FILE_WRITE(thefile, buf, BUFSIZE, MPI_INTEGER, &
                        MPI_STATUS_IGNORE, ierr)
    call MPI_FILE_CLOSE(thefile, ierr)
    call MPI_FINALIZE(ierr)

END PROGRAM main
```

Figure 2.8
MPI I/O to a single file in Fortran

---

int **MPI_File_get_size**(MPI_File fh, MPI_Offset *size)

int **MPI_File_read**(MPI_File fh, void *buf, int count, MPI_Datatype datatype,
                      MPI_Status *status)

Table 2.3
C bindings for some more I/O functions

Figure 2.9 we show a program to read the file we have been writing in our previous examples. This program is independent of the number of processes that run it. The total size of the file is obtained, and then the views of the various processes are set so that they each have approximately the same amount to read.

One new MPI function is demonstrated here: MPI_File_get_size. The first argument is an open file, and the second is the address of a field to store the size of the file in bytes. Since many systems can now handle files whose sizes are too big to be represented in a 32-bit integer, MPI defines a type, MPI_Offset, that is large enough to contain a file size. It is the type used for arguments to MPI functions that refer to displacements in files. In C, one can expect it to be a long or long long—at any rate a type that can participate in integer arithmetic, as it is here, when we compute the displacement used in MPI_File_set_view. Otherwise, the program used to read the file is very similar to the one that writes it.

One difference between writing and reading is that one doesn't always know exactly how much data will be read. Here, although we could compute it, we let every process issue the same MPI_File_read call and pass the address of a real MPI_- Status instead of MPI_STATUS_IGNORE. Then, just as in the case of an MPI_Recv, we can use MPI_Get_count to find out how many occurrences of a given datatype were read. If it is less than the number of items requested, then end-of-file has been reached.

C bindings for the new functions used in this example are given in Table 2.3.

2.2.7   C++ Version

The MPI Forum faced a number of choices when it came time to provide C++ bindings for the MPI-1 and MPI-2 functions. The simplest choice would be to make them identical to the C bindings. This would be a disappointment to C++ programmers, however. MPI is object-oriented in design, and it seemed a shame not to express this design in C++ syntax, which could be done without changing the basic structure of MPI. Another choice would be to define a complete class library that might look quite different from MPI's C bindings.

```
/* parallel MPI read with arbitrary number of processes*/
#include "mpi.h"
#include <stdio.h>
int main(int argc, char *argv[])
{
    int myrank, numprocs, bufsize, *buf, count;
    MPI_File thefile;
    MPI_Status status;
    MPI_Offset filesize;

    MPI_Init(&argc, &argv);
    MPI_Comm_rank(MPI_COMM_WORLD, &myrank);
    MPI_Comm_size(MPI_COMM_WORLD, &numprocs);
    MPI_File_open(MPI_COMM_WORLD, "testfile", MPI_MODE_RDONLY,
                  MPI_INFO_NULL, &thefile);
    MPI_File_get_size(thefile, &filesize); /* in bytes */
    filesize = filesize / sizeof(int);     /* in number of ints */
    bufsize = filesize / numprocs + 1;     /* local number to read */
    buf = (int *) malloc (bufsize * sizeof(int));
    MPI_File_set_view(thefile, myrank * bufsize * sizeof(int),
                      MPI_INT, MPI_INT, "native", MPI_INFO_NULL);
    MPI_File_read(thefile, buf, bufsize, MPI_INT, &status);
    MPI_Get_count(&status, MPI_INT, &count);
    printf("process %d read %d ints\n", myrank, count);
    MPI_File_close(&thefile);
    MPI_Finalize();
    return 0;
}
```

Figure 2.9
Reading the file with a different number of processes

Although the last choice was explored, and one instance was explored in detail [80], in the end the Forum adopted the middle road. The C++ bindings for MPI can almost be deduced from the C bindings, and there is roughly a one-to-one correspondence between C++ functions and C functions. The main features of the C++ bindings are as follows.

- Most MPI "objects," such as groups, communicators, files, requests, and statuses, are C++ objects.
- If an MPI function is naturally associated with an object, then it becomes a method on that object. For example, `MPI_Send(...,comm)` becomes a method on its communicator: `comm.Send(...)`.
- Objects that are not components of other objects exist in an MPI name space. For example, `MPI_COMM_WORLD` becomes `MPI::COMM_WORLD` and a constant like `MPI_-INFO_NULL` becomes `MPI::INFO_NULL`.
- Functions that normally create objects return the object as a return value instead of returning an error code, as they do in C. For example, `MPI::File::Open` returns an object of type `MPI::File`.
- Functions that in C return a value in one of their arguments return it instead as the value of the function. For example, `comm.Get_rank` returns the rank of the calling process in the communicator `comm`.
- The C++ style of handling errors can be used. Although the default error handler remains `MPI::ERRORS_ARE_FATAL` in C++, the user can set the default error handler to `MPI::ERRORS_THROW_EXCEPTIONS`. In this case the C++ exception mechanism will throw an object of type `MPI::Exception`.

We illustrate some of the features of the C++ bindings by rewriting the previous program in C++. The new program is shown in Figure 2.10. Note that we have used the way C++ can defer defining types, along with the C++ MPI feature that functions can return values or objects. Hence instead of

```
int myrank;
MPI_Comm_rank(MPI_COMM_WORLD, &myrank);
```

we have

```
int myrank = MPI::COMM_WORLD.Get_rank();
```

The C++ bindings for basic MPI functions found in nearly all MPI programs are shown in Table 2.4. Note that the new `Get_rank` has no arguments instead of the two that the C version, `MPI_Get_rank`, has because it is a method on a

```cpp
// example of parallel MPI read from single file, in C++
#include <iostream.h>
#include "mpi.h"

int main(int argc, char *argv[])
{
    int bufsize, *buf, count;
    char filename[128];
    MPI::Status status;

    MPI::Init();
    int myrank = MPI::COMM_WORLD.Get_rank();
    int numprocs = MPI::COMM_WORLD.Get_size();
    MPI::File thefile = MPI::File::Open(MPI::COMM_WORLD, "testfile",
                                        MPI::MODE_RDONLY,
                                        MPI::INFO_NULL);
    MPI::Offset filesize = thefile.Get_size();  // in bytes
    filesize    = filesize / sizeof(int);     // in number of ints
    bufsize     = filesize / numprocs + 1;    // local number to read
    buf = (int *) malloc (bufsize * sizeof(int));
    thefile.Set_view(myrank * bufsize * sizeof(int),
                     MPI_INT, MPI_INT, "native", MPI::INFO_NULL);
    thefile.Read(buf, bufsize, MPI_INT, &status);
    count = status.Get_count(MPI_INT);
    cout << "process " << myrank << " read " << count << " ints"
         << endl;
    thefile.Close();
    MPI::Finalize();
    return 0;
}
```

Figure 2.10
C++ version of the example in Figure 2.9

> **void MPI::Init**(int& argc, char**& argv)
>
> **void MPI::Init**()
>
> **int MPI::Comm::Get_size**() const
>
> **int MPI::Comm::Get_rank**() const
>
> **void MPI::Finalize**()

Table 2.4
C++ bindings for basic MPI functions

> **MPI::File MPI::File::Open**(const MPI::Intracomm& comm, const char* filename,
>   int amode, const MPI::Info& info)
>
> **MPI::Offset MPI::File::Get_size** const
>
> **void MPI::File::Set_view**(MPI::Offset disp, const MPI::Datatype& etype,
>   const MPI::Datatype& filetype, const char* datarep,
>   const MPI::Info& info)
>
> **void MPI::File::Read**(void* buf, int count, const MPI::Datatype& datatype,
>   MPI::Status& status)
>
> **void MPI::File::Read**(void* buf, int count, const MPI::Datatype& datatype)
>
> **void MPI::File::Close**

Table 2.5
C++ bindings for some I/O functions

communicator and returns the rank as its value. Note also that there are two versions of `MPI::Init`. The one with no arguments corresponds to the new freedom in MPI-2 to pass (`NULL, NULL`) to the C function `MPI_Init` instead of (`&argc, &argv`).

The C++ bindings for the I/O functions used in our example are shown in Table 2.5. We see that `MPI::File::Open` returns an object of type `MPI::File`, and `Read` is called as a method on this object.

2.2.8   Other Ways to Write to a Shared File

In Section 2.2.4 we used `MPI_File_set_view` to show how multiple processes can be instructed to share a single file. As is common throughout MPI, there are

multiple ways to achieve the same result. MPI_File_seek allows multiple processes
to position themselves at a specific byte offset in a file (move the process's file
pointer) before reading or writing. This is a lower-level approach than using file
views and is similar to the Unix function lseek. An example that uses this approach
is given in Section 3.2. For efficiency and thread-safety, a seek and read operation
can be combined in a single function, MPI_File_read_at; similarly, there is an
MPI_File_write_at. Finally, another file pointer, called the shared file pointer, is
shared among processes belonging to the communicator passed to MPI_File_open.
Functions such as MPI_File_write_shared access data from the current location of
the shared file pointer and increment the shared file pointer by the amount of data
accessed. This functionality is useful, for example, when all processes are writing
event records to a common log file.

2.3   Remote Memory Access

In this section we discuss how MPI-2 generalizes the strict message-passing model of
MPI-1 and provides direct access by one process to parts of the memory of another
process. These operations, referred to as *get*, *put*, and *accumulate*, are called *remote
memory access* (RMA) operations in MPI. We will walk through a simple example
that uses the MPI-2 remote memory access operations.

The most characteristic feature of the message-passing model of parallel computation is that data is moved from one process's address space to another's only by
a cooperative pair of send/receive operations, one executed by each process. The
same operations that move the data also perform the necessary synchronization; in
other words, when a receive operation completes, the data is available for use in
the receiving process.

MPI-2 does not provide a real shared-memory model; nonetheless, the remote
memory operations of MPI-2 provide much of the flexibility of shared memory.
Data movement can be initiated entirely by the action of one process; hence these
operations are also referred to as *one sided*. In addition, the synchronization needed
to ensure that a data-movement operation is complete is decoupled from the (one-
sided) initiation of that operation. In Chapters 5 and 6 we will see that MPI-2's remote memory access operations comprise a small but powerful set of data-movement
operations and a relatively complex set of synchronization operations. In this chapter we will deal only with the simplest form of synchronization.

It is important to realize that the RMA operations come with no particular
guarantee of performance superior to that of send and receive. In particular, they

have been designed to work both on shared-memory machines and in environments without any shared-memory hardware at all, such as networks of workstations using TCP/IP as an underlying communication mechanism. Their main utility is in the flexibility they provide for the design of algorithms. The resulting programs will be portable to all MPI implementations and presumably will be efficient on platforms that do provide hardware support for access to the memory of other processes.

2.3.1   The Basic Idea: Memory Windows

In strict message passing, the send/receive buffers specified by MPI datatypes represent those portions of a process's address space that are exported to other processes (in the case of send operations) or available to be written into by other processes (in the case of receive operations). In MPI-2, this notion of "communication memory" is generalized to the notion of a remote memory access *window*. Each process can designate portions of its address space as available to other processes for both read and write access. The read and write operations performed by other processes are called *get* and *put* remote memory access operations. A third type of operation is called *accumulate*. This refers to the update of a remote memory location, for example, by adding a value to it.

The word *window* in MPI-2 refers to the portion of a single process's memory that it contributes to a distributed object called a *window object*. Thus, a window object is made up of multiple windows, each of which consists of all the local memory areas exposed to the other processes by a collective window-creation function. A collection of processes can have multiple window objects, and the windows contributed to a window object by a set of processes may vary from process to process. In Figure 2.11 we show a window object made up of windows contributed by two processes. The *put* and *get* operations that move data to and from the remote memory of another process are nonblocking; a separate synchronization operation is needed to ensure their completion. To see how this works, let us consider a simple example.

2.3.2   RMA Version of `cpi`

In this section we rewrite the `cpi` example that appears in Chapter 3 of *Using MPI* [32]. This program calculates the value of π by numerical integration. In the original version there are two types of communication. Process 0 prompts the user for a number of intervals to use in the integration and uses `MPI_Bcast` to send this number to the other processes. Each process then computes a partial sum, and the total sum is obtained by adding the partial sums with an `MPI_Reduce` operation.

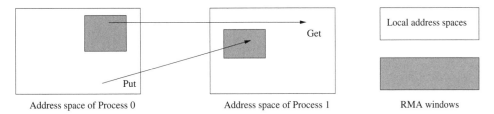

Figure 2.11
Remote memory access window on two processes. The shaded area covers a single window object made up of two windows.

In the one-sided version of this program, process 0 will store the value it reads from the user into its part of an RMA window object, where the other processes can simply *get* it. After the partial sum calculations, all processes will add their contributions to a value in another window object, using *accumulate*. Synchronization will be carried out by the simplest of the window synchronization operations, the *fence*.

Figure 2.12 shows the beginning of the program, including setting up the window objects. In this simple example, each window object consists only of a single number in the memory of process 0. Window objects are represented by variables of type MPI_Win in C. We need two window objects because window objects are made up of variables of a single datatype, and we have an integer n and a double pi that all processes will access separately. Let us look at the first window creation call done on process 0.

```
MPI_Win_create(&n, sizeof(int), 1, MPI_INFO_NULL,
               MPI_COMM_WORLD, &nwin);
```

This is matched on the other processes by

```
MPI_Win_create(MPI_BOTTOM, 0, 1, MPI_INFO_NULL,
               MPI_COMM_WORLD, &nwin);
```

The call on process 0 needs to be matched on the other processes, even though they are not contributing any memory to the window object, because MPI_Win_create is a collective operation over the communicator specified in its last argument. This communicator designates which processes will be able to access the window object.

The first two arguments of MPI_Win_create are the address and length (in bytes) of the window (in local memory) that the calling process is exposing to *put/get* operations by other processes. Here it is the single integer n on process 0 and no

```
/* Compute pi by numerical integration, RMA version */
#include "mpi.h"
#include <math.h>
int main(int argc, char *argv[])
{
    int n, myid, numprocs, i;
    double PI25DT = 3.141592653589793238462643;
    double mypi, pi, h, sum, x;
    MPI_Win nwin, piwin;

    MPI_Init(&argc,&argv);
    MPI_Comm_size(MPI_COMM_WORLD,&numprocs);
    MPI_Comm_rank(MPI_COMM_WORLD,&myid);

    if (myid == 0) {
        MPI_Win_create(&n, sizeof(int), 1, MPI_INFO_NULL,
                       MPI_COMM_WORLD, &nwin);
        MPI_Win_create(&pi, sizeof(double), 1, MPI_INFO_NULL,
                       MPI_COMM_WORLD, &piwin);
    }
    else {
        MPI_Win_create(MPI_BOTTOM, 0, 1, MPI_INFO_NULL,
                       MPI_COMM_WORLD, &nwin);
        MPI_Win_create(MPI_BOTTOM, 0, 1, MPI_INFO_NULL,
                       MPI_COMM_WORLD, &piwin);
    }
```

Figure 2.12
cpi: setting up the RMA windows

memory at all on the other processes, signified by a length of 0. We use MPI_-
BOTTOM as the address because it is a valid address and we wish to emphasize that
these processes are not contributing any local windows to the window object being
created.

The next argument is a *displacement unit* used to specify offsets into memory
in windows. Here each window object contains only one variable, which we will
access with a displacement of 0, so the displacement unit is not really important.
We specify 1 (byte). The fourth argument is an MPI_Info argument, which can be
used to optimize the performance of RMA operations in certain situations. Here
we use MPI_INFO_NULL. See Chapter 5 for more on the use of displacement units
and the MPI_Info argument. The fifth argument is a communicator, which specifies

the set of processes that will have access to the memory being contributed to the window object. The MPI implementation will return an `MPI_Win` object as the last argument.

After the first call to `MPI_Win_create`, each process has access to the data in `nwin` (consisting of the single integer `n`) via *put* and *get* operations for storing and reading, and the *accumulate* operation for updating. Note that we did not have to acquire or set aside special memory for the window; we just used the ordinary program variable `n` on process 0. It is possible, and sometimes preferable, to acquire such special memory with `MPI_Alloc_mem`, but we will not do so here. See Chapter 6 for further information on `MPI_Alloc_mem`.

The second call to `MPI_Win_create` in each process is similar to the first, and creates a window object `piwin` giving each process access to the variable `pi` on process 0, where the total value of π will be accumulated.

Now that the window objects have been created, let us consider the rest of the program, shown in Figure 2.13. It is a loop in which each iteration begins with process 0 asking the user for a number of intervals and continues with the parallel computation and printing of the approximation of π by process 0. The loop terminates when the user enters a 0.

The processes of nonzero rank will *get* the value of `n` directly from the window object without any explicit action on the part of process 0 to send it to them. But before we can call `MPI_Get` or any other RMA communication function, we must call a special synchronization function, `MPI_Win_fence`, to start what is known as an *RMA access epoch*. We would like to emphasize that the function `MPI_Barrier` *cannot* be used to achieve the synchronization necessary for remote memory operations. MPI provides special mechanisms—three of them—for synchronizing remote memory operations. We consider the simplest of them, `MPI_Win_fence`, here. The other two mechanisms are discussed in Chapter 6.

The *fence* operation is invoked by the function `MPI_Win_fence`. It has two arguments. The first is an "assertion" argument permitting certain optimizations; 0 is always a valid assertion value, and so we use it here for simplicity. The second argument is the window the *fence* operation is being performed on. `MPI_Win_fence` can be thought of as a barrier (across all the processes in the communicator used to create the window object) that separates a set of local operations on the window from the remote operations on the window or (not illustrated here) separates two sets of remote operations. Here,

```
MPI_Win_fence(0, nwin);
```

```
    while (1) {
        if (myid == 0) {
            printf("Enter the number of intervals: (0 quits) ");
            fflush(stdout);
            scanf("%d",&n);
            pi = 0.0;
        }
        MPI_Win_fence(0, nwin);

        if (myid != 0)
            MPI_Get(&n, 1, MPI_INT, 0, 0, 1, MPI_INT, nwin);
        MPI_Win_fence(0, nwin);

        if (n == 0)
            break;
        else {
            h   = 1.0 / (double) n;
            sum = 0.0;
            for (i = myid + 1; i <= n; i += numprocs) {
                x = h * ((double)i - 0.5);
                sum += (4.0 / (1.0 + x*x));
            }
            mypi = h * sum;
            MPI_Win_fence( 0, piwin);

            MPI_Accumulate(&mypi, 1, MPI_DOUBLE, 0, 0, 1, MPI_DOUBLE,
                           MPI_SUM, piwin);
            MPI_Win_fence(0, piwin);

            if (myid == 0)
                printf("pi is approximately %.16f, Error is %.16f\n",
                       pi, fabs(pi - PI25DT));
        }
    }
    MPI_Win_free(&nwin);
    MPI_Win_free(&piwin);
    MPI_Finalize();
    return 0;
}
```

Figure 2.13
cpi: main loop

separates the assignment of the value of n read from the terminal from the operations that follow, which are remote operations. The *get* operation, performed by all the processes except process 0, is

```
MPI_Get(&n, 1, MPI_INT, 0, 0, 1, MPI_INT, nwin);
```

The easiest way to think of this argument list is as that of a receive/send pair, in which the arguments for both send and receive are specified in a single call on a single process. The *get* is like a *receive*, so the receive buffer is specified first, in the normal MPI style, by the triple &n, 1, MPI_INT, in the usual (address, count, datatype) format used for receive buffers. The next argument is the rank of the *target* process, the process whose memory we are accessing. Here it is 0 because all processes except 0 are accessing the memory of process 0. The next three arguments define the "send buffer" in the window, again in the MPI style of (address, count, datatype). Here the address is given as a displacement into the remote memory on the target process. In this case it is 0 because there is only one value in the window, and therefore its displacement from the beginning of the window is 0. The last argument is the window object.

The remote memory operations only *initiate* data movement. We are not guaranteed that when MPI_Get returns, the data has been fetched into the variable n. In other words, MPI_Get is a nonblocking operation. To ensure that the operation is complete, we need to call MPI_Win_fence again.

The next few lines in the code compute a partial sum mypi in each process, including process 0. We obtain an approximation of π by having each process update the value pi in the window object by adding its value of mypi to it. First we call another MPI_Win_fence, this time on the piwin window object, to start another RMA access epoch. Then we perform an *accumulate* operation operation using

```
MPI_Accumulate(&mypi, 1, MPI_DOUBLE, 0, 0, 1, MPI_DOUBLE,
               MPI_SUM, piwin);
```

The first three arguments specify the local value being used to do the update, in the usual (address, count, datatype) form. The fourth argument is the rank of the target process, and the subsequent three arguments represent the value being updated, in the form (displacement, count, datatype). Then comes the operation used to do the update. This argument is similar to the op argument to MPI_Reduce, the difference being that only the predefined MPI reduction operations can be used in MPI_Accumulate; user-defined reduction operations cannot be used. In this example, each process needs to add its value of mypi to pi; therefore, we

```
int MPI_Win_create(void *base, MPI_Aint size, int disp_unit, MPI_Info info,
                   MPI_Comm comm, MPI_Win *win)

int MPI_Win_fence(int assert, MPI_Win win)

int MPI_Get(void *origin_addr, int origin_count, MPI_Datatype origin_datatype,
            int target_rank, MPI_Aint target_disp, int target_count,
            MPI_Datatype target_datatype, MPI_Win win)

int MPI_Accumulate(void *origin_addr, int origin_count,
                   MPI_Datatype origin_datatype, int target_rank,
                   MPI_Aint target_disp, int target_count,
                   MPI_Datatype target_datatype,  MPI_Op op, MPI_Win win)

int MPI_Win_free(MPI_Win *win)
```

Table 2.6
C bindings for the RMA functions used in the cpi example

use the operation `MPI_SUM`. The final argument is the window object on which the update is being performed, here `piwin`.

Since `MPI_Accumulate` is a nonblocking function, we call `MPI_Win_fence` to complete the operation. We then print the answer from process 0. Note that if process 0 did not use `MPI_Accumulate` but instead simply used `pi += mypi`, the program would be *wrong* and would produce incorrect results. This is discussed in more detail in Chapter 5.

The program finishes by freeing the window objects it has created, with `MPI_-Win_free`, which takes as argument the address of the window object being freed. `MPI_Win_free` is a collective operation on the same communicator that was used to create the window object in the first place.

C bindings for the RMA functions used in this example are given in Table 2.6.

2.4   Dynamic Process Management

In the process model used in MPI-1, there is a fixed number of processes throughout an MPI computation. This is a conceptually simple model because it puts all of the complexity of interaction with the operating system (which must be involved in the creation of processes) completely outside the scope of the MPI application program. When `MPI_Init` returns, all the processes have been started, `MPI_COMM_WORLD` is fixed once and for all, and every process can communicate with every other process by using MPI_COMM_WORLD. All communicators subsequently created have groups that are subgroups of the group of MPI_COMM_WORLD.

Although this situation makes life easier for MPI implementers, some MPI applications need more flexibility. Part of the interest in a more dynamic approach to process management came from the PVM [24] community, where process startup under application control is commonplace (although not as portable as other parts of PVM that don't have to interact with job schedulers and process managers). Some applications have a genuine need to compute at run time—perhaps after some initial calculations—how many processes should be created to work on the problem at hand. Some applications consist of two MPI programs separately started, which need to connect to one another *after* each has formed its own separate MPI_COMM_-WORLD.

Before we begin with a simple example, we would like to point out that the dynamic process routines make good use of MPI *intercommunicators*, a form of communicator that connects two groups of processes. As we will see in Chapter 7, intercommunicators provide a natural way to describe the spawned processes and their parent(s). However, to keep our first example simple, we will convert the intercommunicator that is created when new processes are started into a more familiar *intracommunicator*, using MPI_Intercomm_merge (merge the two groups in an intercommunicator into one and return a "normal" intracommunicator).

2.4.1 Spawning Processes

In MPI-2, process are created by using the function MPI_Comm_spawn. The key features of MPI_Comm_spawn are the following:

• It is a collective operation over the spawning processes (called the *parents*) and also collective with the calls to MPI_Init in the processes that are spawned (called the *children*).
• It returns an intercommunicator in which, from the point of view of the parents, the local group contains the parents and the remote group contains the children.
• The new processes have their own MPI_COMM_WORLD.
• The function MPI_Comm_parent, called from the children, returns an intercommunicator containing the children as the local group and the parents as the remote group.

These features are illustrated in Figure 2.14.

In the parents   In the children

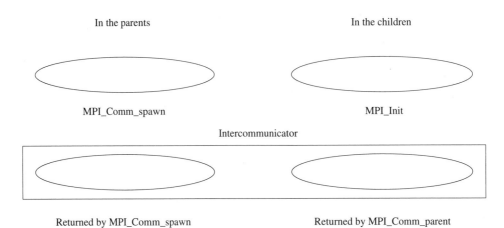

MPI_Comm_spawn   MPI_Init

Intercommunicator

Returned by MPI_Comm_spawn   Returned by MPI_Comm_parent

Figure 2.14
Spawning processes. Ovals are intracommunicators containing several processes.

2.4.2 Parallel cp: A Simple System Utility

Let us consider an example in which processes are created dynamically: a simple utility program that does a parallel copy, that is, copies a file from the local disk of a machine to the local disks of other machines. Such a utility could be needed for the following reason. Before a process can be started on a given machine, an executable file must be present on the machine. In many cases, this requirement is satisfied because a shared file system, such as NFS, makes a single copy of the executable file available to all the machines. In other cases there may be no shared file system and the executable may need to be copied into a specific directory or to /tmp on a (possibly large) set of machines, as a prerequisite to starting an MPI application. Even with shared file-systems, we may want to copy the executable to local disks in a scalable way to reduce the time it takes to access the executable. We may even want to do this inside mpiexec.

How can MPI help? The main way is by providing us with MPI_Bcast to send the file from the root (the process that can read the file) to the other processes. A good implementation can provide a scalable MPI_Bcast, at least on switched networks, by using algorithms such as a spanning tree. We should also be able to achieve extra parallelism through pipelining, as we explain below.

We hypothesize a parallel-computing environment in which we have a "Beowulf" system (a cluster of machines) without a shared file system. Let us suppose that our login- and compile-server is called dion and the "compute" nodes are called

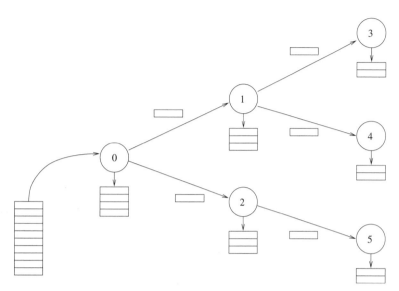

Figure 2.15
Multiple levels of parallelism in `pcp`

`belmont0`, `belmont1`, and so on. We expect to frequently have to copy a file (such as a recently compiled executable) from `dion` to the local file systems of some subset of the `belmonts`. We would like it to look like the ordinary Unix `cp` command, but function as a parallel copy. That is, if we say

```
pcp 0-63 mandelslave /tmp/mandelslave
```

we want the file `mandelslave` to be copied from its local place on `dion` to the `/tmp` directory on the first 64 `belmonts`. The `pcp` program is one of a set of similar parallel versions of familiar Unix commands described in [28].

Figure 2.15 shows our `pcp` program in action. Process 0 is reading the input file and broadcasting it, one block at a time, to all the other processes, who are writing it to local disk. This program has three forms of parallelism.

- All of the processes are doing file I/O in parallel.
- Much of the message passing takes place in parallel (assuming that our MPI implementation implements `MPI_Bcast` in a scalable way). For example, the message from process 1 to process 3 is being transmitted concurrently with the message from process 2 to process 5.
- By breaking the file into blocks, we also achieve *pipeline* parallelism. This type of parallelism arises, for example, from the concurrency of the message from process

0 to process 1 with the message from process 1 to process 3. Enabling pipeline parallelism is one of the reasons that MPI_Bcast is not a synchronizing operation; multiple broadcasts can be occurring in parallel.

In this example, even process 0, which is reading the file, makes a copy of it. This approach makes sense if the file has just been compiled on one file system but now is to be copied to a uniform place in the local file system on each machine. An alternative semantics for pcp would be to assume that the file is already in place on process 0 and, therefore, process 0 does not write the output file.

The code for the beginning of the master part of the pcp program is shown in Figure 2.16. The first step is to parse the expression for the machines to copy the file to and create a file containing those machine names. Let us assume that the function makehostlist parses the first argument and writes out a hostfile (whose name is given by the second argument) that can be understood by our implementation of MPI_Comm_spawn. The number of slaves specified is returned as the third argument of makehostlist. We then pass the name of this file to MPI_Comm_spawn via info, in order to create pcp slaves on each of the target machines. Therefore the call

```
makehostlist( argv[1], "targets", &num_hosts );
```

writes out a file called targets containing the appropriate host names. We need to pass this information to the system that starts up new processes. Since job scheduling and process startup systems have not been standardized, there is no standard MPI format for this information. Instead, this information is passed to MPI_Comm_spawn via an info object. We cover this in more detail in Section 2.5. For now, we show how MPI_Info is used to give information to an MPI call. We create an MPI_Info object containing "targets" as the value of the reserved key (for use with MPI_Comm_spawn) file. This info key simply tells MPI_Comm_spawn to look in the file targets for information, in a format specific to the MPI implementation, about how to perform the operation. We assume here that the file may contain the names of the processors to spawn processes on. The info key soft is also used to allow MPI_Comm_spawn to return successfully even if it was unable to start all of the requested processes. Next, the call

```
MPI_Comm_spawn( "pcp_slave", MPI_ARGV_NULL, num_hosts, hostinfo,
                0, MPI_COMM_SELF, &pcpslaves,
                MPI_ERRCODES_IGNORE );
```

creates the slaves. For simplicity we leave out error checking at this point, passing MPI_ERRCODES_IGNORE instead of an array for returning the error codes.

```
/* pcp from the Scalable Unix Tools, in MPI */
#include "mpi.h"
#include <stdio.h>
#include <sys/types.h>
#include <sys/stat.h>
#include <fcntl.h>
#define BUFSIZE    256*1024
#define CMDSIZE    80
int main( int argc, char *argv[] )
{
    int     num_hosts, mystatus, allstatus, done, numread;
    int     infd, outfd;
    char    outfilename[MAXPATHLEN], controlmsg[CMDSIZE];
    char    buf[BUFSIZE];
    char    soft_limit[20];
    MPI_Info hostinfo;
    MPI_Comm pcpslaves, all_processes;

    MPI_Init( &argc, &argv );

    makehostlist( argv[1], "targets", &num_hosts );
    MPI_Info_create( &hostinfo );
    MPI_Info_set( hostinfo, "file", "targets" );
    sprintf( soft_limit, "0:%d", num_hosts );
    MPI_Info_set( hostinfo, "soft", soft_limit );
    MPI_Comm_spawn( "pcp_slave", MPI_ARGV_NULL, num_hosts,
                    hostinfo, 0, MPI_COMM_SELF, &pcpslaves,
                    MPI_ERRCODES_IGNORE );
    MPI_Info_free( &hostinfo );
    MPI_Intercomm_merge( pcpslaves, 0, &all_processes );
```

Figure 2.16
Beginning of master part of parallel copy program

We immediately convert the intercommunicator `pcpslaves` that contains both the calling process and the processes created by MPI_Comm_spawn into an intra-communicator with `MPI_Intercomm_merge`. The output intracommunicator, `all_-processes`, will be used for all subsequent communication between the slaves and the master.

The code for the middle of the master part of the `pcp` program is shown in Figure 2.17. We attempt to open the input file, and if we fail, we broadcast a message to the slaves telling them to exit immediately. If we succeed, we broadcast a "ready" message instead.

Next we broadcast the name of the output file, and all processes attempt to open it. To test whether the file opened successfully, we use an `MPI_Allreduce` with `MPI_MIN` as the operation. Thus, if any process fails to open the output file, all processes will know (since `allstatus` will be set to `-1`). In this case all processes call `MPI_Finalize` and exit. If all processes receive a 0 in `allstatus` (`MPI_Allreduce` ensures that all processes get the same result), then all files have been successfully opened. (If we replaced `MPI_MIN` as the operation in the `MPI_Allreduce` of the `mystatus` variable with `MPI_MINLOC`, we could indicate the rank of the failed process as well.)

The first part of the slave code is shown in Figure 2.18. This code is quite similar to the code for the master, except that the slaves need to call `MPI_Comm_get_parent` to establish contact with process 0, and slaves do no argument processing and print no messages.

At the end of the sections of code for both master and slave that we have looked at so far, all processes have successfully opened the necessary files. The second part of the master code is shown in Figure 2.19. It simply reads the file a block at a time and broadcasts the blocks to the slaves. Note that before sending each block it sends the length as well. This approach handles the (possibly) short block at the end and the end-of-file condition, since all processes in an `MPI_Bcast` (the root that is sending and the other processes that are receiving) must specify the *same* buffer length.[1] An alternative approach would be to use a structure containing an `int` field for the length of the data and a fixed-sized array of `char` for the buffer; a single `MPI_Bcast` would send both the `numread` value and the data read. Only in the last `MPI_Bcast` call would more data be sent (and ignored) than was needed. The second part of the slave code, which matches this structure, is shown in Figure 2.20. At the end, all processes free the intercommunicator created by MPI_Comm_spawn

---

[1]This is unlike the send/receive case, where the sender specifies the length of data but the receiver specifies the *maximum* buffer length, providing the `MPI_Status` argument to determine the actual size received.

```
strcpy( outfilename, argv[3] );
if ( (infd = open( argv[2], O_RDONLY ) ) == -1 ) {
    fprintf( stderr, "input %s does not exist\n", argv[2] );
    sprintf( controlmsg, "exit" );
    MPI_Bcast( controlmsg, CMDSIZE, MPI_CHAR, 0, all_processes );
    MPI_Finalize();
    return -1 ;
}
else {
    sprintf( controlmsg, "ready" );
    MPI_Bcast( controlmsg, CMDSIZE, MPI_CHAR, 0, all_processes );
}

MPI_Bcast( outfilename, MAXPATHLEN, MPI_CHAR, 0,
          all_processes );
if ( (outfd = open( outfilename, O_CREAT|O_WRONLY|O_TRUNC,
                    S_IRWXU ) ) == -1 )
    mystatus = -1;
else
    mystatus = 0;
MPI_Allreduce( &mystatus, &allstatus, 1, MPI_INT, MPI_MIN,
               all_processes );
if ( allstatus == -1 ) {
    fprintf( stderr, "Output file %s could not be opened\n",
             outfilename );
    MPI_Finalize();
    return 1 ;
}
```

Figure 2.17
Middle of master part of parallel copy program

```
/* pcp from the Scalable Unix Tools, in MPI */
#include "mpi.h"
#include <stdio.h>
#include <sys/types.h>
#include <sys/stat.h>
#include <fcntl.h>
#define BUFSIZE     256*1024
#define CMDSIZE     80
int main( int argc, char *argv[] )
{
    int       mystatus, allstatus, done, numread;
    char      outfilename[MAXPATHLEN], controlmsg[CMDSIZE];
    int       outfd;
    char      buf[BUFSIZE];
    MPI_Comm slavecomm, all_processes;

    MPI_Init( &argc, &argv );

    MPI_Comm_get_parent( &slavecomm );
    MPI_Intercomm_merge( slavecomm, 1, &all_processes );
    MPI_Bcast( controlmsg, CMDSIZE, MPI_CHAR, 0,
               all_processes );
    if ( strcmp( controlmsg, "exit" ) == 0 ) {
        MPI_Finalize();
        return 1;
    }

    MPI_Bcast( outfilename, MAXPATHLEN, MPI_CHAR, 0,
               all_processes );
    if ( (outfd = open( outfilename, O_CREAT|O_WRONLY|O_TRUNC,
                        S_IRWXU ) ) == -1 )
        mystatus = -1;
    else
        mystatus = 0;
    MPI_Allreduce( &mystatus, &allstatus, 1, MPI_INT, MPI_MIN,
                   all_processes );
    if ( allstatus == -1 ) {
        MPI_Finalize();
        return -1;
    }
```

Figure 2.18
First part of slave for parallel copy program

```
    /* at this point all files have been successfully opened */
    done = 0;
    while (!done) {
        numread = read( infd, buf, BUFSIZE );
        MPI_Bcast( &numread, 1, MPI_INT, 0, all_processes );
        if ( numread > 0 ) {
            MPI_Bcast( buf, numread, MPI_BYTE, 0, all_processes );
            write( outfd, buf, numread );
        }
        else {
            close( outfd );
            done = 1;
        }
    }
    MPI_Comm_free( &pcpslaves );
    MPI_Comm_free( &all_processes );
    MPI_Finalize();
    return 0;
}
```

Figure 2.19
End of master part of parallel copy program

and the merged intracommunicator before exiting.

The primary difference between MPI's spawn function and that of earlier message-passing systems is the collective nature of the operation. In MPI, a group of processes collectively creates another group of processes, and all of them synchronize (via MPI_Comm_spawn in the parents and MPI_Init in the children), thus preventing race conditions and allowing the necessary communication infrastructure to be set up before any of the calls return.

We defer to Chapter 7 the rest of the dynamic process management features of MPI-2. These include details on how to use all of the features of MPI_Comm_spawn, as well as how to form communicators connecting two MPI programs that are already running.

C bindings for the dynamic process management functions used in the parallel copy example are given in Table 2.7.

```
    /* at this point all files have been successfully opened */

    done = 0;
    while ( !done ) {
        MPI_Bcast( &numread, 1, MPI_INT, 0, all_processes );
        if ( numread > 0 ) {
            MPI_Bcast( buf, numread, MPI_BYTE, 0, all_processes );
            write( outfd, buf, numread );
        }
        else {
            close( outfd );
            done = 1;
        }
    }
    MPI_Comm_free( &slavecomm );
    MPI_Comm_free( &all_processes );
    MPI_Finalize();
    return 0;
}
```

Figure 2.20
End of slave part of parallel copy program

int **MPI_Comm_spawn**(char *command, char *argv[], int maxprocs, MPI_Info info, int root, MPI_Comm comm, MPI_Comm *intercomm, int array_of_errcodes[])
int **MPI_Comm_get_parent**(MPI_Comm *parent)
int **MPI_Intercomm_merge**(MPI_Comm intercomm, int high, MPI_Comm *newintracomm)

Table 2.7
C bindings for the functions used in the parallel copy example

2.5   More Info on `Info`

In the preceding sections we have several times seen *info* as an argument in a long parameter list but skipped over the details, often by passing `MPI_INFO_NULL` as that argument. In this section we explain the concept of info and give examples of its use in parallel I/O and dynamic process management.

2.5.1   Motivation, Description, and Rationale

MPI-2 contains some complex functions with potentially long and unwieldy argument lists. In addition, some functions interact with external objects such as the operating system or file system in ways that are unlikely to be uniform across the wide range of platforms on which MPI programs are expected to run. In order to preserve at least some measure of portability for MPI programs, some arguments need to be optional.

The answer to all of these problems is the info object. The info object is an opaque object (of type `MPI_Info` in C, `MPI::Info` in C++, and `integer` in Fortran) that provides a flexible mechanism for dealing with complex, optional, or nonportable options on certain MPI-2 function calls. In some ways it is a general "mini-database" of (key, value) pairs. MPI provides functions to create and delete info objects, to access and update an info object by adding and deleting these pairs, and to access the pairs either by key or by number in sequence. Both keys and values are character strings.

This type of functionality (managing sets of strings) doesn't seem to have much to do with message passing; what is it doing as part of the MPI standard? The MPI Forum felt that no existing library provided the flexibility needed, was available on all platforms, and was language neutral. Therefore it had to specify one of its own. We will see how it is used with some examples related to the programs discussed earlier in this chapter; a more through description is given in other chapters where info is used.

2.5.2   An Example from Parallel I/O

Several parallel file systems can benefit from "hints" given to the file system about how the application program will interact with the file system. These hints contain information known to the programmer or user that may be difficult or impossible for the file system to figure out by itself and that may allow the file system to perform useful optimizations in handling the application's I/O requests. For example, optimizations may be possible if the file system knows that the file will be read only once and in a sequential fashion. This hint can be given to the file system via the info object as follows.

```
MPI_Info myinfo;
MPI_File myfile;
MPI_Comm mycomm;

MPI_Info_create(&myinfo);
MPI_Info_set(myinfo, "access_style", "read_once,sequential");
MPI_File_open(mycomm, "myfile", MPI_MODE_RDONLY, myinfo,
              &myfile);
MPI_Info_free(&myinfo);
```

Note that one can free the info object after it has been used in the call to MPI_File_open; the info object belongs to the user, not the system, and its content is extracted by the system when it is used as an argument in an MPI call.

The key access_style is a reserved key in MPI, and the values for it are also reserved. An MPI implementation is free to ignore this hint, but if it recognizes access_style, it should also recognize the values specified in the MPI Standard. It can also recognize additional values not defined in the Standard. The Standard contains all the reserved keys for the info object and describes their possible values. Implementations are allowed to recognize other keys and values as well, at some risk to the portability of programs that use them.

2.5.3   An Example from Dynamic Process Management

In our parallel copy example in Section 2.4, we used an info object to pass information on the processors to spawn the new processes on, without discussing the details of the use of the info routines. We assumed that somehow the implementation could find the executable and make a reasonable choice of working directory for the program to run in. We also used a special info key, file, to provide an implementation-specific list of processors to spawn processes on.

The info object passed to MPI_Comm_spawn can provide more information. For example, suppose we want the slaves in our parallel copy example to be run on host nome.mcs.anl.gov, the executable program slave should be looked for in directory /home/kosh/progs, and each slave process should have /home/kosh/tmp as its working directory when it is started. Then we would use

```
integer spawninfo, ierr
integer slavecomm, numslaves
```

---

int **MPI_Info_create**(MPI_Info *info)

int **MPI_Info_set**(MPI_Info info, char *key, char *value)

int **MPI_Info_free**(MPI_Info *info)

Table 2.8
C bindings for the info functions used in this chapter

MPI_INFO_CREATE(info, ierror)
                 integer info, ierror

MPI_INFO_SET(info, key, value, ierror)
                 integer info, ierror
                 character*(*) key, value

MPI_INFO_FREE(info, ierror)
                 integer info, ierror

Table 2.9
Fortran bindings for the info functions used in this chapter

```
numslaves = 10
call MPI_INFO_CREATE(spawninfo, ierr)
call MPI_INFO_SET(spawninfo, 'host', 'nome.mcs.anl.gov', ierr)
call MPI_INFO_SET(spawninfo, 'path', '/home/kosh/progs', ierr)
call MPI_INFO_SET(spawninfo, 'wdir', '/home/kosh/tmp', ierr)
call MPI_COMM_SPAWN('slave', MPI_ARGV_NULL, numslaves, &
                    spawninfo, 0, MPI_COMM_WORLD, &
                    slavecomm, MPI_ERRCODES_IGNORE, ierr)
call MPI_INFO_FREE(spawninfo, ierr)
```

(We have rewritten this part of the example in Fortran just to provide an example of the info routines and the MPI_Comm_Spawn in Fortran.) The keys host, path, and wdir are reserved; there are other reserved keys, which we will describe in Chapter 7.

C and Fortran bindings for the info functions used above are given in Tables 2.8 and 2.9. We return to info, including the C++ versions of the info routines, in Section 3.7.

2.6 Summary

In this chapter we have presented a quick overview of MPI-2. We have walked
through some simple example programs in the areas of parallel I/O, remote memory access, and dynamic process management. Along the way we have touched on
the C++ bindings and the use of Fortran 90, collective operations on intercommunicators, and the info object. Readers should now have an idea of some of the new
capabilities provided by MPI-2. In the following chapters we will examine these
and other MPI-2 features in greater detail, so that users will be able to apply these
capabilities in more complex MPI applications.

3 Parallel I/O

In this chapter we demonstrate the parallel I/O capabilities of MPI-2, sometimes referred to as MPI-IO. We begin with simple example programs that demonstrate the basic use of MPI for I/O and then move on to programs that demonstrate various advanced I/O features of MPI. We also explain how the I/O features of MPI must be used in order to achieve high performance.

3.1 Introduction

As we discussed in Section 2.2, many parallel applications perform I/O either by having each process write to a separate file or by having all processes send their data to one process that gathers all the data and writes it to a single file. Application developers have chosen these approaches because of historical limitations in the I/O capabilities of many parallel systems: either parallel I/O from multiple processes to a common file was not supported, or, if supported, the performance was poor. On modern parallel systems, however, these limitations no longer exist. With sufficient and appropriately configured I/O hardware and modern parallel/high-performance file systems, such as IBM's PIOFS and GPFS, SGI's XFS, HP's HFS, and NEC's SFS, one can achieve both high performance and the convenience of a single file by having multiple processes directly access a common file. The I/O interface in MPI is specifically designed to support such accesses and to enable implementations to deliver high performance for such accesses. The interface supports various features—such as noncontiguous accesses, collective I/O, and hints—that research projects in parallel I/O have demonstrated to be essential for high performance [4, 5, 10, 13, 16, 17, 19, 26, 41, 48, 52, 64, 65, 69, 73, 74, 77, 82, 83].

We note that the I/O functions in MPI are for unformatted binary file I/O—similar to the Unix I/O functions `read` and `write` or the C library functions `fread` and `fwrite`. MPI does not have any functions for formatted text I/O equivalent to `fprintf` and `fscanf` in C. For formatted text output, one can use tools such as the Parallel Print Function [55].

3.2 Using MPI for Simple I/O

We presented some simple I/O programs in Chapter 2. Let us begin this chapter with another simple example: a parallel program in which processes need to read data from a common file. Let us assume that there are n processes, each needing to read $(1/n)$th of the file as shown in Figure 3.1.

FILE

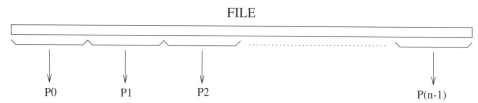

PO   P1   P2   P(n-1)

Figure 3.1
Each process needs to read a chunk of data from a common file

3.2.1 Using Individual File Pointers

Figure 3.2 shows one way of writing such a program with MPI. It has the usual functions one would expect for I/O: an open, a seek, a read, and a close. Let us look at each of the functions closely. MPI_File_open is the function for opening a file. The first argument to this function is a communicator that indicates the group of processes that need to access the file and that are calling this function. We use MPI_COMM_WORLD as the communicator because all processes in this example need to open and thereafter access a common file called /pfs/datafile. The file name is passed as the second argument to MPI_File_open.

The MPI Standard does not specify the format of file names; instead, implementations have the freedom to define the format they support. One can expect that implementations will support familiar naming conventions. For example, implementations running in Unix environments can be expected to support the usual Unix file-naming conventions. In this example and many other examples in this chapter, we use the file name /pfs/datafile (for no particular reason). This name refers to a file called datafile stored in the directory /pfs. Readers can replace this file name with a file name of their choice. The directory name can be expected to be optional in most implementations—if not specified, the implementation will use a default directory such as the directory from where the program is run.

The third argument to MPI_File_open specifies the mode of access; we use MPI_-MODE_RDONLY because this program only reads from the file. The fourth argument, called the *info* argument, allows the user to pass hints to the implementation. In this simple example, we don't pass any hints; instead, we pass a null info argument, MPI_INFO_NULL. In Section 3.7 we will consider in detail the issue of passing hints to the implementation. MPI_File_open returns a *file handle* in the last argument. This file handle is to be used for future operations on the open file.

All I/O functions return an integer error code. For simplicity, we don't check error codes in any of the examples in this chapter; we assume that the functions return successfully. We defer the discussion of error handling to Chapter 9.

```
/* read from a common file using individual file pointers */
#include "mpi.h"

#define FILESIZE (1024 * 1024)

int main(int argc, char **argv)
{
    int *buf, rank, nprocs, nints, bufsize;
    MPI_File fh;
    MPI_Status status;

    MPI_Init(&argc,&argv);
    MPI_Comm_rank(MPI_COMM_WORLD, &rank);
    MPI_Comm_size(MPI_COMM_WORLD, &nprocs);

    bufsize = FILESIZE/nprocs;
    buf = (int *) malloc(bufsize);
    nints = bufsize/sizeof(int);

    MPI_File_open(MPI_COMM_WORLD, "/pfs/datafile", MPI_MODE_RDONLY,
                  MPI_INFO_NULL, &fh);
    MPI_File_seek(fh, rank*bufsize, MPI_SEEK_SET);
    MPI_File_read(fh, buf, nints, MPI_INT, &status);
    MPI_File_close(&fh);

    free(buf);
    MPI_Finalize();
    return 0;
}
```

Figure 3.2
C program to perform the I/O needed in Figure 3.1 using individual file pointers

After opening the file, each process moves its local file pointer, called *individual file pointer* in MPI, to the location in the file from which the process needs to read data. We use the function `MPI_File_seek` for this purpose. The first argument to `MPI_File_seek` is the file handle returned by `MPI_File_open`. The second argument specifies the offset in the file to seek to, and the third argument `MPI_SEEK_SET` specifies that the offset must be calculated from the head of the file. File offsets in C are of an implementation-defined type called `MPI_Offset`. The implementation will define `MPI_Offset` to be an integer type of size large enough to represent the largest file size supported by the implementation (for example, `long` or `long long`). We specify the offset to `MPI_File_seek` as a product of the rank of the process and the amount of data (in bytes) to be read by each process. (The offset to `MPI_-File_seek` in this example must be specified as a number of bytes because we are using what is known as the default file view. We will consider the issue of file views in detail in Section 3.3.)

We use the function `MPI_File_read` for reading data. On each process, this function reads data from the current location of the process's individual file pointer for the open file. The first argument to `MPI_File_read` is the file handle. The second argument is the address of the buffer in memory into which data must be read. The next two arguments specify the amount of data to be read. Since the data is of type integer, we specify it as a count of the number of integers to be read. The final argument is a status argument, which is the same as the status argument in MPI communication functions, such as `MPI_Recv`. One can determine the amount of data actually read by using the functions `MPI_Get_count` or `MPI_Get_elements` on the status object returned by `MPI_File_read`, but we don't bother to do so in this example. `MPI_File_read` increments the individual file pointer on each process by the amount of data read by that process. Finally, we close the file using the function `MPI_File_close`.

The five functions, `MPI_File_open`, `MPI_File_seek`, `MPI_File_read`, `MPI_File_-write`, and `MPI_File_close`, are actually sufficient to write any I/O program. In addition, these functions are quite similar in functionality to their Unix counterparts. The other I/O functions in MPI are for performance, portability, and convenience. Although these five functions can be used as a quick start to using MPI for I/O and for easily porting Unix I/O programs to MPI, we strongly recommend that users not stop here. For real benefits with using MPI for I/O, one must use its special features, such as support for noncontiguous accesses and collective I/O, described in the rest of this chapter.

The C, Fortran, and C++ bindings for the five basic I/O functions in MPI are given in Tables 3.1, 3.2, and 3.3. Note that `MPI_File_read` and `MPI_File_-`

---

int **MPI_File_open**(MPI_Comm comm, char *filename, int amode, MPI_Info info,
              MPI_File *fh)

int **MPI_File_seek**(MPI_File fh, MPI_Offset offset, int whence)

int **MPI_File_read**(MPI_File fh, void *buf, int count, MPI_Datatype datatype,
              MPI_Status *status)

int **MPI_File_write**(MPI_File fh, void *buf, int count, MPI_Datatype datatype,
              MPI_Status *status)

int **MPI_File_close**(MPI_File *fh)

Table 3.1
C bindings for the five basic I/O functions in MPI

`write` (and other functions in this chapter that take a status argument) have two bindings in C++. This is because MPI allows the user to indicate that the status argument is not to be filled in. Unlike in C and Fortran where the user provides a special parameter, `MPI_STATUS_IGNORE`, in C++ the same is achieved by having two bindings for a function: one with the status argument and one without.

3.2.2 Using Explicit Offsets

`MPI_File_read` and `MPI_File_write` are called *individual-file-pointer functions* because they use the current location of the individual file pointer of each process as the location from where to read/write data. MPI also provides another set of functions, called *explicit-offset functions* (`MPI_File_read_at` and `MPI_File_write_at`), which don't use the individual file pointer. In these functions, the file offset is passed directly as an argument to the function. A separate seek is therefore not needed. If multiple threads of a process are accessing the same file, the explicit-offset functions, rather than the individual-file-pointer functions, must be used for thread safety.

Figure 3.3 shows how the same example of Figure 3.1 can be implemented by using `MPI_File_read_at` instead of `MPI_File_read`. We use Fortran this time in order to show how the I/O functions in MPI can be used from Fortran. Other than a difference in programming language, the only difference in this example is that `MPI_File_seek` is not called; instead, the offset is passed as an argument to `MPI_File_read_at`. We also check how much data was actually read by using `MPI_Get_count` on the status object returned by `MPI_File_read_at`. The individual file

---

MPI_FILE_OPEN(comm, filename, amode, info, fh, ierror)
               character*(*) filename
               integer comm, amode, info, fh, ierror

MPI_FILE_SEEK(fh, offset, whence, ierror)
               integer fh, whence, ierror
               integer(kind=MPI_OFFSET_KIND) offset

MPI_FILE_READ(fh, buf, count, datatype, status, ierror)
               <type> buf(*)
               integer fh, count, datatype, status(MPI_STATUS_SIZE), ierror

MPI_FILE_WRITE(fh, buf, count, datatype, status, ierror)
               <type> buf(*)
               integer fh, count, datatype, status(MPI_STATUS_SIZE), ierror

MPI_FILE_CLOSE(fh, ierror)
               integer fh, ierror

Table 3.2
Fortran bindings for the five basic I/O functions in MPI

MPI::File MPI::File::Open(const MPI::Intracomm& comm, const char* filename,
               int amode, const MPI::Info& info)

void MPI::File::Seek(MPI::Offset offset, int whence)

void MPI::File::Read(void* buf, int count, const MPI::Datatype& datatype,
               MPI::Status& status)

void MPI::File::Read(void* buf, int count, const MPI::Datatype& datatype)

void MPI::File::Write(void* buf, int count, const MPI::Datatype& datatype,
               MPI::Status& status)

void MPI::File::Write(void* buf, int count, const MPI::Datatype& datatype)

void MPI::File::Close()

Table 3.3
C++ bindings for the five basic I/O functions in MPI

```fortran
! read from a common file using explicit offsets
PROGRAM main
    include 'mpif.h'

    integer FILESIZE, MAX_BUFSIZE, INTSIZE
    parameter (FILESIZE=1048576, MAX_BUFSIZE=1048576, INTSIZE=4)
    integer buf(MAX_BUFSIZE), rank, ierr, fh, nprocs, nints
    integer status(MPI_STATUS_SIZE), count
    integer (kind=MPI_OFFSET_KIND) offset

    call MPI_INIT(ierr)
    call MPI_COMM_RANK(MPI_COMM_WORLD, rank, ierr)
    call MPI_COMM_SIZE(MPI_COMM_WORLD, nprocs, ierr)

    call MPI_FILE_OPEN(MPI_COMM_WORLD, '/pfs/datafile', &
                    MPI_MODE_RDONLY, MPI_INFO_NULL, fh, ierr)
    nints = FILESIZE/(nprocs*INTSIZE)
    offset = rank * nints * INTSIZE
    call MPI_FILE_READ_AT(fh, offset, buf, nints, MPI_INTEGER, &
                    status, ierr)
    call MPI_GET_COUNT(status, MPI_INTEGER, count, ierr)
    print *, 'process ', rank, 'read ', count, 'integers'

    call MPI_FILE_CLOSE(fh, ierr)
    call MPI_FINALIZE(ierr)
END PROGRAM main
```

Figure 3.3
Fortran program to perform the I/O needed in Figure 3.1 using explicit offsets

pointer is neither used nor incremented by the explicit-offset functions.

File offsets are of type `integer (kind=MPI_OFFSET_KIND)` in Fortran. `MPI_OFFSET_KIND` is a constant defined by the MPI implementation in the include file `mpif.h` and in the Fortran-90 module `mpi`. `MPI_OFFSET_KIND` defines an integer of size large enough to represent the maximum file size supported by the implementation.

Notice how we have passed the file offset to `MPI_File_read_at` in Fortran. We did not pass the expression `rank*nints*INTSIZE` directly to the function. Instead we defined a variable `offset` of type `integer (kind=MPI_OFFSET_KIND)`, assigned the value of the expression to it, and then passed `offset` as a parameter to `MPI_File_read_at`. We did so because, in the absence of function prototypes, if we

---

int **MPI_File_read_at**(MPI_File fh, MPI_Offset offset, void *buf, int count,
                        MPI_Datatype datatype, MPI_Status *status)

int **MPI_File_write_at**(MPI_File fh, MPI_Offset offset, void *buf, int count,
                        MPI_Datatype datatype, MPI_Status *status)

Table 3.4
C bindings for the explicit-offset functions

MPI_FILE_READ_AT(fh, offset, buf, count, datatype, status, ierror)
                        \<type\> buf(*)
                        integer fh, count, datatype, status(MPI_STATUS_SIZE), ierror
                        integer(kind=MPI_OFFSET_KIND) offset

MPI_FILE_WRITE_AT(fh, offset, buf, count, datatype, status, ierror)
                        \<type\> buf(*)
                        integer fh, count, datatype, status(MPI_STATUS_SIZE), ierror
                        integer(kind=MPI_OFFSET_KIND) offset

Table 3.5
Fortran bindings for the explicit-offset functions

passed the expression directly to the function, the compiler would pass it as an argument of type `integer`. The MPI implementation expects an argument of type `integer (kind=MPI_OFFSET_KIND)`, which could be (and often is) of size larger than `integer`. For example, on many machines integers are of size four bytes, whereas file offsets may be defined to be of size eight bytes in order to support large files. In such cases, passing an integer expression as the offset parameter in Fortran would result in a runtime error that is hard to debug. Many users make this mistake; for example, they directly pass 0 as the offset. The problem can be avoided either by passing only variables of the correct type (`integer (kind=MPI_-OFFSET_KIND)`) to functions that take file offsets or displacements as arguments or by using the Fortran-90 module "mpi" that has the MPI function prototypes (that is, by replacing "`include 'mpif.h'`" by "`use mpi`").

C, Fortran, and C++ bindings for the explicit-offset functions are given in Tables 3.4, 3.5, and 3.6.

> **void MPI::File::Read_at**(MPI::Offset offset, void* buf, int count,
>   const MPI::Datatype& datatype, MPI::Status& status)
>
> **void MPI::File::Read_at**(MPI::Offset offset, void* buf, int count,
>   const MPI::Datatype& datatype)
>
> **void MPI::File::Write_at**(MPI::Offset offset, void* buf, int count,
>   const MPI::Datatype& datatype, MPI::Status& status)
>
> **void MPI::File::Write_at**(MPI::Offset offset, void* buf, int count,
>   const MPI::Datatype& datatype)

Table 3.6
C++ bindings for the explicit-offset functions

3.2.3 Writing to a File

In the above example, if we wanted to write to the file instead of reading, we would simply replace `MPI_File_read` with `MPI_File_write` in Figure 3.2 and `MPI_File_read_at` with `MPI_File_write_at` in Figure 3.3. In addition, in both programs, we would need replace the flag `MPI_MODE_RDONLY` that was passed to `MPI_File_open` with the two flags `MPI_MODE_CREATE` and `MPI_MODE_WRONLY`. `MPI_MODE_CREATE` is necessary to create the file if it doesn't already exist. `MPI_MODE_WRONLY` indicates that the file is being opened for writing only. In C, we can pass two (or more) flags by using the bitwise-or operator as follows: `MPI_MODE_CREATE | MPI_MODE_WRONLY`. In Fortran, we can use the addition operation: `MPI_MODE_CREATE + MPI_MODE_WRONLY`. The flag `MPI_MODE_RDWR` must be used if the file is being opened for both reading and writing.

We note that to create a file with `MPI_File_open`, most implementations would require that the directory containing the file (specified in the file name) exist before the call to `MPI_File_open`. (The Unix `open` function also requires this.) Users can create the directory, for example, with the Unix command `mkdir` before running the program.

3.3 Noncontiguous Accesses and Collective I/O

In the preceding section we saw how to use MPI for a simple example where the I/O request of each process is contiguous. I/O of this kind can also be done equally well with regular Unix I/O functions. In many real parallel applications, however, each process needs to access lots of small pieces of data located noncontiguously in the file [4, 17, 65, 77, 78, 85]. One way to access noncontiguous data is to use a separate function call to read/write each small contiguous piece, as in Unix I/O. Because of high I/O latency, however, accessing small amounts of data at a time is *very* expensive. A great advantage of MPI over Unix I/O is the ability in MPI to access noncontiguous data with a single function call. Combined with that is the ability to specify—with the help of a class of read/write functions called *collective I/O functions*—that a group of processes need to access a common file at about the same time. By using these two features, the user can provide the implementation with the entire (noncontiguous) access information of a process as well as information about which set of processes are accessing the file simultaneously. The implementation can use this information to perform certain optimizations that can improve performance significantly. These optimizations typically involve merging several small accesses and making few large requests to the file system [87].

3.3.1   Noncontiguous Accesses

Let us first see how MPI supports noncontiguous accesses in the file. MPI has a notion of a *file view*, which we did not explain in the two example programs so far, but it was implicitly used nonetheless. A file view in MPI defines which portion of a file is "visible" to a process. A read or write function can access data only from the visible portion of the file; all other data will be skipped. When a file is first opened, the entire file is visible to the process, and MPI treats the file as consisting of all bytes (not integers, floating-point numbers, etc.). The user can read any byte or write to any byte in the file. The individual file pointer of each process and also the shared file pointer (discussed in Section 3.6) are set to offset 0 when the file is opened.

It is possible and often desirable to change a process's file view by using the function `MPI_File_set_view`. This may be done for two reasons:

• To indicate the type of data that the process is going to access, for example, integers or floating-point numbers, rather than just bytes. This is particularly necessary for file portability, that is, if the user wants to access the file later on from a different machine with a different data representation. We will consider this issue further in Section 3.9.

• To indicate which parts of the file should be skipped, that is, to specify noncontiguous accesses in the file.

For accessing data using the individual file pointer or explicit offsets, each process can specify a different view if it needs to. For accessing data with the shared file pointer, however, all processes must specify the same view (see Section 3.6). The function for setting the file view is MPI_File_set_view; the view can be changed any number of times during the program.

MPI datatypes, both basic and derived, are used to specify file views. File views are specified by a triplet: *displacement*, *etype*, and *filetype*. The displacement indicates the number of bytes (always bytes!) to be skipped from the start of the file. It can be used, for example, to skip reading the header portion of a file if the file contains a header. The etype is the basic unit of data access. It can be any MPI basic or derived datatype. All file accesses are performed in units of etype (no less). All offsets in the file (for example, file-pointer locations, offsets passed to the explicit-offset functions) are specified in terms of the number of etypes. For example, if the etype is set to MPI_INT, the individual and shared file pointers can be moved by a number of integers, rather than bytes.

The filetype is an MPI basic or derived datatype that specifies which portion of the file is visible to the process and of what type is the data. The filetype must be either the same as the etype or must be a derived datatype constructed out of etypes.[1] The file view of a process begins from the displacement and consists of multiple contiguous copies of the filetype. This is similar to the use of the datatype argument in the MPI_Send function, with the additional displacement.

When a file is first opened, the displacement is 0, and the etype and filetype are both MPI_BYTE. This is known as the default file view. The two programs we considered in the preceding section (Figures 3.2 and 3.3) use the default file view.

Figure 3.4 shows an example of a file view consisting of a displacement of five integers, an etype of MPI_INT, and a filetype consisting of two integers followed by a gap of four integers. The figure shows how the file is "tiled" with this filetype. Once this view is set, only the shaded portions of the file will be read/written by any read/write function; the blank unshaded portions will be skipped. Figure 3.5 shows the corresponding C code for setting this view. We first create a contiguous derived datatype consisting of two integers. We then set a gap of four integers at the end of this datatype, by using the function MPI_Type_create_resized with a lower bound of zero and an extent of 6 * sizeof(int). (The MPI-2 Standard states that this is the new preferred way of setting the upper bound of a datatype. The old MPI-1 way of doing the same by using MPI_Type_struct with an explicit MPI_UB marker has been deprecated [32].) We commit the resized datatype, and

---

[1]A restriction on filetypes is that a filetype must specify only monotonically nondecreasing offsets in the file. For example, a derived datatype that specifies offsets in the order {2, 6, 5, 7, 4} cannot be used as a valid filetype. We consider this issue further in Section 3.4.5.

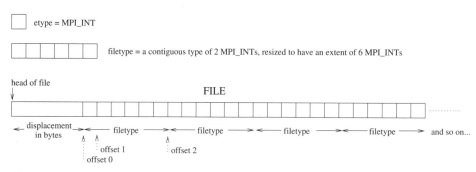

Figure 3.4
Example of file view

---

int **MPI_File_set_view**(MPI_File fh, MPI_Offset disp, MPI_Datatype etype,
MPI_Datatype filetype, char *datarep, MPI_Info info)

int **MPI_Type_create_resized**(MPI_Datatype oldtype, MPI_Aint lb,
MPI_Aint extent, MPI_Datatype *newtype)

Table 3.7
C bindings for `MPI_File_set_view` and `MPI_Type_create_resized`

the committed datatype is used as the filetype. The etype is `MPI_INT`, and the displacement is `5 * sizeof(int)`.

The arguments passed to `MPI_File_set_view` are the file handle, displacement, etype, filetype, data representation, and info (hints). We consider data representation and hints in Sections 3.9 and 3.7, respectively. Here we set the data representation to the default value `native`, which means the data representation in the file is the same as in memory, and we pass `MPI_INFO_NULL` as the info argument.

When this program is run, the single `MPI_File_write` call will result in 1,000 integers written to the file in a noncontiguous fashion as defined by the file view: an initial gap of size equal to five integers, then two integers of data, then a gap of size four integers, followed again by two integers of data, then a gap of size four integers, and so forth. File views thus provide a powerful way of specifying noncontiguous accesses in the file. Any noncontiguous access pattern can be specified because any MPI derived datatype can be used to define the file view.

C, Fortran, and C++ bindings for `MPI_File_set_view` and `MPI_Type_create_-resized` are given in Tables 3.7, 3.8, and 3.9.

```
MPI_Aint lb, extent;
MPI_Datatype etype, filetype, contig;
MPI_Offset disp;
MPI_File fh;
int buf[1000];

MPI_File_open(MPI_COMM_WORLD, "/pfs/datafile",
              MPI_MODE_CREATE | MPI_MODE_RDWR, MPI_INFO_NULL, &fh);

MPI_Type_contiguous(2, MPI_INT, &contig);
lb = 0;
extent = 6 * sizeof(int);
MPI_Type_create_resized(contig, lb, extent, &filetype);
MPI_Type_commit(&filetype);

disp = 5 * sizeof(int);    /* assume displacement in this file view
                              is of size equal to 5 integers */
etype = MPI_INT;

MPI_File_set_view(fh, disp, etype, filetype, "native",
                  MPI_INFO_NULL);
MPI_File_write(fh, buf, 1000, MPI_INT, MPI_STATUS_IGNORE);
```

Figure 3.5
C code to set the view shown in Figure 3.4.

MPI_FILE_SET_VIEW(fh, disp, etype, filetype, datarep, info, ierror)
        integer fh, etype, filetype, info, ierror
        character*(*) datarep
        integer(kind=MPI_OFFSET_KIND) disp

MPI_TYPE_CREATE_RESIZED(oldtype, lb, extent, newtype, ierror)
        integer oldtype, newtype, ierror
        integer(kind=MPI_ADDRESS_KIND) lb, extent

Table 3.8
Fortran bindings for MPI_File_set_view and MPI_Type_create_resized

> **void MPI::File::Set_view**(MPI::Offset disp, const MPI::Datatype& etype,
> const MPI::Datatype& filetype, const char datarep[],
> const MPI::Info& info)
>
> **MPI::Datatype MPI::Datatype::Resized**(const MPI::Datatype& oldtype,
> const MPI::Aint lb, const MPI::Aint extent)

Table 3.9
C++ bindings for `MPI_File_set_view` and `MPI_Type_create_resized`

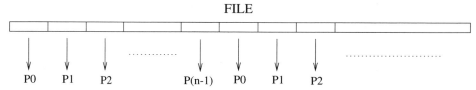

Figure 3.6
Each process needs to read blocks of data from the file, the blocks being distributed in a
round-robin (block-cyclic) manner among processes.

3.3.2 Collective I/O

Now let us consider the use of *collective* I/O functions together with noncontiguous
accesses. We use a different example, shown in Figure 3.6. The difference between
this example and the first example we considered in this chapter (Figure 3.1) is that
each process in this case reads smaller blocks of data distributed in a round-robin
(block-cyclic) manner in the file. With Unix I/O, the only way to read this data
would be to read each block separately, because the Unix **read** function allows the
user to access only a single contiguous piece of data at a time. One can also do
the same with MPI (by using the default file view), but one can do better. Instead
of making several read calls, one can define the noncontiguous file view of each
process in order to read data with a single function, and one can use a collective
read function to specify that all processes need to read data. The corresponding
code is given in Figure 3.7. A good MPI implementation will be able to deliver much
better performance if the user expresses the I/O in the program in this manner,
rather than if the user performed Unix-style I/O. Let's go through this program in
detail.

The constant `FILESIZE` specifies the size of the file in bytes. `INTS_PER_BLK` specifies the size of each of the blocks that a process needs to read; the size is specified
as the number of integers in the block. Each process needs to read several of these
blocks distributed in a cyclic fashion in the file. We open the file using `MPI_File_-`

```
/* noncontiguous access with a single collective I/O function */
#include "mpi.h"

#define FILESIZE        1048576
#define INTS_PER_BLK    16

int main(int argc, char **argv)
{
    int *buf, rank, nprocs, nints, bufsize;
    MPI_File fh;
    MPI_Datatype filetype;

    MPI_Init(&argc,&argv);
    MPI_Comm_rank(MPI_COMM_WORLD, &rank);
    MPI_Comm_size(MPI_COMM_WORLD, &nprocs);

    bufsize = FILESIZE/nprocs;
    buf = (int *) malloc(bufsize);
    nints = bufsize/sizeof(int);

    MPI_File_open(MPI_COMM_WORLD, "/pfs/datafile", MPI_MODE_RDONLY,
                  MPI_INFO_NULL, &fh);

    MPI_Type_vector(nints/INTS_PER_BLK, INTS_PER_BLK,
                    INTS_PER_BLK*nprocs, MPI_INT, &filetype);
    MPI_Type_commit(&filetype);
    MPI_File_set_view(fh, INTS_PER_BLK*sizeof(int)*rank, MPI_INT,
                      filetype, "native", MPI_INFO_NULL);

    MPI_File_read_all(fh, buf, nints, MPI_INT, MPI_STATUS_IGNORE);
    MPI_File_close(&fh);

    MPI_Type_free(&filetype);
    free(buf);
    MPI_Finalize();
    return 0;
}
```

Figure 3.7
C program to perform the I/O needed in Figure 3.6. Each process reads noncontiguous data
with a single collective read function.

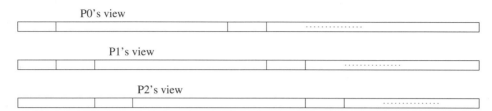

Figure 3.8
The file views created by the program in Figure 3.7

open and specify MPI_COMM_WORLD as the communicator, because all processes access a common file /pfs/datafile. Next we construct the file view. For specifying the filetype, we create a derived datatype of type "vector" by using the function MPI_-Type_vector. The first argument to this function is the number of blocks each process needs to read. The second argument is the number of integers in each block. The third argument is the number of integers between the starting elements of two consecutive blocks that a process needs to read. The fourth argument is the type of each data item—MPI_INT in this case. The newly created vector datatype is returned in the fifth argument. We commit this datatype and then use it as the filetype argument for MPI_File_set_view. The etype is MPI_INT. Note how we use the displacement argument of MPI_File_set_view to specify the file offset from where the view of each process begins. The displacement is specified (in bytes, always) as the product of the size of the block and the rank of the process. As a result, the file view of each process is a vector datatype starting from the displacement, as illustrated in Figure 3.8.

I/O is performed by using the collective version of MPI_File_read, called MPI_-File_read_all. Notice that there is no difference in the parameter list of MPI_-File_read and MPI_File_read_all. The only difference is that MPI_File_read_-all is defined to be a *collective I/O function*, as suggested by the _all in its name. Collective means that the function must be called by every process in the communicator that was passed to the MPI_File_open function with which the file was opened. This communicator information is implicitly contained in the file handle passed to MPI_File_read_all. MPI_File_read, on the other hand, may be called independently by any subset of processes and is therefore known as an *independent I/O function*.

When a process calls an independent I/O function, the implementation has no idea what other processes might do and must therefore satisfy the request of each process individually. When a process calls a collective I/O function, however, the

---

int **MPI_File_read_all**(MPI_File fh, void *buf, int count, MPI_Datatype datatype,
                    MPI_Status *status)

int **MPI_File_write_all**(MPI_File fh, void *buf, int count, MPI_Datatype datatype,
                    MPI_Status *status)

Table 3.10
C bindings for `MPI_File_read_all` and `MPI_File_write_all`

MPI_FILE_READ_ALL(fh, buf, count, datatype, status, ierror)
                <type> buf(*)
                integer fh, count, datatype, status(MPI_STATUS_SIZE), ierror

MPI_FILE_WRITE_ALL(fh, buf, count, datatype, status, ierror)
                <type> buf(*)
                integer fh, count, datatype, status(MPI_STATUS_SIZE), ierror

---

Table 3.11
Fortran bindings for `MPI_File_read_all` and `MPI_File_write_all`

implementation knows exactly which other processes will also call the same collective I/O function, each process providing its own access information. The implementation may, therefore, choose to wait for all those processes to reach the function, in order to analyze the access requests of different processes and service the combined request efficiently. Although the request of one process may consist of numerous small noncontiguous pieces the combined request of all processes may be large and contiguous, as in Figure 3.6. Optimization of this kind is broadly referred to as collective I/O [19, 48, 73, 87], and it can improve performance significantly. Therefore, the user should, when possible, use the collective I/O functions instead of independent I/O functions. We consider this issue further in Section 3.10.

C, Fortran, and C++ bindings for `MPI_File_read_all` and `MPI_File_write_all` are given in Tables 3.10, 3.11, and 3.12. Collective versions also exist for the explicit-offset functions, `MPI_File_read_at` and `MPI_File_write_at`.

3.4 Accessing Arrays Stored in Files

In this section we demonstrate how MPI makes it easy to access subarrays and distributed arrays (both regularly and irregularly distributed) stored in files. I/O of this kind is very commonly needed in parallel programs.

void MPI::File::Read_all(void* buf, int count, const MPI::Datatype& datatype,
                 MPI::Status& status)

void MPI::File::Read_all(void* buf, int count, const MPI::Datatype& datatype)

void MPI::File::Write_all(const void* buf, int count,
                 const MPI::Datatype& datatype, MPI::Status& status)

void MPI::File::Write_all(const void* buf, int count,
                 const MPI::Datatype& datatype)

Table 3.12
C++ bindings for MPI_File_read_all and MPI_File_write_all

Many parallel programs have one or more multidimensional arrays distributed among processes in some manner. Each array must be read from or written to a file in which the storage order corresponds to that of the global array in either row-major order (as in C programs) or column-major order (as in Fortran programs). Figure 3.9 shows such an example. A two-dimensional array of size m rows and n columns is distributed among six processes arranged as a 2×3 logical grid. The array must be written to a common file containing the global array in row-major (C) order. Clearly the local array of each process is not located contiguously in the file: each row of the local array of a process is separated by rows of the local arrays of other processes. MPI provides a convenient way of describing I/O of this kind and performing it with a single I/O function call. If the user uses the collective I/O functions, the MPI implementation may also be able to deliver high performance for this kind of access, even though the accesses are noncontiguous.

Two new datatype constructors, called *darray* and *subarray*, are defined in MPI-2. These functions facilitate the creation of derived datatypes describing the location of a local array within a linearized global array. These datatypes can be used as the filetype to describe the noncontiguous file-access pattern when performing I/O for distributed arrays. Let's first see how the array in Figure 3.9 can be written by using the darray datatype, and then we will do the same by using the subarray datatype.

3.4.1   Distributed Arrays

Figure 3.10 shows the program for writing the array shown in Figure 3.9 by using the darray datatype constructor. The only difference between this program and the others we have seen in this chapter so far is the way in which the filetype is con-

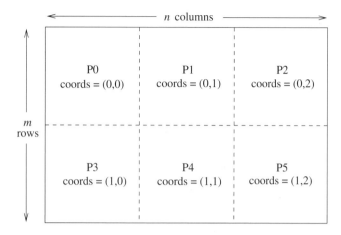

2D array distributed on a 2 x 3 process grid

Figure 3.9
A 2D array of size m rows and n columns is distributed among six processes arranged as a 2×3
logical grid. The array is to be written to a common file containing the global array in
row-major order (as in C).

structed. The darray datatype constructor provides an easy way to create a derived
datatype describing the location of the local array of a process within a linearized
multidimensional global array for common regular distributions. The distributions
supported are the array distributions defined in High Performance Fortran (HPF),
namely, block, cyclic, and the general block-cyclic or cyclic(k) distribution [47].

The array can have any number of dimensions, and each dimension can be distributed in any of the above ways, or the dimension can be replicated (that is, not
distributed). The input to the darray constructor consists of the array size and
distribution information and the rank of the process whose local array is the one to
be described. The output is a derived datatype describing the layout of the local
array of that process within the linearized global array for the specified distribution. It is possible to create such a derived datatype by using other MPI datatype
constructors, but it is more difficult. Therefore, these new datatype constructors
were added in MPI-2 as convenience functions.

The first argument to MPI_Type_create_darray is the number of processes over
which the array is distributed, six in this case. The second argument is the rank
of the process whose local array is the one to be described, which in this case is
the process calling the function. The third argument is the number of dimensions
of the global array (and also the local array). The fourth argument is an array

```
gsizes[0] = m;    /* no. of rows in global array */
gsizes[1] = n;    /* no. of columns in global array*/

distribs[0] = MPI_DISTRIBUTE_BLOCK;  /* block distribution */
distribs[1] = MPI_DISTRIBUTE_BLOCK;  /* block distribution */

dargs[0] = MPI_DISTRIBUTE_DFLT_DARG; /* default block size */
dargs[1] = MPI_DISTRIBUTE_DFLT_DARG; /* default block size */

psizes[0] = 2;  /* no. of processes in vertical dimension
                   of process grid */
psizes[1] = 3;  /* no. of processes in horizontal dimension
                   of process grid */

MPI_Comm_rank(MPI_COMM_WORLD, &rank);
MPI_Type_create_darray(6, rank, 2, gsizes, distribs, dargs,
                   psizes, MPI_ORDER_C, MPI_FLOAT, &filetype);
MPI_Type_commit(&filetype);

MPI_File_open(MPI_COMM_WORLD, "/pfs/datafile",
           MPI_MODE_CREATE | MPI_MODE_WRONLY,
           MPI_INFO_NULL, &fh);

MPI_File_set_view(fh, 0, MPI_FLOAT, filetype, "native",
                  MPI_INFO_NULL);

local_array_size = num_local_rows * num_local_cols;
MPI_File_write_all(fh, local_array, local_array_size,
                  MPI_FLOAT, &status);

MPI_File_close(&fh);
```

Figure 3.10
C program for writing the distributed array of Figure 3.9 to a common file using a "darray"
datatype as the filetype

that specifies the size of the global array in each dimension. The fifth argument is an array specifying the way in which the global array is distributed in each dimension. In this example, we specify a block distribution using `MPI_DISTRIBUTE_-BLOCK`. The sixth argument specifies the distribution parameter for each dimension, that is, the k in a cyclic(k) distribution. For block and cyclic distributions, which don't need this parameter, this argument is specified as `MPI_DISTRIBUTE_DFLT_-DARG`. The seventh argument is an array specifying the number of processes along each dimension of the logical process grid over which the array is distributed. The process grid is always assumed to have the same number of dimensions as the global array. If the array is not distributed along a particular dimension, the number of processes for that dimension must be specified as 1. For example, a 100×100 array can be distributed over 4 processes arranged as a 2×2 grid, or 1×4 grid, or 4×1 grid. The ordering of processes in the grid is *always* assumed to be row-major, as in the case of virtual Cartesian process topologies in MPI-1 [32]. If a program assumes a different ordering of processes, one cannot use the darray constructor but instead must use subarray or other derived datatype constructors. We discuss this issue further in Section 3.4.2.

The eighth argument to `MPI_Type_create_darray` specifies the storage order of the local array in memory and also of the global array in the file. It can be specified as either `MPI_ORDER_C` or `MPI_ORDER_FORTRAN`, which correspond to row-major ordering as in C or column-major ordering as in Fortran. The ninth argument is the datatype describing the type of each array element, which in this example is `MPI_FLOAT`. The function returns in the last argument a derived datatype that describes the layout of the local array of the specified process within the linearized global array for the specified distribution. We commit this datatype and set the file view using this datatype as the filetype. For maximum performance, we call the collective write function `MPI_File_write_all` and not an independent write function. Note that the count and datatype passed to `MPI_File_write_all` describe the memory layout of the local array. In this example we assume that the local array is contiguously allocated in memory. We therefore specify the datatype as `MPI_FLOAT` and the count as the number of elements in the local array. In Section 3.4.4, we will consider an example in which the local array is noncontiguous in memory and see how to construct a derived datatype that describes the memory layout.

3.4.2   A Word of Warning about Darray

Although the darray datatype is very convenient to use, one must be careful about using it because it assumes a very specific definition of data distribution—the exact definition of the distributions in HPF [47]. This assumption matters particularly when in a block distribution the size of the array in any dimension is not evenly divisible by the number of processes in that dimension. In such a case, HPF defines the block size to be obtained by a ceiling division of the array size and the number of processes.[2] If one assumes a different definition in a program, such as floor division (which is regular integer division, for example, $\lfloor 5/4 \rfloor = 1$), one cannot use the darray constructor because the resulting datatype will not match the distribution. Furthermore, darray assumes that the ordering of processes in the logical grid is always row-major as in the virtual Cartesian process topologies of MPI-1 (see Figure 3.9). If a program follows a different ordering, such as column-major, the datatype returned by darray will be incorrect for that program.

If one follows a different definition of distribution or a different process-grid ordering, one can use the subarray datatype instead. For this datatype, the location (starting coordinates) of the local array in the global array must be specified explicitly. The subarray datatype, however, will work only for block distributions, not cyclic or cyclic(k) distributions (because one cannot specify a stride in any dimension). In cases where subarray is also not applicable, one can create the derived datatype explicitly by using some of the general constructors defined in MPI-1, such as indexed or struct. *Any* data layout can be specified by (recursively) using the MPI-1 constructors; it's just easier to use darray or subarray wherever it works.

3.4.3 Subarray Datatype Constructor

The subarray datatype constructor can be used to create a derived datatype that describes the layout of a subarray within a linearized array. One describes the subarray by its starting coordinates and size in each dimension. The example of Figure 3.9 can also be written by using subarray instead of darray, because the local array of each process is effectively a subarray of the global array. Figure 3.11 shows the "subarray version" of the program in Figure 3.10. This program is a bit more complicated than the darray version because we have to specify the subarray explicitly. In darray, the subarray is implicitly specified by specifying the data distribution.

We use the MPI-1 process-topology function `MPI_Cart_create` to create a virtual Cartesian process grid. We do this purely for convenience: it allows us to find the coordinates of each process within the two-dimensional grid (with the function `MPI_Cart_coords`) and use these coordinates to calculate the global indices of the first element of the local array of each process.

---

[2]The ceiling division of two integers i and j is defined as $\lceil i/j \rceil = (i + j - 1)/j$. For example, $\lceil 5/4 \rceil = 2$. Therefore, a block distribution of an array of size 5 on 4 processes is defined as 2 elements on processes 0 and 1, 1 element on process 2, and 0 elements on process 3.

```
gsizes[0] = m;  /* no. of rows in global array */
gsizes[1] = n;  /* no. of columns in global array*/

psizes[0] = 2;  /* no. of processes in vertical dimension
                   of process grid */
psizes[1] = 3;  /* no. of processes in horizontal dimension
                   of process grid */

lsizes[0] = m/psizes[0];   /* no. of rows in local array */
lsizes[1] = n/psizes[1];   /* no. of columns in local array */

dims[0] = 2;
dims[1] = 3;
periods[0] = periods[1] = 1;
MPI_Cart_create(MPI_COMM_WORLD, 2, dims, periods, 0, &comm);
MPI_Comm_rank(comm, &rank);
MPI_Cart_coords(comm, rank, 2, coords);

/* global indices of the first element of the local array */
start_indices[0] = coords[0] * lsizes[0];
start_indices[1] = coords[1] * lsizes[1];

MPI_Type_create_subarray(2, gsizes, lsizes, start_indices,
                         MPI_ORDER_C, MPI_FLOAT, &filetype);
MPI_Type_commit(&filetype);

MPI_File_open(MPI_COMM_WORLD, "/pfs/datafile",
              MPI_MODE_CREATE | MPI_MODE_WRONLY,
              MPI_INFO_NULL, &fh);
MPI_File_set_view(fh, 0, MPI_FLOAT, filetype, "native",
                  MPI_INFO_NULL);

local_array_size = lsizes[0] * lsizes[1];
MPI_File_write_all(fh, local_array, local_array_size,
                   MPI_FLOAT, &status);

MPI_File_close(&fh);
```

Figure 3.11
C program for writing the distributed array of Figure 3.9 to a common file using a "subarray" datatype as the filetype

The first argument to `MPI_Type_create_subarray` is the number of dimensions of the array. The second argument is the size of the array in each dimension. The third argument is the size of the subarray in each dimension. The fourth argument specifies the starting coordinates of the subarray in each dimension of the array. The starting coordinates are always specified assuming that the array is indexed beginning from zero (even for Fortran arrays). For example, if a Fortran program contains an array `A(1:100,1:100)` and one wants to specify the subarray `B(4:50,10:60)`, then the starting coordinates of B must be specified as `(3,9)`. In other words, the C convention is always used. (Some convention is needed because Fortran allows arrays to be defined starting from any number, for example, `X(50:100, 60:120)`.)

In the program in Figure 3.11, we calculate the starting index of the local array of a process in the global array as a function of the coordinates of the process in the process grid. For this we use the MPI-1 virtual-process-topology functions, `MPI_-Cart_create` and `MPI_Cart_coord`. `MPI_Cart_create` creates the specified 2×3 logical process grid and returns a new communicator. `MPI_Cart_coord` returns the coordinates of a process in the process grid. The coordinates are as shown in Figure 3.9. We multiply the coordinates of the process by the size of the local array in each dimension to obtain the starting location of the process's local array in the global array.

The fifth argument to `MPI_Type_create_subarray` is the same as the `order` argument in `MPI_Type_create_darray`: it specifies the array storage order in memory and file. The sixth argument is the type of each element in the array, which could be any MPI basic or derived datatype. The function returns in the last argument a derived datatype corresponding to the layout of the subarray in the global array. We use this datatype as the filetype in `MPI_File_set_view`. In this example, the array is contiguously allocated in memory. Therefore, in the `MPI_File_write_all` call, we specify the memory datatype as `MPI_FLOAT` and the count as the number of floats in the local array.

C, Fortran, and C++ bindings for the darray and subarray datatype constructors are given in Tables 3.13, 3.14, and 3.15.

3.4.4   Local Array with Ghost Area

In many applications with distributed arrays, the local array is allocated with a few extra rows and columns in each dimension. This extra area, which is not really part of the local array, is often referred to as a *ghost area*. (For examples of the use of ghost areas, see Chapter 4 of [32] and Chapter 5 of this book.) The ghost area is used to store rows or columns belonging to neighboring processes that have been

int **MPI_Type_create_darray**(int size, int rank, int ndims, int array_of_gsizes[],
                    int array_of_distribs[], int array_of_dargs[], int array_of_psizes[],
                    int order, MPI_Datatype oldtype, MPI_Datatype *newtype)

int **MPI_Type_create_subarray**(int ndims, int array_of_sizes[],
                    int array_of_subsizes[], int array_of_starts[], int order,
                    MPI_Datatype oldtype, MPI_Datatype *newtype)

Table 3.13
C bindings for darray and subarray datatype constructors

MPI_TYPE_CREATE_DARRAY(size, rank, ndims, array_of_gsizes,
                    array_of_distribs, array_of_dargs, array_of_psizes, order, oldtype,
                    newtype, ierror)
                    integer size, rank, ndims, array_of_gsizes(*), array_of_distribs(*),
                        array_of_dargs(*), array_of_psizes(*), order, oldtype, newtype,
                        ierror

MPI_TYPE_CREATE_SUBARRAY(ndims, array_of_sizes, array_of_subsizes,
                    array_of_starts, order, oldtype, newtype, ierror)
                    integer ndims, array_of_sizes(*), array_of_subsizes(*),
                        array_of_starts(*), order, oldtype, newtype, ierror

Table 3.14
Fortran bindings for darray and subarray datatype constructors

MPI::Datatype MPI::Datatype::Create_darray(int size, int rank, int ndims,
                    const int array_of_gsizes[], const int array_of_distribs[],
                    const int array_of_dargs[], const int array_of_psizes[], int order) const

MPI::Datatype MPI::Datatype::Create_subarray(int ndims,
                    const int array_of_sizes[], const int array_of_subsizes[],
                    const int array_of_starts[], int order) const

Table 3.15
C++ bindings for darray and subarray datatype constructors

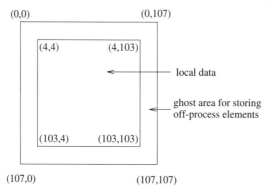

Figure 3.12
A local array of size (100,100) is actually allocated as a (108,108) array to provide a "ghost"
area along the boundaries for storing off-process elements. The real data is stored starting from
index (4,4). The local array is therefore noncontiguous in memory.

communicated via interprocess communication. These rows and columns are stored
in the ghost area, and not in a separate buffer, in order to make the computational
part of the code compact, convenient, and cache friendly and to avoid splitting any
"do loops" that loop across the rows or columns of the local array. Figure 3.12
illustrates the idea of a ghost area.

If a local array has a ghost area around it, the local data is not located contiguously in memory. In the case of C arrays, for example, the rows of the local array
in memory are separated by a few elements of ghost area. When such an array
is written to a file, one usually does not want the ghost area to be written to the
file since the data corresponding to that area will be written by another process.
Instead of writing each row of the local array with a separate function, resulting
in many I/O function calls, we can describe this noncontiguous memory layout in
terms of an MPI derived datatype and specify this derived datatype as the datatype argument to a single MPI_File_write_all function. The entire data transfer,
which is noncontiguous in both memory and file, can therefore be performed with
a single function.

As Figure 3.12 illustrates, the local array is effectively a subarray of a larger
array that includes the ghost area. Therefore, we can use a subarray datatype to
describe the layout of the local array in the allocated memory space. The code for
doing this is given in Figure 3.13.

Assume that the ghost area is of size four elements on each side in each dimension;
in other words, there are four extra rows and columns on each side of the local array.
We first create the filetype using a subarray datatype, open the file, and set the

```
gsizes[0] = m;    gsizes[1] = n;
/* no. of rows and columns in global array*/
psizes[0] = 2;    psizes[1] = 3;
/* no. of processes in vertical and horizontal dimensions
   of process grid */
lsizes[0] = m/psizes[0];   /* no. of rows in local array */
lsizes[1] = n/psizes[1];   /* no. of columns in local array */
dims[0] = 2;    dims[1] = 3;
periods[0] = periods[1] = 1;
MPI_Cart_create(MPI_COMM_WORLD, 2, dims, periods, 0, &comm);
MPI_Comm_rank(comm, &rank);
MPI_Cart_coords(comm, rank, 2, coords);
/* global indices of the first element of the local array */
start_indices[0] = coords[0] * lsizes[0];
start_indices[1] = coords[1] * lsizes[1];
MPI_Type_create_subarray(2, gsizes, lsizes, start_indices,
                         MPI_ORDER_C, MPI_FLOAT, &filetype);
MPI_Type_commit(&filetype);
MPI_File_open(MPI_COMM_WORLD, "/pfs/datafile",
              MPI_MODE_CREATE | MPI_MODE_WRONLY,
              MPI_INFO_NULL, &fh);
MPI_File_set_view(fh, 0, MPI_FLOAT, filetype, "native",
                  MPI_INFO_NULL);
/* create a derived datatype that describes the layout of the local
   array in the memory buffer that includes the ghost area. This is
   another subarray datatype! */
memsizes[0] = lsizes[0] + 8; /* no. of rows in allocated array */
memsizes[1] = lsizes[1] + 8; /* no. of columns in allocated array */
start_indices[0] = start_indices[1] = 4;
/* indices of the first element of the local array in the
   allocated array */
MPI_Type_create_subarray(2, memsizes, lsizes, start_indices,
                         MPI_ORDER_C, MPI_FLOAT, &memtype);
MPI_Type_commit(&memtype);
MPI_File_write_all(fh, local_array, 1, memtype, &status);
MPI_File_close(&fh);
```

Figure 3.13
C program for writing a distributed array that is also noncontiguous in memory because of a ghost area

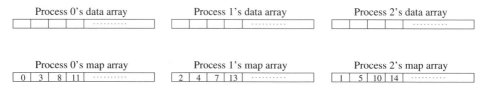

map array describes the location of each element of data array in the (common) file

Figure 3.14
Example of irregular file access. Each process has a local data array and a local map array. Each
element of the map array indicates the location in the file of the corresponding element in the
data array.

view to this type. This portion of the code is identical to the previous program in
Figure 3.11. Then we create another subarray datatype to describe the memory
layout of the local array. For this, we specify the size of the allocated array as
the local array size plus eight in each dimension (four on each side). The starting
location of the local array in the allocated array is (4,4), assuming zero-based
indexing as required. We commit the resulting datatype returned by MPI_Type_-
create_subarray and use it as the datatype argument in MPI_File_write_all.
(Recall that this argument describes memory layout, not file layout; the file layout
is specified by the file view.) Since the entire local array is described by this
datatype, we specify the count argument of MPI_File_write_all as 1.

3.4.5 Irregularly Distributed Arrays

MPI can also be used for accessing irregularly distributed arrays—by specifying the
filetype appropriately. If combined with the use of collective I/O functions, an
MPI implementation may even be able to deliver high performance for such accesses,
which are normally considered difficult to optimize. An irregular distribution is one
that cannot be expressed mathematically by a compact formula, unlike a block or
cyclic distribution. Therefore, another array—called a *map array*—that specifies
the mapping of each element of the local array to the global array is needed. An
example of a map array is the output of a graph partitioner that partitions an
unstructured mesh among processes based on some load-balancing criteria.

Let's consider an example in which an irregularly distributed array is to be written to a common file containing the global array in canonical order, as shown in
Figure 3.14. Figure 3.15 shows the Fortran subroutine for performing this I/O.
The main difference between this program and the ones we considered above for
regularly distributed arrays is the construction of the datatype to be used as the
filetype.

```
SUBROUTINE write_irreg_array(buf, map, bufsize)
    use mpi

    integer bufsize
    double precision buf(bufsize)
    integer map(bufsize), fh, filetype, status(MPI_STATUS_SIZE)
    integer (kind=MPI_OFFSET_KIND) disp
    integer i, ierr

    call MPI_FILE_OPEN(MPI_COMM_WORLD, '/pfs/datafile', &
                    MPI_MODE_CREATE + MPI_MODE_RDWR, &
                    MPI_INFO_NULL, fh, ierr)

    call MPI_TYPE_CREATE_INDEXED_BLOCK(bufsize, 1, map, &
                    MPI_DOUBLE_PRECISION, filetype, ierr)
    call MPI_TYPE_COMMIT(filetype, ierr)
    disp = 0
    call MPI_FILE_SET_VIEW(fh, disp, MPI_DOUBLE_PRECISION, &
                        filetype, 'native', MPI_INFO_NULL, ierr)

    call MPI_FILE_WRITE_ALL(fh, buf, bufsize, &
                        MPI_DOUBLE_PRECISION, status, ierr)

    call MPI_FILE_CLOSE(fh, ierr)

    return
END SUBROUTINE write_irreg_array
```

Figure 3.15
Fortran program for writing an irregularly distributed array

We note that the MPI Standard specifies that the filetype used by any process must specify only monotonically nondecreasing offsets in the file (see Section 9.1.1 in [59]). For example, a derived datatype that specifies offsets in the order {2, 6, 5, 7, 4} cannot be used as a valid filetype. No such restriction exists on the datatype used to describe data layout in memory; it can specify memory offsets in any order. Therefore, the filetype created for an irregular distribution must always specify monotonically nondecreasing offsets. If the entries in the map array are not in nondecreasing order, the map array must first be reordered into nondecreasing order before it is used to create the filetype. The datatype describing the memory layout must be correspondingly permuted so that the desired distribution is still

```
int MPI_Type_create_indexed_block(int count, int blocklength,
            int array_of_displacements[], MPI_Datatype oldtype,
            MPI_Datatype *newtype)
```

Table 3.16
C binding for MPI_Type_create_indexed_block

```
MPI_TYPE_CREATE_INDEXED_BLOCK(count, blocklength,
            array_of_displacements, oldtype, newtype, ierror)
            integer count, blocklength, array_of_displacements(*), oldtype,
            newtype, ierror
```

Table 3.17
Fortran binding for MPI_Type_create_indexed_block

specified correctly.

Let us assume for simplicity that, in the program in Figure 3.15, the map array is already in monotonically nondecreasing order. We can therefore directly use the map array as an index into the file and use an indexed datatype as the filetype. Let us assume further that the map array specifies the location in units of local-array elements—double-precision numbers in this case—and not in bytes. We use the datatype constructor MPI_Type_create_indexed_block , a new constructor defined in MPI-2, to create the indexed datatype. It is the same as the datatype constructor MPI_Type_indexed defined in MPI-1, except that it uses a constant blocklength for all blocks. We pass as the first argument to MPI_Type_create_indexed_block the number of elements in the local data array. The second argument is the number of elements in each block, which we set to 1. The third argument is an array specifying the displacement of each block in the datatype; we pass the map array as this argument. The fourth argument is the type of each element, MPI_DOUBLE_-PRECISION in this case. The function returns the resulting derived datatype in the fifth argument. We commit this datatype and use it as the filetype in MPI_File_-set_view. We use a single collective write function, MPI_File_write_all, to write the entire array.

C, Fortran, and C++ bindings for MPI_Type_create_indexed_block are given in Tables 3.16, 3.17, and 3.18.

MPI::Datatype MPI::Datatype::Create_indexed_block(int count,
int blocklength, const int array_of_displacements[]) const

Table 3.18
C++ binding for `MPI_Type_create_indexed_block`

3.5   Nonblocking I/O and Split Collective I/O

MPI supports nonblocking versions of all independent read/write functions. The mechanism MPI provides for nonblocking I/O is similar to that for nonblocking communication. The nonblocking I/O functions are all named `MPI_File_ixxx`, for example, `MPI_File_iread` and `MPI_File_iwrite_at`, similar to the names `MPI_-Isend` and `MPI_Irecv`. The nonblocking I/O functions return an `MPI_Request` object, as do the nonblocking communication functions. One can use the usual MPI test/wait functions (`MPI_Test`, `MPI_Wait`, `MPI_Testany`, etc.) on the returned request object to test or wait for the completion of nonblocking I/O operations. By using nonblocking I/O functions, one can potentially overlap I/O with other computation/communication in the program, for example as shown below.

```
MPI_Request request;

MPI_File_iwrite_at(fh, offset, buf, count, datatype, &request);
for (i=0; i<1000; i++) {
    /* perform computation */
}
MPI_Wait(&request, &status);
```

How well I/O can be overlapped depends of course on the quality of the implementation.

For collective I/O, MPI supports only a restricted form of nonblocking I/O, called *split collective I/O*. To use split collective I/O, the user must call a "begin" function (for example, `MPI_File_read_all_begin`) to start the collective I/O operation and an "end" function (for example, `MPI_File_read_all_end`) to complete the operation. The restriction is that the user can have only one split collective I/O operation active at a time on any given file handle. In other words, the user cannot issue two begin functions on the same file handle without calling an end function to complete the first begin. Since this restriction exists, a split collective begin does not return an `MPI_Request` object or any other object. A split collective end, by definition, matches the previously called split collective begin on that file

---

int **MPI_File_iwrite_at**(MPI_File fh, MPI_Offset offset, void *buf, int count,
                   MPI_Datatype datatype, MPI_Request *request)

int **MPI_File_write_all_begin**(MPI_File fh, void *buf, int count,
                   MPI_Datatype datatype)

int **MPI_File_write_all_end**(MPI_File fh, void *buf, MPI_Status *status)

Table 3.19
C bindings for MPI_File_iwrite_at, MPI_File_write_all_begin, and MPI_File_write_all_end

---

MPI_FILE_IWRITE_AT(fh, offset, buf, count, datatype, request, ierror)
            <type> buf(*)
            integer fh, count, datatype, request, ierror
            integer(kind=MPI_OFFSET_KIND) offset

MPI_FILE_WRITE_ALL_BEGIN(fh, buf, count, datatype, ierror)
            <type> buf(*)
            integer fh, count, datatype, ierror

MPI_FILE_WRITE_ALL_END(fh, buf, status, ierror)
            <type> buf(*)
            integer fh, status(MPI_STATUS_SIZE), ierror

Table 3.20
Fortran bindings for MPI_File_iwrite_at, MPI_File_write_all_begin, and
MPI_File_write_all_end

handle. The MPI standard allows an implementation to perform the collective I/O operation entirely during the begin function, or entirely during the end function, or in the "background," between the begin and end functions.

An example of using split collective I/O is as follows:

```
MPI_File_write_all_begin(fh, buf, count, datatype);
for (i=0; i<1000; i++) {
    /* perform computation */
}
MPI_File_write_all_end(fh, buf, &status);
```

C, Fortran, and C++ bindings for MPI_File_iwrite_at, MPI_File_write_all_-
begin, and MPI_File_write_all_end are given in Tables 3.19, 3.20, and 3.21.

> **MPI::Request MPI::File::Iwrite_at**(MPI::Offset offset, const void* buf,
>   int count, const MPI::Datatype& datatype)
>
> **void MPI::File::Write_all_begin**(const void* buf, int count,
>   const MPI::Datatype& datatype)
>
> **void MPI::File::Write_all_end**(const void* buf, MPI::Status& status)
>
> **void MPI::File::Write_all_end**(const void* buf)

Table 3.21
C++ binding for `MPI_File_iwrite_at`, `MPI_File_write_all_begin`, and `MPI_File_write_all_end`

3.6   Shared File Pointers

Thus far, we have seen two ways of specifying to MPI the location in the file from where data must be read/written: individual file pointers and explicit offsets. MPI also supports a third way of specifying the location: via the shared file pointer. The shared file pointer is a file pointer whose value is shared among the processes belonging to the communicator passed to `MPI_File_open`. MPI provides functions, `MPI_File_read_shared` and `MPI_File_write_shared`, that read/write data starting from the current location of the shared file pointer. After a call to one of these functions, the shared file pointer is updated by the amount of data read/written. The next call to one of these functions from *any* process in the group will result in data being read/written from the new location of the shared file pointer. Contrast this with individual file pointers: a read/write operation on one process using the individual file pointer has no effect on the individual file pointer on any other process.

A process can explicitly move the shared file pointer (in units of etypes) by using the function `MPI_File_seek_shared`. MPI requires that all processes specify the same file view when using the shared file pointer. This restriction does not exist for individual file pointers and explicit offsets. Examples of applications where shared file pointers are useful are work sharing and writing log files.

Figure 3.16 shows a C++ example in which all processes need to write to a common log file and the order in which the writes appear in the file does not matter. We simply use the shared-file-pointer function `MPI_File_write_shared`. Therefore, we do not need to calculate file offsets. C, Fortran, and C++ bindings for `MPI_File_write_shared` are given in Tables 3.22, 3.23, and 3.24.

Nonblocking versions of the shared-file-pointer functions also exist, called `MPI_`

```
// writing to a common file using the shared file pointer
#include "mpi.h"

int main(int argc, char *argv[])
{
    int buf[1000];
    MPI::File fh;

    MPI::Init();

    MPI::File fh = MPI::File::Open(MPI::COMM_WORLD, "/pfs/datafile",
                                   MPI::MODE_RDONLY, MPI::INFO_NULL);
    fh.Write_shared(buf, 1000, MPI_INT);
    fh.Close();

    MPI::Finalize();
    return 0;
}
```

Figure 3.16
A C++ example that uses the shared file pointer

---

int **MPI_File_write_shared**(MPI_File fh, void *buf, int count,
                    MPI_Datatype datatype, MPI_Status *status)

Table 3.22
C binding for MPI_File_write_shared

MPI_FILE_WRITE_SHARED(fh, buf, count, datatype, status, ierror)
                    <type> buf(*)
                    integer fh, count, datatype, status(MPI_STATUS_SIZE), ierror

---

Table 3.23
Fortran binding for MPI_File_write_shared

---

void **MPI::File::Write_shared**(const void* buf, int count,
                    const MPI::Datatype& datatype)

void **MPI::File::Write_shared**(const void* buf, int count,
                    const MPI::Datatype& datatype, MPI::Status& status)

Table 3.24
C++ binding for MPI_File_write_shared

File_iread_shared and MPI_File_iwrite_shared. The collective I/O functions that use shared file pointers are called MPI_File_read_ordered and MPI_File_write_ordered. With these functions, data will be read or written in the file as if the shared file pointer was accessed in order of process rank, hence the name "ordered." For example, in the case of MPI_File_write_ordered, process 0's data will appear first in the file, followed by process 1's data, and so on. Note that the implementation can still perform this I/O in parallel: since the function is collective, the implementation can determine the sizes of the requests of all processes, calculate the offsets in the file corresponding to a rank ordering of the writes, and then perform all the writes concurrently. As in the case of individual file pointers and explicit offsets, split collective versions are available, for example, MPI_File_read_ordered_begin and MPI_File_read_ordered_end.

3.7 Passing Hints to the Implementation

MPI provides users the option to pass "hints" to the implementation. For I/O, this can be done via the info argument to the functions MPI_File_open, MPI_File_set_view, and MPI_File_set_info. In all programs so far, we have passed MPI_INFO_NULL as the info argument because we did not want to pass any hints. There are, however, many instances where one might want to pass hints. Examples of hints include the number of disks to stripe a file across, the striping unit, access pattern information, and file permissions. We briefly introduced the info argument in Chapter 2. Here we will see how info is used for I/O.

Recall that info is an opaque MPI object of type MPI_Info in C, MPI::Info in C++, and integer in Fortran. Any number of (key, value) pairs can be added to an info object. When the info object is passed to an I/O function, such as MPI_File_open, MPI_File_set_view, or MPI_File_set_info, each (key, value) pair serves as a hint associated with the file handle passed to the function. For example, if a key is striping_unit and the value is 65536, the user is requesting a striping unit of 65536 (64 Kbytes). Keys and values are both specified as character strings. MPI has reserved a set of keys whose meanings are defined in the Standard; an implementation is free to define additional keys whose meanings are implementation specific. All hints are optional: a user need not provide any hints, and even if hints are provided, an implementation is free to ignore them. Hints do not change the semantics of a program, but they may help an implementation improve performance.

Figure 3.17 shows a simple program in which various hints are set, both predefined hints and hints specific to our implementation of the I/O functions in MPI, called ROMIO [84, 87, 88, 89]. The function `MPI_Info_create` creates an info object. `MPI_Info_set` adds (key, value) pairs to the info object. `MPI_Info_set` is called several times in the program, each time to add a different (key, value) pair to the info object. The first four hints are predefined hints in MPI; the next six are ROMIO specific. Note that this program can be run with any MPI implementation: if an implementation does not understand a particular hint, it will just ignore the hint.

The key `striping_factor` specifies the number of I/O devices (for example, disks) across which the file should be striped. `striping_unit` specifies the number of consecutive bytes of a file that are stored on a particular I/O device when a file is striped across I/O devices. The `striping_factor` and `striping_unit` hints are useful only if specified at the time the file is created in an `MPI_File_open` call with the mode `MPI_MODE_CREATE`. The key `cb_buffer_size` specifies the size of the temporary buffer that the implementation can use on each process when performing collective I/O. The key `cb_nodes` specifies the number of processes that should actually perform disk accesses during collective I/O.

The key `start_iodevice` is a ROMIO-specific hint that specifies the I/O device from which file striping should begin. The keys `ind_rd_buffer_size` and `ind_wr_buffer_size` specify the size of the temporary buffer ROMIO uses for data sieving, which is an optimization ROMIO performs in the case of noncontiguous, independent accesses. We demonstrate the utility of these two hints in Section 3.10.3. The keys `direct_read` and `direct_write` are hints ROMIO accepts on SGI's XFS file system as directives from the user to use direct I/O (an XFS optimization) wherever possible.

Hints can be specified when the file is opened with `MPI_File_open`, or when setting the file view with `MPI_File_set_view`, or explicitly with the function `MPI_File_set_info`.

Querying the values of hints. One can also query the values of hints being used by the implementation, if any, as shown in the code in Figure 3.18. `MPI_File_get_info` returns a new info object containing the hints currently being used for the specified file. In this example, it contains the default values of hints being used. `MPI_Info_get_nkeys` returns the number of keys associated with the info object. We loop over the number of keys and, for each iteration of the loop, retrieve one key with the function `MPI_Info_get_nthkey` and its associated value with `MPI_Info_get`. Since `MPI_File_get_info` returns a new info object, we must free it using `MPI_Info_free`.

```
MPI_File fh;  MPI_Info info;

MPI_Info_create(&info);

/* FOLLOWING HINTS ARE PREDEFINED IN MPI */

/* no. of I/O devices across which the file should be striped */
MPI_Info_set(info, "striping_factor", "4");

/* the striping unit in bytes */
MPI_Info_set(info, "striping_unit", "65536");

/* buffer size for collective I/O */
MPI_Info_set(info, "cb_buffer_size", "8388608");

/* no. of processes that should perform disk accesses
   during collective I/O */
MPI_Info_set(info, "cb_nodes", "4");

/* FOLLOWING ARE ADDITIONAL HINTS SUPPORTED BY ROMIO */

/* the I/O-device from which to start striping the file */
MPI_Info_set(info, "start_iodevice", "2");

/* buffer size for data sieving in independent reads */
MPI_Info_set(info, "ind_rd_buffer_size", "2097152");

/* buffer size for data sieving in independent writes */
MPI_Info_set(info, "ind_wr_buffer_size", "1048576");

/* use direct I/O on SGI's XFS file system
   (platform-specific hints) */
MPI_Info_set(info, "direct_read", "true");
MPI_Info_set(info, "direct_write", "true");

/* NOW OPEN THE FILE WITH THIS INFO OBJECT */
MPI_File_open(MPI_COMM_WORLD, "/pfs/datafile",
              MPI_MODE_CREATE | MPI_MODE_RDWR, info, &fh);

MPI_Info_free(&info);  /* free the info object */
```

Figure 3.17
Example of passing hints to the implementation

```
/* query the default values of hints being used */
#include "mpi.h"
#include <stdio.h>

int main(int argc, char **argv)
{
    int i, nkeys, flag, rank;
    MPI_File fh;
    MPI_Info info_used;
    char key[MPI_MAX_INFO_KEY], value[MPI_MAX_INFO_VAL];

    MPI_Init(&argc,&argv);
    MPI_Comm_rank(MPI_COMM_WORLD, &rank);

    MPI_File_open(MPI_COMM_WORLD, "/pfs/datafile",
                  MPI_MODE_CREATE | MPI_MODE_RDWR,
                  MPI_INFO_NULL, &fh);

    MPI_File_get_info(fh, &info_used);
    MPI_Info_get_nkeys(info_used, &nkeys);

    for (i=0; i<nkeys; i++) {
        MPI_Info_get_nthkey(info_used, i, key);
        MPI_Info_get(info_used, key, MPI_MAX_INFO_VAL,
                     value, &flag);
        printf("Process %d, Default: key = %s, value = %s\n",
               rank, key, value);
    }

    MPI_File_close(&fh);
    MPI_Info_free(&info_used);

    MPI_Finalize();
    return 0;
}
```

Figure 3.18
Querying the values of hints being used by the implementation

---

int **MPI_Info_create**(MPI_Info *info)

int **MPI_Info_set**(MPI_Info info, char *key, char *value)

int **MPI_Info_get**(MPI_Info info, char *key, int valuelen, char *value, int *flag)

int **MPI_Info_get_nkeys**(MPI_Info info, int *nkeys)

int **MPI_Info_get_nthkey**(MPI_Info info, int n, char *key)

int **MPI_Info_free**(MPI_Info *info)

int **MPI_File_get_info**(MPI_File fh, MPI_Info *info_used)

Table 3.25
C bindings for the info functions used in Figures 3.17 and 3.18

Note that we have defined `key` and `value` as character strings of length MPI_MAX_-INFO_KEY and MPI_MAX_INFO_VAL, respectively. These two MPI constants specify the maximum lengths of info key and value strings supported by the implementation. In C and C++, the length specified by these constants includes the null terminating character. Therefore, there is no need to allocate a character buffer of size (MPI_MAX_INFO_KEY+1) or (MPI_MAX_INFO_VAL+1). In Fortran, there is no null terminating character; therefore, the values of the constants MPI_MAX_INFO_KEY and MPI_MAX_INFO_VAL in Fortran are one less than in C.

Tables 3.25, 3.26, and 3.27 give the C, Fortran, and C++ bindings for the info functions used in Figures 3.17 and 3.18. We refer readers to the MPI Standard for a complete list of the info keys predefined in MPI [27].

3.8 Consistency Semantics

MPI's consistency semantics for I/O specify the results when multiple processes perform I/O. Several scenarios are possible. We consider the common ones and explain them with the help of examples. We refer readers to the MPI Standard for a complete specification of the consistency semantics [27].

3.8.1 Simple Cases

There are two scenarios where consistency is not an issue. They are:

MPI_INFO_CREATE(info, ierror)
        integer info, ierror

MPI_INFO_SET(info, key, value, ierror)
        integer info, ierror
        character*(*) key, value

MPI_INFO_GET(info, key, valuelen, value, flag, ierror)
        integer info, valuelen, ierror
        character*(*) key, value
        logical flag

MPI_INFO_GET_NKEYS(info, nkeys, ierror)
        integer info, nkeys, ierror

MPI_INFO_GET_NTHKEY(info, n, key, ierror)
        integer info, n, ierror
        character*(*) key

MPI_INFO_FREE(info, ierror)
        integer info, ierror

MPI_FILE_GET_INFO(fh, info_used, ierror)
        integer fh, info_used, ierror

Table 3.26
Fortran bindings for the info functions used in Figures 3.17 and 3.18

MPI::Info MPI::Info::Create()

void MPI::Info::Set(const char* key, const char* value)

bool MPI::Info::Get(const char* key, int valuelen, char* value) const

int MPI::Info::Get_nkeys() const

void MPI::Info::Get_nthkey(int n, char* key) const

void MPI::Info::Free()

MPI::Info MPI::File::Get_info() const

Table 3.27
C++ bindings for the info functions used in Figures 3.17 and 3.18

1. *Read-only access*: If all processes are only reading from files and not performing any writes, each process will see exactly the data that is present in the file. This is true regardless of which communicator was used to open the file (`MPI_COMM_SELF`, `MPI_COMM_WORLD`, or some other).

2. *Separate files*: If each process accesses a *separate* file (that is, no file is shared among processes), MPI guarantees that the data written by a process can be read back by the same process at any time after the write.

It gets more interesting when multiple processes access a *common* file and at least one process *writes* to the file. From the perspective of consistency semantics, a lot depends on which communicator was used to open the file. In general, MPI guarantees stronger consistency semantics if the communicator correctly specifies every process that is accessing the file (for example, `MPI_COMM_WORLD`) and weaker consistency semantics if the communicator specifies only a subset of the processes accessing the common file (for example, `MPI_COMM_SELF`). In either case, the user can take steps to guarantee consistency when MPI does not automatically guarantee consistency, as we shall see below.

3.8.2   Accessing a Common File Opened with `MPI_COMM_WORLD`

Let us first consider the case where all processes access a common file and specify the communicator as `MPI_COMM_WORLD` when they open the file, and at least one process needs to write to the file. The simplest case of such access is when each process accesses a *separate portion* of the file, that is, there are no overlapping regions (bytes) in the file between the accesses of any two processes. In such cases, MPI automatically guarantees that a process can read back the data it wrote without any extra synchronization. An example is shown below:

Process 0	Process 1
MPI_File_open(MPI_COMM_WORLD, "file", ... , &fh1)	MPI_File_open(MPI_COMM_WORLD, "file", ... , &fh2)
MPI_File_write_at(fh1, 0, buf, 100, MPI_BYTE, ...)	MPI_File_write_at(fh2, 100, buf, 100, MPI_BYTE, ...)
MPI_File_read_at(fh1, 0, buf, 100, MPI_BYTE, ...)	MPI_File_read_at(fh2, 100, buf, 100, MPI_BYTE, ...)

Here, two processes open a common file with `MPI_COMM_WORLD`. Each process writes 100 bytes to different locations in the file and reads back only the data it just wrote. MPI guarantees that the data will be read correctly.

Now let's consider the same example but with a difference: let's assume that each process needs to read the data just written by the other process. In other words, the accesses of the two processes overlap in the file. With respect to consistency semantics, the situation now is dramatically different. When the accesses (or portions of the accesses) of any two processes overlap in the file, MPI does *not* guarantee that the data will automatically be read correctly. The user must take some extra steps to ensure correctness. There are three choices:

1. *Set atomicity to true*: Before the write on each process, change the file-access mode to *atomic* by using the function `MPI_File_set_atomicity` as follows.

Process 0	Process 1
MPI_File_open(MPI_COMM_WORLD, "file", ... , &fh1)	MPI_File_open(MPI_COMM_WORLD, "file", ... , &fh2)
MPI_File_set_atomicity(fh1, 1)	MPI_File_set_atomicity(fh2, 1)
MPI_File_write_at(fh1, 0, buf, 100, MPI_BYTE, ...)	MPI_File_write_at(fh2, 100, buf, 100, MPI_BYTE, ...)
MPI_Barrier(MPI_COMM_WORLD)	MPI_Barrier(MPI_COMM_WORLD)
MPI_File_read_at(fh1, 100, buf, 100, MPI_BYTE, ...)	MPI_File_read_at(fh2, 0, buf, 100, MPI_BYTE, ...)

In the atomic mode, MPI guarantees that the data written by one process can be read immediately by another process. This is not guaranteed in the nonatomic mode, which is the default mode when the file is opened. In the above program, a barrier is used after the writes to ensure that each process has completed its write before the read is issued from the other process.

2. *Close the file and reopen it*: Another way to read the data correctly is to close the file after the write, reopen it, and then read the data written by the other process, as shown below.

Process 0	Process 1
MPI_File_open(MPI_COMM_WORLD, "file", ... , &fh1)	MPI_File_open(MPI_COMM_WORLD, "file", ... , &fh2)
MPI_File_write_at(fh1, 0, buf, 100, MPI_BYTE, ...)	MPI_File_write_at(fh2, 100, buf, 100, MPI_BYTE, ...)
MPI_File_close(&fh1)	MPI_File_close(&fh2)
MPI_Barrier(MPI_COMM_WORLD)	MPI_Barrier(MPI_COMM_WORLD)
MPI_File_open(MPI_COMM_WORLD, "file", ... , &fh1)	MPI_File_open(MPI_COMM_WORLD, "file", ... , &fh2)
MPI_File_read_at(fh1, 100, buf, 100, MPI_BYTE, ...)	MPI_File_read_at(fh2, 0, buf, 100, MPI_BYTE, ...)

By doing so, we ensure that there are no overlapping operations on the file handles returned from one collective open. The reads are performed with a different set of file handles that did not exist when the writes were performed. A barrier is used in this program for a similar reason as above: to ensure that each process has completed its close before the other process reopens the file.

3. *Ensure that no "write sequence" on any process is concurrent with any sequence (read or write) on another process*: This is a more complicated way of ensuring correctness. The words *sequence* and *write sequence* have a specific meaning in this context. A *sequence* is defined as a set of file operations bracketed by any pair of the functions `MPI_File_sync`,[3] `MPI_File_open`, and `MPI_File_close`. A

---

[3]The function `MPI_File_sync` explicitly synchronizes any cached file data with that on the storage device; `MPI_File_open` and `MPI_File_close` also have the same effect.

sequence is called a *write sequence* if any of the data-access operations in the sequence are write operations. For example, the following three sets of operations are all sequences, and the first two are write sequences: sync–write–read–sync, open–write–write–close, and sync–read–read–close. It is important to note that the first and last operations must be a sync, open, or close for the set of operations to be called a sequence. MPI guarantees that the data written by a process can be read by another process if the user arranges the program such that a *write* sequence on one process is not concurrent (in time) with *any* sequence (read or write) on any other process.

Figure 3.19 shows how to apply this rule to the above example where each process needs to read the data just written by the other process. To ensure that no write sequence on a process is concurrent with any sequence on the other process, we have to add sync functions to create a write sequence and use a barrier to separate them (in time) from the write sequence on the other process. We choose to let the write on process 0 occur first; we could have chosen the other way around. We add a sync after the write on process 0 in order to create the sequence open–write_at–sync. Since `MPI_File_sync` is collective over the communicator with which the file was opened, namely, `MPI_COMM_WORLD`, the function must also be called on process 1. Then we call a barrier to separate this write sequence from the write sequence on process 1. Since the write sequence on process 1 must begin after this barrier, we first have to create a sequence by calling a sync on process 1 immediately after the barrier. Then we do the write, followed by another sync to complete the sequence. Because of the collective nature of `MPI_File_sync`, the function must be called on process 0 as well. Next we call a barrier to separate the write sequence on process 1 from the read sequence on process 0. Since the read sequence on process 0 must start after the barrier, we add a sync after the barrier, followed by the read. If we did not add this sync, the read sequence would start from the sync that is just before the barrier and, therefore, would not be time-separated from the write sequence on process 1. The sync after the barrier on process 1 is needed because it is collective with the corresponding sync on process 0. It is not needed for consistency semantics because the read sequence on process 1 that starts from just before the barrier is already nonconcurrent with the previous write sequence on process 0.

We note that if the program had used the collective versions of the read/write functions, namely, `MPI_File_write_at_all` and `MPI_File_read_at_all`, we could not have used this method for achieving consistency. The reason is that since it is erroneous to separate collective operations among processes by inserting barriers in between, there is no way to make the write sequence on one process nonconcurrent

Process 0	Process 1
MPI_File_open(MPI_COMM_WORLD, "file", ... , &fh1)	MPI_File_open(MPI_COMM_WORLD, "file", ... , &fh2)
MPI_File_write_at(fh1, 0, buf, 100, MPI_BYTE, ...)	
MPI_File_sync(fh1)	MPI_File_sync(fh2) *(needed for collective operation)*
MPI_Barrier(MPI_COMM_WORLD)	MPI_Barrier(MPI_COMM_WORLD)
MPI_File_sync(fh1) *(needed for collective operation)*	MPI_File_sync(fh2)
	MPI_File_write_at(fh2, 100, buf, 100, MPI_BYTE, ...)
MPI_File_sync(fh1) *(needed for collective operation)*	MPI_File_sync(fh2)
MPI_Barrier(MPI_COMM_WORLD)	MPI_Barrier(MPI_COMM_WORLD)
MPI_File_sync(fh1)	MPI_File_sync(fh2) *(needed for collective operation)*
MPI_File_read_at(fh1, 100, buf, 100, MPI_BYTE, ...)	MPI_File_read_at(fh2, 0, buf, 100, MPI_BYTE, ...)
MPI_File_close(&fh1)	MPI_File_close(&fh2)

Figure 3.19
Two processes open a common file with MPI_COMM_WORLD and use the default nonatomic mode of access. Each process writes to the file and then needs to read the data just written by the other process. The syncs and barriers are needed for the data to be correctly written and read.

with any other sequence on the other process. Therefore, in cases where multiple collective operations overlap, only the first two options for achieving consistency are available, namely, setting atomicity or closing and then reopening the file.

3.8.3   Accessing a Common File Opened with MPI_COMM_SELF

Now let's consider the case where all processes access a common file but specify MPI_COMM_SELF as the communicator when they open it. (It's legal to do so, but we don't recommend it in general.) In this case, there is only one way to achieve consistency: the user must take steps to ensure that no write sequence on any process is concurrent with any sequence (read or write) on any other process. This is needed even if there are no overlapping accesses among processes, that is, even if each process accesses separate parts of the file. Changing the file-access mode to atomic does not help in this case.

Therefore, for our example where one process needs to read the data written by the other process, the only way to do it correctly when the file is opened with MPI_COMM_SELF is as shown in Figure 3.20. This is similar to Figure 3.19, the only difference being the communicator passed to MPI_File_open. Because of MPI_-COMM_SELF, all collective operations, such as MPI_File_sync, effectively become local operations. Therefore, the syncs that were needed in Figure 3.19 for matching the corresponding collective sync on the other process are not needed here. Only those syncs needed for consistency semantics, that is, for creating sequences, are needed.

Process 0	Process 1
MPI_File_open(MPI_COMM_SELF, "file", ... , &fh1)	MPI_File_open(MPI_COMM_SELF, "file", ... , &fh2)
MPI_File_write_at(fh1, 0, buf, 100, MPI_BYTE, ...)	
MPI_File_sync(fh1)	
MPI_Barrier(MPI_COMM_WORLD)	MPI_Barrier(MPI_COMM_WORLD)
	MPI_File_sync(fh2)
	MPI_File_write_at(fh2, 100, buf, 100, MPI_BYTE, ...)
	MPI_File_sync(fh2)
MPI_Barrier(MPI_COMM_WORLD)	MPI_Barrier(MPI_COMM_WORLD)
MPI_File_sync(fh1)	
MPI_File_read_at(fh1, 100, buf, 100, MPI_BYTE, ...)	MPI_File_read_at(fh2, 0, buf, 100, MPI_BYTE, ...)
MPI_File_close(&fh1)	MPI_File_close(&fh2)

Figure 3.20
The example in Figure 3.19 when the file is opened with MPI_COMM_SELF

```
int MPI_File_set_atomicity(MPI_File fh, int flag)

int MPI_File_sync(MPI_File fh)
```

Table 3.28
C bindings for MPI_File_set_atomicity and MPI_File_sync

3.8.4 General Recommendation

Although it is legal for multiple processes to access a common file by opening it with MPI_COMM_SELF as the communicator, it is not advisable to do so. Users should strive to specify the right communicator to MPI_File_open—one that specifies all the processes that need to access the open file. Doing so not only provides the benefit of the stronger consistency semantics that MPI guarantees in such cases, but it can also result in higher performance. For example, one can then use the collective I/O functions, which allow the implementation to perform collective optimizations.

Tables 3.28, 3.29, and 3.30 give the C, Fortran, and C++ bindings for the two functions introduced in this section, MPI_File_set_atomicity and MPI_File_sync.

3.9 File Interoperability

Unlike messages, files are persistent entities; they remain after the program ends. Therefore, some questions must be answered about MPI files, such as:

MPI_FILE_SET_ATOMICITY(fh, flag, ierror)
        integer fh, ierror
        logical flag

MPI_FILE_SYNC(fh, ierror)
        integer fh, ierror

Table 3.29
Fortran bindings for MPI_File_set_atomicity and MPI_File_sync

---

void MPI::File::Set_atomicity(bool flag)

void MPI::File::Sync()

Table 3.30
C++ bindings for MPI_File_set_atomicity and MPI_File_sync

- Are MPI files any different from the files normally created by the file system? In other words, can an MPI file be read by a non-MPI program?
- How can MPI files created on one machine be moved to another machine?
- How can MPI files written on one machine be read on another machine with a different data representation?

We answer these questions in this section.

3.9.1   File Structure

MPI files contain no more information about the application than what the application explicitly stores in the files. In other words, MPI files are not self-describing in any way; they are just like ordinary files in content.

For performance reasons, MPI does not specify how an implementation should physically create files, although logically an MPI program will always see the file as a linear sequence of bytes. For example, an implementation is free to store a file physically in a compressed format or divide the file into smaller files stored on the local disks of different machines or in some other way, as long as the user is able to access the file as a linear sequence of bytes from an MPI program.

If files created by an MPI implementation are different from regular files in the underlying file system, the MPI Standard requires that the implementation provide a utility for users to convert an MPI file into a linear sequence of bytes. It must also provide utilities to perform familiar file operations, such as copying, deleting, and moving. Therefore, it is always possible to access the data written by an

MPI program from a non-MPI program—by converting the MPI file into a linear sequence of bytes if necessary.

In many implementations, including ours (ROMIO [84, 87, 88, 89]), the files created are no different from the files created by the underlying file system. Therefore, for files created by such implementations, one can directly use the regular file-system commands, such as `cp`, `rm`, `mv`, `ls`, and one also can directly access the files from a non-MPI program.

3.9.2   File Data Representation

Since different machines have different binary data representations—byte ordering, sizes of datatypes, etc.—files created on one machine may not be directly portable to other machines, unless these differences are accounted for. MPI provides users the option of creating portable files that can be read on other machines. This is done via the `datarep` parameter to `MPI_File_set_view`.

In all the examples we have considered so far in this chapter, we have used `native` as the value for the `datarep` parameter to `MPI_File_set_view`. This parameter specifies the data representation used to store various datatypes (integers, floating-point numbers) in the file. MPI supports multiple data representations. Three types of data representations are predefined in MPI, called `native`, `internal`, and `external32`. Implementations are free to support additional representations. MPI also allows users to define new data representations and add them to an MPI implementation at run time (by providing the necessary conversion functions, see Section 9.1).

In the `native` representation, data is stored in the file as it is in memory; no data conversion is performed. This is the default data representation. Since there is no data conversion, there is no loss in I/O performance or data precision. This representation cannot be used in heterogeneous environments where the processes accessing a file have different data representations in memory. Similarly, a file created with this representation cannot be read on a machine with a different data representation. In other words, files created with the `native` representation are not portable.

The `internal` representation is an implementation-defined representation that may provide some (implementation-defined) degree of file portability. For example, an MPI implementation can define an `internal` representation that is portable to any machine where that MPI implementation is supported. A different MPI implementation may or may not be able to read the file.

The `external32` representation is a specific data representation defined in MPI. It is basically a 32-bit big-endian IEEE format, with the sizes of all basic data-

types specified by MPI. For a complete specification of `external32`, see the MPI
Standard [27]. A file written with `external32` can be read with any MPI implementation on any machine. Since using `external32` may require the implementation
to perform data conversion, however, it may result in lower I/O performance and
some loss in data precision. Therefore, this representation should be used only if
file portability is needed.

Note that an implementation may choose to use `external32` as the `internal`
representation.

3.9.3   Use of Datatypes for Portability

Although `internal` and `external32` data representations enable file portability,
portability is possible only if the user specifies the correct datatypes, and not `MPI_-`
`BYTE`, to the read/write functions and to `MPI_File_set_view`. This allows the implementation to know what kind of datatype is being accessed and therefore perform
the necessary type conversions. For example, to write an array of 100 integers,
you should specify `count=100` and `datatype=MPI_INT` to the write function. You
should not specify it as `count=400` and `datatype=MPI_BYTE` as you would with the
Unix I/O interface.

Care must also be taken in constructing file views with derived datatypes because
some derived-datatype constructors, such as `MPI_Type_struct`, take displacements
in bytes. For constructing derived datatypes to be used in file views, these byte
displacements must be specified in terms of their values for the file data representation, not for the data representation in memory. The function `MPI_File_get_-`
`type_extent` is provided for this purpose. It returns the extent of a datatype in
the file data representation selected. Similarly, the initial displacement in the file
view (the `disp` argument to `MPI_File_set_view`), which is also specified in bytes,
must be specified in terms of its value for the file data representation.

We note that the datatypes passed as arguments to read/write functions specify
the data layout in memory. They must always be constructed using displacements
corresponding to displacements in the memory data representation.

Let us now revisit the example of Figure 3.4 in which a process needs to access noncontiguous data located in a file as follows: an initial displacement of five
integers, followed by groups of two contiguous integers separated by gaps of four integers. We saw in Figure 3.5 how to set the view for this example for a nonportable
file using the `native` data representation. Now let's do the same for a portable file
using `external32`. The code is shown in Figure 3.21.

When a file is first opened, the default data representation is `native`. To change
the data representation to `external32`, we have to call the function `MPI_File_-`

```
MPI_Aint lb, extent, extent_in_file;
MPI_Datatype etype, filetype, contig;
MPI_Offset disp;
MPI_File fh;
int buf[1000];

MPI_File_open(MPI_COMM_WORLD, "/pfs/datafile",
              MPI_MODE_CREATE | MPI_MODE_RDWR,
              MPI_INFO_NULL, &fh);

MPI_File_set_view(fh, 0, MPI_BYTE, MPI_BYTE, "external32",
    '             MPI_INFO_NULL);
MPI_File_get_type_extent(fh, MPI_INT, &extent_in_file);

MPI_Type_contiguous(2, MPI_INT, &contig);
lb = 0;
extent = 6 * extent_in_file;
MPI_Type_create_resized(contig, lb, extent, &filetype);
MPI_Type_commit(&filetype);

disp = 5 * extent_in_file;
etype = MPI_INT;

MPI_File_set_view(fh, disp, etype, filetype, "external32",
                  MPI_INFO_NULL);
MPI_File_write(fh, buf, 1000, MPI_INT, MPI_STATUS_IGNORE);
```

Figure 3.21
Writing portable files

set_view. But in this example, we run into a small problem. To create the derived datatype to be used as the filetype, we need to know the extent of an integer in the external32 data representation. We can, of course, look up the value in the MPI Standard, but we would like to find it at run time using the function specifically provided for the purpose, namely, MPI_File_get_type_extent. The problem is that this function takes a file handle (and not a data representation) as argument, which means that the data representation for the file must be set before calling this function. Hence, we need to call MPI_File_set_view twice: once just to set the data representation to external32 (with dummy values for displacement, etype, and filetype) and once again with the real displacement, etype, and filetype after the extent of an integer in the file has been determined by using MPI_File_get_type_-

---

int **MPI_File_get_type_extent**(MPI_File fh, MPI_Datatype datatype,
MPI_Aint *extent)

Table 3.31
C binding for MPI_File_get_type_extent

MPI_FILE_GET_TYPE_EXTENT(fh, datatype, extent, ierror)
integer fh, datatype, ierror
integer(kind=MPI_ADDRESS_KIND) extent

Table 3.32
Fortran binding for MPI_File_get_type_extent

MPI::Aint MPI::File::Get_type_extent(const MPI::Datatype& datatype) const

---

Table 3.33
C++ binding for MPI_File_get_type_extent

extent.[4] Instead of using sizeof(int) as in Figure 3.4, we use extent_in_file to calculate disp and to create the filetype. The file created by this program can be read with any MPI implementation on any machine.

C, Fortran, and C++ bindings for MPI_File_get_type_extent are given in Tables 3.31, 3.32, and 3.33.

3.9.4 User-Defined Data Representations

MPI also allows the user to define new data representations and register them with the MPI implementation. The user must provide the necessary conversion functions, which the implementation will use to convert from memory to file format and vice versa. This provides a powerful method for users to write data in a representation that an MPI implementation may not support by default. This is an advanced feature of MPI; we explain it with the help of an example in Chapter 9.

---

[4]This could have been avoided if MPI had a function that took a data-representation string and a communicator as arguments (instead of a file handle) and returned the extent of a datatype in that representation. Alas, since MPI has no such function, we have to do it in this roundabout fashion.

3.10   Achieving High I/O Performance with MPI

In this section we describe how MPI must be used in order to achieve high I/O performance. The I/O in an application can be written with MPI in many different ways, with different performance implications. We examine the different ways of writing an I/O application with MPI and see how these choices affect performance.

3.10.1   The Four "Levels" of Access

Any application has a particular "I/O access pattern" based on its I/O needs. The same I/O access pattern, however, can be presented to the I/O system in different ways, depending on which I/O functions the application uses and how. We classify the different ways of expressing I/O access patterns in MPI into four "levels," level 0 through level 3 [86]. We explain this classification with the help of a simple example, accessing a distributed array from a file, which is a common access pattern in parallel applications. The principle applies to other access patterns as well.

Consider a two-dimensional array distributed among 16 processes in a (block, block) fashion as shown in Figure 3.22. The array is stored in a file corresponding to the global array in row-major order, and each process needs to read its local array from the file. The data distribution among processes and the array storage order in the file are such that the file contains the first row of the local array of process 0, followed by the first row of the local array of process 1, the first row of the local array of process 2, the first row of the local array of process 3, then the second row of the local array of process 0, the second row of the local array of process 1, and so on. In other words, the local array of each process is located noncontiguously in the file.

Figure 3.23 shows four ways in which a user can express this access pattern in MPI. In level 0, each process does Unix-style accesses—one independent read request for each row in the local array. Level 1 is similar to level 0 except that it uses collective I/O functions, which indicate to the implementation that all processes that together opened the file will call this function, each with its own access information. Independent I/O functions, on the other hand, convey no information about what other processes will do. In level 2, each process creates a derived datatype to describe the noncontiguous access pattern, defines a file view, and calls independent I/O functions. Level 3 is similar to level 2 except that it uses collective I/O functions.

The four levels represent increasing amounts of data per request, as illustrated

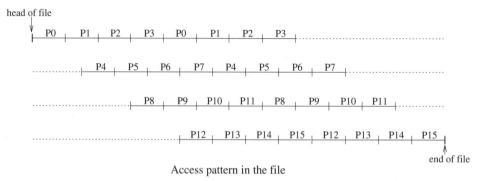

Figure 3.22

Distributed-array access

in Figure 3.24.[5] The more the amount of data per request, the greater is the opportunity for the implementation to deliver higher performance. Users must therefore strive to express their I/O requests as level 3 rather than level 0. How good the performance is at each level depends, of course, on how well the implementation takes advantage of the extra access information at each level.

If an application needs to access only large, contiguous pieces of data, level 0 is equivalent to level 2, and level 1 is equivalent to level 3. Users need not create derived datatypes in such cases, as level-0 requests themselves will likely perform well. Most real parallel applications, however, do not fall into this category. Several studies of I/O access patterns in parallel applications [4, 17, 65, 77, 78, 85] have shown that each process in a parallel program may need to access a number of relatively small, noncontiguous portions of a file. From a performance perspective, it is critical that this access pattern be expressed in the I/O interface, as it enables

---

[5]In this figure, levels 1 and 2 represent the same amount of data per request, but, in general, when the number of noncontiguous accesses per process is greater than the number of processes, level 2 represents more data than level 1.

```
MPI_File_open(..., "filename", ..., &fh)
for (i=0; i<n_local_rows; i++) {
    MPI_File_seek(fh, ...)
    MPI_File_read(fh, row[i], ...)
}
MPI_File_close(&fh)
```

Level 0
(many independent, contiguous requests)

```
MPI_File_open(MPI_COMM_WORLD, "filename", ..., &fh)
for (i=0; i<n_local_rows; i++) {
    MPI_File_seek(fh, ...)
    MPI_File_read_all(fh, row[i], ...)
}
MPI_File_close(&fh)
```

Level 1
(many collective, contiguous requests)

```
MPI_Type_create_subarray(..., &subarray, ...)
MPI_Type_commit(&subarray)
MPI_File_open(..., "filename", ..., &fh)
MPI_File_set_view(fh, ..., subarray, ...)
MPI_File_read(fh, local_array, ...)
MPI_File_close(&fh)
```

Level 2
(single independent, noncontiguous request)

```
MPI_Type_create_subarray(.., &subarray, ...)
MPI_Type_commit(&subarray)
MPI_File_open(MPI_COMM_WORLD, "filename", ..., &fh)
MPI_File_set_view(fh, ..., subarray, ...)
MPI_File_read_all(fh, local_array, ...)
MPI_File_close(&fh)
```

Level 3
(single collective, noncontiguous request)

Figure 3.23
Pseudo-code that shows four ways of accessing the data in Figure 3.22 with MPI

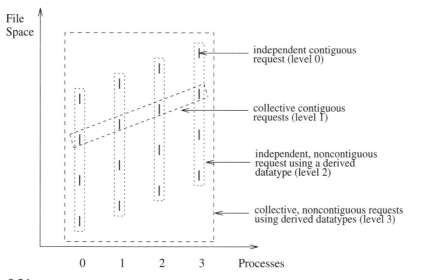

Figure 3.24
The four levels representing increasing amounts of data per request

```
gsizes[0] = num_global_rows;
gsizes[1] = num_global_cols;
distribs[0] = distribs[1] = MPI_DISTRIBUTE_BLOCK;
dargs[0] = dargs[1] = MPI_DISTRIBUTE_DFLT_DARG;
psizes[0] = psizes[1] = 4;
MPI_Comm_rank(MPI_COMM_WORLD, &rank);
MPI_Type_create_darray(16, rank, 2, gsizes, distribs, dargs, psizes,
                       MPI_ORDER_C, MPI_FLOAT, &filetype);
MPI_Type_commit(&filetype);
local_array_size = num_local_rows * num_local_cols;
MPI_File_open(MPI_COMM_WORLD, "/pfs/datafile", MPI_MODE_RDONLY,
              MPI_INFO_NULL, &fh);
MPI_File_set_view(fh, 0, MPI_FLOAT, filetype, "native",
                  MPI_INFO_NULL);
MPI_File_read_all(fh, local_array, local_array_size,
                  MPI_FLOAT, &status);
MPI_File_close(&fh);
```

Figure 3.25
Detailed code for the distributed-array example of Figure 3.22 using a level-3 request

the implementation to optimize the I/O request. The optimizations typically allow the physical I/O to take place in large, contiguous chunks, with higher performance, even though the user's request may be noncontiguous.

For example, our implementation, ROMIO, performs an optimization called *data sieving* for level-2 requests. The basic idea is as follows: instead of reading noncontiguous data with lots of separate read calls to the file system, ROMIO reads large chunks from the file and extracts, in memory, the data that is really needed. For level-3 requests, ROMIO performs collective I/O: it analyzes the requests of different processes, merges the requests as much as possible, and makes large parallel reads/writes for the combined request. Details of both these optimizations can be found in [87].

Users, therefore, must ensure that they describe noncontiguous access patterns in terms of a file view and then call a single I/O function; they must not try to access each contiguous portion separately as in Unix I/O. Figure 3.25 shows the detailed code for creating a derived datatype, defining a file view, and making a level-3 I/O request for the distributed-array example of Figure 3.22. It is similar to the example in Figure 3.10.

We note that the MPI standard does not *require* an implementation to perform any of these optimizations. Nevertheless, even if an implementation does not perform any optimization and instead translates level-3 requests into several level-0 requests to the file system, the performance would be no worse than if the user directly made level-0 requests. Therefore, there is no reason not to use level-3 requests (or level-2 requests where level-3 requests are not possible).

3.10.2   Performance Results

We present some performance results that show how the choice of level of request affects performance. We wrote the distributed-array access example using level-0, level-2, and level-3 requests and ran the three versions *portably* on five different parallel machines—HP Exemplar, SGI Origin2000, IBM SP, Intel Paragon, and NEC SX-4—using ROMIO. (For this particular application, level-1 requests do not contain sufficient information for any useful optimizations, and ROMIO therefore internally translates level-1 requests into level-0 requests.) These machines cover almost the entire spectrum of state-of-the-art high-performance systems, and they represent distributed-memory, shared-memory, and parallel vector architectures. They also represent a wide variation in I/O architecture, from the "traditional" parallel file systems on distributed-memory machines such as the SP and Paragon, to the so-called high-performance file systems on shared-memory machines such as the Origin2000, Exemplar, and SX-4. We used the native file systems on each machine: HFS on the Exemplar, XFS on the Origin2000, PIOFS on the SP, PFS on the Paragon, and SFS on the SX-4.

We note that the machines had varying amounts of I/O hardware. Some of the differences in performance results among the machines are due to these variations. Our goal in this experiment was to compare the performance of the different levels of requests on a given machine, rather than comparing the performance of different machines.

Figures 3.26 and 3.27 show the read and write bandwidths for distributed-array access. The performance with level-0 requests was, in general, very poor because level-0 requests result in too many small read/write calls. For level-2 requests—for which ROMIO performs data sieving—the read bandwidth improved over level-0 requests by a factor ranging from 2.6 on the HP Exemplar to 453 on the NEC SX-4. Similarly, the write bandwidth improved by a factor ranging from 2.3 on the HP Exemplar to 121 on the NEC SX-4. The performance improved considerably with level-3 requests because ROMIO performs collective I/O in this case. The read bandwidth improved by a factor of as much as 793 over level-0 requests (NEC SX-4) and as much as 14 over level-2 requests (Intel Paragon). Similarly, with level-3 requests, the write performance improved by a factor of as much as 721 over level-0

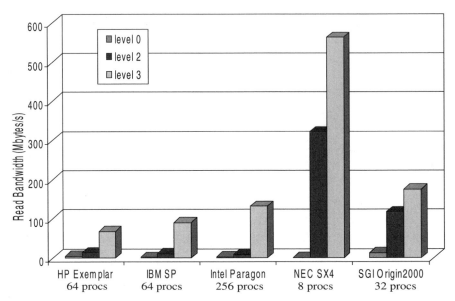

Figure 3.26
Read performance of distributed array access (array size 512x512x512 integers = 512 Mbytes)

requests (NEC SX-4) and as much as 40 over level-2 requests (HP Exemplar). It is clearly advantageous to use level-3 requests rather than any other kind of request.

3.10.3   Upshot Graphs

We present some Upshot plots that illustrate the reduction in time obtained by using level-2 and level-3 requests instead of level-0 requests for writing a three-dimensional distributed array of size 128 × 128 × 128 on 32 processors on the Intel Paragon at Caltech. We instrumented the ROMIO source code to measure the time taken for each file-system call made by ROMIO and also for the computation and communication required for collective I/O. The instrumented code created trace files, which we visualized using a performance-visualization tool called *Upshot* [38].

Figure 3.28 shows the Upshot plot for level-0 requests, where each process makes a separate write function call to write each row of its local array. The numerous small bands represent the numerous writes in the program, as a result of which the total time taken is about 125 seconds. The large white portions are actually lots of writes clustered together, which become visible when you zoom in to the region using Upshot.

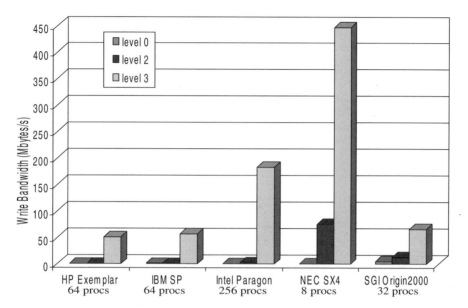

Figure 3.27
Write performance of distributed array access (array size 512x512x512 integers = 512 Mbytes)

Figure 3.29 shows the Upshot plot for level-2 requests, for which ROMIO performs performs data sieving. In this case it performed data sieving in blocks of 4 Mbytes at a time. As mentioned in Section 3.7, we can vary this block size via the ROMIO-specific hint `ind_wr_buffer_size`. Notice that the total time has decreased to about 16 seconds compared with 125 seconds for level-0 requests. For writing with data sieving, each process must perform a read-modify-write and also lock the region of the file being written. Because of the need for file locking and a buffer size of 4 Mbytes, many processes remain idle waiting to acquire locks. Therefore, only a few write operations take place concurrently. It should be possible to increase parallelism, however, by decreasing the size of the buffer used for data sieving. Figure 3.30 shows the results for a buffer size of 512 Kbytes. Since more I/O operations take place in parallel, the total time decreased to 10.5 seconds. A further reduction in buffer size to 64 Kbytes (Figure 3.31) resulted in even greater parallelism, but the I/O time increased because of the smaller granularity of each I/O operation. The performance of data sieving can thus be tuned by varying the size of the buffer used for data sieving, which can be done via the hints mechanism in MPI.

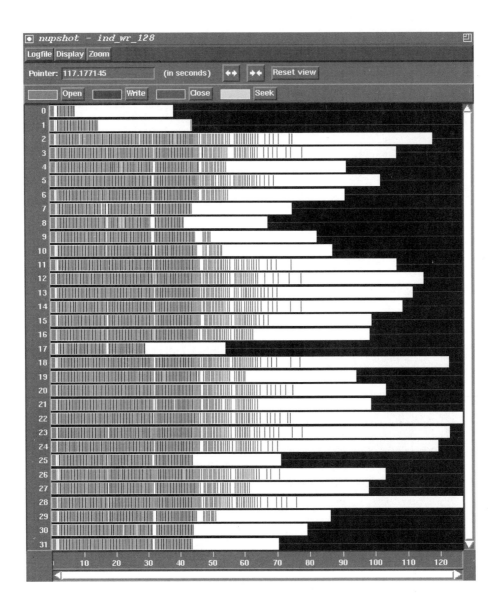

Figure 3.28
Writing a $128 \times 128 \times 128$ distributed array on the Intel Paragon using level-0 requests (Unix-style independent writes). Elapsed time = 125 seconds.

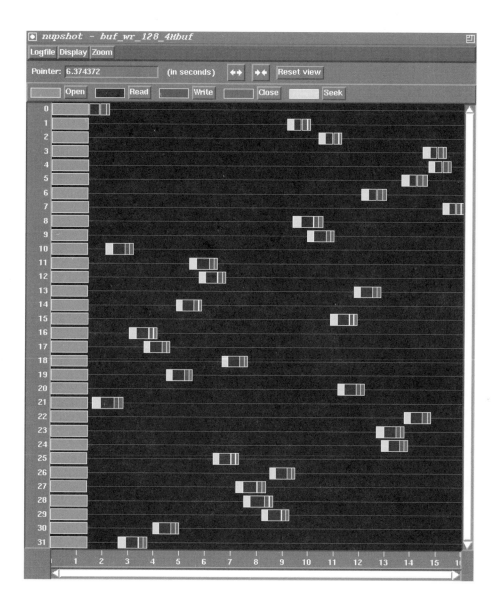

Figure 3.29
Writing a $128 \times 128 \times 128$ distributed array on the Intel Paragon using level-2 requests, with the buffer size for data sieving = 4 Mbytes. Elapsed time = 16 seconds.

110   Chapter 3

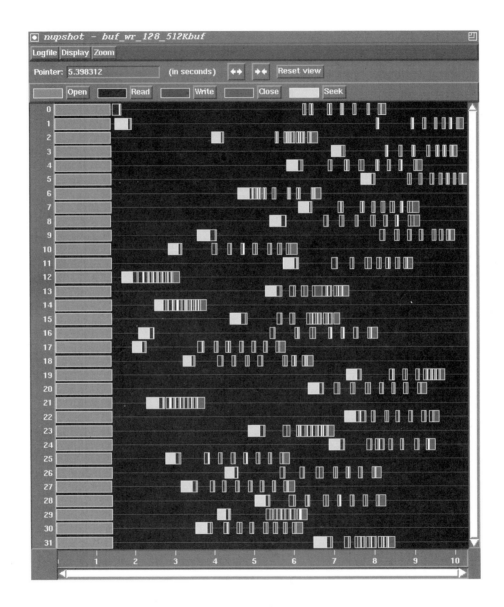

Figure 3.30
Writing a $128 \times 128 \times 128$ distributed array on the Intel Paragon using level-2 requests, with the buffer size for data sieving = 512 Kbytes. Elapsed time = 10.5 seconds.

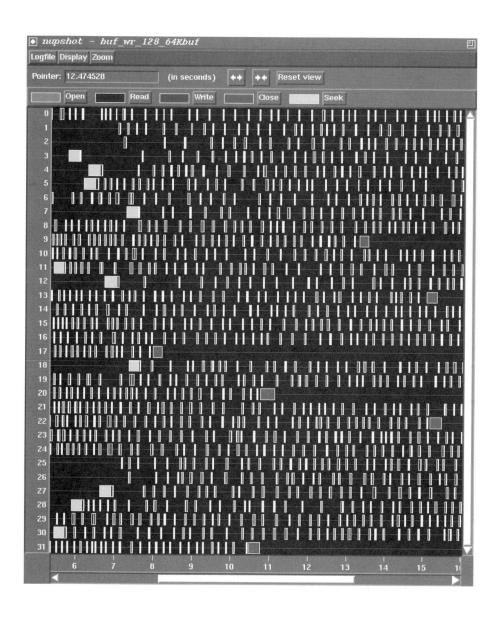

Figure 3.31
Writing a $128 \times 128 \times 128$ distributed array on the Intel Paragon using level-2 requests, with the buffer size for data sieving = 64 Kbytes. Elapsed time = 20 seconds.

Figure 3.32 shows the Upshot plot for level-3 requests, for which ROMIO performs collective I/O. The total time decreased to about 2.75 seconds, which means that level-3 requests were about 45 times faster than level-0 requests and about four times faster than the best performance with level-2 requests. The reason for the improvement is that the numerous writes of each process were coalesced into a *single* write at the expense of some extra computation (to figure how to merge the requests) and interprocess communication. With collective I/O, the actual write time was only a small fraction of the total I/O time; for example, file open took longer than the write.

3.11   An Astrophysics Example

As an example, we consider an astrophysics application from the University of Chicago, called ASTRO3D. This application studies the mechanism by which intergalactic gases condense to form new stars. We describe how to perform the I/O needed by this application using MPI. Details of the application and its I/O requirements can be found in [85].

3.11.1   ASTRO3D I/O Requirements

The application uses several three-dimensional arrays that are distributed among processes using a block distribution in all three dimensions. The arrays fit entirely in memory. Every few iterations, some of the arrays must be written to files for three purposes: data analysis, checkpointing (for later restart), and visualization. The storage order of data in all files is required to be the same as it would be if the program were run with a single process. In other words, the arrays must be stored in column-major order of the global array. There are two reasons for this requirement. The developers of the application want to be able to restart the program with a different number of processes from the program that created the restart file [53]. They also want to analyze and visualize the data with sequential (uniprocess) tools on regular workstations [53]. The easiest way to achieve these goals is to write the data to a single file in some canonical order. The alternative way of writing to separate files and postprocessing them is clumsy and inconvenient.

   The data in the data-analysis and restart files is organized as follows. Each file begins with a small "header" consisting of six floating-point variables that have the same values on all processes. Following this header are six arrays appended one after another in the same file. The visualization data is stored in four separate files, each of which has a six-variable header followed by a single array. Every few

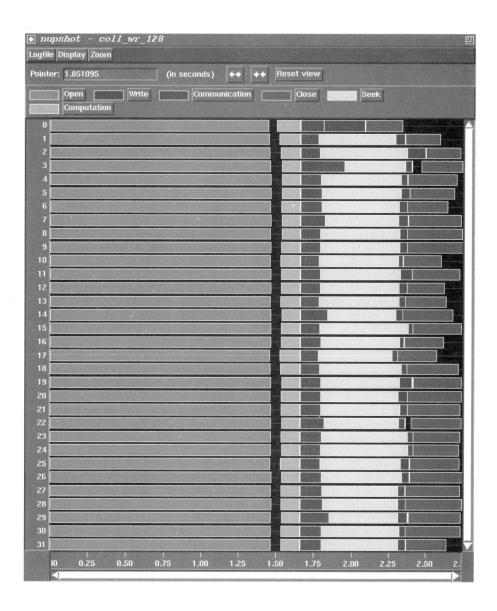

Figure 3.32
Writing a 128 × 128 × 128 distributed array on the Intel Paragon using level-3 requests. Elapsed time = 2.75 seconds.

iterations, the application writes out new data-analysis and visualization files and overwrites the previously written restart file.

3.11.2 Implementing the I/O with MPI

We describe how to write the restart file using MPI; the data-analysis file is identical, and the visualization file is similar—actually simpler, as it has only one array.

Figure 3.33 shows the code for writing the restart file. We first write the six-variable header (assume that the six variables have already been collected into a single buffer called header). Since all processes have the same values for the header, any one process can write it. We choose to let process 0 write the header. Now we need to define the file view in a way that the header is automatically skipped and the arrays can be written with a single function call each. We create a darray datatype for use as the filetype, similar to the one in the program in Figure 3.10. We fill in various one-dimensional arrays, which are used as parameters to the darray datatype constructor. gsizes contains the size of the global array in each dimension. distribs specifies that the distribution is a block distribution in each dimension. dargs specifies the default distribution argument. We set all entries in psizes to zero for use in the function MPI_Dims_create. MPI_Dims_create creates a logical process grid of the specified number of dimensions. If psizes specifies a nonzero value in any dimension, MPI_Dims_create will use that value as the number of processes in that dimension. We want MPI_Dims_create to calculate the number of processes in each dimension; therefore, we pass a zero-filled psizes.

MPI_Type_create_darray returns a datatype, which we first commit and then use as the filetype to MPI_File_set_view. The displacement is specified as the size of the header in bytes, namely, six times the size of a floating-point number. This will cause the header portion of the file to be skipped in subsequent writes. The etype is specified as MPI_FLOAT. Recall that the file view is defined as a *tiling* of the file, starting at the displacement, followed by multiple copies of the filetype appended contiguously one after another. Therefore, with this view, we can simply write all six arrays with six calls to MPI_File_write_all. local_array_size is the size of the local array in terms of the number of floating-point numbers. After each write, the individual file pointer on each process is automatically incremented by the number of etypes written, skipping all holes. The file pointer will therefore point to the offset in the file where the write of the next array from this process should begin. Consequently, no explicit file-pointer manipulation is needed.

We note that we have used the darray datatype and MPI_Dims_create for simplicity. All the warnings about darray mentioned in Section 3.4.2 apply here. If an application does not follow the same definition of data distribution or logical-

```
MPI_File_open(MPI_COMM_WORLD, "/pfs/restartfile",
              MPI_MODE_CREATE | MPI_MODE_WRONLY,
              MPI_INFO_NULL, &fh);

MPI_Comm_size(MPI_COMM_WORLD, &nprocs);
MPI_Comm_rank(MPI_COMM_WORLD, &rank);
if (rank == 0)
    MPI_File_write(fh, header, 6, MPI_FLOAT, &status);

for (i=0; i<3; i++) {
    gsizes[i] = global_size_in_each_dim;
    distribs[i] = MPI_DISTRIBUTE_BLOCK;
    dargs[i] = MPI_DISTRIBUTE_DFLT_DARG;
    psizes[i] = 0;
}
MPI_Dims_create(nprocs, 3, psizes);
MPI_Type_create_darray(nprocs, rank, 3, gsizes, distribs, dargs,
                       psizes, MPI_ORDER_FORTRAN, MPI_FLOAT,
                       &filetype);
MPI_Type_commit(&filetype);

MPI_File_set_view(fh, 6*sizeof(float), MPI_FLOAT, filetype,
                  "native", MPI_INFO_NULL);

MPI_File_write_all(fh, array1, local_array_size, MPI_FLOAT,
                   MPI_STATUS_IGNORE);
MPI_File_write_all(fh, array2, local_array_size, MPI_FLOAT,
                   MPI_STATUS_IGNORE);
MPI_File_write_all(fh, array3, local_array_size, MPI_FLOAT,
                   MPI_STATUS_IGNORE);
MPI_File_write_all(fh, array4, local_array_size, MPI_FLOAT,
                   MPI_STATUS_IGNORE);
MPI_File_write_all(fh, array5, local_array_size, MPI_FLOAT,
                   MPI_STATUS_IGNORE);
MPI_File_write_all(fh, array6, local_array_size, MPI_FLOAT,
                   MPI_STATUS_IGNORE);
MPI_File_close(&fh);
```

Figure 3.33
Writing the restart file in ASTRO3D

process ordering as the darray datatype, one must not use darray but must use subarray instead.

3.11.3 Header Issues

As mentioned above, the header in this application consists of six variables with the same values on all processes. It is customary in most applications to write such a header at the start of the file. For performance reasons, however, it may be better to write the header at the *end* of the file. High-performance file systems typically stripe files across multiple disks in units of 64 Kbytes or some such number. By storing a small header at the start of a file and large arrays following it, accesses to data in the large arrays are not likely to be aligned to disk blocks or striping units. These skewed accesses may result in loss of performance. A better alternative (although somewhat counterintuitive) is to store the large arrays first and store the header at the end of the file. With such a storage order, accesses to the large array are more likely to be aligned with file-system boundaries, and the performance is likely to be better.

Figure 3.34 shows the code for writing the ASTRO3D restart file with the header at the end of the file. For writing the six arrays, the only difference in the specification of the file view compared with the previous program is that the displacement is specified as zero because there is no header to skip. The arrays are then written one after another with MPI_File_write_all. To write the header at the end of the file, we create a new file view in which we specify the displacement as the size of the six arrays (global size) in bytes and the etype and filetype both as MPI_FLOAT. With this view, all six arrays will be skipped, and the header will be written contiguously after the arrays. Process 0 writes the header.

Reading the header.   When the header needs to be read from a file, for example during a restart, the read can be implemented in one of the following ways:

- Process 0 can read the header and broadcast it to all other processes.
- All processes can read the header directly by using a collective read function, such as MPI_File_read_all.
- All processes can read the header directly by using an independent read function, such as MPI_File_read.

Since headers are usually small, the read-broadcast method is usually the best method to use. In the case of collective reads, the implementation may analyze the request and then choose to implement it using a read-broadcast. Analyzing the request involves interprocess communication, and hence overhead, which can be

```
MPI_File_open(MPI_COMM_WORLD, "/pfs/restartfile",
              MPI_MODE_CREATE | MPI_MODE_WRONLY,
              MPI_INFO_NULL, &fh);

for (i=0; i<3; i++) {
    gsizes[i] = global_size_in_each_dim;
    distribs[i] = MPI_DISTRIBUTE_BLOCK;
    dargs[i] = MPI_DISTRIBUTE_DFLT_DARG;
    psizes[i] = 0;
}
MPI_Dims_create(nprocs, 3, psizes);
MPI_Comm_size(MPI_COMM_WORLD, &nprocs);
MPI_Comm_rank(MPI_COMM_WORLD, &rank);

MPI_Type_create_darray(nprocs, rank, 3, gsizes, distribs, dargs,
                       psizes, MPI_ORDER_FORTRAN, MPI_FLOAT,
                       &filetype);
MPI_Type_commit(&filetype);
MPI_File_set_view(fh, 0, MPI_FLOAT, filetype, "native",
                  MPI_INFO_NULL);
MPI_File_write_all(fh, array1, local_array_size, MPI_FLOAT,
                   MPI_STATUS_IGNORE);
MPI_File_write_all(fh, array2, local_array_size, MPI_FLOAT,
                   MPI_STATUS_IGNORE);
MPI_File_write_all(fh, array3, local_array_size, MPI_FLOAT,
                   MPI_STATUS_IGNORE);
MPI_File_write_all(fh, array4, local_array_size, MPI_FLOAT,
                   MPI_STATUS_IGNORE);
MPI_File_write_all(fh, array5, local_array_size, MPI_FLOAT,
                   MPI_STATUS_IGNORE);
MPI_File_write_all(fh, array6, local_array_size, MPI_FLOAT,
                   MPI_STATUS_IGNORE);
global_array_size = gsizes[0]*gsizes[1]*gsizes[2];
MPI_File_set_view(fh, 6*global_array_size*sizeof(float), MPI_FLOAT,
                  MPI_FLOAT, "native", MPI_INFO_NULL);
if (rank == 0)
    MPI_File_write(fh, header, 6, MPI_FLOAT, &status);

MPI_File_close(&fh);
```

Figure 3.34
Writing the ASTRO3D restart file with the header at the end of the file rather than at the beginning

avoided if the user does the read-broadcast directly. The third option, independent
reads from each process, will result in too many small I/O requests.

3.12   Summary

The I/O interface in MPI provides many features that can help users achieve high
I/O performance in parallel applications. The most important of these features
are the ability for users to specify noncontiguous data layouts in memory and file
using MPI datatypes, the ability to specify the group of processes participating
in collective I/O operations, and the ability to pass hints to the implementation.
To achieve high I/O performance with MPI, users must use these features. In
particular, in applications with noncontiguous access patterns, users must strive to
express the I/O in terms of level-3 requests (noncontiguous, collective), rather than
level-0 requests (Unix-style).

For further information on parallel I/O in general, we refer readers to [20, 21,
43, 49]. We also recommend the Parallel I/O Archive on the World Wide Web
at `http://www.cs.dartmouth.edu/pario`, which contains links to a number of
research projects in the area, a comprehensive bibliography, and other useful information.

4 Understanding Synchronization

Parallel programming involves more than just transferring data between two processes. The receiver of the data must know when the data is available. In the message-passing programming model, these two operations (data transfer and indicating that the data is available) are tightly connected. This is not true of some other parallel programming models. In addition, the fact that these two steps are combined in message passing can have unexpected performance consequences. In this chapter we will explore some of the issues of synchronization between senders and receivers of data, both for message passing and shared memory, before venturing away from the message-passing model in Chapter 5.

4.1 Introduction

In this short chapter, we will not introduce any new MPI routines. Instead, we will look in more detail at what happens—and what must happen—when data is moved between processes. In Section 4.2, we present another view of the ghost-cell-exchange problem, where we consider not just the individual point-to-point messages, but the performance effect of interactions between the delivery of messages. In Section 4.3, we change gears and look briefly at the shared-memory programming model and address some of the issues in writing correct shared-memory programs. These two sections will motivate the design of MPI's remote memory access routines, introduced in the next chapter.

4.2 Synchronization in Message Passing

A common use of message passing is to exchange ghost point values on a grid or mesh that is distributed among processes. We have discussed such an example in Chapter 4 of *Using MPI* [32]. We will revisit this example to illustrate performance problems caused by unintended synchronization and discuss how to improve the performance of this example using only MPI-1 point-to-point message passing.

For concreteness, consider the 4×3 array of meshes (on twelve processes) shown in Figure 4.1. Each process must exchange data with its neighbors; two of the processes have four neighbors, six have three neighbors, and four have two neighbors.

The simplest code to send the ghost points between the processes is shown in Figure 4.2. As we showed in Chapter 4 of *Using MPI* [32], this code can perform poorly or even deadlock because the `MPI_Send` calls can block, each waiting for another process to issue the matching receive. Variations of this code that order

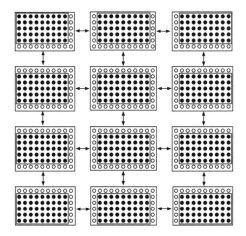

Figure 4.1
4 × 3 array of meshes. Open circles are ghost cells; arrows indicate data exchanges needed to fill ghost cells.

the send and receive pairs, for example, first sending down and then receiving from above, also have poor performance because most of the sends will block, except for the processes at the very bottom. These have no process to send to and hence will issue their receives, matching the send for the process immediately above them. In a very real sense, the code in Figure 4.2 has so much synchronization that it will deadlock (a sort of interlocking synchronization).

To eliminate the possibility of deadlock or serialization, one should use nonblocking operations. Often, the easiest strategy is to replace the `MPI_Recv` operations with the nonblocking version, `MPI_Irecv`, as shown in Figure 4.3. This code will work, but in practice its performance may be significantly poorer than you might expect. To understand why, we use a simple performance model.

Let us assume that a process can receive from several senders at the same time, but that the total rate at which it can receive data is fixed. That is, if one process can send it data at 100 MBytes/sec, then two processes can send data at only 50 MBytes/sec each. This is a very reasonable model; it assumes that the rate at which a process can receive data is controlled by the receiving process's ability to move data from its interconnection network with other processes into memory. To simplify the analysis, let us assume that it takes one time period to send the ghost-cell data from one process to a neighboring process for an entire edge. Since there are four edges, it should take four steps to send all of the ghost cell data.

Figures 4.4 through 4.9 show what might happen given the timing model that

```
do i=1,n_neighbors
    call MPI_SEND(edge(1,i), len, MPI_REAL,&
                    nbr(i), tag, comm, ierr)
enddo
do i=1,n_neighbors
    call MPI_RECV(inedge(1,i), len, MPI_REAL,&
                    nbr(i), tag, comm, status, ierr)
enddo
```

Figure 4.2
Sending ghost-point values in a way that is straightforward, but performs poorly and may even deadlock

```
do i=1,n_neighbors
    call MPI_IRECV(inedge(1,i), len, MPI_REAL, nbr(i), tag,&
                    comm, requests(i), ierr)
enddo
do i=1,n_neighbors
    call MPI_SEND(edge(1,i), len, MPI_REAL, nbr(i), tag,&
                    comm, ierr)
enddo
call MPI_WAITALL(n_neighbors, requests, statuses, ierr)
```

Figure 4.3
Code to send ghost-point values using nonblocking receives

has receivers controlling the rate at which data may be delivered. In the first step, shown in Figure 4.4, most of the processes are sending down to the neighbor below. However, the bottom row of processes have no neighbor below, and so they begin to send to another neighbor on the right or above, depending on the location. The processes that are the destinations for these messages must share their memory bandwidth among the different senders.

In Figure 4.5 we begin to see the consequences of using MPI_Send. MPI_Send cannot return until the message has been moved from the user's buffer. Because several processes in Figure 4.4 are the targets of two MPI_Send operations, these sends can run only at half speed each, and so do not complete in a single step. We see these data transfers continuing in Figure 4.5.

At the end of the fourth step, the communication could be complete if full use has been made of every process's interconnect. Because of the synchronization requirements of MPI_Send, however, some communication steps did not take place at full speed, and we are not yet done. In fact, two more steps are required, as shown

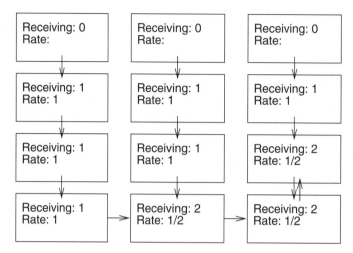

Figure 4.4
Step 1. All processes send to first neighbor; three processes are each targets of two sends.

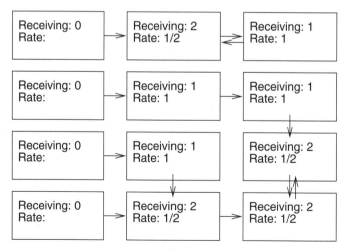

Figure 4.5
Step 2. Some sends to first neighbors are still continuing.

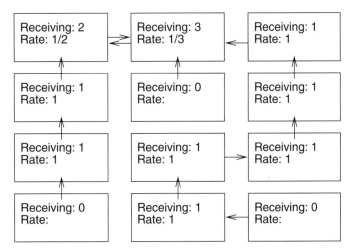

Figure 4.6
Step 3. One process is now receiving only at 1/3 of peak rate.

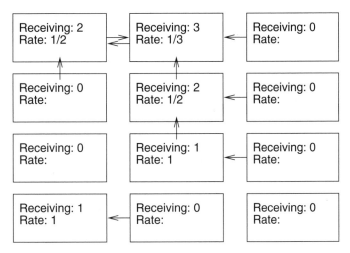

Figure 4.7
Step 4. Two processes have become completely idle.

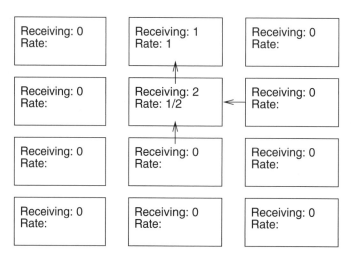

Figure 4.8
Step 5. Eight processes are idle!

in Figures 4.8 and 4.9. For simplicity in exposition, in the case where there are three processes sending to a single process, we have "rounded down" the performance of transfers into that process (on the top center). Making this more precise changes the predictions of the timing model slightly, but does not change the qualitative behavior.

We can validate our theoretical analysis by running this program and examining its performance with a tool such as Upshot [38, 46]. An Upshot view of one iteration of this program, run on an IBM SP, is shown in Figure 4.10. We can see from Figure 4.10 that processes five and six, the two processes in the interior of the mesh, are the last to send, and processes one and two are the last to receive, just as our model predicts. Furthermore, the time to send an edge (shown as a black bar in Figure 4.10) is not the same for each process; rather, there are roughly two different times. The longer time is roughly twice a long as the short send time; this can be seen in a histogram of the MPI_Send times (Figure 4.11). The source of this loss of performance is our insistence that the communication operations complete in a certain order. In this example, we do not need to send the ghost-point values in any particular order, but by choosing MPI_Send to send the data, we have, without really thinking about it, specified a certain order for the motion of data. As we have seen in Figures 4.4 through 4.9, this order of operations causes conflicts for shared resources (in this case, the resource for receiving data), causing a loss in performance.

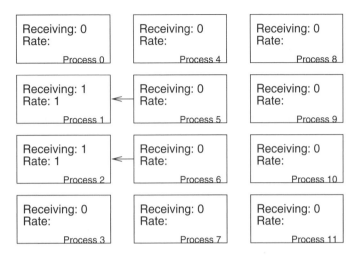

Figure 4.9
Step 6. Communication finally completes, delayed by excessive synchronization. Only four processes are busy during the last step.

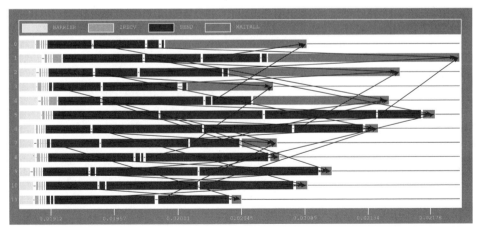

Figure 4.10
Upshot view of one iteration

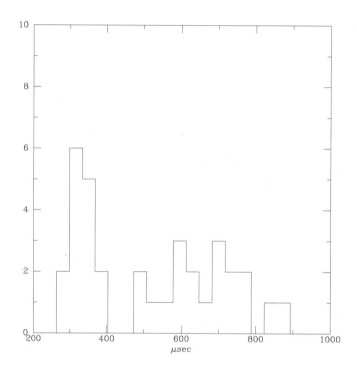

Figure 4.11
Histogram of send times

To fix this problem, we need to relax our requirement of a particular order of execution. We can replace the `MPI_Send` calls with `MPI_Isend` as shown in Figure 4.12. Now, all of the sends may proceed; a sophisticated MPI implementation will ensure that all of the `MPI_Isend` operations effectively share the available memory resources, and the data transfer will take four time steps. When we do this, Upshot does indeed show us a more balanced view, as shown in Figure 4.13.

This approach is an example of a general technique for high-performance programming called *deferred synchronization*. By waiting until the last possible moment to require that an operation (such as an `MPI_Isend`) be completed, we give the system the greatest opportunity to order operations for best performance.

```
      do i=1,n_neighbors
         call MPI_IRECV(inedge(1,i), len, MPI_REAL, nbr(i), tag, &
                        comm, requests(i), ierr)
      enddo
      do i=1,n_neighbors
         call MPI_ISEND(edge(1,i), len, MPI_REAL, nbr(i), tag, &
                        comm, requests(n_neighbors+i), ierr)
      enddo
      call MPI_WAITALL(2*n_neighbors, requests, statuses, ierr)
```

Figure 4.12
Better version of code to exchange ghost points

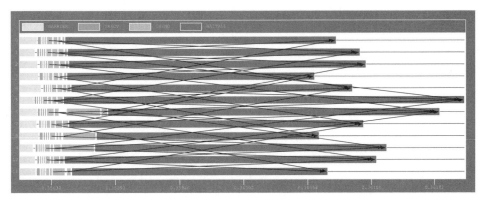

Figure 4.13
Upshot view of exchange with nonblocking operations

4.3 Comparison with Shared Memory

In shared-memory programming, data transfer between two threads of control (you can think of threads as processes sharing memory if you are unfamiliar with threads) is often described as being as simple as reading from a variable or writing to a variable. This is almost true. Consider the two threads that are counting up to 10 with a shared counter variable i (i starts at zero) and a private (nonshared) variable j, using the code in Figure 4.14.

What can we say about the values of j that the two threads might print out? We are tempted to say that the sum of the values of j printed by the two processes would equal 10, since i has been incremented ten times. But this isn't the only result that can happen. Many values for the sum of the j values that are greater

```
int j = 0;
while (i < 10) {
    i = i + 1;
    j = j + 1;
}
print ("j = %d\n", j );
```

Figure 4.14
Code to increment i until it reaches 10

thread 1	thread 2
read i (value 0) into register r1	read i (value 0) into register r1
increment r1 and j	increment r1 (value 1) and j
store r1 into i	
read i (value 1) into r1	
increment r1 and j	
store r1 into i	
read i (value 2) into r1	
increment r1 and j	
store r1 into i	
	store r1 into i (value 1)

Figure 4.15
One possible sequence of operations for the first few steps of the code in 4.14

than ten are possible, and in fact the value of j on a single thread may exceed ten!

The reason is that as the two threads read and write to the shared variable i, the value set by one thread can be overwritten by the other thread. For example, consider the sequence of operations shown in Figure 4.15.

At the end of the sequence of operations in Figure 4.15, the value of i is one, but the value of j on thread 1 is three! This is a well-known and understood problem. The solution is to ensure that only one thread at a time can modify a variable and that a thread does not read a variable until the value in the variable is guaranteed to be ready to be read. In other words, the read-modify-write of i must be made *atomic*.

Consider the following modification. We use a shared variable token to alternate the threads: the value of token is 1 to start, the value of myid is the number of the executing thread (either 1 or 2), and the value of otherid is the number of the other thread (either 2 or 1, respectively). The code is shown in Figure 4.16.

This code is more likely to produce the correct value, but it too isn't guaranteed. There are two problems: volatile variables and write ordering.

4.3.1 Volatile Variables

First, the compiler may decide that `token` can be placed into a register. That is, the compiler may read the value of `token` from memory, place it into a register, and then refer to the value in that register rather than re-reading the value from memory. In that case, any change to the value of `token` that is made by the other thread will not be seen by the first thread. To fix this problem, at least in C and C++, we can declare `token` as `volatile`:

```
volatile int token;
```

Note that we really need to declare `i` as volatile as well. Some Fortran compilers accept a similar extension, for example,

```
integer token
volatile token
```

(in many Fortran 77 compilers) or

```
integer, volatile :: token
```

(in some Fortran 90 compilers). The Fortran 2000 draft standard includes `volatile`. This tells the compiler that the value of this variable may be changed by another agent, such as another thread, and ensures that the compiler won't reuse a value that has been put in a register.

However, note that declaring a variable as `volatile` will cause the compiler to reload it into register before every use. In some programs, this can result in a significant loss of performance.

```
int j = 0;
while (i < 10) {
    while (token != myid) ;
    i = i + 1;
    token = otherid;
    j = j + 1;
}
print ("j = %d\n", j );
```

Figure 4.16
Code to increment i until it reaches 10 using a flag

4.3.2   Write Ordering

The second problem is more subtle. There is no reason why the compiler can't choose to implement

```
i     = i + 1
token = otherid
```

as

```
token = otherid
i     = i + 1
```

As far as the compiler is concerned, the results are the same since the language doesn't say anything about multiple threads of execution, and since such reorderings can be important for performance in other contexts. Furthermore, even if the compiler didn't reorder the statements, modern microprocessors may reorder writes to memory. That is, the *hardware* may decide to write to memory in a different order than the compiler asked for, again to improve performance.

The concept of *sequential consistency* [50] is used to describe a parallel execution where the results are the same as if the statements were executed by a single process (hence the sequential) according to some interleaving (without reordering) of the statements from each process. The above compiler optimization or hardware reordering violates sequential consistency. The slightly weaker *processor consistency* describes the intent of the code fragment above: on any processor, the writes (and reads) occur in the order shown in the program. A discussion of several different consistency models, including much weaker ones than these, is found in [25].

Avoiding the problems of write reordering requires great care. For example, to ensure that the value of i has been written to memory before the value of token is modified in Figure 4.16, many systems require that a write synchronization instruction be issued. Unfortunately, neither C nor Fortran has a portable way to write this (in some C compilers, you can issue assembly language instructions with a directive such as `asm(wsync)`, but this is not portable). As a result, correct shared-memory programming often requires calling special routines to ensure that operations are properly synchronized.

A third problem has to do with performance rather than correctness. The solution proposed above requires each thread to do the same amount of work. In many cases, we prefer for each thread to be able to work at its own pace.

The most common solution is to all three of these problems is to use *locks*. Only one thread may hold the lock at any time, and the implementation of a lock is

```
int j = 0;
while (i < 10) {
    lock();
    i = i + 1;
    unlock();
    j = j + 1;
}
print ("j = %d\n", j );
```

Figure 4.17
Code to increment i until it reaches 10 using locks

guaranteed to avoid all of the problems that we've discussed. An example is shown in Figure 4.17.

There are other solutions, including semaphores and monitors. Another approach is to carefully implement abstractions such as queues, stacks, and lists in such a way that all operations on those data structures behave correctly even when multiple processes (or threads) are accessing them (see, for example, [54, 93, 60]). Unfortunately, the efficient implementation of these operations often requires assembly language programming.

4.3.3   Comments

One advantage of shared memory is that, other than the issues that we've raised above, no special programming is needed—a program may access data anywhere simply by referring to it. There is another advantage: even when tools such as lock()/unlock() must be used to guarantee that data has been transferred, a single such operation may be used for any number of data transfers. In other words, in shared-memory programming, the steps of transferring the data and synchronizing access to the data have been separated. A single synchronization step may "complete" an arbitrary number of data transfers.

This analysis leads us to the next two chapters, in which we study the MPI approach to separating data transfer from synchronization. In Chapter 5, we consider a simple barrier-style synchronization model. In Chapter 6, we look at two more complex synchronization models.

5 Introduction to Remote Memory Operations

Two principal approaches exist for communicating data between cooperating processes: message passing and direct access to the memory in the remote process. MPI-1 provides a powerful and complete interface for the message-passing approach. The remote memory operations of MPI-2 provide a way to directly access memory in another process, through operations that *put* data to, *get* data from, or *update* data at a remote process. Unlike message passing, the program running on the remote process does not need to call any routines to match the put or get operations. Thus, remote memory operations can offer both greater performance (when there is sufficient support in hardware for the operations) and greater functionality, simplifying some kinds of parallel programming.

The MPI-2 remote memory operations grew out of several approaches for parallel programming based on remote memory operations,[1] just as MPI-1 standardized message passing by drawing on experiences with research systems and commercial message-passing systems,

Perhaps the most important of the research systems is *bulk synchronous parallel*, often abbreviated as BSP [39, 76, 92]. In the BSP style of parallel programming, programs are divided into sections, one where there is no communication between the processes, and one where there is only communication; the sections are separated by barriers. Communication of data between processes is handled by remote memory operations that put or get data, and these operations are all nonblocking (in the MPI sense). Completion of these operations is handled by a single communication barrier, hence the term "bulk synchronous."

Several commercial systems have been delivered with remote memory operations. The most significant is undoubtedly the Cray *shmem* [18] interface introduced with the Cray T3D. There were earlier commercial remote memory programming systems, for example, CMMD Version 3 on the Thinking Machines CM-5. IBM has introduced LAPI [75] for distributed-memory systems such as the IBM SP. All of these systems have demonstrated that a remote memory programming model both can be expressive in terms of supporting complex parallel applications and can offer high performance, particularly when supported by fast hardware such as on the Cray T3D and T3E.

A related development has been in the use of remote memory operations to provide faster (particularly lower latency) "user-space" networking as an alternative to TCP/IP. A number of successful research systems, including U-Net [96], demon-

---

[1] These are also called one-sided operations because only one of the two processes is directly involved, from the programmer's standpoint, in the operation.

strated the potential of this approach. Recently, an industry group has proposed VIA [95], or Virtual Interface Architecture, as an industry standard model for network interfaces that directly support remote memory operations.

All of the above contributed to the design of the MPI-2 remote memory programming model. In addition, the MPI-2 design makes the remote memory operations have the same "look and feel" as other MPI routines, including permitting the use of datatypes and allowing collective operations on any communicator, not just `MPI_COMM_WORLD` (which is a restriction of many of the prior systems). Finally, the MPI model is designed to be implementable on a wide range of systems, from workstation networks with no special hardware for remote memory operations to tightly coupled parallel computers with fast, fully coherent shared-memory hardware.

The MPI-2 remote memory operations must be distinguished from the shared-memory programming model. In the usual shared-memory model, there is a single address space, shared by multiple threads of execution. References to memory, regardless of location, are accomplished simply by referencing variables. A major advantage of this model is that programs can be written by using familiar variable reference and assignment statements; new syntax or routines are not required. However, the model has several disadvantages. The most obvious is that supporting this model efficiently requires special hardware. A less obvious problem is that simultaneous access by several different threads to the same memory location can lead to hard-to-find errors; correcting this problem requires providing a way to control or synchronize access to shared data as we saw in Section 4.3. The approach used in shared-memory models uses some combination of sophisticated compilers and special routines to provide, for example, locks to synchronize access to shared variables.

This chapter introduces the MPI remote memory model. Rather than covering all of the functions in each category, as the MPI-2 Standard [58] and the MPI Complete Reference [27] do, this chapter introduces functions as they are needed to illustrate their use. Specifically, we cover here the routines used to initiate remote memory operations and the simplest of the three methods provided by MPI for completing remote memory operations.

The following chapter continues the discussion of more general models of memory access and completes the coverage of the remote memory access routines.

5.1   Introduction

The message-passing model provides a *cooperative* way of moving data from one process to another: one process performs a send, and the destination process performs a receive. Only when the receive completes does the destination process have the data. This approach has a number of important properties. One is that changes in the memory of the receiver can happen only when the receiver allows them (by calling one of the MPI receive routines) and only in the memory locations that are specified as the receive buffer in those routines. Thus, it is clear from the program both what memory locations can be modified by another process (often called a *remote* process) and at what points in the program this can happen. These properties can aid in ensuring that the program is correct and in debugging it if it isn't.

The requirement of message passing that data transfers be cooperative has its disadvantages as well. There are two main areas of limitation: expressiveness (the ease with which programs may be written) and performance.

While in principle any parallel program can be written using message passing, in practice some programs are much harder to write than others. The requirement that every send be matched with a receive demands careful planning and can add complexity to a code. It is difficult to provide with message passing a way for one process to access or modify data held by another process, since both processes must cooperate to perform the operation. An example is a single counter (for example, a counter of the number of errors seen) that is shared by many processes. How can a process add a value to this counter? With message passing, it must send a message to the process that "owns" the counter, asking that process to update the value. That process in turn must check for these messages. This greatly complicates the program, particularly if the MPI implementation is single threaded or does not want to use a thread solely to update this value (as in Section 8.3).

In addition, as we saw in Section 4.2, the cooperative nature of message passing introduces an order into the delivery of data; in some cases, the order isn't important to the application. Enforcing the order has performance costs, in terms of both the effect described in Section 4.2 and of extra overhead in implementing message matching.

MPI-2 introduces a new approach for moving data from one process to another that eliminates the drawbacks of message passing while retaining many of the advantages. This approach, called *remote memory access* (RMA), provides a way to move data from one process to another with a single routine that specifies both where the data is coming from and where it is going to. An RMA operation is a kind of combined send and receive; the calling process specifies both the send buffer and the receive buffer. Because a single call is used, these routines are also called *one-sided communication* routines.

Using the RMA approach involves three main steps:

1. Define the memory of the process that can be used for RMA operations, preserving the advantage of limiting what memory can be modified by a remote process. This is accomplished by defining a *memory window* and creating a new MPI object, the MPI window object `MPI_Win`. See Section 5.3 for details.

2. Specify the data to be moved and where to move it. The MPI routines that may be used are `MPI_Put`, `MPI_Get`, and `MPI_Accumulate`. See Section 5.4 for details.

3. Specify how we know that the data is available. In other words, what is the RMA equivalent to the completion of a receive? There are three different ways to accomplish this in MPI. The simplest, which corresponds to the simplest BSP and shmem models, is described in Section 5.5 and is the only method described in this chapter. The others are described in the next chapter.

Section 5.2 contrasts message passing with remote memory access. The MPI functions introduced are described in more detail in the following three sections (Sections 5.3 through 5.5). Section 5.6 contains two examples: an alternative to the Poisson problem described in Chapter 4 of *Using MPI* [32], and a dense matrix-vector multiply. The chapter closes with some discussion of memory coherence and RMA performance issues.

5.2 Contrast with Message Passing

Before going into the details of remote memory operations, we begin with a simple RMA example and compare it with point-to-point message passing. In this example, unlike the example for computing π in Section 2.3, we will concentrate on the RMA routines most closely related to `MPI_Send` and `MPI_Recv`. This example emphasizes the similarities between RMA and message-passing operations. Later we will see how to use RMA in situations where a message-passing solution is much more difficult.

To see the similarities between RMA and message passing, let us consider sending data from one process to another. Specifically, process 0 is sending n ints in outbuf to the variable inbuf in process 1.

```
/* Create communicator for separate context for processes
   0 and 1 */
MPI_Comm_rank( MPI_COMM_WORLD, &rank );
MPI_Comm_split( MPI_COMM_WORLD, rank <= 1, rank, &comm );

/* Only processes 0 and 1 execute the rest of this */
if (rank > 1) return;

/* Process 0 sends and Process 1 receives */
if (rank == 0) {
    MPI_Isend( outbuf, n, MPI_INT, 1, 0, comm, &request );
}
else if (rank == 1) {
    MPI_Irecv( inbuf, n, MPI_INT, 0, 0, comm, &request );
}
/* Allow other operations to proceed (communication or
   computation) */
...
/* Complete the operation */
MPI_Wait( &request, &status );

/* Free communicator */
MPI_Comm_free( &comm );
```

Figure 5.1
Example code for sending data from one process to another with nonblocking message passing

Figures 5.1 and 5.2 show the correspondence between the message-passing operations and remote memory operations. For example, the memory window object serves a role similar to that of a communicator in message passing. MPI_Put, like MPI_Isend, initiates a data transfer. MPI_Win_fence completes the data transfer initiated by MPI_Put, much as MPI_Wait completes the transfer initiated by MPI_Isend.

These figures also show some of the differences. Note that this example uses no remote memory operation corresponding to MPI_Irecv; instead, the destination of the data is specified as arguments to the window creation on process 1. There is also an MPI_Win_fence call *before* the MPI_Put call. These differences will be covered below. An alternative version of Figure 5.2 is possible that uses MPI_Get on process 1 instead of MPI_Put on process 0. In this case, there is an RMA routine corresponding to MPI_Irecv, but not to MPI_Isend.

```
/* Create memory window for separate context for processes
   0 and 1 */
MPI_Comm_rank( MPI_COMM_WORLD, &rank );
MPI_Comm_split( MPI_COMM_WORLD, rank <= 1, rank, &comm );
if (rank == 0) {
    MPI_Win_create( NULL, 0, sizeof(int),
                    MPI_INFO_NULL, comm, &win );
}
else if (rank == 1 ) {
    MPI_Win_create( inbuf, n * sizeof(int), sizeof(int),
                    MPI_INFO_NULL, comm, &win );
}
/* Only processes 0 and 1 execute the rest of this */
if (rank > 1) return;

/* Process 0 puts into process 1 */
MPI_Win_fence( 0, win );
if (rank == 0)
    MPI_Put( outbuf, n, MPI_INT, 1, 0, n, MPI_INT, win );

/* Allow other operations to proceed (communication or
   computation) */
...

/* Complete the operation */
MPI_Win_fence( 0, win );

/* Free the window */
MPI_Win_free( &win );
```

Figure 5.2
Example code for sending data from one process to another with remote memory operations

A more subtle issue that has been passed over here has to do with when a program may access variables that are also used in RMA operations. With message passing, the rules are (relatively) natural and easy to follow: between the beginning of the message-passing operation and the end of the operation, whether it is a send or a receive, the buffer for the data should not be accessed.[2] With shared memory and RMA, the rules are more complex because of the one-sided nature of the operation: when can data in the process that is not directly involved (via an `MPI_Put` or `MPI_Get` call) in the data transfer be used? While the general rules are somewhat complex, there are simple rules that will ensure a correct program; some of these are presented in Section 5.7.

This example makes remote memory operations look more complex than message passing. The reason is that the operation is "sending data from one process to another." Message passing is very natural for this operation, whereas RMA is not the most natural approach, although it can be implemented with RMA. We will see later other operations that are more natural with RMA.

In addition, this example has used a collective routine (`MPI_Win_fence`) to complete the remote memory operations. This provides a very simple RMA model, but it is not the most general. A method that does not involve collective completion operations is described in the next chapter.

5.3 Memory Windows

The first step in using RMA is to define the memory that will be available for remote memory operations. The memory in a process that can be accessed by another process through the use of the RMA routines is called a *memory window* into the process. It is called a window because MPI limits what part of a process's memory is accessible to other processes. That is, just as `MPI_Recv` limits where a message can be received (in the buffer specified by arguments to `MPI_Recv`), a memory window limits where data may be written (with `MPI_Put` or `MPI_Accumulate`) or read from (with `MPI_Get`). A memory window is local memory (memory in the calling MPI process) that is made available to RMA operations. It is a contiguous section of memory, described as base address plus size in bytes.

The routine `MPI_Win_create` is used to tell MPI what memory windows are available. Following the analogy with the message-passing operations, in addition

---

[2]This applies even to reading from a buffer used for sends, even though many MPI programmers are unaware of this requirement in the MPI Standard (see Section 3.7.2, Communication Initiation, in [56]).

to specifying where data may be stored or read, we need also specify which MPI processes have access to that data. Since one of the reasons for using the RMA interface is to allow several different processes to access (read, set, or update) a memory location, the most natural way to describe the processes that can access a memory window is with an MPI group.

Since an MPI group is involved, it is not surprising that the MPI group used is the group of an MPI (intra)communicator. Since a communicator is involved, it isn't surprising that the operation to create the memory windows is collective over the communicator.

This is enough to define the memory that forms the local memory window and the processes that can access that memory window (also called window or local window). Two additional arguments must be provided. The first is the displacement unit. This is used to simplify accesses with a single datatype, particularly in heterogeneous applications. Typical values are either 1 (all accesses are in terms of byte *offsets*) or the size of a data item (e.g., `sizeof(double)`). Sections 5.4.1 through 5.4.3 covers this argument in more detail.

The second required argument is an info argument that can be used to improve performance. This is covered in more detail in Section 5.8. It is always correct to use `MPI_INFO_NULL` for this argument.

The value returned is called an MPI *window object*, which represents the collection of windows defined by the collective `MPI_Win_create` call. This window object must be passed to all RMA routines that perform RMA operations. The window object serves the same role for RMA operations that the MPI communicator does for message-passing operations. The bindings for `MPI_Win_create` are shown in Tables 5.1, 5.2, and 5.3.

A note on terminology. A *window* refers to a region of memory within a single process. The output `MPI_Win` object from a `MPI_Win_create` is called a "window object" and describes the collection of windows that are the input to the `MPI_Win_-create` call. It might have been easier if the individual regions of memory were called something like facets or panes (as in window panes), but that is not what was chosen in the MPI Standard. Instead, the term "window object" is always used for the object returned by a call to `MPI_Win_create`, and the term "window" for the local memory region.

When a window object is no longer needed, it should be freed with a call to `MPI_Win_free`. This is a collective call; all of the processes that formed the original window must call `MPI_Win_free` collectively. `MPI_Win_free` should be called

---

int **MPI_Win_create**(void *base, MPI_Aint size, int disp_unit, MPI_Info info,
                MPI_Comm comm, MPI_Win *win)

int **MPI_Win_free**(MPI_Win *win)

Table 5.1
C bindings for memory window routines

MPI_WIN_CREATE(base, size, disp_unit, info, comm, win, ierror)
                <type> base(*)
                integer(kind=MPI_ADDRESS_KIND) size
                integer disp_unit, info, comm, win, ierror

MPI_WIN_FREE(win, ierror)
                integer win, ierror

Table 5.2
Fortran bindings for memory window routines

MPI::Win MPI::Win::Create(const void* base, Aint size, int disp_unit,
                const Info& info, const Intracomm& comm)

void MPI::Win::Free()

Table 5.3
C++ bindings for memory window routines

only when all RMA operations are complete; the completion of RMA operations is described in Section 5.5 and in Sections 6.2 and 6.11. As with the other routines that free an MPI opaque object, the address of the object is passed; on return, it will be set to MPI_WIN_NULL.

5.3.1   Hints on Choosing Window Parameters

This section covers some suggestions for picking the parameters for MPI_Win_-create. Choices related to performance are covered separately in Section 5.8. The use of the displacement unit for heterogeneous RMA communication is covered in Section 5.4.1.

Local window and displacement unit.   Often, the local window should be chosen as a single array, declared or allocated in the calling program. The size of the window should be the size of the array. If the local window is a simple type, such as `double` in C or `DOUBLE PRECISION` in Fortran, then the displacement should be the size of that type. Otherwise, a displacement of one should be used.

Info. The info argument is used only to provide performance-tuning options. A value of `MPI_INFO_NULL` is always valid. See Section 5.8.1 for an info value that can be used when only `MPI_Win_fence` is used to complete RMA operations.

5.3.2   Relationship to Other Approaches

Other (non-MPI) RMA approaches use a function similar to `MPI_Win_create` to make a local memory area available for RMA operations. In BSP [39], the routine `BSP_push_reg` (`reg` is short for "register") is similar to `MPI_Win_create` called over `MPI_COMM_WORLD`, and `BSP_pop_reg` is similar to `MPI_Win_free`.

In Cray shmem [18], the single program model is exploited; variables that are statically declared (e.g., most variables in Fortran) are guaranteed (by the Cray compiler and the loader) to have the same local address. Thus, a program can use the address of a local variable as the address of that same variable (in the single program model) in another process. In this case, no special routines are needed to indicate what local memory is available for RMA operations; all memory is "preregistered." Accessing dynamically allocated memory requires communicating the addresses between the processes; in this case, the programmer is responsible for keeping track of the location of a remote memory area (remote memory window in MPI terms). In MPI, this is handled for the programmer by MPI through `MPI_Win_create`.

In IBM's LAPI [75], memory is allocated specifically for RMA operations. This roughly combines `MPI_Alloc_mem` (see Section 6.3) with `MPI_Win_create`.

5.4   Moving Data

Now that we've identified the memory that can participate in remote memory operations, we need to specify how to move data between two processes. MPI provides three routines that specify what data to move: `MPI_Put` to put data into a remote memory window, `MPI_Get` to get data from a remote memory window, and `MPI_Accumulate` to update data in a remote window. `MPI_Put` is like "store to remote memory" or "write to remote memory."

The specification of the data to put is identical to that in an `MPI_Send`: buffer address, count, and datatype. The data can be anywhere in memory; it does not

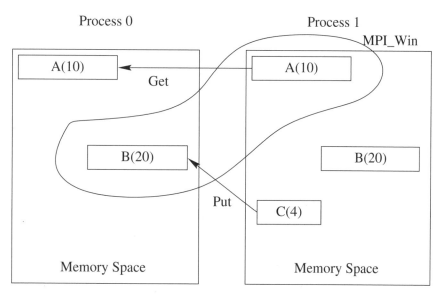

Figure 5.3
Windows, put, and get. Process 0 gets data from A on process 1. Process 1 puts data into B on process 0. The window object is made up of the array B on process 0 and the array A on process 1.

need to be in a window. This is called the *origin address*; origin here refers to the process making the call, not the source of the data.

The specification of where to put the data on the remote node is slightly different from that of where the data comes from. The destination of the data is always relative to the memory window on the destination process. Thus, instead of a buffer address, the location to put the data is specified with the triple of offset in window, count, and datatype. The offset argument is combined with the displacement unit that was specified when the window was created (the `disp_unit` parameter to `MPI_-Win_create`) to determine exactly where the data will be placed (see Section 5.4.1). The remote process is specified with a relative rank in the window object, just as the destination of an `MPI_Send` is specified with a relative rank in a communicator. The relationship between window objects, local windows, and RMA operations is shown in Figure 5.3. A more detailed diagram of an `MPI_Put` operation is shown in Figure 5.4.

We've said that `MPI_Put` is like a combined send and receive. This isn't quite correct. It is more like a combined nonblocking send and nonblocking receive. That is, `MPI_Put` is a nonblocking communication routine. There is no blocking version

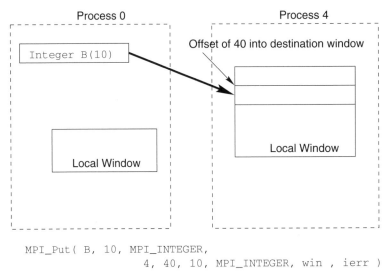

MPI_Put(B, 10, MPI_INTEGER,
                    4, 40, 10, MPI_INTEGER, win , ierr)

Figure 5.4
Illustration of an MPI put operation. Note that the data sent is *not* in the local window.

of `MPI_Put`. This is a deliberate choice in MPI, and it is worth spending some time
to explain why the RMA communication routines are nonblocking.

One of the benefits of nonblocking RMA operations is that they allow many data
motion operations to be completed with a single operation (the `MPI_Win_fence` that
we've seen in the examples in Section 5.2). One of the contributions to the latency
of point-to-point message passing is the need to complete each message-passing operation separately (even when using multiple completion operations, such as `MPI_-`
`Waitall`, the MPI implementation must be prepared to complete each individually
with `MPI_Wait`). Separating the initiation of data motion from the completion of
that data motion is important in achieving high performance, as we have seen in
Chapter 4. With the MPI RMA operations, any number of `MPI_Put` operations can
be completed efficiently by a single `MPI_Win_fence` call.

Section 6.2.1 shows how to implement a kind of blocking put operation. There
could also be a buffered put (the analogue of `MPI_Bsend`); again, this is easy for
an application programmer to do and isn't needed. The BSP `bsp_put` routine is
in fact a buffered put; the BSP counterpart to `MPI_Put` is `BSP_hpput` (hp for "high
performance"). The Cray `shmemput` is nonblocking in the same way `MPI_Put` is.

A counterpart to `MPI_Put` is the routine `MPI_Get`, which gets data *from* the
remote process and returns that data to the calling process. This takes the same

```
int MPI_Put(void *origin_addr, int origin_count, MPI_Datatype origin_datatype,
            int target_rank, MPI_Aint target_disp, int target_count,
            MPI_Datatype target_datatype, MPI_Win win)

int MPI_Get(void *origin_addr, int origin_count, MPI_Datatype origin_datatype,
            int target_rank, MPI_Aint target_disp, int target_count,
            MPI_Datatype target_datatype, MPI_Win win)
```

Table 5.4
C bindings for RMA put and get routines

```
MPI_PUT(origin_addr, origin_count, origin_datatype, target_rank, target_disp,
        target_count, target_datatype, win, ierror)
        <type> origin_addr(*)
        integer(kind=MPI_ADDRESS_KIND) target_disp
        integer origin_count, origin_datatype, target_rank, target_count,
            target_datatype, win, ierror

MPI_GET(origin_addr, origin_count, origin_datatype, target_rank, target_disp,
        target_count, target_datatype, win, ierror)
        <type> origin_addr(*)
        integer(kind=MPI_ADDRESS_KIND) target_disp
        integer origin_count, origin_datatype, target_rank, target_count,
            target_datatype, win, ierror
```

Table 5.5
Fortran bindings for RMA put and get routines

```
void MPI::Win::Put(const void* origin_addr, int origin_count,
            const Datatype& origin_datatype, int target_rank, Aint target_disp,
            int target_count, const Datatype& target_datatype) const

void MPI::Win::Get(void *origin_addr, int
            origin_count, const MPI::Datatype& origin_datatype,
            int target_rank, MPI::Aint target_disp, int target_count,
            const MPI::Datatype& target_datatype) const
```

Table 5.6
C++ bindings for RMA put and get routines

arguments as `MPI_Put`, but the data moves in the opposite direction. The bindings for `MPI_Put` and `MPI_Get` are shown in Tables 5.4, 5.5, and 5.6.

5.4.1 Reasons for Using Displacement Units

We will see that there are two reasons why MPI memory windows have a displacement unit. (rather than defining everything in terms of byte displacements). One reason is clarity in programming (byte offsets can be confusing), and the second is correctness for heterogeneous systems. To understand both of these, consider the following task: put four `int`s into a remote window, starting at the 11th `int` (10th numbering from zero). Let the remote window be created on process three with this code:

```
int A[20];
disp_unit = 1;  /* displacements in bytes */
MPI_Win_create( A, 20*sizeof(int), disp_unit, ..., &win );
```

Then, to store into `A[10]` through `A[13]`, process 1 would call

```
target_offset = 10 * sizeof(int);
MPI_Put( B, 4, MPI_INT, 3, target_offset, 4, MPI_INT, win );
```

Because process 3 specified a displacement unit in bytes (`disp_unit = 1`), the `target_offset` used by process 1 must be computed in bytes.

If, instead, process 3 creates the window explicitly as an array of integers with

```
int A[20];
disp_unit = sizeof(int); /* displacements in ints */
MPI_Win_create( A, 20*sizeof(int), disp_unit, ..., &win );
```

then process 1 can put data into `A[10]` through `A[13]` with

```
target_offset = 10;
MPI_Put( B, 4, MPI_INT, 3, target_offset, 4, MPI_INT, win );
```

Certainly the second approach is more *convenient* for RMA communication operations. However, it is *essential* when the MPI processes use different data representations, such as in a heterogeneous cluster of workstations. For example, in the above case, let us assume that process 1 uses 4-byte integers and process 3 uses 8-byte integers. In the first case, the use of a byte offset displacement unit leads to the wrong action: process 1 is specifying a byte offset of `10*sizeof(int)`, but the size of an `int` on process 1 is 4 bytes, leading to an offset of 40 bytes. But on

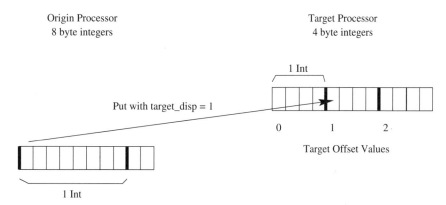

Figure 5.5
Data size offset computation

process 3, with its 8-byte integers, this refers to `A[5]` (`5*sizeof(int)`). Using displacement units in terms of the local type at the time the window object is created ensures that programs will be portable to heterogeneous environments. Figure 5.5 shows how an `MPI_Put` operation can move data to the correct location, even when the two processes have different data lengths, when the displacement unit is set to the size of the data item (an integer in this case) rather than a single byte.

Given this, why ever use a displacement unit of 1 (byte displacement)? One case is with a window that contains several different data types. For example, a sparse matrix is often represented as three separate arrays: two of type integer and one of type double precision. If these arrays were in a single window (for example, they were allocated in a single Fortran common block), it would be easiest to use byte displacements to access the individual elements.[3] However, if byte displacements are used, the application is not portable to heterogeneous systems where the basic datatypes have different lengths.

5.4.2 Cautions in Using Displacement Units

Note that the location in a remote memory window that is accessed by an RMA operation depends on combining the offset specified on the *origin* process with the displacement unit that was specified on the *target* process. This is a potential source of error: the displacement unit used is *not* the one specified in the `MPI_Win_create` call on the process that is originating the RMA (e.g., `MPI_Put`) call.

---

[3]We say easiest because Fortran defines the ratio of sizes of numeric types; thus a displacement size of type integer could also be used, even with the double-precision entries.

```
MPI_SIZEOF(x,size,ierror)
              <type> x
              integer size, ierror
```

Table 5.7
Fortran binding for finding the size of a variable

To avoid potential problems in understanding RMA code, the displacement units should either be one for all processes in the window or the size of the same basic type.

5.4.3   Displacement Sizes in Fortran

Fortran has no counterpart to the C `sizeof` operator. In order to get the size of a datatype to be used in computing a displacement, the function `MPI_Type_size` may be used with MPI predefined datatypes such as `MPI_REAL` and `MPI_INTEGER`. In Fortran 90, the MPI routine `MPI_Sizeof` can also be used. This routine takes as input a variable of any numeric intrinsic type and returns the size in bytes of that type. The variable may be a scalar or an array; the size returned is the size of a single element of that type. This routine may be used only when using the `mpi` module. The binding for `MPI_Sizeof` is shown in Table 5.7.

5.5   Completing Data Transfers

MPI provides many different ways to complete data transfers. This section discusses a simple barrier-like method. Other methods are described in Chapter 6.

In many computations, data exchange happens in phases; computation occurs between communication phases. In the MPI RMA model described in this chapter, these phases are separated with `MPI_Win_fence`. `MPI_Win_fence` is collective over all processes in the group associated with the window object passed to `MPI_Win_-fence`. `MPI_Win_fence` completes any RMA operations that started since the last call to `MPI_Win_fence` and ensures that any local stores to the memory window will be visible to RMA operations (i.e., code like `a(10) = 3` where `a` is part of the local window) before any RMA operations that follow the `MPI_Win_fence` call. A good rule for using `MPI_Win_fence` is to ensure that between any pair of successive `MPI_Win_fence` calls, there may be either local stores (assignments to variables in the process) to the (local) memory window or RMA put or accumulate operations (or neither), but not both local stores and RMA put or accumulate operations. If

```
int MPI_Win_fence(int assert, MPI_Win win)
```

Table 5.8
C binding for window fence

```
MPI_WIN_FENCE(assert, win, ierror)
              integer assert, win, ierror
```

Table 5.9
Fortran binding for window fence

```
void MPI::Win::Fence(int assert) const
```

Table 5.10
C++ binding for window fence

there are no RMA put operations between a pair of `MPI_Win_fence` calls, there may be both load and RMA get operations on the memory window.

Programming remote memory operations using `MPI_Win_fence` is much like the BSP model or SGI/Cray shmem programming model. It is the *least* like shared memory. It is most suitable for "data parallel" applications, where each process is performing operations on a shared, distributed data structure.

`MPI_Win_fence` has an additional argument (beyond the window), named `assert`, that provides information about the fence that can be used by some MPI implementations to provide better performance. A value of zero for the `assert` argument is always valid. Other values are described in Section 5.8.2. The bindings for `MPI_Win_fence` are shown in Tables 5.8, 5.9, and 5.10.

One common use of `MPI_Win_fence` is to alternate between RMA accesses to a memory window and accesses by local loads and stores from the local process. When used this way, `MPI_Win_fence` can be thought of a "toggling" between the two kinds of accesses. However, `MPI_Win_fence` is more general. `MPI_Win_fence` separates RMA accesses (particularly `MPI_Put` and `MPI_Accumulate`) from non-RMA accesses that store data into any local window. The `assert` argument can be used to indicate exactly what kind of operations `MPI_Win_fence` is separating; this is covered in detail in Section 5.8.2.

The code fragment in Figure 5.6 shows an example of using `MPI_Win_fence` to complete RMA operations and to separate RMA operations from local loads and stores. Note that in this example, `MPI_Win_fence` is not a toggle between RMA and local accesses. To be more specific, when using `MPI_Win_fence` for RMA synchronization, all RMA operations must be bracketed by `MPI_Win_fence` calls; an `MPI_Win_fence` is needed both to start and to complete any RMA operation.

5.6   Examples of RMA Operations

In this section we present two examples that use RMA operations. The first is a ghost-cell update, similar to those used for finite difference, finite volume, and finite element computations. The second computes a matrix-vector product using a distributed dense matrix and vector.

5.6.1   Mesh Ghost Cell Communication

This section provides an alternative approach to the Poisson problem, a simple partial differential equation, described in Section 4.1 of [32]. In that chapter, the problem is solved with a finite difference method, using MPI's point-to-point communication routines to communicate data between processes. The reader is referred to that section for details of the Poisson problem. We will briefly review the operations that are needed to implement a finite difference method on a mesh that is distributed among processes.

In solving partial differential equations, the solution often is approximated on a mesh of points that is distributed among the processes. In the simplest case, shown in Figure 5.7, the mesh is regular, and it is partitioned among the processes with a simple, one-dimensional decomposition. In more complex cases, the decomposition among processes can be multidimensional, and the grid itself can be irregular. We will start with the simple decomposition. To compute the discretization at every point on the part of the mesh that is local to the process, we need the value of the neighboring points; these are called the *ghost cells* or *ghost points*. An example is illustrated in Figure 5.8.

We will declare the local part of the distributed mesh with

```
double precision a(0:nx+1,s-1:e+1)
```

We let `a(i,j)` stand for $a(x_i, y_j)$, where the coordinates of a mesh point are given by (x_i, y_j). As discussed in *Using MPI* [32], this follows the natural representation of a mesh but is different from the "matrix" interpretation of a two-dimensional array. See Appendix E in *Using MPI* for more details. The declaration of `a` represents a slice of the mesh, where each process has rows (that is, ranges of the mesh in the y-coordinate) `s` to `e` (for *start* to *end*), and there are `nx` columns (ranges of the mesh in the x-coordinate), plus a column for the boundary conditions on the left and right.

```
MPI_Win_create( A, ..., &win );
MPI_Win_fence( 0, win );
if (rank == 0) {
    /* Process 0 puts data into many local windows */
    MPI_Put( ... , win );
    MPI_Put( ... , win );
}
/* This fence completes the MPI_Put operations initiated
   by process 0 */
MPI_Win_fence( 0, win );

/* All processes initiate access to some window to extract data */
MPI_Get( ... , win );
/* The following fence completes the MPI_Get operations */
MPI_Win_fence( 0, win );

/* After the fence, processes can load and store
   into A, the local window */
A[rank] = 4;
printf( "A[%d] = %d\n", 0, A[0] );
MPI_Win_fence( 0, win );

/* We need a fence between stores and RMA operations */
MPI_Put( ... , win );
/* The following fence completes the preceding Put */
MPI_Win_fence( 0, win );
```

Figure 5.6
An example using `MPI_Win_fence` to separate RMA operations from local load/stores and to complete RMA operations

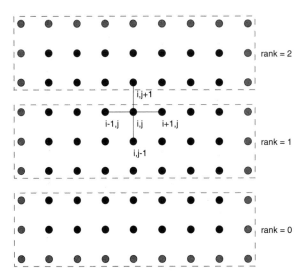

Figure 5.7
1-D decomposition of the domain. Gray circles represent boundary condition cells; black circles are cells interior to the physical domain. A sample computational stencil is shown.

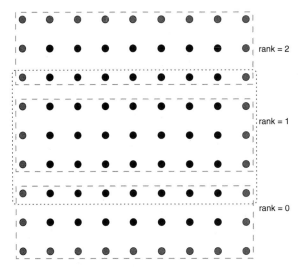

Figure 5.8
The computational domain, with ghost points, for one of the processes

```
subroutine exchng1( a, nx, s, e, comm1d, &
                    bottom_nbr, top_nbr )
use mpi
integer nx, s, e
double precision a(0:nx+1,s-1:e+1)
integer comm1d, bottom_nbr, top_nbr
integer status_array(MPI_STATUS_SIZE,4), ierr, req(4)

call MPI_IRECV ( &
     a(1,s-1), nx, MPI_DOUBLE_PRECISION, bottom_nbr, 0, &
     comm1d, req(1), ierr )
call MPI_ISEND ( &
     a(1,e), nx, MPI_DOUBLE_PRECISION, top_nbr, 0, &
     comm1d, req(3), ierr )
call MPI_IRECV ( &
     a(1,e+1), nx, MPI_DOUBLE_PRECISION, top_nbr, 1, &
     comm1d, req(2), ierr )
call MPI_ISEND ( &
     a(1,s), nx, MPI_DOUBLE_PRECISION, bottom_nbr, 1, &
     comm1d, req(4), ierr )

call MPI_WAITALL ( 4, req, status_array, ierr )
return
end
```

Figure 5.9
Code using point-to-point message passing to exchange ghost cell values

The algorithm for communicating the neighbor information to the ghost cells can be summarized as follows:

1. Initiate send a(*,e) in the local process to a(*,s-1) in the top neighbor.

2. Initiate send a(*,s) in the local process to a(*,e+1) in the bottom neighbor.

3. Complete all data transfers.

An implementation of this algorithm that uses point-to-point message passing is shown in Figure 5.9. To convert this to use remote memory operations, it is quite obvious that the pairs of MPI_Irecv and MPI_Isend can be combined into either MPI_Put or MPI_Get operations. The third step of the algorithm requires a simple MPI_Win_fence call, replacing the MPI_Waitall in Figure 5.9.

To use the RMA routines, we must first define an MPI window object in which
the data will be moved (with either `MPI_Put` or `MPI_Get`). The following code
creates a window where each local window is the (local part of the) mesh, including
the ghost cells:

```
integer sizedouble, ierr, win
double precision A(0:nx+1,s-1:e+1)

call MPI_TYPE_SIZE( MPI_DOUBLE_PRECISION, sizedouble, ierr )
call MPI_WIN_CREATE( A, (nx+2)*(e-s+3)*sizedouble, sizedouble, &
                     MPI_INFO_NULL, MPI_COMM_WORLD, win, ierr )
```

The code to use RMA to exchange ghost-cell values is shown in Figure 5.10. The
displacements at the targets are offset by one; this is necessary to skip the first
ghost cell on the left. It corresponds to `a(0,s-1)` and `a(0,e+1)` which is used to
store the boundary conditions and does not need to be transferred (note that the
point-to-point version in Figure 5.9 sent and received with `a(1,*)`). Note that we
can store into `A` both with `MPI_Put` and read values from `A`; we don't need separate
windows for the different parts of `A`. However, if we wanted to both store into `A` with
statements such as `A(i,j) = ...` and with `MPI_Put`, we must either separate the
stores into the local window and the `MPI_Put` operations with a `MPI_Win_fence` or
put the parts of `A` that we access with `MPI_Put` into separate MPI window objects.

The RMA code in Figure 5.10 is very similar to the point-to-point version in
Figure 5.9. We have replaced two send-receive pairs with two `MPI_Put` operations,
and we have replaced the `MPI_Waitall` on four requests with a simple `MPI_Win_-`
`fence`. The major difference is that there is an `MPI_Win_fence` at the *beginning* of
the code to indicate that local stores to `A` must complete and that RMA operations
can now take place.

Determining the target displacement. In the example above, the first `MPI_-`
`Put` call appears to take the leftmost edge of the mesh on the calling process and
put it into the rightmost ghost edge of the destination (or target) process. But does
it? In the example, the displacement for the target window (`right_ghost_disp`) is
computed by using the *local process*'s window. In other words, the code computes
the location of the right ghost cells on process `left_nbr` using the calling process's
parameters. As Figure 5.11 shows, this strategy can lead to errors if each process
does not have an identically sized mesh. In our example, if the values of `s` and `e`
are not the same on all processes, the wrong value of `right_ghost_disp` will be
computed.

```
subroutine exchng1( a, nx, s, e, win, &
                    bottom_nbr, top_nbr )
use mpi
integer nx, s, e
double precision a(0:nx+1,s-1:e+1)
integer win, bottom_nbr, top_nbr
integer ierr
integer(kind=MPI_ADDRESS_KIND) bottom_ghost_disp, top_ghost_disp

call MPI_WIN_FENCE( 0, win, ierr )
! Put bottom edge into bottom neighbor's top ghost cells
! See text about top_ghost_disp
top_ghost_disp = 1 + (nx+2)*(e-s+2)
call MPI_PUT( a(1,s), nx, MPI_DOUBLE_PRECISION, &
              bottom_nbr, top_ghost_disp, nx, &
              MPI_DOUBLE_PRECISION, win, ierr )
! Put top edge into top neighbor's bottom ghost cells
bottom_ghost_disp = 1
call MPI_PUT( a(1,e), nx, MPI_DOUBLE_PRECISION, &
              top_nbr, bottom_ghost_disp, nx, &
              MPI_DOUBLE_PRECISION, win, ierr )
call MPI_WIN_FENCE( 0, win, ierr )
return
end
```

Figure 5.10
Code using RMA to exchange ghost cell values

To obtain the correct target displacement for the ghost cells on the right edge of the neighbor's mesh, it may be necessary to communicate this information to the process that is performing the MPI_Put operation. The easiest way to do this is with point-to-point message passing: as part of the process of setting up the windows and preparing to communicate, every process sends to its right neighbor the value to use for the target displacement in the MPI_Put. This code is shown in Figure 5.12. The one in the expression for my_top_ghost_disp puts the displacement at the first ghost point in the mesh (skipping the mesh point representing the boundary).

An alternative approach is to communicate the mesh parameters s and e; then the appropriate displacements can be computed. We have shown the communication of the displacements to illustrate the general case and the care that must be taken when communicating data of type MPI_Aint or MPI_ADDRESS_KIND integers.

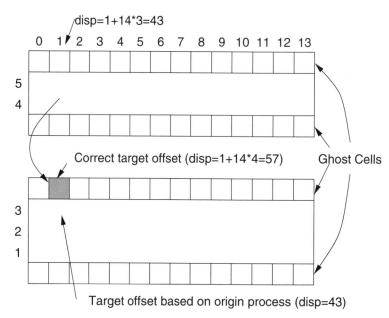

Figure 5.11
Illustration of the different target displacements needed when each local mesh is of a different size

```
integer sizedouble, ierr, win
integer my_top_ghost_disp
integer top_ghost_disp_int
integer (kind=MPI_ADDRESS_KIND) top_ghost_disp
double precision A(0:nx+1,s-1:e+1)

call MPI_TYPE_SIZE( MPI_DOUBLE_PRECISION, sizedouble, ierr )
call MPI_WIN_CREATE( A, (nx+2)*(e-s+3)*sizedouble, sizedouble, &
                     MPI_INFO_NULL, MPI_COMM_WORLD, win, ierr )
! Compute the displacement into my top ghost cells
my_top_ghost_disp = 1 + (nx+2)*(e-s+2)
call MPI_SEND( my_top_ghost_disp, 1, MPI_INTEGER, right_nbr, &
               0, MPI_COMM_WORLD, ierr )
call MPI_RECV( top_ghost_disp_int, 1, MPI_INTEGER, left_nbr, &
               0, MPI_COMM_WORLD, status, ierr )
! Since INTEGER may not be the same as an MPI_ADDRESS_KIND integer
top_ghost_disp = top_ghost_disp_int
```

Figure 5.12
Code to send to neighboring processes the displacement values to be used in MPI_Put operations

---

int **MPI_Type_create_f90_integer**(int r, MPI_Datatype *newtype)

int **MPI_Type_match_size**(int typeclass, int size, MPI_Datatype *type)

Table 5.11
C binding for routine to return the MPI datatype corresponding to a Fortran integer with **r** digits and for the routine to return a datatype of a particular size

More on the target displacement. The type of the target displacement is INTEGER (kind=MPI_ADDRESS_KIND) in Fortran, MPI_Aint in C, and MPI::Aint in C++. Unfortunately, no native MPI datatype corresponds to the type MPI_Aint or INTEGER (kind=MPI_ADDRESS_KIND). In many cases, as shown above, one can use an INTEGER in Fortran or an int or long in C and C++ to communicate target displacements between processes. Care must be taken, however, to pass the correct type of integer in the call to MPI_Put. This is especially important in Fortran when not using the MPI module, since type mismatches will not be caught by the compiler.

The following code shows how to create a datatype that may be used to send values of type INTEGER (kind=MPI_ADDRESS_KIND) for Fortran:

```
integer (kind=MPI_ADDRESS_KIND) sample
integer address_type, r, ierr

r = DIGITS(sample)
call MPI_TYPE_CREATE_F90_INTEGER( r, address_type, ierr )
```

The function DIGITS is a Fortran intrinsic function that provides the number of digits in a variable. The MPI routine MPI_Type_create_f90_integer returns the predefined MPI datatype that has the specified number of digits. Since this is a predefined MPI datatype, you must not free the datatype nor commit it with MPI_Type_commit. The bindings for MPI_Type_create_f90_integer are shown in Tables 5.11, 5.12, and 5.13.

In C and C++, MPI_Type_match_size can be used to return a predefined MPI datatype with a specific size. This function takes two input arguments: the *typeclass* of the datatype, which may have values MPI_TYPECLASS_REAL, MPI_TYPECLASS_INTEGER, and MPI_TYPECLASS_COMPLEX, and the size (in bytes) of the desired variable. The output value is a reference to a predefined MPI datatype. This datatype must not be freed. For example, to find an MPI datatype in C++ that corresponds to MPI::Aint, the following code may be used:

MPI_TYPE_CREATE_F90_INTEGER(r, newtype, ierror)
　　　　　integer r, newtype, ierror

MPI_TYPE_MATCH_SIZE(typeclass, size, type, ierror)
　　　　　integer typeclass, size, type, ierror

Table 5.12
Fortran binding for routine to return the MPI datatype corresponding to a Fortran integer with
r digits and for the routine to return a datatype of a particular size

---

MPI::Datatype MPI::Datatype::Create_f90_integer(int r)

MPI::Datatype MPI::Datatype::Match_size(int typeclass, int size)

Table 5.13
C++ binding for routine to return the MPI datatype corresponding to a Fortran integer with r
digits and to return a datatype of a particular size

```
newtype = MPI::Datatype::Match_size( MPI::TYPECLASS_INTEGER,
                                      sizeof(MPI::Aint )
```

In a heterogeneous environment, neither MPI_Type_create_f90_integer nor
MPI_Type_match_size should be used because systems of different type may return different MPI datatypes. In that case, your best bet is to find an integer
type whose size is at least as large as as the size of char * and use that integer
type when sending displacements. Alternatively, if the C or C++ implementation
supports the long long type, you can use that, taking advantage of the rule in C
that sizeof(long long) is at least as large as the size of any other integer type,
and is almost always large enough to hold a pointer. The MPI datatype that corresponds with long long is MPI_LONG_LONG_INT[4] (in C++, MPI:LONG_LONG). Make
sure that you send a variable of the correct type. MPI_LONG_LONG_INT should not
be used to send data declared as MPI_Aint because long long may be longer than
an MPI_Aint.

An alternative to sending displacements. In the example above, we had to
send the displacement value needed for the MPI_Put operation for the ghost cells
on the top edge because the displacement needed at the origin process (the process
calling MPI_Put), in the general case, might not be easy to calculate. There is

---

[4]MPI_LONG_LONG is used in [79] but is not in the Standard, except in the I/O chapter where
the external32 format is being defined. MPI implementations are likely to accept both, but
MPI_LONG_LONG_INT is a more portable choice, because that MPI datatype is part of MPI-1.

```fortran
subroutine exchng1( a, nx, s, e, win, &
                    bottom_nbr, top_nbr )
use mpi
integer nx, s, e
double precision a(0:nx+1,s-1:e+1)
integer win, bottom_nbr, top_nbr
integer ierr

call MPI_WIN_FENCE( 0, win, ierr )
! Get top edge from top neighbor's first column
call MPI_GET( a(1,e+1), nx, MPI_DOUBLE_PRECISION, &
             top_nbr, nx + 1, nx, MPI_DOUBLE_PRECISION, win, ierr )
! Put bottom edge into bottom neighbor's ghost cells
call MPI_PUT( a(1,e), nx, MPI_DOUBLE_PRECISION, &
             bottom_nbr, 1, nx, MPI_DOUBLE_PRECISION, win, ierr )
call MPI_WIN_FENCE( 0, win, ierr )

return
end
```

Figure 5.13
Alternative code for exchanging ghost cells that mixes puts and gets

an alternative to this approach. Instead of putting data into ghost cells only on remote processes, we can put data into the ghost cells of the process on the top, starting at a displacement of one, and we can get the ghost cells for our part of the grid on the bottom edge by getting grid data from the first column of the process on the bottom. That is, for the ghost values, we can put into the bottommost row (displacement of one), and for the top ghost cells, we get from the first row (displacement of (nx+2)+1 double-precision values). The routine that we use to get the data is MPI_Get, and the code for this is shown in Figure 5.13.

Note that we can use both MPI_Put and MPI_Get operations on the window. We can do this because the memory locations being accessed as targets of the MPI_Put and MPI_Get operations do not overlap (see Section 5.7.3 and Section 4.7 of [27]). Also note that there is no explicit reference to the left_nbr in the above code: the "get from right neighbor" replaces the "put to left neighbor."

Playing with the displacement unit. In our example, we used a displacement unit of sizedouble, the number of bytes in a DOUBLE PRECISION data item. This is the most obvious choice, but there are others. One choice is to make the displacement unit the size of an entire row[5] of A, rather than a single element of A. If the window is defined with a displacement unit of (nx+2)*sizedouble, then the offset that is used in MPI_Put is just the row number. In other words, instead of (nx+2)*(m+1), we can use simply m+1. If we do this, however, we must send an extra element, not just the interior part (e.g., we must send nx+1 values starting from a(0,m) rather than nx values starting from a(1,m). Even the need to send nx+1 elements instead of nx elements can be avoided by a careful definition of the local window; we leave that as an exercise for the reader.

Using datatypes. The simple one-dimensional decomposition is not scalable to a large number of processes. In that case, it is important to use a higher-dimensional decomposition. In the case of our two-dimensional mesh, we might declare the local mesh as

```
double precision a(sx-1:ex+1,sy-1:sy+1)
```

This includes ghost cells on all four sides. When sending the top and bottom row of ghost cells, we can use essentially the same code as before. However, for the left and right edges, the data is not contiguous in memory. This is a perfect place to use MPI datatypes, specifically the MPI_Type_vector routine to construct a datatype for columns of the local mesh. The code to construct the window object and the datatypes for the columns is shown in Figures 5.14 and 5.15. Just as in the previous cases, we also need to send the offsets to be used as the target displacements and the strides needed for the target datatypes (if every local mesh has exactly the same size, we can dispense with this step; we include it to show what is needed in the general case).

With the window object and datatype for a row defined, we can now write the code to fill the ghost cells on all four sides (this is assuming a five-point stencil). The code is shown in Figure 5.16. In a Fortran 90 environment, the variables describing the displacements and datatypes to use for the neighbors could be placed in a derived type, much as a C programmer would put them into a structure.

Performance issues. Using MPI datatypes is certainly the clearest and simplest approach and offers the possibility of good performance. In practice, unfortunately, many MPI implementations do not provide high performance when using derived

---

[5]Recall that we have defined a row of the array a as a row of the mesh, that is, the elements corresponding to constant y value. Readers who are used to the matrix interpretation of two-dimensional arrays are reminded that the jth row of the mesh, corresponding to y_j, is a(:,j), which in the *matrix* interpretation of a, is a column. We use the mesh interpretation because no matrices are involved in our example.

```
integer win, sizedouble, ierr
integer (kind=MPI_ADDRESS_KIND) right_ghost_disp, &
        left_ghost_disp, top_ghost_disp
integer my_right_ghost_disp, my_left_ghost_disp, &
        my_top_ghost_disp, right_ghost_disp_int, &
        left_ghost_disp_int, top_ghost_disp_int
double precision a(sx-1:ex+1,sy-1:ey+1)

! nx is the number of (non-ghost) values in x, ny in y
nx = ex - sx + 1
ny = ey - sy + 1
call MPI_TYPE_SIZE( MPI_DOUBLE_PRECISION, sizedouble, ierr )
call MPI_WIN_CREATE( a, (ex-sx+3)*(ey-sy+3)*sizedouble, &
                     sizedouble, MPI_INFO_NULL, MPI_COMM_WORLD, &
                     win, ierr )
! Exchange information on the offsets
! Compute the displacement into my right ghost cells
my_right_ghost_disp = 2*(nx+2)-1
call MPI_SEND( my_right_ghost_disp, 1, MPI_INTEGER, right_nbr, &
               0, MPI_COMM_WORLD, ierr )
call MPI_RECV( right_ghost_disp_int, 1, MPI_INTEGER, left_nbr, &
               0, MPI_COMM_WORLD, status, ierr )
! Compute the displacement into my top ghost cells
my_top_ghost_disp = (nx + 2)*(ny + 1) + 1
call MPI_SEND( my_top_ghost_disp, 1, MPI_INTEGER, top_nbr, &
               0, MPI_COMM_WORLD, ierr )
call MPI_RECV( top_ghost_disp_int, 1, MPI_INTEGER, bottom_nbr, &
               0, MPI_COMM_WORLD, status, ierr )
! Compute the displacement into my left ghost cells
my_left_ghost_disp = nx + 2
call MPI_SEND( my_left_ghost_disp, 1, MPI_INTEGER, left_nbr, &
               0, MPI_COMM_WORLD, ierr )
call MPI_RECV( left_ghost_disp_int, 1, MPI_INTEGER, right_nbr, &
               0, MPI_COMM_WORLD, status, ierr )
! Just in case INTEGER is not the same as MPI_ADDRESS_KIND integer
right_ghost_disp = right_ghost_disp_int
top_ghost_disp   = top_ghost_disp_int
left_ghost_disp  = left_ghost_disp_int
```

Figure 5.14
Code to exchange displacement values in preparation for using MPI_Put in the example in
Figure 5.16

```
integer coltype, left_coltype, right_coltype

! Vector type used on origin
call MPI_TYPE_VECTOR( 1, ny, nx+2, MPI_DOUBLE_PRECISION, &
                      coltype, ierr )
call MPI_TYPE_COMMIT( coltype, ierr )

! Exchange stride information needed to build the left and right
! coltypes
call MPI_SENDRECV( nx, 1, MPI_INTEGER, left_nbr, 2, &
                   right_nx, 1, MPI_INTEGER, right_nbr, 2, &
                   MPI_COMM_WORLD, status, ierr )
call MPI_SENDRECV( nx, 1, MPI_INTEGER, right_nbr, 3, &
                   left_nx, 1, MPI_INTEGER, left_nbr, 3, &
                   MPI_COMM_WORLD, status, ierr )
call MPI_TYPE_VECTOR( 1, ny, left_nx + 2, MPI_DOUBLE_PRECISION, &
                      left_coltype, ierr )
call MPI_TYPE_COMMIT( left_coltype, ierr )
call MPI_TYPE_VECTOR( 1, ny, right_nx + 2, MPI_DOUBLE_PRECISION, &
                      right_coltype, ierr )
call MPI_TYPE_COMMIT( right_coltype, ierr )
```

Figure 5.15
Code to create vector datatypes to be used at the origin and at the targets in the example in
Figure 5.16

datatypes for communication [33]. If the highest performance is required, it may
be necessary to avoid the use of derived datatypes. In this case, there are two
approaches.

The first is to move the data into a buffer, collecting the data from a row in A
into contiguous memory locations. For example, to move the top row of A into a
buffer on the neighboring process, the code in Figure 5.17 code could be used. This
approach replaces the single MPI_Put call that uses the coltype datatype. Note
that it uses a different window object, winbuf, from that used to move columns of
A. This requires a separate set of MPI_Win_fence calls.

An alternative is to put all of the ghost cells into contiguous memory locations,
even the ones that were moved into columns of A. That is, rather than put the ghost
cells in A, we put them into a different array, aghost. This array has 2*nx+2*ny
elements. We can create the window with the following code:

```
integer winbuf, ierr
```

```
subroutine exchng2( a, sx, ex, sy, ey, win, &
    left_nbr, right_nbr, top_nbr, bot_nbr, &
    right_ghost_disp, left_ghost_disp, &
    top_ghost_disp, coltype, right_coltype, left_coltype )
use mpi
integer sx, ex, sy, ey, win, ierr
integer left_nbr, right_nbr, top_nbr, bot_nbr
integer coltype, right_coltype, left_coltype
double precision a(sx-1:ex+1,sy-1:ey+1)
integer (kind=MPI_ADDRESS_KIND) right_ghost_disp, &
        left_ghost_disp, top_ghost_disp, bot_ghost_disp
integer nx

nx = ex - sx + 1

call MPI_WIN_FENCE( 0, win, ierr )
! Put bottom edge into bottom neighbor's top ghost cells
call MPI_PUT( a(sx,sy), nx, MPI_DOUBLE_PRECISION, bot_nbr, &
              top_ghost_disp, nx, MPI_DOUBLE_PRECISION, &
              win, ierr )
! Put top edge into top neighbor's bottom ghost cells
bot_ghost_disp = 1
call MPI_PUT( a(sx,ey), nx, MPI_DOUBLE_PRECISION, top_nbr, &
              bot_ghost_disp, nx, MPI_DOUBLE_PRECISION, &
              win, ierr )
! Put right edge into right neighbor's left ghost cells
call MPI_PUT( a(ex,sy), 1, coltype, &
              right_nbr, left_ghost_disp, 1, right_coltype, &
              win, ierr )
! Put left edge into the left neighbor's right ghost cells
call MPI_PUT( a(sx,sy), 1, coltype, &
              left_nbr, right_ghost_disp, 1, left_coltype, &
              win, ierr )
call MPI_WIN_FENCE( 0, win, ierr )
return
end
```

Figure 5.16
Code to exchange ghost values for a two-dimensional decomposition of the mesh

```
! Create a special window for the ghost cells
call MPI_WIN_CREATE( abuf, ..., winbuf, ierr )
...
ny = ey - sy + 1
do i=1,ny
    buf(i) = a(1,i-sy+1)
enddo
call MPI_WIN_FENCE( 0, winbuf, ierr )
call MPI_PUT( buf, ny, MPI_DOUBLE_PRECISION, top_nbr, &
              0, ny, MPI_DOUBLE_PRECISION, winbuf, ierr )
... similar code for the bottom edge
call MPI_WIN_FENCE( 0, winbuf, ierr )
... code to unpack the data in the local memory to the ghost
... cells
```

Figure 5.17
Code to move ghost cell data without using derived datatypes but using a second window object

```
double precision aghost(MAX_GHOST)

nx = ex - sx + 1
ny = ey - sy + 1
! MAX GHOST must be at least 2*nx + 2*ny
call MPI_TYPE_SIZE( MPI_DOUBLE_PRECISION, sizedouble, ierr )
call MPI_WIN_CREATE( aghost, (2*nx+2*ny)*sizedouble, &
                     sizedouble, MPI_INFO_NULL, &
                     MPI_COMM_WORLD, winbuf, ierr )
```

Figure 5.18 shows the corresponding code to collect data into buffer arrays and then move it with `MPI_Put`. Note that two separate local buffer arrays, `buf1` and `buf2`, are used. Recall that RMA data movement operations (`MPI_Put` here) are all nonblocking in the MPI sense. That is, the data buffer must not be modified until the operation completes. Thus, just as separate buffers are needed for `MPI_Isend`, they are needed for the `MPI_Put` calls here.

For unstructured grid problems, a slight variation of the separate ghost array is to put all of the "ghost" points at the end of the local array.

5.6.2 Combining Communication and Computation

In many applications, a common step is to receive data and then combine that data with other local data with a simple operation, such as addition. We saw a simple

```
call MPI_WIN_FENCE( 0, winbuf, ierr )
! Put bottom edge into bottom neighbor's ghost cells
nx = ex - sx + 1
call MPI_PUT( a(sx,sy), nx, MPI_DOUBLE_PRECISION, &
              bottom_nbr, 0, nx, MPI_DOUBLE_PRECISION, winbuf, ierr )
! Put top edge into top neighbor's ghost cells
call MPI_PUT( a(sx,ey), nx, MPI_DOUBLE_PRECISION, &
              top_nbr, nx, nx, MPI_DOUBLE_PRECISION, winbuf, ierr  )
! Put left edge into left neighbor's ghost cells
ny = ey - sy + 1
do i=sy,ey
    buf1(i-sy+1) = a(sx,i)
enddo
call MPI_PUT( buf1, ny, MPI_DOUBLE_PRECISION, &
              left_nbr, 2*nx, ny, MPI_DOUBLE_PRECISION, &
              winbuf, ierr )
! Put right edge into right neighbor's ghost cells
do i=sy,ey
    buf2(i-sy+1) = a(ex,i)
enddo
call MPI_PUT( buf2, ny, MPI_DOUBLE_PRECISION, &
              right_nbr, 2*nx+ny, ny, MPI_DOUBLE_PRECISION, &
              winbuf, ierr )
call MPI_WIN_FENCE( 0, winbuf, ierr )
... use data in aghost ...
```

Figure 5.18
Code to exchange ghost cell information in a 2-d decomposition without using derived datatypes

example of this in Section 2.3.2, where π was computed using RMA routines. In this section, we consider a slightly more elaborate example: forming a matrix-vector product with the matrix and the vector distributed across two processes.

We can write this as follows, with the lines indicating the division of data among the two processes.

$$\left(\frac{w_0}{w_1}\right) = \left(\begin{array}{c|c} A_{00} & A_{01} \\ A_{10} & A_{11} \end{array}\right)\left(\frac{v_0}{v_1}\right)$$

We can expand this to show the four separate matrix-vector multiplications:

$$w_0 = A_{00}v_0 + A_{01}v_1$$
$$w_1 = A_{10}v_0 + A_{11}v_1$$

Assume that process 0 has w_0, v_0, and the first block column of A: A_{00} and A_{10} and that process 1 has w_1, v_1, and the second block column of A: A_{01} and A_{11}. Process 0 can thus compute $t_0^0 = A_{00}v_0$ and $t_1^0 = A_{10}v_0$; process 1 can compute $t_0^1 = A_{01}v_1$ and $t_1^1 = A_{11}v_1$. The temporary t_i^j stands for the result on the jth process of multiplying the ith block of the matrix times the ith block of the vector. The computation of w is then

$$w_0 = t_0^0 + t_0^1$$
$$w_1 = t_1^0 + t_1^1$$

where the superscript on t indicates which process computed the value.

If this was implemented with message passing, the natural approach would look something like the following for process 0, and where there are only two processes.

```
double t[2][VEC_SIZE], buf[VEC_SIZE], w[VEC_SIZE];
... each process computes  t_i^rank for i = 0, 1.
if (rank == 0) {
    // Send  t_1^0 = t[1] to process 1
    req[0] = MPI::COMM_WORLD.Isend(t[1], n, MPI::DOUBLE, 1, 0);
    // Receive  t_0^1 from process 1 into buf
    req[1] = MPI::COMM_WORLD.Irecv(buf, n, MPI::DOUBLE, 1, 0);
    // We can also use req[0].Waitall() or
    // even  MPI::REQUEST_NULL.Waitall().
    MPI::Request::Waitall( 2, req );
    for (i=0; i<n; i++) w[i] = t[0][i] + buf[i];
}
```

We have seen how to replace the message-passing part of this code with RMA operations. However, this involves moving the data in t[] twice: once from process 1 to process 0, ending up in the temporary vector buf, and then once more as it is loaded and added to t[0] in the for-loop. This can be inefficient. Each time data is moved, the opportunity is lost to do some computing. It would be better to move the data in t and immediately add it to s to form w.

MPI-2 provides a way to accomplish a move and combine as a single operation. The routine MPI_Accumulate allows data to be moved and combined, at the destination, using any of the predefined MPI reduction operations, such as MPI_SUM. The arguments to MPI_Accumulate have the same form as for MPI_Put, with the addition of an MPI_Op op argument. The bindings for MPI_Accumulate are shown in Tables 5.14, 5.15, and 5.16.

int **MPI_Accumulate**(void *origin_addr, int origin_count,
                    MPI_Datatype origin_datatype, int target_rank,
                    MPI_Aint target_disp, int target_count,
                    MPI_Datatype target_datatype,MPI_Op op, MPI_Win win)

Table 5.14
C bindings for RMA accumulate routine

MPI_ACCUMULATE(origin_addr, origin_count,origin_datatype, target_rank,
                    target_disp, target_count,target_datatype, op, win, ierror)
                    <type> origin_addr(*)
                    integer(kind=MPI_ADDRESS_KIND) target_disp
                    integer origin_count, origin_datatype, target_rank, target_count,
                    target_datatype, op, win, ierror

Table 5.15
Fortran bindings for RMA accumulate routine

void MPI::Win::Accumulate(const void* origin_addr, int origin_count,
                    const MPI::Datatype& origin_datatype, int target_rank,
                    Aint target_disp,int target_count,
                    const Datatype& target_datatype, const Op& op) const

Table 5.16
C++ bindings for RMA accumulate routine

Using `MPI_Accumulate`, we can replace the message passing *and* remove the for-loop, as shown in the following code (again, this is for process 0):

```
MPI::Win win;
// Create a window with w
win = MPI::Win_create( w, n*sizeof(double), sizeof(double),
                    MPI::INFO_NULL, MPI::COMM_WORLD );
if (rank == 0) {
    // compute  t^0_0 in w and  t^0_1  in buf
    ...
    // Add this value to w on the remote process
    win.Fence( 0 );
    win.Accumulate( buf, n, MPI::DOUBLE, 1, 0, n, MPI::DOUBLE,
                    MPI::SUM );
```

```
        win.Fence( 0 );
    }
```

`MPI_Accumulate` is not quite as general as the MPI-1 collective computation routines (`MPI_Reduce`, `MPI_Allreduce`, `MPI_Reduce_scatter`, and `MPI_Scan`) because only the predefined reduction operations, such as `MPI_SUM` and `MPI_LAND`, are allowed. User-defined operations may not be used with `MPI_Accumulate`. This restriction was made by the MPI Forum to allow and encourage more efficient implementations of `MPI_Accumulate`. In addition, there are restrictions on the datatype arguments. It is always correct to use the basic MPI datatypes.

Concurrent updates using accumulate. Now consider the case where there are more than two processes. If there are p processes, then the result w_i on the ith process is computed from the local contribution $A_{ii}v_i$ and $p-1$ contributions from the other $p-1$ processes. With message passing[6] (e.g., `MPI_Isend` and `MPI_Irecv`), or the RMA routines `MPI_Put`, and `MPI_Get`, one buffer is needed to receive data from each process that is contributing data. With `MPI_Accumulate`, each process can contribute directly to the result vector `w`, as shown below:

```
double t[MAX_RANK][MAX_VEC];
MPI::Win win;
// Create a window with w
win = MPI::Win_create( w, n*sizeof(double), sizeof(double),
                       MPI::INFO_NULL, MPI::COMM_WORLD );
// compute t_i^rank in t[i] and t_rank^rank in w
...
// Add this value to w on the remote process
win.Fence( 0 );
for (i=0; i<p; i++) {
    if (i != myrank)
        win.Accumulate( t[i], n, MPI::DOUBLE, i,
                        0, n, MPI::DOUBLE, MPI::SUM );
}
win.Fence( 0 );
```

A special operation allowed for `MPI_Accumulate` is `MPI_REPLACE`. The effect of this operation is to replace the value at the target with the value provided on the origin process. We do not need this operation for this example, but it can come

---

[6]See Section 7.3.2 in *Using MPI* [32] for how this can be implemented with `MPI_Reduce_scatter`.

in handy. In addition, it emphasizes that the `MPI_Accumulate` function is the only one of the three RMA operations that may be used to update the same locations in a memory window with multiple calls without separating the calls with an `MPI_-Win_fence` (or other window synchronization routine). The next section helps us understand the reason for this, as well as the rules for when a memory location may be accessed with RMA operations and when with local loads and stores.

5.7   Pitfalls in Accessing Memory

In order to understand the rules for access to data in memory windows, that is, when can one use an RMA operation and when a local load or store, it is necessary to consider in more detail what might happen when data in memory is referenced. The issues here are quite subtle; it is important to remember that the MPI Standard is designed to be implementable on a wide range of hardware platforms, even those that do not have any hardware support for shared- or remote memory operations. Understanding the reasons for the rules in this section often requires thinking of things that can go wrong, as in the examples in Section 4.3.

5.7.1   Atomicity of Memory Operations

When can a program access a variable with local load or store? That is, when can the operations for using a value in a variable (load) or assigning a value in a variable (store) be used without interfering with RMA operations? Consider the code in Figure 5.19. What is the value of `b[2]` at the end of the code?

A number of possibilities arise. The most obvious is that `b[2]` is either the value `1/3` or `12.0`. But that assumes that either `b[2] = 1./3.` or that the `MPI_Put` for `b[2]` succeeds completely, that is, that either one of the operations to store a value into `b[2]` succeeds, and the other does not. Unfortunately, that may not be what happens within the computer (this also applies to shared-memory programming, by the way). For example, assume that the hardware moves only four bytes at a time and that a `double` is eight bytes long. Then putting a value into `b[2]` will require two separate operations by the computer hardware. In the code in Figure 5.19, there are four possibilities for the result, not two, depending on the order in which each of the two parts of `b[2]` are stored. These four possibilities are shown in Figure 5.20.

This example may seem a little contrived, since many computers will guarantee to store even an eight-byte `double` or `DOUBLE PRECISION` in a single operation. But

```
    /* This code is erroneous */
double b[10];

for (i=0; i<10; i++) b[i] = rank * 10.0 + i;

MPI_Win_create( b, 10*sizeof(double), sizeof(double),
                MPI_INFO_NULL, MPI_COMM_WORLD, &win );
MPI_Win_fence( 0, win );
if (rank == 0) {
  b[2] = 1./3.;
}
else if (rank == 1) {
  /* Store my value of b into process 0's window, which is
     process 0's array b */
  MPI_Put( b, 10, MPI_DOUBLE, 0, 0, 10, MPI_DOUBLE, win );
}
MPI_Win_fence( 0, win );
```

Figure 5.19
Example of conflicting put and store operations. This code is erroneous.

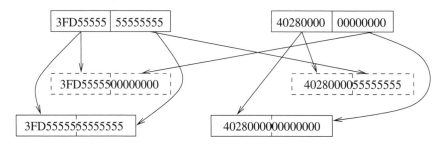

Figure 5.20
The four possible results for b[2] in Figure 5.19. The dashed boxes show possible, but incorrect, results. The box on the top left contains 1/3 (as a floating-point value) and is the value stored by process 0 in the example in Figure 5.19. The box on the top right contains 12 (also in floating point) and is the value MPI_Put by process 1.

even for double-precision complex values, two operations may be required. And for a structure, of course, a number of operations will be required.

This illustrates an important point: Operations in a programming language that appear to be a single operation, such as a store to a variable, an increment (e.g., i++ in C), or an array operation (e.g., A = 0 for an array A in Fortran, may not be a single operation in the hardware. Operations that are performed as a single operation, without any possibility of another operation modifying the result of the operation, are called *atomic*, because they are the smallest, indivisible operations.

5.7.2   Memory Coherency

Some computer systems do not even provide memory systems that are fully coherent. For example, data in cache (representing a copy of data in memory) that is updated may not cause data in memory or in another cache (representing the same memory address) to be updated before some other process references the same memory locations. Such systems are said to *not* have coherent memory caches. Most computers today do provide coherent caches, but there are performance implications, and some special high-performance systems may trade memory coherency for greater performance. The MPI RMA is designed to work with both memory coherent and incoherent systems; this promotes maximum portability but does introduce some restrictions to allow relatively efficient implementation even when there is no hardware support for coherent memory.

5.7.3   Some Simple Rules for RMA

We have seen that maintaining the consistency of memory when two different agents may modify a word can be difficult. On some systems, sophisticated hardware is used to ensure that updates are atomic and memory is coherent and to give the expected results. However, MPI is designed so that RMA can be used even when such hardware support is not available. In order to accomplish this, certain rules must be followed when using the RMA operations. A complete description is given in the MPI-2 Standard, Section 6.7, and in [27], Section 4.7. In this section, we provide rules that are sufficient for writing correct code, but may be slightly stricter than required.

Also, as is clear from above, reading from memory with either local loads or MPI_Get is less restrictive that writing to memory with either local stores or MPI_-Put and MPI_Accumulate. For that reason, we divide the cases to consider into whether the memory window merely is accessed (that is, MPI_Get and load) or is modified (that is, MPI_Put, MPI_Accumulate, or store).

Overlapping put and accumulate operations. The targets of two `MPI_Put` operations in the same destination window must not overlap. This rule prevents problems such as the one illustrated in Figure 5.19 (but involving two put operations rather than a put and a local store).

Note that `MPI_Accumulate` allows (and even encourages) overlapping operations. There are a few restrictions here as well. When the targets overlap, both the basic MPI datatype (for example, `MPI_INT`) and the operation (for example, `MPI_SUM`) must be the same.

It is possible to make remote memory stores to overlapping locations by using the operation `MPI_REPLACE` in `MPI_Accumulate`. Note, however, that if two `MPI_Accumulate` operations are accessing the same locations in the target window, MPI does not specify in which order they make their replacements. For example, if two processes are making calls like this

```
MPI_Accumulate( a, 2, MPI_DOUBLE, ..., MPI_REPLACE );
```

then at the target, the location at displacement 0 may get the value from one process and the location at displacement 1 may get its value from the other process. MPI guarantees only that the updates don't break a basic datatype.[7] Put and accumulate operations between two `MPI_Win_fence` calls must not overlap under any circumstances.

Local stores and RMA updates. Stores into the local window and `MPI_Put` or `MPI_Accumulate` operations into that window must be separated by an `MPI_Win_fence` call.

Local loads and RMA get. Local loads and `MPI_Get` operations may access any part of the window that has not been updated by an RMA update (`MPI_Put` or `MPI_Accumulate`) or local store operation.

The easy rule. The simplest rule is as follows:

1. Do not overlap accesses on windows (except for `MPI_Accumulate`).

2. Separate non-RMA access from RMA access with `MPI_Win_fence`.

This is stricter than required by MPI, but it is often easy to accomplish.

So far, we have referred only to `MPI_Win_fence` as the routine to use in separating RMA updates, accesses, local loads, and local stores. In the next chapter, we will

---

[7]The MPI Standard refers to "locations" and says that the results may vary only as much as computer arithmetics are not commutative or associative. This suggests the interpretation that we have used here, but the actual text is unclear.

introduce some additional MPI routines that may be used to separate the accesses. In those cases, these same rules apply.

5.7.4   Overlapping Windows

It is possible to have several MPI window objects whose local windows overlap. The rules in MPI for using these windows are very restrictive; see item 3, page 132, in [27], Section 4.7 (Semantics and Correctness). The restrictions were made by the MPI Forum to allow for relatively efficient implementations on systems without hardware support for shared-memory coherency. Because of the performance issues and the complexities of the rules for correct use, we recommend avoiding the use of overlapping windows.[8]

5.7.5   Compiler Optimizations

As we saw in Section 4.3, when one process modifies data in another process, there is a risk that, because the compiler has placed the variable into a register, the modified result won't be seen by the target process. The simplest fix for this in C and C++ (and in many Fortran implementations) is to declare the variable that is given to `MPI_Win_create` as the local memory window as `volatile`.[9] For example, in the grid example, we might use

```
integer sizedouble, ierr, win
double precision, volatile :: a(0:nx+1,s-1:e+1)

call MPI_TYPE_SIZE( MPI_DOUBLE_PRECISION, sizedouble, ierr )
call MPI_WIN_CREATE( a, (nx+2)*(e-s+3)*sizedouble, sizedouble, &
                     MPI_INFO_NULL, MPI_COMM_WORLD, win, ierr )
```

In addition, if the array `A` is then passed to other routines, it may be necessary to declare it as `volatile` in those routines as well.

The approach of using `volatile` has its drawbacks, however. Most important, it forces the compiler to reload any element of the variable from memory rather than using a previously loaded value that is already in a register. This can cause a significant loss in performance. Fortunately, there is a work-around. The key is that the MPI RMA operations (that are completed by `MPI_Win_fence`) can update the local window any time between the two `MPI_Win_fence` calls that separate them

---

[8]These rules are the reason that there is no `MPI_Win_dup`, since a duplicated window object would involve overlapping memory windows.

[9]We will see shortly that for C/C++ and `MPI_Win_fence` synchronization, `volatile` is not necessary.

from other operations. Thus, a correct MPI program cannot rely on the updates happening before the `MPI_Win_fence` that completes the RMA operations. For C and C++ this is enough: since the local window is an argument to the `MPI_Win_-create` routine that returned the window object, and the window object is an input to `MPI_Win_fence`, the C or C++ compiler must take into account the possibility that `MPI_Win_fence` will access the local window through a pointer stored in the window object. Thus, we do not need `volatile` in C or C++ when using `MPI_Win_-fence` synchronization. Note that we are *not* saying that `MPI_Win_fence` actually performs the updates, only that it *could* do so. The C/C++ compilers must assume the same, and therefore reload the value of any part of the local memory window that is in the register after the call to `MPI_Win_fence`.

The situation is different in Fortran. Fortran pointers are much more restrictive (to allow the compiler more flexibility in generating code), and in this case the Fortran compiler will not conclude that `MPI_Win_fence` might update the variable provided to `MPI_Win_create` as the local memory window. There is a simple fix that the programmer can use. Consider the routine

```
subroutine MPE_WIN_FENCE( base, assert, win, ierr )
use mpi
double precision base(*)
integer assert, win, ierr
call MPI_WIN_FENCE( assert, win, ierr )
end
```

If we call this routine from our Fortran program instead of just `MPI_Win_fence`, passing it the same array (as `base`) that we used with `MPI_Win_create`, then the Fortran compiler will assume that we might have changed the variable `base` (the local window), particularly if we define `MPE_Win_fence` with the following interface definition:

```
INTERFACE MPE_WIN_FENCE
    subroutine MPE_WIN_FENCE( base, assert, win, ierr )
    double precision, intent(inout) :: base(*)
    integer, intent(in) :: assert, win
    integer, intent(out) :: ierr
    end subroutine MPE_WIN_FENCE
END INTERFACE
```

5.8   Performance Tuning for RMA Operations

MPI-2 provides a number of ways to aid an MPI implementation in performing
RMA operations efficiently. This section discusses how to specify special cases to
`MPI_Win_create` and `MPI_Win_fence` to allow the MPI implementation to optimize
the RMA operations.

5.8.1   Options for `MPI_Win_create`

The `MPI_Win_create` call has an info argument that can be used to provide hints to
the MPI implementation. There is one predefined hint: the info key `no_locks`, if set
to true, states that this local window is never used with locks (see Section 6.2 for a
discussion of locks). None of the examples in this chapter use locks. This hint may
be used with any RMA code that uses only `MPI_Win_fence` for synchronization.

The following example shows how to use `no_locks` with the info argument to
`MPI_Win_create`.

```
MPI_Info info;
MPI_Info_create( &info );
MPI_Info_set( info, "no_locks", "true" );
MPI_Win_create( ..., info, ... );
MPI_Info_free( &info );
```

MPI implementations may ignore the `no_locks` key; however, it never hurts to
provide this info value when creating a window object when locks are not used.

The MPI-2 Standard, in an "advice to users," mentions that `MPI_Win_free` internally requires a barrier to ensure that all operations, from any source, have
completed. This applies in general, but not if every process involved in creating a
window sets `no_locks` to `true`. Thus, while `MPI_Win_free` is collective over all of
the processes in the group that formed the window object, it need not be a barrier.

Choice of local window.   The memory in a computer is organized into a hierarchy of elements, each with its own size. At the very top of the hierarchy are
registers that hold a single word (often 32 or 64 bits) of data. The next level of
hierarchy is usually one or more levels of cache. Each level of cache is made up
of *cache lines*. Each cache line is 4 to 128 (or more) bytes in length. Below the
cache memory are *memory pages*, which are typically 4K to 16K bytes (but may
be larger) in size. Data motion in a computer usually happens in units of these
natural sizes. For example, data is moved between memory and cache in units of
the cache line size.

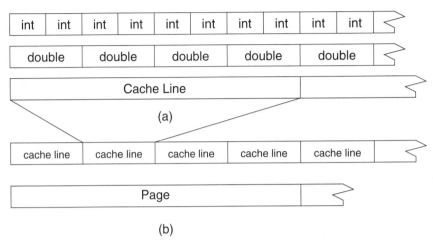

Figure 5.21
Alignments of data items. Part (a) shows how a basic datatypes such as `int` and `double` fit into
a cache line. Part (b) shows how cache lines fit into a memory page.

In addition, each larger item is *aligned* to begin at the start of the next smallest
item. That is, a page always starts at the beginning of a cache line, and a cache
line always starts at the beginning of a memory word. Another way to say this
is that a smaller item never crosses a boundary between two larger items. This is
shown in Figure 5.21. Note that the sizes and alignments are all nested.

Some MPI implementations will be more efficient if the base address is aligned on
one of these boundaries; aligning on a page boundary will guarantee that the base
address is also aligned on word and cache boundaries. It may also help if the size
of the local window is an exact multiple of the page size. This applies particularly
to systems without hardware support for shared memory.

On some Unix systems, C users may use `memalign` instead of `malloc` to get good
data alignments for dynamically allocated data. The page size can be determined
with the Unix function `getpagesize`.[10] One Unix system provides the function
`valloc`, which returns memory aligned with the system page size.

Another option is to allocate the memory used for the local memory window
with `MPI_Alloc_mem` and `MPI_Free_mem`. Because these routines are required for
memory used with RMA lock and unlock routines, we discuss both the `MPI_Alloc_-
mem` and `MPI_Free_mem` routines with lock and unlock in the next chapter.

---

[10]`getpagesize` returns the system page size, which may be different from the page size used by
the hardware. However, the system page size is likely to be a good size to use because the system
will want to size and align pages for efficient operation.

5.8.2 Options for MPI_Win_fence

MPI_Win_fence provides a very general collective RMA synchronization, which makes it relatively simple to use. In the general case, each call to MPI_Win_fence will complete any RMA operations that were started since the last call to MPI_-Win_fence. In addition, MPI_Win_fence must ensure that any local load and store operations are also complete before any RMA operations that follow the MPI_-Win_fence call access the memory window. Ensuring that everything is in order is potentially expensive; for example, it may require flushing caches or making a copy of the memory window. To allow an implementation to optimize for cases where such operations are unnecessary because of the structure of the user's code, the MPI_Win_fence call has an argument, assert, that allows the user to provide information to MPI about how much work MPI_Win_fence may need to perform. The assert argument can contain any combination of the following four values; they can be combined using bitwise or (|) in C and C++ and integer addition in Fortran.

MPI_MODE_NOSTORE. The local window was not updated by local stores (or local get or receive calls) since the last call to MPI_Win_fence. This refers to operations that occurred *before* the fence call.

MPI_MODE_NOSTORE may be used, for example, for the ghost cells in a mesh computation, where the local window that contains the ghost cells is read only with local loads. This works only if the ghost cells are all that is exposed, or if the entire array is used as read only and writes are done to another array.

Consider the case where the data is read from the array b, the corresponding window is called win_b, and the data is computed in the array a; a is not in a memory window (or not in an overlapping memory window, as discussed in Section 5.7.4). Since there are no stores to b between the two calls to MPI_Win_fence, the MPI_-MODE_NOSTORE assertion may be used on the second call to MPI_Win_fence. This is shown below:

```
MPI_Win_create( b, n*sizeof(double), sizeof(double),
                MPI_INFO_NULL, MPI_COMM_WORLD, &win_b );
...
MPI_Win_fence( 0, win_b );
MPI_Put( buf, m, MPI_DOUBLE, nbr, 0, m, MPI_DOUBLE, win_b );
...   update array a using information in array b
...   EXCEPT for any ghost cells
```

```
MPI_Win_fence( MPI_MODE_NOSTORE, win_b );
...   update the parts of a that depend on the ghost cells
...   in b
```

MPI_MODE_NOPUT. The local window will not be updated by put or accumulate calls between this fence call and the next fence call.

This basically says that no changes will be made by remote processes to the local window before the *next* fence call. The local process can modify the data in the local memory window using stores. Another name for this mode could have been "no RMA update."

This flag can help implementations that do not have hardware support for memory coherency, by informing them that the memory window will not be changed by any RMA operations (this includes hardware where a cache-flush might otherwise be required to maintain correct operations).

MPI_MODE_NOPRECEDE. The fence will not complete any sequence of RMA calls made by the process calling `MPI_Win_fence`. If this assertion is given by any process in the window group, then it must be given by all processes in the group. Thus, no RMA calls can be made by *any* process in the group of the window, on this window object, since the last `MPI_Win_fence` call. This refers to the operations that occurred *before* the fence call. It used to state that no process in the window object's group made any RMA calls on this window. In other words, there isn't anything to complete. Another name for this mode could have been "no RMA completion."

MPI_MODE_NOSUCCEED. No RMA calls will be made on this window between this fence call and the next fence call. If the assertion is given by any process in the window group, then it must be given by all processes in the group. This is used to indicate that following this fence, no RMA calls will be made by any process in this window object's group before the next fence call. Another name for this mode could have been "no RMA start."

The C++ names of these modes have the form `MPI::MODE_NOSTORE` and so on.

These assert flags may be combined where it makes sense. As an example, the code in Figure 5.10 can be augmented with all four of the assertion values:

```
call MPI_WIN_FENCE( MPI_MODE_NOPRECEDE, win, ierr )
! Put bottom edge into bottom neighbor's top ghost cells
top_ghost_disp = 1 + (nx+2)*(e-s+2)
```

```
call MPI_PUT( a(1,s), nx, MPI_DOUBLE_PRECISION, &
              bottom_nbr, top_ghost_disp, nx, &
              MPI_DOUBLE_PRECISION, win, ierr )
! Put top edge into top neighbor's bottom ghost cells
bottom_ghost_disp = 1
call MPI_PUT( a(1,e), nx, MPI_DOUBLE_PRECISION, &
              top_nbr, bottom_ghost_disp, nx, &
              MPI_DOUBLE_PRECISION, win, ierr )
call MPI_WIN_FENCE( MPI_MODE_NOSTORE + MPI_MODE_NOPUT + &
                    MPI_MODE_NOSUCCEED, win, ierr )
```

The first `MPI_Win_fence` call does not complete any RMA operations, and so `MPI_MODE_NOPRECEDE` may be used. Note that the window may have been updated by local stores; in fact, it almost certainly was, so `MPI_MODE_NOSTORE` must not be used in the first fence call.

The second fence call completes only RMA operations. Thus, `MPI_MODE_NOSTORE` can be used. Since no RMA calls follow the fence, we can use `MPI_MODE_NOSUCCEED`. `MPI_MODE_NOPUT` is redundant here because `MPI_MODE_NOSUCCEED` states that there are no RMA calls of any kind between this fence call and the next one. `MPI_MODE_-NOPUT` could be used where `MPI_Get` operations were being made between two fence calls but no `MPI_Put` or `MPI_Accumulate` operations.

Almost every use of `MPI_Win_fence` can specify some assert values. It is good practice to specify assert values because it allows the MPI implementation to optimize the performance of `MPI_Win_fence` and because it forces the programmer to examine closely how the MPI RMA operations are being used. Such examination will help detect any erroneous use of RMA that violates the rules set forth in Section 5.7.

6 Advanced Remote Memory Access

This chapter introduces two new mechanisms for synchronizing and completing remote memory access (RMA) operations. The first mechanism is called *locks*; locks allow one process to access a window in another process without the target process making any RMA calls, providing for truly one-sided operations. The second mechanism is a scalable, noncollective alternative to `MPI_Win_fence`.

6.1 Introduction

In the preceding chapter, we introduced MPI's remote memory access operations. One requirement of the RMA routines in that chapter was the need for all processes that created a window object to call `MPI_Win_fence` to separate RMA operations from local loads and stores and to complete RMA operations. In other words, while the individual `MPI_Put`, `MPI_Get`, and `MPI_Accumulate` operations are one sided and are called by a single process (instead of the two processes required to use send-receive-style message passing), we required a collective operation (`MPI_Win_fence`) to complete the RMA operations. In this chapter, we will relax this requirement in two different ways.

6.2 Lock and Unlock

In Chapter 5, both the origin and target processes of an RMA operation must call the `MPI_Win_fence` to complete the RMA call (along with all of the processes that are in the window object's group). This is called *active target* synchronization, because the target is actively involved in the process. In many cases, however, a process may want to access data in a remote (target) process without that process being required to call any MPI routines. This is called *passive target* synchronization. In MPI, passive target synchronization is accomplished by using `MPI_Win_lock` and `MPI_Win_unlock` at the origin process.

To perform a passive target RMA operation, you use `MPI_Put`, `MPI_Get`, and/or `MPI_Accumulate`, just as when using active target synchronization. However, instead of surrounding the RMA calls with calls to `MPI_Win_fence`, you begin the sequence of RMA calls with `MPI_Win_lock` and end the sequence of RMA calls with `MPI_Win_unlock`. The lock and unlock operations apply only to a specific remote window (specified by a rank), not the entire window object (that is, not all ranks); the specific window is indicated by a `rank` in the group of the window object. These two calls define an *access epoch*: between `MPI_Win_lock` and `MPI_Win_unlock`, a

```
int MPI_Win_lock(int lock_type, int rank, int assert, MPI_Win win)

int MPI_Win_unlock(int rank, MPI_Win win)
```

Table 6.1
C binding for locks

```
MPI_WIN_LOCK(lock_type, rank, assert, win, ierror)
              integer lock_type, rank, assert, win, ierror

MPI_WIN_UNLOCK(rank, win, ierror)
              integer rank, win, ierror
```

Table 6.2
Fortran binding for locks

```
void MPI::Win::Lock(int lock_type, int rank, int  assert) const

void MPI::Win::Unlock(int rank) const
```

Table 6.3
C++ binding for locks

process may access the memory window of a remote process. The bindings for
`MPI_Win_lock` and `MPI_Win_unlock` are shown in Tables 6.1, 6.2, and 6.3.

The name `lock` is an unfortunate one, as these MPI operations do not behave the
way shared-memory locks do. Instead, they are really "begin passive target access"
and "end passive target access." Specifically, when referring to a remote window, all
that the `MPI_Win_lock` and `MPI_Win_unlock` pair says is that the RMA operations
between them will be complete when `MPI_Win_unlock` returns, and, depending
on the lock type (see below), they may occur atomically with respect to other
accesses to the same remote memory window. We will discuss this in more detail in
Section 6.5. Only when referring to the local window (that is, when the `rank` in the
lock call is the rank of the calling process in the window object's group) do these
routines behave like conventional locks. That is because, when using passive target
synchronization, you must use `MPI_Win_lock` and `MPI_Win_unlock` around accesses
to your own local window to ensure that RMA operations from other processes do
not modify the data unexpectedly.

```
int MPE_Blocking_put( void *buf, int count, MPI_Datatype dtype,
                      int target_rank, MPI_Aint target_offset,
                      int target_count, MPI_Datatype target_dtype,
                      MPI_Win win )
{
    int err;

    MPI_Win_lock( MPI_LOCK_SHARED, target_rank, 0, win );
    err = MPI_Put( buf, count, dtype, target_rank, target_offset,
                   target_count, target_dtype, win );
    MPI_Win_unlock( target_rank, win );
    return err;
}
```

Figure 6.1
Blocking, independent (passive target) put operation

6.2.1   Implementing Blocking, Independent RMA Operations

The most elementary use of lock and unlock is to create a blocking version of the
RMA data-movement commands that do not require the target to make any MPI
calls. To do this, we simply surround the RMA call with lock and unlock. Figure 6.1
shows an implementation of a blocking put operation.

The use of `MPI_LOCK_SHARED` allows several RMA operations to act on the same
window (not just window object) at the same time. If it is necessary to ensure
that only one RMA operation at a time can act on the target window, `MPI_LOCK_-`
`EXCLUSIVE` must be used. This guarantees that no other RMA operation has any
access, either put, get, or accumulate, to the window at the target process.

Put another way, `MPI_LOCK_SHARED` is used when the purpose of the lock is simply
to allow one or more RMA operation to complete, independently of any action by
the target or other process. When it is essential to guarantee atomic (undivided)
access to a window on a particular process, `MPI_LOCK_EXCLUSIVE` must be used.
We will see in Section 6.5 an example where `MPI_LOCK_EXCLUSIVE` is required.

Note that when `MPI_LOCK_SHARED` is used, the user must ensure that no concurrent operations modify the same or overlapping parts of the window, with the
exception of multiple `MPI_Accumulate` calls that all use the same type signatures
and same operation (these are the same restrictions on `MPI_Accumulate` as in the
previous chapter). `MPI_LOCK_SHARED` should be used primarily with `MPI_Get` when
there is no chance that a `MPI_Put` or `MPI_Accumulate` operation will be changing

the contents of the window.

Locks in MPI protect only the window at a specific rank within a window object. This feature improves scalability: a distributed data structure is thus protected by separate locks on each process.

6.3 Allocating Memory for MPI Windows

In Chapter 5, any variable or memory location could be used as the local window for RMA operations. Passive target operations, however, can be more difficult to implement. Realizing this, the MPI Standard allows implementations to restrict the use of passive target RMA (that is, using `MPI_Win_lock` and `MPI_Win_unlock`) to memory windows that have been allocated with `MPI_Alloc_mem`. This routine allocates `size` bytes of memory and returns a pointer to the allocated memory in `baseptr`.

6.3.1 Using MPI_Alloc_mem from C/C++

The C version of `MPI_Alloc_mem` uses the type `void *` for the returned type, even though the actual parameter that must be passed is the address of a pointer. This choice of binding makes it easier to pass the address of a pointer to a particular datatype. For example, the following code allocates 10 doubles:

```
double *d_ptr;
MPI_Alloc_mem( 10 * sizeof(double), MPI_INFO_NULL, &d_ptr );
```

If the last formal argument was typed as `void **`, the third actual argument would need to be cast to that type:

```
MPI_Alloc_mem( 10, MPI_INFO_NULL, (void **)&d_ptr )
```

The MPI Forum felt that the convenience of avoiding the extra cast outweighed the potential confusion in the binding, since returning a pointer to an `int`, for example, requires an argument of type `int **`. The same approach is used by `MPI_Buffer_-detach`, which also returns a pointer, and in the copy callback function used in attribute caching (see Section 9.4).

The `info` argument is provided to allow the user to specify, for example, different locations or properties for the allocated memory. For example, on a distributed-shared-memory machine such as an SGI Origin2000, specifying the node that should contain the shared memory might offer performance advantages. The null value, `MPI_INFO_NULL`, is always valid and will be the only value that we will use in our examples. There are no predefined info keys for use with `MPI_Alloc_mem`; implementations define the keys that they support.

To free memory allocated with `MPI_Alloc_mem`, one must use the routine `MPI_-Free_mem`. The bindings for the memory allocation routines are shown in Tables 6.4, 6.5, and 6.6.

6.3.2 Using `MPI_Alloc_mem` from Fortran

Fortran doesn't have pointers of the same kind that C and C++ do. However, some Fortran implementations provide an extension, often referred to as "Cray pointers" or "integer pointers," that may be used. A "Cray pointer" is very much like a C pointer rather than a Fortran 90 pointer. In the declaration, a "Cray pointer" is named, and the Fortran variable that the pointer will point at is also named. The space for this second variable is not allocated. In the following example, the pointer is p and the variable it points to is u(0:50,0:20).

```
double precision u
pointer (p, u(0:50,0:20))
integer (kind=MPI_ADDRESS_KIND) size
integer sizeofdouble, ierror
! careful with size (must be MPI_ADDRESS_KIND)
call MPI_SIZEOF(u,sizeofdouble,ierror)
size = 51 * 21 * sizeofdouble
call MPI_ALLOC_MEM( size, MPI_INFO_NULL, p, ierror )
...
... program may now refer to u, including passing it
... to MPI_WIN_CREATE
...
call MPI_FREE_MEM( u, ierror )   ! not p!
```

Note that in `MPI_Free_mem`, the variable that the pointer points at, not the pointer itself, is passed.

If "Cray pointers" are not available, then the best approach is often to use a C program to allocate the array with `MPI_Alloc_mem` and then pass this array as an argument to a Fortran routine.

6.4 Global Arrays

As an example of how an existing high-level library for one-sided operations can be implemented using the standard MPI one-sided operations, we consider the Global

---

int **MPI_Alloc_mem**(MPI_Aint size, MPI_Info info, void *baseptr)

int **MPI_Free_mem**(void *baseptr)

Table 6.4
C bindings for memory allocation and deallocation routines. The pointer is returned in `baseptr`
in `MPI_Alloc_mem`; see text.

MPI_ALLOC_MEM(size, info, baseptr, ierror)
       integer info,ierror
       integer (kind=MPI_ADDRESS_KIND) size, baseptr

MPI_FREE_MEM(base, ierror)
       <type> base(*)
       integer ierror

Table 6.5
Fortran bindings for memory allocation and deallocation routines

---

void *MPI::Alloc_mem(Aint size,const Info &info)

void MPI::Free_mem(void *base)

Table 6.6
C++ bindings for memory allocation and deallocation routines

Arrays library [62, 63].

The Global Arrays library is a collection of routines that allows the user to define and manipulate an array that is distributed across all processes of a parallel program. In the versions 1 and 2 of the Global Arrays library, the global array had two dimensions, whose individual elements could be of `integer`, `double precision`, or `double complex`. Version 3 of the Global Arrays library allows for arrays with more than two dimensions. The Global Arrays library is large and powerful; in addition to operations for writing to and reading from any part of a global array, it provides a range of operations from linear algebra, including `GA_DIAG` for solving the generalized eigenvalue problem, `GA_LU_SOLVE` for solving a system of linear equations by LU factorization, and `GA_DGEMM` for performing matrix-matrix multiplies.

In this section we will describe an implementation of a small subset of a library similar to the Global Arrays library. Our simple subset has the following routines:

ga_create Creates a new global array.

ga_free Frees a global array.

ga_put Puts data into an arbitrary 2-dimensional subsection of a global array.

ga_get Gets data from an arbitrary 2-dimensional subsection of a global array.

ga_acc Accumulates data into an arbitrary 2-dimensional subsection of a global array. Unlike `MPI_Accumulate`, the entire accumulation is atomic.

ga_read_inc Reads data from the `(i,j)` element of a global array of integers, returns that value, and increments the `(i,j)` element by a given increment. This is a fetch-and-add operation.

ga_create_mutexes Creates mutex variables that can be used for mutual exclusion.

ga_lock Locks a mutex (see below).

ga_unlock Unlocks a mutex.

ga_destroy_mutexes Frees the mutex variables created with `ga_create_mutexes`.

The major differences between our library and the Global Arrays library, beyond offering far fewer capabilities, are the simpler distribution of the global array among processes (to simplify the code that we present) and the more general datatypes and process groups. The latter come essentially "for free" by exploiting the datatypes and groups in MPI.

Most of these operations are fairly obvious. The `ga_create` and `ga_free` are needed to manage the global array itself. The routines `ga_put`, `ga_get`, and `ga_-acc` are similar to `MPI_Put`, `MPI_Get`, and `MPI_Accumulate`. The remaining five routines introduce new functionality that we describe briefly here and in more detail below. The operation `ga_read_inc` provides a basic operation for implementing shared data structures. The remaining four routines provide for *mutexes*: these are variables that allow one process to ensure that it has exclusive access to a shared resource (such as a memory window). Mutex is short for "mutual exclusion."

One reason for considering such a large set of operations is that the presence of some operations, particularly `ga_read_inc`, introduces some complications into the implementation of the others.

Let's begin with an overview of the design. We use a pointer to a structure, called GA,[1] which contains information about the global array. For simplicity in the examples, we require that the array have two dimensions and that the array be decomposed into groups of columns as shown in Figure 6.2. We also assume Fortran ordering and indexes that start from one. Thus, the local rectangles on each process are stored in contiguous memory locations.

This immediately gives us most of the members of the data pointed at by GA: we need an MPI window object to contain the global array and some ints to hold the sizes of the array and how it is decomposed among the processes. It is also useful to know the MPI datatype that corresponds to the data type for the array and the size of an element of this data type. For cases where the datatype is MPI_INTEGER, MPI_DOUBLE_PRECISION, or MPI_DOUBLE_COMPLEX, this matches the original Global Arrays library. In our version, we can allow any contiguous datatype (we will use the size, not the extent, of the datatype in our example code, again for simplicity). The ga->lock_win element is explained in Section 6.7.1. The contents of a GA are shown in the header file in Figure 6.3. The implementation of our GA library is in C; a Fortran interface may be provided by using tools such as bfort [34].

6.4.1   Create and Free

Now that we have all of the members of GA, we can describe the code to create and free a new global array.

The code for ga_create is shown in Figure 6.4. The routine MPE_Mutex_create is used to initialize a special synchronization operation and is explained in Section 6.6.

The code to free a global array is shown in Figure 6.5. This code uses a window attribute to discover the base address of the window. Window attributes are much like communicator attributes; the function to access window attributes, MPI_Win_-get_attr, is much like its communicator counterpart (MPI_Attr_get in MPI 1; MPI_Comm_get_attr in MPI 2). Three predefined window attributes are set; these are MPI_WIN_BASE for the base address of the local window, MPI_WIN_SIZE for the size (in bytes) of the local memory window, and MPI_WIN_DISP_UNIT for the displacement unit chosen when the window object was created. In addition, users can create their own window object keyvals and attributes (see Section 6.5.3). The bindings for MPI_Win_get_attr are shown in Tables 6.7, 6.8, and 6.9.

---

[1]We use a pointer to the structure instead of the structure itself so that the users always see the pointer. This improves modularity and makes it easier to modify the implementation without forcing the users to rebuild all their code.

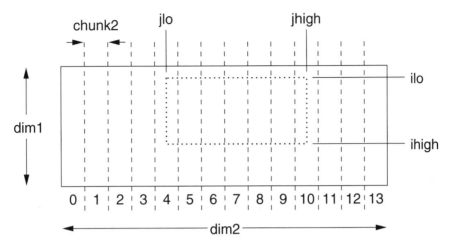

Figure 6.2
Decomposition of a global two-dimensional array. The rectangle given by coordinates (`ilo`,`jlo`)
to (`ihigh`,`jhigh`) shows a typical region that can be accessed or modified with the global array
routines. Vertical dashed lines show the decomposition of the global array across 14 processes.
The global array has dimensions `dim1` by `dim2`.

```
/* We make GA a pointer to this structure so that users always
   have a pointer, never the actual structure */
typedef struct _GA {
    MPI_Win       ga_win;
    MPI_Win       lock_win;
    /* Datatype and size */
    MPI_Datatype dtype;
    int          dtype_size;
    /* sizes of the global array */
    int          dim1, dim2, chunk2;
} *GA;
```

Figure 6.3
Header file for global arrays. Additional information, such as the address and size of the local
memory window, could be stored here as well.

---

int **MPI_Win_get_attr**(MPI_Win win, int win_keyval, void *attribute_val, int *flag)

Table 6.7
C binding for routine to access window attributes

```
#include "ga.h"
int ga_create( MPI_Comm comm, int dim1, int dim2,
               MPI_Datatype dtype, GA *ga )
{
    GA      new_ga;
    int     size, chunk2, sizeoftype;
    MPI_Aint local_size;
    void    *ga_win_ptr;

    /* Get a new structure */
    new_ga = (GA)malloc( sizeof(struct _GA) );
    if (!new_ga) return 0;

    /* Determine size of GA memory */
    MPI_Comm_size( comm, &size );
    chunk2 = dim2 / size;
    /* Require size to exactly divide dim2 */
    if ((dim2 % size) != 0) MPI_Abort( comm, 1 );
    MPI_Type_size( dtype, &sizeoftype );
    local_size = dim1 * chunk2 * sizeoftype;

    /* Allocate memory my ga_win and create window */
    MPI_Alloc_mem( local_size, MPI_INFO_NULL, &ga_win_ptr );

    MPI_Win_create( ga_win_ptr, local_size, sizeoftype,
                    MPI_INFO_NULL, comm, &new_ga->ga_win );

    /* Create critical section window */
    MPE_Mutex_create( comm, size, &new_ga->lock_win );

    /* Save other data and return */
    new_ga->dtype      = dtype;
    new_ga->dtype_size = sizeoftype;
    new_ga->dim1       = dim1;
    new_ga->dim2       = dim2;
    new_ga->chunk2     = chunk2;
    *ga                = new_ga;

    return 1;
}
```

Figure 6.4
Code to create a global array

MPI_WIN_GET_ATTR(win, win_keyval, attribute_val, flag, ierror)
             integer win, win_keyval, ierror
             integer(kind=MPI_ADDRESS_KIND) attribute_val
             logical flag

Table 6.8
Fortran binding for routine to access window attributes

---

bool MPI::Win::Get_attr(const Win& win, int win_keyval,
             void* attribute_val) const

Table 6.9
C++ binding for routine to access window attributes

```
#include "ga.h"
int ga_free( GA ga )
{
    int flag;
    void *ga_win_ptr;

    MPI_Win_get_attr( ga->ga_win, MPI_WIN_BASE, &ga_win_ptr,
                      &flag );
    if (!flag) return 1;
    MPI_Win_free( &ga->ga_win );
    MPE_Mutex_free( &ga->lock_win );
    MPI_Free_mem( ga_win_ptr );

    free(ga);
    return 0;
}
```

Figure 6.5
Code to free a global array

An alternative to using a `GA` structure is to use the MPI window object, specifically `ga_win`, and use window attributes to store the rest of the data. We will see an example of this approach in Section 6.5.

6.4.2   Put and Get

The routines for `ga_put` and `ga_get` are relatively simple. The code for `ga_put` is shown in Figure 6.6; `ga_get` is very similar. The basic algorithm is as follows:

1.   Determine the rank of process holding the leftmost column to update (`ga_-put`) or get (`ga_get`).

2.   Begin an access epoch for that rank.

3.   For each column of data to be updated or fetched from that target process, perform the RMA (put or get) operation.

4.   Complete the RMA.

5.   Continue to the next rank until the last specified column (`jhigh`) has been reached.

For simplicity, these routines put or get one column of data at a time; a more sophisticated implementation would check for special cases such as entire columns or use an MPI datatype created with `MPI_Type_vector` to access all of the required columns on a remote process with a single RMA call. Using an MPI datatype eliminates the `for` loop and replaces a set of `MPI_Put` or `MPI_Get` operations with a single `MPI_Put` or `MPI_Get`.

These routines have two tricky parts. The first is the computation of the address of the buffer to pass to the RMA routines. The code presented here assumes that a `char *` pointer is in bytes (this is common but not universal and is not required by the C standard). The other tricky part is the calls to `MPE_Mutex_lock` and `MPE_Mutex_unlock`. These routines establish a critical section (mutex is short for "mutual exclusion") and are necessary to ensure proper operation when `ga_acc` and `ga_read_inc` are used. We will see how to implement these routines below in Section 6.6. We will call these mutex locks or mutual exclusion locks to emphasize that they are different from the locks provided by `MPI_Win_lock`.

In these examples, an assert argument of `MPI_MODE_NOCHECK` is provided to `MPI_-Win_lock`. This value may be used when it is known that no other process will attempt to call `MPI_Win_lock` on the same window object and process. In our case, because of the call to `MPE_Mutex_lock`, we know that no other process can

```
#include "ga.h"
int ga_put( GA ga, int ilo, int ihigh, int jlo, int jhigh,
            void *buf )
{
    int      jcur, jfirst, jlast, j, rank;
    MPI_Aint disp;

    jcur = jlo;
    while (jcur <= jhigh) {
        rank   = (jcur - 1) /ga->chunk2;
        jfirst = rank * ga->chunk2 + 1;
        jlast  = (rank + 1) * ga->chunk2;
        if (jlast > jhigh) jlast = jhigh;

        MPE_Mutex_lock( rank, ga->lock_win );

        /* Using lock_shared allows get accesses to proceed */
        MPI_Win_lock( MPI_LOCK_SHARED, rank, MPI_MODE_NOCHECK,
                      ga->ga_win );
        for (j=jcur; j<=jlast; j++) {
            disp = (j - jfirst) * ga->dim1 + (ilo - 1);
            MPI_Put( buf, ihigh - ilo + 1, ga->dtype,
                     rank, disp, ihigh - ilo + 1, ga->dtype,
                     ga->ga_win );
            buf = (void *)( ((char *)buf) +
                            (ihigh - ilo + 1) * ga->dtype_size );
        }
        MPI_Win_unlock( rank, ga->ga_win );

        MPE_Mutex_unlock( rank, ga->lock_win );
        jcur = jlast + 1;
    }
    return 0;
}
```
Figure 6.6
The code for ga_put

call `MPI_Win_lock` for this process and window. The `MPI_Win_lock` and `MPI_Win_-unlock` calls in this case are used only to complete the RMA operations between them.

6.4.3 Accumulate

The global array version of accumulate, `ga_acc`, is a bit more interesting. In the Global Arrays library, `ga_acc` is both one sided and atomic. By atomic, we mean that the action is indivisible; if there are multiple accumulate operations to the same part of a global array, all elements contributed by a single `ga_acc` operation are accumulated before another `ga_acc` operation is allowed to modify any of the same elements of the global array. To implement this, we first acquire *all* of the mutual exclusion locks that we are going to need and then perform the accumulate operations. We can release the mutual exclusion locks as we complete the accumulate operations in each window. The code for `ga_acc` is shown in Figure 6.7.

It is often dangerous for a routine to depend on acquiring several mutexes, as `ga_acc` does here. In the general case, if there are several processes each of which needs several mutexes, each process may acquire one of the mutexes needed by the others and then wait forever for one of the other mutexes. This is the *dining philosophers* problem, where processes are replaced by philosophers and mutexes by forks, with each philosopher needing two forks to eat; if each philosopher siezes a fork, the philosophers starve, each waiting for another the relinquish a fork.

The current code does not suffer from this problem because the mutexes are acquired in strict rank-increasing order: if a process requires several mutexes, it either acquires all that it needs, or blocks because a process has gotten the mutex ahead of it. If it has blocked, it cannot interfere with the success of the process that already holds the mutex. However, if we made major changes to our library, such as providing more general decompositions of the global array among the processes, this algorithm would have to be reevaluated.

To implement the remaining parts of our simple global array library, we will need to discuss the implementation of mutexes. We will use a fetch-and-add operation to implement a mutex.

6.5 Another Version of NXTVAL

In *Using MPI* [32], Section 7.1.2, we introduced the `NXTVAL` routine. This routine provided a shared counter; any process could request a value from this counter, which was then incremented. This is a "fetch-and-add" operation, a common build-

```
#include "ga.h"
int ga_acc(GA ga, int ilo, int ihigh, int jlo, int jhigh, void *buf)
{
    int       jcur, jfirst, jlast, j, rank, rank_first, rank_last;
    MPI_Aint disp;

    /* In order to ensure that the entire update is atomic, we must
       first mutex-lock all of the windows that we will access */
    rank_first = (jlo - 1) / ga->chunk2;
    rank_last  = (jhigh - 1) / ga->chunk2;
    for (rank = rank_first; rank <= rank_last; rank++) {
        MPE_Mutex_lock( rank, ga->lock_win );
    }

    jcur = jlo;
    while (jcur <= jhigh) {
        rank   = (jcur - 1) /ga->chunk2;
        jfirst = rank * ga->chunk2 + 1;
        jlast  = (rank + 1) * ga->chunk2;
        if (jlast > jhigh) jlast = jhigh;

        MPI_Win_lock( MPI_LOCK_SHARED, rank, MPI_MODE_NOCHECK,
                    ga->ga_win );
        for (j=jcur; j<=jlast; j++) {
            disp = (j - jfirst) * ga->dim1 + (ilo - 1);
            MPI_Accumulate( buf, ihigh - ilo + 1, ga->dtype,
                    rank, disp, ihigh - ilo + 1, ga->dtype,
                    MPI_SUM, ga->ga_win );
            buf = (void *)( ((char *)buf) +
                    (ihigh - ilo + 1) *  ga->dtype_size );
        }
        MPI_Win_unlock( rank, ga->ga_win );

        MPE_Mutex_unlock( rank, ga->lock_win );
        jcur = jlast + 1;
    }
    return 0;
}
```

Figure 6.7
Code for global array accumulate. Note that all target processes are locked with MPE_Mutex_lock before any is updated.

ing block for certain types of distributed algorithms. The versions presented in *Using MPI* used point-to-point message passing and required either a separate process or thread or periodic polling by one process. In this section, we will see how to implement a fetch-and-add operation using RMA.

Our first attempt might look something like the following:

```
/* This code is erroneous */
int one = 1;
MPI_Win_create( ..., &win );
...
MPI_Win_lock( MPI_LOCK_EXCLUSIVE, 0, 0, win );
MPI_Get( &value, 1, MPI_INT, 0, 0, 1, MPI_INT, win );
MPI_Accumulate( &one, 1, MPI_INT,
                0, 0, 1, MPI_INT, MPI_SUM, win );
MPI_Win_unlock( 0, win );
```

However, this would not be correct. There are two problems. First, the MPI Standard explicitly prohibits accessing (with `MPI_Get` or a local load) and updating (with either `MPI_Put` or `MPI_Accumulate`) the same location in the same access epoch (the time between two `MPI_Win_fence` calls or `MPI_Win_lock` and `MPI_Win_unlock`). Even if the MPI Standard permitted overlapping accesses by `MPI_Accumulate` and `MPI_Get`, these functions are nonblocking and can complete in any order as long as they complete by the time `MPI_Win_unlock` returns. The MPI Standard does not specify an order in which RMA operations must complete.

In some implementations, these operations may complete in the order that they appear, particularly on loosely coupled systems with no shared-memory hardware support. On other systems, enforcing an ordering may be expensive, and hence the MPI Forum decided not to require it (also see Section 4.3.2). For applications such as the ghost-point exchange in Section 5.6.1, ordering is not required, and, as mentioned in Section 4.2, enforcing an ordering can reduce performance. However, for operations such as fetch and add, the lack of ordered operations is inconvenient. Specifically, the lack of ordering means that loosening the access restrictions to allow overlapping access from the same origin process isn't sufficient to allow us to use the above code to implement fetch and add.

Because of the very weak synchronization provided by `MPI_Win_lock` and `MPI_Win_lock` and the restrictions on overlapping access to memory windows by RMA operations, it turns out to be surprisingly hard to implement a fetch and add operation using the MPI RMA operations. We will present two solutions, but first we will start with another approach that doesn't work. Understanding why it doesn't work will provide a better understanding of `MPI_Win_lock` and `MPI_Win_-unlock`.

We will present the solutions as part of an MPI extension library we call MPE. These functions are not part of the MPI standard but are designed to utilize any MPI implementation.

6.5.1 The Nonblocking Lock

An obvious approach for implementing fetch and add is to use two locks: one is used to complete the `MPI_Get` and, in a separate step, the `MPI_Accumulate` operations, and the other is used to establish a *critical section*. Only one process is allowed to be "in" the critical section at any time; in shared-memory code it is common to use locks to implement critical sections. Thus, at first glance, it looks like we could use a window object where rank 0 contained a single integer that was accessed with `MPI_Get` and `MPI_Accumulate`, and where a lock on rank 1 was used solely to provide the critical section. The code for `NXTVAL` might then look like that in Figure 6.8.

But this code will not work because `MPI_Win_lock`, except when called with the target rank the same as the rank of the calling process, may be *nonblocking*. That is, just as the `MPI_Put`, `MPI_Get`, and `MPI_Accumulate` operations are nonblocking, so may `MPI_Win_lock` be nonblocking. All the `MPI_Win_lock` call does is to establish an access epoch, indicating that RMA calls on the specified window object and rank may be made, until the matching `MPI_Win_unlock`. If the lock type is `MPI_LOCK_-EXCLUSIVE`, it also ensures that the RMA operations are performed atomically with respect to other processes at the target.

Note that when `MPI_Win_lock` is called with the rank of the calling process (so the lock is being acquired for the local memory window), the MPI Standard specifies that `MPI_Win_lock` must block until the lock is acquired. This is because, when using passive target RMA operations, you must call `MPI_Win_lock` and `MPI_Win_-unlock` around any local loads and stores. Since the local loads and stores may happen at any time, the `MPI_Win_lock` call in this particular case must block until the lock is acquired. But in all other cases, `MPI_Win_lock` may be nonblocking.

6.5.2 A Nonscalable Implementation of `NXTVAL`

How can we implement a fetch-and-add operation using RMA? Here is one simple algorithm. The value of the counter is the sum of the contributions from each process. Since a process always knows the sum of its own contributions, a process needs only get the contributions from all other processes and add that to its own.

```
/* Erroneous code */
int MPE_Counter_nxtval( MPI_Win counter_win, int *value )
{
    int one = 1;

    /* Acquire access to the counter */
    MPI_Win_lock( MPI_LOCK_EXCLUSIVE, 1, 0, counter_win );

    /* Once we get the lock, we can fetch the counter value */
    MPI_Win_lock( MPI_LOCK_SHARED, 0, MPI_MODE_NOCHECK, counter_win );
    MPI_Get( value, 1, MPI_INT, 0, 0, 1, MPI_INT, counter_win );
    MPI_Win_unlock( 0, counter_win );

    /* And update the value */
    MPI_Win_lock( MPI_LOCK_SHARED, 0, MPI_MODE_NOCHECK, counter_win );
    MPI_Accumulate( &one, 1, MPI_INT, 1, 0, 1, MPI_INT, MPI_SUM,
                    counter_win );
    MPI_Win_unlock( 0, counter_win );

    /* Release the counter */
    MPI_Win_unlock( 1, counter_win );
    return 0;
}
```

Figure 6.8
An (erroneous) attempt to implement NXTVAL using two locks

This suggests that instead of a single integer for the counter, we use an array that
has one element for each participating process. We will use an array of integers on
the process with rank 0. The ith element of this array will contain the contribution
of the process with rank i to the counter. The algorithm for the process at rank i
is then as follows:

1. Lock the window at rank zero.

2. Get all elements of the array *except* for the ith element (our rank).

3. Increment the ith element.

4. Unlock the window.

---

int **MPI_Win_get_group**(MPI_Win win, MPI_Group *group)

Table 6.10
C routine for accessing the group of a window object

MPI_WIN_GET_GROUP(win, group, ierror)
          integer win, group, ierror

Table 6.11
Fortran routine for accessing the group of a window object

MPI::Group MPI::Win::Get_group() const

Table 6.12
C++ routine for accessing the group of a window object

5.   Sum the elements in the array (except for the ith element); add the number of times this routine has been called (that is, the sum of contributions to the counter by this process).

This code is shown in Figure 6.9.

In this implementation of NXTVAL, we have chosen to store the additional information (myval_p, the pointer to the contributions from the local process to the counter) that we need in the window object itself. This approach allows us to illustrate how information may be cached on a window object. An alternative approach would be to define a mutex object that would contain fields for the window object, the size of the window object's group, the rank of the process in that group, and the sum of the contributions to the counter from this process.

To determine the number of processes in the window object's group, and the rank of the calling process in this group, we can access the window object's group with MPI_Win_get_group. This call returns a group that is the same as the group of the communicator that was used in creating the window object. Once we have this group, we can find the size and rank of the calling process by using MPI_Group_size and MPI_Group_rank, respectively. We free the group with MPI_Group_free. This example does not include the code to create the window object or initialize the window memory. Bindings for MPI_Win_get_group are shown in Tables 6.10, 6.11, and 6.12.

```
extern int MPE_COUNTER_KEYVAL;
int MPE_Counter_nxtval( MPI_Win counter_win, int *value )
{
    MPI_Group group;
    int       rank, size, myval, flag, i, *val, one = 1;
    MPI_Aint  *myval_p;

    MPI_Win_get_group( counter_win, &group );
    MPI_Group_rank( group, &rank );
    MPI_Group_size( group, &size );
    MPI_Group_free( &group );
    MPI_Win_get_attr( counter_win, MPE_COUNTER_KEYVAL, &myval_p,
                      &flag );
    myval = *myval_p;

    val = (int *)malloc( size * sizeof(int) );
    MPI_Win_lock( MPI_LOCK_EXCLUSIVE, 0, 0, counter_win );
    for (i=0; i<size; i++) {
        if (i == rank)
            MPI_Accumulate( &one, 1, MPI_INT, 0, i, 1, MPI_INT,
                            MPI_SUM, counter_win );
        else
            MPI_Get( &val[i], 1, MPI_INT, 0, i, 1, MPI_INT,
                     counter_win );
    }
    MPI_Win_unlock( 0, counter_win );
    /* Add to our contribution */
    *myval_p = *myval_p + 1;

    /* Compute the overall value.
       Storing *myval_p into val[rank] and starting *value at zero
       would eliminate the if test */
    *value = myval;
    for (i=0; i<size; i++) {
        if (i != rank) *value = *value + val[i];
    }
    free( val );
    return 0;
}
```

Figure 6.9
A nonscalable version of NXTVAL

---

int **MPI_Win_create_keyval**(MPI_Win_copy_attr_function *win_copy_attr_fn,
    MPI_Win_delete_attr_function *win_delete_attr_fn, int *win_keyval,
    void *extra_state)

int **MPI_Win_free_keyval**(int *win_keyval)

int **MPI_Win_set_attr**(MPI_Win win, int win_keyval, void *attribute_val)

int **MPI_Win_delete_attr**(MPI_Win win, int win_keyval)

Table 6.13
C bindings for window object attribute routines (see Table 6.7 for MPI_Win_get_attr)

6.5.3   Window Attributes

One complication in the code in Figure 6.9 is the need to store the local contribution
to the counter. In this code, we have stored this value in the counter window itself,
using a window attribute. Window attributes are very similar to communicator
attributes (see Section 9.4 and *Using MPI* [32], Section 6.2). Attributes allow
information to be cached on a window object according to a keyval. The functions
for window attributes are shown in Tables 6.13, 6.14, and 6.15.

With these functions, we can create a keyval (MPE_COUNTER_KEYVAL in our example) that is known only to the NXTVAL routines. We allocate an int to hold the
local contribution to the counter and store the pointer to this value as the attribute
associated with MPE_COUNTER_KEYVAL.

The code to create the MPI_Win for NXTVAL is shown in Figure 6.10. Note that
we have used MPI_Alloc_mem to create the counter memory.

A curious feature.   The MPI_Win_create_keyval routine contains a MPI_Win_-
copy_attr_fn. However, there is no circumstance when this routine would be
called. For communicators and datatypes, the respective duplicate functions (MPI_-
Comm_dup, MPI::Comm::Clone, and MPI_Type_dup) are the only functions that
cause a keyval's copy function to be invoked. But as we have mentioned before,
the rules for overlapping accesses make any kind of "duplicate window" operation
nearly useless. Thus, as the MPI Standard is currently written, the copy function
provided when creating a keyval for a window object has no purpose.

If the MPI Standard were to be extended, it is possible that a MPI_Win_dup function could be defined, perhaps by loosening the restrictions on overlapping access
to memory windows or by having MPI_Win_dup allocate new memory windows. In
that case, a copy function would become important. By providing the copy func-

---

MPI_WIN_CREATE_KEYVAL(win_copy_attr_fn, win_delete_attr_fn, win_keyval,
      extra_state, ierror)
      external win_copy_attr_fn, win_delete_attr_fn
      integer win_keyval, ierror
      integer(kind=MPI_ADDRESS_KIND) extra_state

MPI_WIN_FREE_KEYVAL(win_keyval, ierror)
      integer win_keyval, ierror

MPI_WIN_SET_ATTR(win, win_keyval, attribute_val, ierror)
      integer win, win_keyval, ierror
      integer(kind=MPI_ADDRESS_KIND) attribute_val

MPI_WIN_DELETE_ATTR(win, win_keyval, ierror)
      integer win, win_keyval, ierror

Table 6.14
Fortran bindings for window object attribute routines (see Table 6.8 for `MPI_Win_get_attr`)

tion argument now, the MPI Forum has ensured that future extensions are not constrained.

Improving the NXTVAL Routine. One of the drawbacks of attaching all of the local data to a window object rather than a separate structure is that a user could erroneously delete the counter with `MPI_Win_free` rather than `MPE_Counter_free`. We can turn this drawback into an advantage by using the `MPI_Win_delete_fn` argument of the keyval. When the window object for the counter is freed, we want all of the memory that we have allocated to be freed. The code to do this is shown in Figure 6.11. With this code, a separate `MPE_Counter_delete` routine is

---

int MPI::Win::Create_keyval(MPI::Win::Copy_attr_function* win_copy_attr_fn,
      MPI::Win::Delete_attr_function* win_delete_attr_fn,
      void* extra_state)

void MPI::Win::Free_keyval(int& win_keyval)

void MPI::Win::Set_attr(int win_keyval, const void* attribute_val)

void MPI::Win::Delete_attr(int win_keyval)

Table 6.15
C++ bindings for window object attribute routines (see Table 6.9 for `MPI::Win::Get_attr`)

```
extern int MPE_COUNTER_KEYVAL;

void MPE_Counter_create( MPI_Comm old_comm, MPI_Win *counter_win )
{
    int size, rank, *counter_mem, i, *myval_p;

    MPI_Comm_rank(old_comm, &rank);
    MPI_Comm_size(old_comm, &size);

    if (rank == 0) {
        MPI_Alloc_mem( size * sizeof(int), MPI_INFO_NULL,
                       &counter_mem );
        for (i=0; i<size; i++) counter_mem[i] = 0;
        MPI_Win_create( counter_mem, size * sizeof(int), sizeof(int),
                        MPI_INFO_NULL, old_comm, counter_win );

    }
    else {
        MPI_Win_create( NULL, 0, 1, MPI_INFO_NULL, old_comm,
                        counter_win );
    }
    /* Create my local counter */
    if (MPE_COUNTER_KEYVAL == MPI_KEYVAL_INVALID) {
        MPI_Win_create_keyval( MPI_WIN_NULL_COPY_FN,
                               MPI_WIN_NULL_DELETE_FN,
                               &MPE_COUNTER_KEYVAL, NULL );
    }
    myval_p = (int *)malloc( sizeof(int) );
    MPI_Win_set_attr( *counter_win, MPE_COUNTER_KEYVAL, myval_p );
}
```

Figure 6.10
Code to create the window object and counter memory used for NXTVAL

```
int MPE_Counter_attr_delete( MPI_Win counter_win, int keyval,
                             void *attr_val, void *extra_state )
{
    int counter_flag, *counter_mem, *myval_p = (int *)attr_val;

    MPI_Win_get_attr( counter_win, MPI_WIN_BASE,
                      &counter_mem, &counter_flag );

    /* Free the memory used by the counter and local value */
    if (counter_flag && counter_mem)
        MPI_Free_mem( counter_mem );
    free( myval_p );

    return MPI_SUCCESS;
}
```

Figure 6.11
Routine to free memory allocated in NXTVAL, using the delete function on the keyval
MPE_COUNTER_KEYVAL

unnecessary; the user may simply use MPI_Win_free on the counter window.

Another improvement is to replace the for loop of MPI_Get calls with a single MPI_Get using a datatype created with MPI_Type_indexed. The code in Figure 6.12 shows the use of the block_length argument to MPI_Type_indexed to define an efficient datatype for this transfer. The first block is of length rank (the number of members before the location that is accumulated into with MPI_Accumulate. The second block contains the number of remaining members after that location. Note that blens[0] will be zero for rank = 0 and blens[1] will be zero for rank = size - 1.

6.5.4   A Scalable Implementation of NXTVAL

Our implementation of NXTVAL is correct but not scalable: for p processes, we need to read or modify p locations in remote memory and perform $p - 1$ local additions. This strategy is acceptable for small numbers of processes but is unworkable when the number of processes reaches hundreds or thousands. To develop a scalable implementation of NXTVAL, we look at the task of forming the sum of the contributions from each process. The most obvious way to improve the scalability is to use a tree, where the internal nodes of the tree hold the sums of the contributions of their children.

We can develop the algorithm recursively. Figure 6.13 shows the trees needed for

```
int blens[2], disps[2];
MPI_Datatype get_type;

blens[0] = rank;
disps[0] = 0;
blens[1] = size - rank - 1;
disps[1] = rank + 1;
MPI_Type_indexed( 2, blens, disps, MPI_INT, &get_type );
MPI_Type_commit( &get_type );
...
/* The following code replaces the RMA accesses in
   MPE_Counter_nxtval */
MPI_Win_lock( MPI_LOCK_EXCLUSIVE, 0, 0, counter_win );
MPI_Accumulate( &one, 1, MPI_INT, 0, rank, 1, MPI_INT,
                MPI_SUM, counter_win );
MPI_Get( &val[0], 1, get_type, 0, 0, 1, get_type, counter_win );
MPI_Win_unlock( 0, counter_win );
```

Figure 6.12
Using an indexed datatype to reduce the number of RMA calls

two processes (a) and four processes (b). The trees are stored in the local window on a single process; for concreteness in the discussion of the algorithm, we will assume that the tree is stored as an array that is contained in the local memory window on process 0. We describe below how the tree is represented in the array. In Figure 6.13(a), we can see that for process 1 to compute the value, it need only get the value that process 0 has contributed. Adding that to its own value gives it the value of the counter. By using MPI_Accumulate to add its component to the its element in the tree (the right child), process 1 ensures that process 0 will get the correct value for the counter the next time process 0 executes a fetch and increment.

In Figure 6.13(b), the tree for four processes shows where the scalability comes from: Process 1 needs to read only two nodes (the right child of the root and its own sibling, process 0) and increment one node (the parent of processes 0 and 1). These operations are shown with black (MPI_Get) and grey (MPI_Accumulate) boxes.

The full algorithm follows. The root of each subtree contains the sum of the values of each leaf. This is applied recursively. Then to get the value of the counter, we need only get the values of the two children. Of the two children, one child will be an ancestor of the process and the other will not be an ancestor. For the child

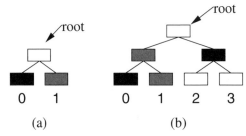

Figure 6.13
Fetch and increment trees for 2 processes (a) and 4 processes (b), where process 1 is performing the fetch and increment. In both cases, the black boxes are read with `MPI_Get` and the grey boxes are incremented with `MPI_Accumulate`. The root box (shown with slanted lines) is neither read nor updated. The numbers under the leaf boxes indicate the number of the process that contributes to that leaf.

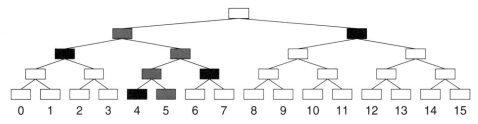

Figure 6.14
Example showing scalable implementation of fetch and increment. Black boxes are read with `MPI_Get`; grey boxes are incremented with `MPI_Accumulate`. The RMA accesses used by process 5 are shown.

that is *not* an ancestor, we read its value with `MPI_Get`. For the child that is an ancestor, we get the value by recursively applying this algorithm to that child, and use `MPI_Accumulate` to increment the value of that child. Thus, to compute the sum, we need only add up the contributions from the sibling of the node, its parents, and the parent's siblings. This is shown in Figure 6.14. The code requires only a single lock and unlock, and for p processes, uses $2p - 2$ words of memory and requires that $\log_2 p$ words be fetched with `MPI_Get`, $\log_2 p$ words be incremented with `MPI_Accumulate`, and $\log_2 p$ local additions be made.

Our code, particularly to set up the counter, is now more complex. We store the tree in an array, following these rules:

1.   The root is at index zero.

2.   For any node, the left child is at index (node + 1) and the right child is at index (node + 2^{m-l-1}), where the tree has m levels and the node is on level l. The

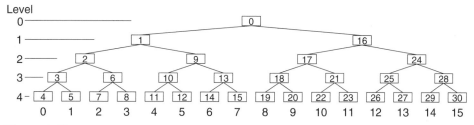

Figure 6.15
Example showing how the tree in Figure 6.14 is mapped into an array. The numbers in the boxes are the indexes into the array.

levels are defined recursively: the level of the children of a node is one greater than the level of a node, and the level of the root is zero. The level of the tree is given by $\lfloor \log_2 p \rfloor$, when there are p processes.

This mapping of the tree onto an array for the tree in Figure 6.14 is shown in Figure 6.15. That tree has five levels, numbered from zero to four.

For a process of rank i, we thus need to access only the nodes on the path from the root to the leaf representing that process. We place these indices into two integer arrays: `get_idx` holds the indices of the entries that we need to get, and `acc_idx` holds the indices of the entries that we need to add one to. The code to determine these values is shown in Figure 6.16. For Fortran programmers, the expression `mask <<= 1` means "shift left by one" and is equivalent to the Fortran code `mask = mask * 2`.

Since we have these arrays, we can build datatypes with them that allow us to use a single `MPI_Get` and `MPI_Accumulate` call as follows:

```
MPI_Type_create_indexed_block( level, 1, get_idx, MPI_INT,
                               &get_type );
MPI_Type_create_indexed_block( level, 1, acc_idx, MPI_INT,
                               &acc_type );
MPI_Type_commit( &get_type );
MPI_Type_commit( &acc_type );
```

The code that we have shown applies only when the number of processes is a power of two. The modifications to allow this code to work with any number of processes are straightforward and left to the reader.

```
/* Get the largest power of two smaller than size */
mask = 1;
while (mask < size) mask <<= 1;
mask >>= 1;

/* Find the path to the leaf from the root */
level = 0;
idx   = 0;
while (mask > 1) {
    if (rank < mask) {
        /* Go left */
        get_idx[level] = idx + mask;
        acc_idx[level] = idx + 1;
        idx = idx + 1;
    }
    else {
        /* Go Right */
        rank           = rank - mask;
        get_idx[level] = idx + 1;
        acc_idx[level] = idx + mask;
        idx = idx + mask;
    }
    level ++;
    mask <<= 1;
}
```

Figure 6.16
Code to find the path through the tree for the counter value

6.6 An RMA Mutex

For many operations, it is important to be able to establish a critical section or
mutual exclusion among the processes. With a small modification to the MPE_-
Counter_nxtval routine, we can implement such an operation. We change MPE_-
Counter_nxtval so that the value added to the counter is the third argument to
the routine, rather than always being one. This simply means changing the first
parameter in the call to MPI_Accumulate to point to the value to add, and changing

```
    *myval_p = *myval_p + 1;
```

to

```
*myval_p = *myval_p + increment;
```

Call this new routine `MPE_Counter_inc_simple`. With this simple change, we can implement a simple mutex as follows:

```
void MPE_Mutex_lock_simple( MPI_Win win )
{
    int value;
    MPE_Counter_inc_simple( win, &value, 1 );
    while (value != 0) {
        MPE_Counter_inc_simple( win, &value, -1 );
        MPE_Counter_inc_simple( win, &value, 1 );
    }
}
```

What this does is continually try to add one to the counter. If the value returned was zero, it returns. Now, any other attempt to acquire a mutex on the same window (window object and rank) will return one (or greater, if several processes are trying to acquire the mutex). Otherwise, it subtracts one from the counter (ignoring the returned value) and calls `MPE_Counter_inc_simple` to get the current value and add one to the counter. The routine to unlock the mutex is even simpler; we need only decrement the counter:

```
void MPE_Mutex_unlock_simple( MPI_Win win )
{
    int value;
    MPE_Counter_inc_simple( win, &value, -1 );
}
```

These implementations are very simple and have their drawbacks. But they are correct and reliable. The implementation of fast, fair, and scalable mutexes and other shared data structures is a major area of study; see [2, 60, 93] for some examples of the issues that arise in different environments.

For the Global Arrays library, we need a slightly more general version of these mutex routines. We need a separate mutex for each process in the window. Where we used process 0 to hold the fetch-and-add tree in `MPE_Counter_nxtval`, we generalize this to use a separate tree on each process of the window; this provides a separate fetch-and-add counter on each process. We define a new routine `MPE_Counter_inc` by adding a rank argument that indicates which process to perform a fetch-and-add on, and define a `MPE_Mutex_lock` and `MPE_Mutex_unlock` that also take a rank argument as the first argument; the window that is used for the fetch-and-increment is the second argument. Finally, we are ready to define `MPE_Mutex_create`. This routine creates a window object that contains a fetch-and-increment tree at the first `size` processes in the window, where `size` is the second argument and the communicator used to create the window object is the first argument. `MPE_Mutex_create` returns the new window object as the third argument.

6.7   The Rest of Global Arrays

Now that we have a scalable fetch and increment and a mutex routine, we can complete our implementation of our simplified Global Arrays library.

6.7.1   Read and Increment

The `ga_read_inc` is a fetch and increment operation. We have seen in Section 6.5 that we cannot simply use `MPI_Get` and `MPI_Accumulate` to implement a fetch and increment. In addition, our solution used multiple memory locations for a single counter. Obviously, we cannot use this approach for a global array with many elements. Our solution is to use the `MPE_Mutex_lock` and `MPE_Mutex_unlock` to establish a critical section around any access to the global array, whether by `ga_-put`, `ga_get`, or `ga_acc`. The window object `ga->lock_win` holds the window used to implement the mutual exclusion; this is the sole purpose of this window object. Note that if we did not allow `ga_read_inc` to modify an arbitrary member of the global array and did not require atomicity of the `ga_acc` operation, we would not need the second MPI window object `ga->lock_win`. The code for `ga_read_inc` is shown in Figure 6.17. The only interesting part of this code is the computation for the rank of the process holding the designated element and the displacement of that element in the local window (see *Using MPI* [32], Appendix E, for a discussion about the computation).

Another approach is to use a single mutex for all accesses to the global array, rather than having one for each local window (that is, there are as many locks as there were processes in the communicator with which the window object was created). The approach that we are taking is more scalable, since nonoverlapping operations on different processes can occur concurrently.

6.7.2   Mutual Exclusion for Global Arrays

Like many libraries that provide shared objects, the Global Arrays library provides routines to create, use, and destroy mutexes for mutual exclusion. Once these mutexes are created, they can be used to lock and unlock access to data or code.

```
#include "ga.h"
int ga_read_inc( GA ga, int i, int j, int inc )
{
    int buf, rank;
    MPI_Aint disp;

    rank    = (j - 1) / ga->chunk2;

    /* disp depends on the displacement unit being sizeof(int) */
    disp = (j - 1 - (rank * ga->chunk2)) * ga->dim1 + i - 1;

    MPE_Mutex_lock( rank, ga->lock_win );

    MPI_Win_lock( MPI_LOCK_SHARED, rank, MPI_MODE_NOCHECK,
                  ga->ga_win );
    MPI_Get( &buf, 1, MPI_INT, disp, 1, MPI_INT, rank, ga->ga_win );
    MPI_Win_unlock( rank, ga->ga_win );

    MPI_Win_lock( MPI_LOCK_SHARED, rank, MPI_MODE_NOCHECK,
                  ga->ga_win );
    MPI_Accumulate( &inc, 1, MPI_INT,
                    disp, 1, MPI_INT, rank, MPI_SUM, ga->ga_win );
    MPI_Win_unlock( rank, ga->ga_win );

    MPE_Mutex_unlock( rank, ga->lock_win );

    return buf;
}
```

Figure 6.17
Code for read and increment, using the MPE mutex routines

The implementation of these mutexes is based on the `MPE_Mutex_lock` introduced in the preceding section.

To provide the best scalability, we place only one mutex per local window. If the number of requested mutexes is larger than the size of `MPI_COMM_WORLD`, we create enough window objects to provide one mutex per process per window object. This code, as well as the code to lock a particular mutex, is shown in Figure 6.18.

6.7.3 Comments on the MPI Version of Global Arrays

The absence of a read-modify-write operation or of ordered RMA operations makes the implementation of a Global Array library less straightforward than it would be if MPI RMA provided those operations. Furthermore, it is not clear yet whether the MPI RMA operations will be implemented efficiently enough to provide a fast enough implementation of libraries such as Global Arrays, particularly when mutual exclusion is needed. In addition, operations such as fetch and increment, while very valuable, are not the most powerful [37]; operations such as compare and swap provide more powerful building blocks. This is one area where enhancements to the MPI Standard may be necessary.

6.8 Differences between RMA and Shared Memory

To understand the similarities and differences between RMA and shared-memory programming, it is helpful to contrast MPI window objects with shared-memory approaches that involve separate processes (rather than separate threads in a single process). There are two widely used and relatively portable models in Unix. One uses `mmap` (memory map) and `fork` (create a new process), and the other uses `shmget` (shared memory get) and `shmat` (shared memory attach).[2] In both cases, the shared memory is a *new* region of memory, not one that exists in the application already. In other words, it is similar to requiring that all shared memory be allocated with `MPI_Alloc_mem`.

The most significant difference, however, is in how the memory is accessed. There are no separate routines to put/get/accumulate with this shared memory; it is part of the address space of the process and can be accessed with the normal language facilities. For example, Figure 6.19 shows one way for a process to create a 4kByte

---

[2]None of these approaches is entirely portable. The version shown in Figure 6.19 relies on using `mmap` without a real file; versions that use `shmat` often run into limits on the amount of available shared memory and race conditions in managing shared-memory segments.

```
#include "ga.h"
/* Instead of using a static variable, we could attach these to
   a communicator, using a communicator attribute */
static MPI_Win *GA_mutex_wins = 0;
static int      GA_mutex_nwins = 0;

int ga_create_mutexes( int num )
{
    int size, nwin, i;

    MPI_Comm_size( MPI_COMM_WORLD, &size );

    nwin = (num + size - 1) / size;

    GA_mutex_wins = (MPI_Win *)malloc( nwin * sizeof(MPI_Win) );
    if (!GA_mutex_wins) return 1;

    for (i=0; i<nwin; i++) {
        if (num < size) size = num;
        MPE_Mutex_create( MPI_COMM_WORLD, size, &GA_mutex_wins[i] );
        num -= size;
    }

    GA_mutex_nwins = nwin;
    return 0;
}

void ga_lock( int n )
{
    int size, rank, win_num;

    MPI_Comm_size( MPI_COMM_WORLD, &size );
    win_num = n / size;
    rank    = n % size;
    MPE_Mutex_lock( rank, GA_mutex_wins[win_num] );
}
```

Figure 6.18
Code for mutex creation and locking a mutex

```
int     *memloc;
int     *shared_int, fd, am_parent;

fd = open("/dev/zero",O_RDWR);
memloc = (int *) mmap( (caddr_t)0, 4096,
                       PROT_READ|PROT_WRITE|PROT_EXEC,
                       MAP_SHARED, fd, (off_t) 0);
shared_int = memloc;
*shared_int = 12;
am_parent = fork();
if (am_parent) {
    /* parent code */
}
else {
    /* child code */
    printf( "The shared integer is %d", *shared_int );
    *shared_int += 1;
}
```

Figure 6.19
Creating two process that communicate with shared memory

shared-memory region with `mmap`, use `fork` to create a second process, and have
both processes access an `int` in this shared region.

The figure illustrates the differences between shared memory and the MPI RMA
model. In MPI, no shared memory is visible to the user. Rather, with `MPI_Put`,
`MPI_Get`, or `MPI_Accumulate`, the user can access memory in a defined memory
window object in another process. This approach is both more general (it provides
more flexibility over the memory that is accessible) and more limited (the user must
use special routines to access memory).

In addition, MPI addresses the issue of data-access synchronization. Consider the
following small change to the code in Figure 6.19, in which the initial assignment
`*shared_int = 12` is moved into the parent code part of the `if`:

```
am_parent = fork();
if (am_parent) {
    /* parent code */
    *shared_int = 12;
}
else {
```

```
      /* child code */
      printf( "The shared integer is %d", *shared_int );
      *shared_int += 1;
}
```

What value is printed out now? The answer is either 0 or 12, depending on exactly how fast the parent and the child run. This is a classic *race condition*, where the answer depends on a race between two threads of control (the two processes, in this case). To avoid this, one must add routines that ensure that data is available when needed. Many Unix implementations provide `semop` (semaphore operation) for this; they may also provide vendor-specific mutual-exclusion operations. In MPI, data synchronization is accomplished by completing an RMA routine using, for example, `MPI_Win_fence` or `MPI_Win_unlock`.

6.9 Managing a Distributed Data Structure

To understand more clearly the differences between the MPI RMA model and shared memory, particularly the use of pointers in shared memory, let us look at the implementation of a list containing character keys and values that is distributed among all the processes in an MPI communicator. We first describe a shared-memory implementation of a routine that searches for a given key and returns the corresponding value. We then show what must be changed to implement the same operations using MPI RMA. We follow this by adding the ability to allow some processes to insert elements in the list while others may be searching the list, again showing both shared-memory and RMA implementations.

6.9.1 A Shared-Memory Distributed List Implementation

In this section, we consider a list distributed among processes as shown in Figure 6.20. We also assume that the list is unchanging (i.e., that the list was constructed in an earlier phase of the program). For this section, the only operation on the list is thus a search through the list for a particular element. We describe the routine `FindElm` that searches through the list.

A shared-memory implementation is relatively simple. We start with a simple list element defined by the structure `ListElm`, shown in Figure 6.21. We also include a pointer to the head of the list and code to initialize the head to point to an empty element (this will simplify some code when we add the ability to modify the list). We assume that all processes can access the `head` pointer, as well as the character

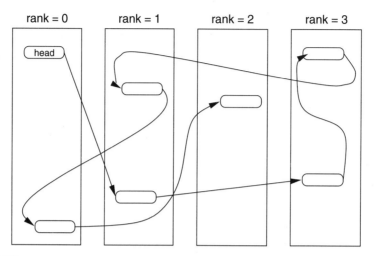

Figure 6.20
A example of a list distributed among four processes

```
typedef struct _listelm {
    struct _listelm *next;
    char *key, *value; } ListElm;
ListElm headval = { 0, 0, 0 };
static ListElm *head = &headval;
```

Figure 6.21
Definition of a list element and list pointer for the shared-memory implementation of a
distributed list. These definitions are stored in the include file `list.h`.

strings pointed at by the `key` and `value` fields in each list element (because they
are all stored in shared memory).

The code to find an element in the list that matches a particular key is then quite
simple, as shown in Figure 6.22. C programmers might reduce the code to three
lines by replacing the `while` loop with a `for` loop that handles the initialization,
test, and advancement to the next list element, but the form here is easier for
Fortran programmers to follow and, more important, will be easier to compare
with the MPI RMA version that we consider next.

6.9.2   An MPI Implementation of a Distributed List

In MPI, we cannot directly access the list elements on other processes. Instead,
we must use RMA operations to access them. In addition, we cannot use a simple
pointer to identify a list element. In the distributed case, we need to know

```
#include "list.h"

char *FindElm( const char *key )
{
    ListElm *ptr;

    ptr = head->next;
    while (ptr) {
        if (strcmp( ptr->key, key ) == 0)
            return ptr->value;
        ptr = ptr->next;
    }
    return 0;
}
```

Figure 6.22
Shared-memory version of `FindElm` for a static list

1. the rank of the process that holds the element, and

2. the displacement within the window of the element.

Thus, instead of using a pointer (`ListELM *`) to access elements, we define a structure `RemotePointer`, shown in Figure 6.23. This structure also includes a `local_pointer` field. If the list element is on the local process, this field is the address of the list element and is used only on that process. It is not required, since the address of an element on a local process can be computed from the displacement, but having this data precomputed can improve the performance of the RMA implementation of `FindElm`. The header file that contains the definition of `RemotePointer` also contains a definition of a list element that replaces the pointer to the next list element (`struct _listelm *next` in the shared-memory case) with a `RemotePointer`. In addition, the list elements themselves contain character arrays for the `key` and `value` rather than pointers to `key` and `value` strings. These could also have been implemented by using `RemotePointer` to point to the storage locations in a memory window, but for many applications, it is both simpler and more efficient (in time if not in memory) to store these directly within the list element.[3]

The head of this list is slightly different, even though it looks nearly the same as the shared-memory case in Figure 6.21. In the shared-memory case, there was one `head` variable that every process could access directly. In the MPI RMA case, there

---

[3]The same efficiency argument often holds in the shared-memory case as well, but for simplicity we have used the simplest and most general form in this case.

```
#define MAX_KEY_SIZE 64
#define MAX_VALUE_SIZE 256

typedef struct {
    MPI_Aint disp;              /* Displacement in window */
    int      owner_rank;        /* Rank (process) */
    void     *local_pointer;    /* Local address of data pointed
                                   at (if data local) */
    } RemotePointer;
typedef struct {
    RemotePointer next;
    /* For simplicity, we make the key and value stay within the
       structure.  In a more general case, they too could use
       RemotePointer */
    char         key[MAX_KEY_SIZE],
                 value[MAX_VALUE_SIZE];
    } ListElm;

/* The head starts on process 0 at displacement 0 */
static RemotePointer head = {0,0,0};

MPI_Datatype ListElm_type;
```

Figure 6.23
Header file Dlist.h for distributed list code. The local_pointer field is declared as void * to
provide a general "remote pointer;" however, in the code in these examples, we could also have
used ListElm *local_pointer.

are no shared variables; each process has (direct) access only to its own variables.
In the RMA case, *each* process has its *own* head variable. This is defined as a
RemotePointer that points at displacement zero on process zero. Thus, the RMA
version of the distributed list always starts on process zero.

The last part of Dlist.h is an MPI datatype that will be used to access a list
element (ListElm). Since a ListElm contains a remote pointer as well as character
arrays, we use an MPI datatype to access a ListElm on a remote process. Not
shown here is the list element that head points to; this is a ListElm on process 0
with displacement 0, and with key = "\relax0".

The code to construct this datatype is fairly simple. The only problem is how
to handle the MPI_Aint field in the RemotePointer because there is no predefined
MPI datatype corresponding to MPI_Aint, as discussed in Section 5.6.1 (we do
not need to transfer the void *local_pointer field, of course). We can use the

function `MPI_Type_match_size` as we did in Section 5.6.1 to find the corresponding MPI datatype. An alternative that maintains portability is to use a tool such as GNU `autoconf` [51] to determine the appropriate datatype.

The rest of the `ListElm_type` datatype is constructed with the following code:

```
/* Create a type for the RemotePointer */
blens[0] = 1;
displs[0] = 0;
MPI_Type_match_size( MPI_TYPECLASS_INTEGER, sizeof(MPI_Aint),
                     &dtypes[0] );
blens[1] = 1;
MPI_Get_address( &head.disp, &disp_base );
MPI_Get_address( &head.owner_rank, &displs[1] );
displs[1] = displs[1] - disp_base;
dtypes[1] = MPI_INT;
MPI_Type_create_struct( 2, blens, displs, dtypes, &rempointer );

/* Create the datatype for ListElm */
dtypes[0] = rempointer;  blens[0] = 1;
dtypes[1] = MPI_CHAR;    blens[1] = MAX_KEY_SIZE;
dtypes[2] = MPI_CHAR;    blens[2] = MAX_VALUE_SIZE;
MPI_Type_create_struct( 3, blens, displs, dtypes,
                        &ListElm_type );
MPI_Type_free( &rempointer );
MPI_Type_commit( &ListElm_type );
```

This example takes advantage of the fact that in MPI, an object may be freed once the user no longer needs it explicitly. Any reference to the object by another MPI operation (in this case, the datatype `ListElm_type`) ensures that the object itself is not deleted until all references to it are freed (in this case, until `ListElm_type` is deleted).

With these preliminaries, we are ready to describe the RMA version of `FindElm`. The code in Figure 6.24 parallels the shared-memory code, but with some important differences.

• Because we must use a `MPI_Win_lock`/`MPI_Win_unlock` to complete any `MPI_-Get` operation, we get an entire list element, including the `key` and `value`, in a single operation, rather than first checking the `key` and then obtaining either the `value` (if the `key` matched) or the `next` pointer (if the `key` did not match). We also make a copy of the list element that we will look at. This is more efficient that using multiple lock/get/unlock operations.

• We get the remote list element into a `local_copy`. This `local_copy` is declared `static` so that we can return it as the value found by `FindElm`. This is a simple approach, but cannot be used if there are multiple threads per process.

• In the case where the data is local, we use the `local_pointer` field of the `RemotePointer` rather than either using `MPI_Get` on the local process or computing the local pointer from the window base and displacement.

• The end of the list is indicated by an `owner_rank` of -1. We use this rather than using a window displacement of zero (`disp` in `RemotePointer`) because a displacement of zero is a valid location.

6.9.3   Handling Dynamically Changing Distributed Data Structures

How does our code change if the list can be updated and searched at the same time? Just as before, we start with shared-memory code. Since the list can be updated by one thread while another thread is searching it, we may need to establish a critical section around the list. We start by defining an `InsertElm` routine that may be used to insert an element into the list; this code is shown in Figure 6.25. We assume that the list is sorted by key; the insert routine inserts the element into the correct location in the list. The code is straightforward; the `while` loop finds the pointer to the list elements before (`lastptr`) and after (`ptr`) the element to be inserted (here is where having `head` point to a first element helps; there is no special code for handling the `head`). No element is inserted if `key` is found. Note that a mutex lock is used around access to the list to prevent concurrent inserts from corrupting the list data structures. We do not define the routines `lock_mutex` and `unlock_mutex`; we simply assume that they exist for the shared-memory case. In addition, the function `DupString` is used to allocate space (in shared memory) for a string and copy the argument to that space; the implementation of this simple function is not shown. Finally, we assume that `malloc` may be used to allocate shared memory.

A `DeleteElm` routine has a similar form, with the code first finding the element (based on `key`) to remove, then linking around it and freeing the storage used by the deleted list element.

The `FindElm` routine for a dynamic list is slightly different from the static list version shown in Figure 6.22. In particular, if elements can be deleted as well as inserted, we cannot simply return the `value` element from a list entry, since that storage could be freed by another process executing `DeleteElm`. Instead, we make a copy of the value before returning it. Of course, this requires that the user free

```
#include "Dlist.h"

char *FindElm( MPI_Win win, const char *key )
{
    static ListElm local_copy;
    ListElm        *local_copy_ptr;
    RemotePointer  ptr;
    int            my_rank;
    MPI_Group      win_group;

    /* my_rank could also be precomputed, of course */
    MPI_Win_get_group( win, &win_group );
    MPI_Group_rank( win_group, &my_rank );
    MPI_Group_free( &win_group );

    ptr = head;
    while (ptr.owner_rank >= 0) {
        /* Make sure we have the data */
        if (ptr.owner_rank != my_rank) {
            MPI_Win_lock( MPI_LOCK_SHARED, ptr.owner_rank, 0, win );
            MPI_Get( &local_copy, 1, ListElm_type,
                        ptr.owner_rank, ptr.disp, 1, ListElm_type, win );
            MPI_Win_unlock( ptr.owner_rank, win );
            local_copy_ptr = &local_copy;
        }
        else
            local_copy_ptr = (ListElm *)(ptr.local_pointer);

        if (strcmp( local_copy_ptr->key, key ) == 0)
            return local_copy_ptr->value;
        ptr = local_copy_ptr->next;
    }
    /* Did not find key */
    return 0;
}
```

Figure 6.24
Code to find an element in an unchanging distributed list using RMA. Note that this code is not thread safe because it uses a static variable (local_copy).

```
#include "list.h"

extern char *DupString( const char * );

void InsertElm( const char *key, const char *value )
{
    ListElm *ptr, *last_ptr, *new_ptr;
    int      compare;

    /* Lock list, find insertion point, and insert element */
    lock_mutex();

    last_ptr = head;
    ptr      = head->next;
    while (ptr) {
        compare = strcmp( ptr->key, key );
        if (compare == 0) {
            /* Duplicate key. Ignore */
            unlock_mutex(); return; }
        if (compare > 0) {
            break;
        }
        last_ptr = ptr;
        ptr      = ptr->next;
    }

    /* Create new element */
    if ( !(new_ptr = (ListElm *)malloc( sizeof(ListElm) )) )
        abort();
    new_ptr->key   = DupString( key );
    new_ptr->value = DupString( value );
    new_ptr->next  = ptr;
    last_ptr->next = new_ptr;

    unlock_mutex();
}
```

Figure 6.25
Shared-memory code to insert an element into a list

```
#include "list.h"
extern char *DupString( const char * );

char *FindElm( const char *key )
{
    ListElm *ptr;
    char    *local_value;
    int     compare;

    lock_mutex( );
    ptr = head->next;
    while (ptr) {
        compare = strcmp( ptr->key, key );
        if (compare == 0) {
            local_value = DupString( ptr->value );
            unlock_mutex( );
            return local_value;
        }
        else if (compare > 0)
            break;
        ptr = ptr->next;
    }
    unlock_mutex( );
    return 0;
}
```

Figure 6.26
Shared-memory routine to find an element in a list that may be modified by other processes

the result returned by FindElm when it is no longer needed. The other change is the addition of lock_mutex and unlock_mutex calls to ensure that the list is not modified by another process while FindElm is searching through the list. The code for the shared-memory version of FindElm for dynamic lists is shown in Figure 6.26.[4]

These two shared-memory codes are fairly simple, but they illustrate one of the more subtle issues in writing parallel programs. In both InsertElm and FindElm, a

---

[4]If write ordering is enforced, that is, stores to memory occur in the order they are written and are not reordered by the compiler or the memory system hardware (see Section 4.3.2), we may be able to avoid locks in the FindElm routine by carefully ordering the updates to the list elements in InsertElm. However, such code is fragile because write ordering is not a requirement of C, C++, or Fortran, and code that runs on one system may fail on another.

single mutex lock is used to protect the list. As a result, only one process at a time can use the list. This restriction makes this code *nonscalable*: as more processes are added, the program may not run faster. Note that if there is no DeleteElm, only an InsertElm, we do not need to use a mutex around the FindElm routine because we can ensure that the list is always valid (this is why the last pointer operation is the assignment to last_ptr->next in InsertElm).

6.9.4 An MPI Implementation of a Dynamic Distributed List

The RMA version of the dynamic list routines is very similar to the shared-memory version, with the same changes that we made for a static list (that is, we read the entire list element into a copy).

Our first task is to provide a way to dynamically allocate memory to be used by InsertElm. Since MPI provides no routines to allocate memory from a local memory window, we must write our own. Fortunately, we have chosen to use fixed-sized list elements, so we can use a simple list allocator. The following code shows the initial list element allocation and window creation.

```
ListElm *avail;
MPI_Alloc_mem( MAX_LOCAL_LIST * sizeof(ListElm),
               MPI_INFO_NULL, &avail );
for (i=0; i<MAX_LOCAL_LIST; i++) {
    avail[i].next.local_pointer = avail + i + 1;
    avail[i].next.disp          = i;
    }
avail[MAX_LOCAL_LIST-1].next.local_pointer = 0;
MPI_Win_create( avail, MAX_LOCAL_LIST * sizeof(ListElm),
                sizeof(ListElm), ... );
```

With this code, allocating an element simply requires using avail and resetting avail to avail->next.local_pointer. We use avail[i].next.disp to hold the displacement in the local window of that item (not the next item) while in the avail list.

The major change in FindElm is the use of MPE_Mutex_lock and MPE_Mutex_-unlock to provide the mutex needed to safely read the list, just as lock_mutex and unlock_mutex were used in the shared-memory version. These use a separate window object, winlock, which is created with MPE_Mutex_create. Similarly, InsertElm also requires a mutex to modify the list safely. In the RMA versions, shown in Figures 6.27, 6.28, and 6.29, a single mutex is used. As this is not scalable, we could use an approach similar to the one used in the Global Arrays library earlier in this chapter—one mutex per process. This allows multiple processes to access the list at the same time, as long as they are accessing parts of the list that are on different processes. Care must be taken to avoid a deadly embrace if this approach is used, since it may be necessary to acquire several locks. Note that because we are using `MPE_Mutex_lock` to ensure exclusive access to the memory window, we can use the assert value `MPI_MODE_NOCHECK` in the call to `MPI_Win_lock`.

There are some important differences between the RMA versions as well. In the static (unchanging) list version of `FindElm` (Figure 6.24), the `MPI_Win_lock` and `MPI_Win_unlock` calls surround only the `MPI_Get` call (in order to provide an access epoch and to complete the `MPI_Get` call). In the dynamic list case shown in Figure 6.27, the lock *must* surround both remote and local accesses to the memory, because in the case where a remote process updates the local window, the update may not become visible to the local process until it begins an access epoch. In the static case, there were no updates, and hence no local access epochs were necessary.

The code for inserting an element, shown in Figures 6.28 and 6.29, has more differences with its shared-memory counterpart than `FindElm` does. Most important, the RMA version of `InsertElm` reads an entire element and saves the previous element (in `local_copy_last`), with `RemotePointer last_ptr` the RMA pointer to the previous element. When an element is inserted, we replace the entire list element, not just the `RemotePointer next` field in it. This is done to keep the example code simple. Note that by using a displacement unit of `sizeof(ListElm)`, we simplify the displacement calculations but lose the flexibility in making updates to specific parts of a `ListElm`.

6.10 Compiler Optimization and Passive Targets

In Section 5.7.5 we discussed the danger that a value updated in memory may be ignored because the compiler is using a copy placed in a register. The same issues apply to passive target synchronization. Fortran programmers should consider either using a `volatile` statement, where available, or passing the local memory window to a dummy or near-dummy routine (e.g., an `MPE_Win_lock` that takes the local window, as well as the window object, as an argument). However, C and C++ programmers don't need to use `volatile`, at least when the lock type is `MPI_LOCK_-EXCLUSIVE`, since accesses to the local window still require using `MPI_Win_lock` and `MPI_Win_unlock`.

```
#include "Dlist.h"
extern char *DupString( const char * );
extern MPI_Win winlock;

char *FindElm( MPI_Win win, const char *key )
{
    ListElm        local_copy, *local_copy_ptr;
    char           *local_value = 0;
    RemotePointer  ptr;
    int            my_rank;
    MPI_Group      win_group;

    /* my_rank could also be precomputed, of course */
    MPI_Win_get_group( win, &win_group );
    MPI_Group_rank( win_group, &my_rank );
    MPI_Group_free( &win_group );

    MPE_Mutex_lock( 0, winlock );
    ptr = head;

    while (ptr.owner_rank >= 0) {
        /* Make sure we have the data */
        MPI_Win_lock( MPI_LOCK_SHARED, ptr.owner_rank,
                    MPI_MODE_NOCHECK, win );
        if (ptr.owner_rank != my_rank) {
            MPI_Get( &local_copy, 1, ListElm_type,
                    ptr.owner_rank, ptr.disp, 1, ListElm_type, win );
            local_copy_ptr = &local_copy;
        }
        else
            local_copy_ptr = (ListElm *)(ptr.local_pointer);
        MPI_Win_unlock( ptr.owner_rank, win );

        if (strcmp( local_copy_ptr->key, key ) == 0) {
            local_value = DupString( local_copy_ptr->value );
            break;
        }
        ptr = local_copy_ptr->next;
    }
    MPE_Mutex_unlock( 0, winlock );
    return local_value;
}
```

Figure 6.27
An RMA routine to find an element in a list that may be modified by other processes

```
#include "Dlist.h"
ListElm *avail;
extern MPI_Win winlock;

void InsertElm( MPI_Win win, const char *key, const char *value )
{
    ListElm       local_copy, local_copy_last, *new_local_ptr;
    MPI_Aint      new_local_ptr_disp;
    RemotePointer last_ptr, ptr;
    int           compare, my_rank;
    MPI_Group     win_group;

  /* my_rank could also be precomputed, of course */
    MPI_Win_get_group( win, &win_group );
    MPI_Group_rank( win_group, &my_rank );
    MPI_Group_free( &win_group );

    /* Lock list, find insertion point, and insert element */
    MPE_Mutex_lock( 0, winlock );

    ptr = head;
    while (ptr.owner_rank >= 0) {
        /* This code could use local_pointer as FindElm does, but this
           shorter version is used to reduce the size of the example */
        MPI_Win_lock( MPI_LOCK_SHARED, ptr.owner_rank,
                      MPI_MODE_NOCHECK, win );
        MPI_Get( &local_copy, 1, ListElm_type,
                 ptr.owner_rank, ptr.disp, 1,
                 ListElm_type, win );
        MPI_Win_unlock( ptr.owner_rank, win );

        compare = strcmp( local_copy.key, key );
        if (compare == 0) {   /* duplicate entry.  Do nothing */
            MPE_Mutex_unlock( 0, winlock ); return; }
        if (compare > 0) {
            break;
        }
        /* Save entire list element that "last_ptr" points to */
        local_copy_last    = local_copy;
        last_ptr           = ptr;
        ptr                = local_copy.next;
    }
```

Figure 6.28
An RMA routine to insert an element in a list that may be modified by other processes: code to find the insert location

```
/* Create new element.  The new element must be allocated from
   the local memory window.  Note that each process has its own
    list of available list elements */
if (! (new_local_ptr = avail) ) MPI_Abort( MPI_COMM_WORLD, 1 );
avail = (ListElm *)avail->next.local_pointer;
strcpy( new_local_ptr->key, key );
strcpy( new_local_ptr->value, value );

new_local_ptr_disp  = new_local_ptr->next.disp;
new_local_ptr->next = local_copy_last.next;
/* Set the remote pointer field of the previous entry to point to
   the new entry */
local_copy_last.next.owner_rank    = my_rank;
local_copy_last.next.disp          = new_local_ptr_disp;
local_copy_last.next.local_pointer =
        (my_rank == last_ptr.owner_rank) ? new_local_ptr : 0;

MPI_Win_lock( MPI_LOCK_SHARED, last_ptr.owner_rank,
            MPI_MODE_NOCHECK, win );
MPI_Put( &local_copy_last, 1, ListElm_type,
        last_ptr.owner_rank, last_ptr.disp, 1, ListElm_type, win );
MPI_Win_unlock( ptr.owner_rank, win );

MPE_Mutex_unlock( 0, winlock );
}
```

Figure 6.29
An RMA routine to insert an element in a list that may be modified by other processes: code to
insert the element into the proper location

6.11 Scalable Synchronization

A third approach may be used to synchronize MPI RMA operations. This approach
is a more scalable version of `MPI_Win_fence`. Like `MPI_Win_fence`, it is an active
target synchronization method. Unlike `MPI_Win_fence`, however, the approach is
not collective over the group of the window object. Instead, these routines are
called only for the processes that are origins, targets, or both for RMA operations.

From the grid ghost-point exchange used in Chapter 5 to introduce the RMA
operations, it should be clear that collective synchronization is stronger than necessary. A process can continue past the ghost-point exchange once two things
have happened: the RMA operations to the neighbors (that is, with the neighbors
as targets) have completed, and any RMA operations targeting this process have
also completed. The third MPI synchronization approach allows us to express this

---

int **MPI_Win_start**(MPI_Group to_group, int assert, MPI_Win win)

int **MPI_Win_complete**(MPI_Win win)

int **MPI_Win_post**(MPI_Group from_group, int assert, MPI_Win win)

int **MPI_Win_wait**(MPI_Win win)

Table 6.16
C routines for scalable active target synchronization

degree of synchronization.

6.11.1 Exposure Epochs

To understand this approach, we first introduce the concept of an *exposure epoch*. This is the period of time when a local window may be the target of RMA operations. In other words, it is the time when the local window is exposed to changes made by other processes. This is the counterpart to the access epoch first mentioned in Section 6.2. The routine `MPI_Win_post` begins an exposure epoch and `MPI_Win_wait` ends an exposure epoch for the local window. These calls take as an argument the window object whose local window is being exposed. In addition, `MPI_Win_post` takes an MPI group as an argument. This is the group of processes that will be making RMA operations with this local window as the target. We emphasize this in the argument list by using the name `from_group` for this group: it is the group from which RMA calls will be coming.

An access epoch is simply the period of time when a process is making RMA calls on a window object. Most of this chapter has discussed the use of `MPI_Win_lock` and `MPI_Win_unlock` to establish an access epoch for passive target synchronization. For active target synchronization, an access epoch is started with `MPI_Win_start` and completed with `MPI_Win_complete`. Just like `MPI_Win_post`, `MPI_Win_start` takes an MPI group as an argument; this group indicates the processes that will be targets of RMA calls made by this process. We emphasize this by using the name `to_group` in the argument list: it is the group to which RMA calls are being made. The bindings for all four routines are shown in Tables 6.16, 6.17, and 6.18.

6.11.2 The Ghost-Point Exchange Revisited

We can rewrite the ghost-point exchange code from Section 5.6.1 by replacing the `MPI_Win_fence` calls that surround the RMA operations with combinations of `MPI_Win_start`, `MPI_Win_post`, `MPI_Win_wait`, and `MPI_Win_complete`. There

MPI_WIN_START(to_group, assert, win, ierror)
          integer to_group, assert, win, ierror

MPI_WIN_COMPLETE(win, ierror)
          integer win, ierror

MPI_WIN_POST(from_group, assert, win, ierror)
          integer from_group, assert, win, ierror

MPI_WIN_WAIT(win, ierror)
          integer win, ierror

Table 6.17
Fortran routines for scalable active target synchronization

void MPI::Win::Start(const MPI::Group& to_group, int assert) const

void MPI::Win::Complete(void) const

void MPI::Win::Post(const MPI::Group& from_group, int assert) const

void MPI::Win::Wait(void) const

Table 6.18
C++ routines for scalable active target synchronization

are two parts to this. First, we must construct the groups for the `MPI_Win_start` and `MPI_Win_post` calls. In the code in Figure 5.10, the targets (neighbors) for the `MPI_Put` operations are `top_nbr` and `bottom_nbr`.

The code to create the group is simply

```
MPI_Win_get_group( win, &group );
ranks[0] = bottom_nbr;
ranks[1] = top_nbr;
MPI_Group_incl( group, 2, ranks, &nbr_group );
MPI_Group_free( &group );
```

(This code ignores the possibility that either `bottom_nbr` or `top_nbr` is `MPI_PROC_-NULL`; in that case, the size of the group `nbr_group` must be reduced.) Because the ghost points are exchanged, this group is also the group of processes that are the origin processes for `MPI_Put` calls that target this process. Thus, the `to_group` of `MPI_Win_start` and the `from_group` of `MPI_Win_post` are the same in this case.

Second, we replace the `MPI_Win_fence` that precedes the RMA operations in Figure 5.10 with

```
MPI_Win_post( nbr_group, 0, win );
MPI_Win_start( nbr_group, 0, win );
```

and we replace the `MPI_Win_fence` that follows the RMA operations with

```
MPI_Win_complete( win );
MPI_Win_wait( win );
```

6.11.3 Performance Optimizations for Scalable Synchronization

The two calls that are used to initiate scalable synchronization for RMA (`MPI_-Win_start` and `MPI_Win_post`) take an `assert` argument. This assert value can be used by an MPI implementation to provide improved performance in the same way that the `assert` argument to `MPI_Win_fence` can be used (see Section 5.8.2).

Three `assert` values may be used with `MPI_Win_post`. Recall that `MPI_Win_-post` begins an exposure epoch for the local window; thus, assert values that tell the implementation about changes to the local window before or after the `MPI_-Win_post` call may be helpful. The three assert values are the following:

`MPI_MODE_NOSTORE:` The local window was not updated by local stores (or local get or receive calls) since the last call to `MPI_Win_complete`.

`MPI_MODE_NOPUT:` The local window will not be updated by put or accumulate calls between this `MPI_Win_post` call and the matching `MPI_Win_complete` call.

`MPI_MODE_NOCHECK:` The matching `MPI_Win_start` calls have not been issued by any process that is an origin of RMA operations that have this process as the target. In addition, those `MPI_Win_start` calls *must* also specify `MPI_MODE_NOCHECK` as their `assert` value.

The only `assert` value defined for `MPI_Win_start` is `MPI_MODE_NOCHECK`, which can be used only when the matching `MPI_Win_post` calls on the target processes have already been called and have specified `MPI_MODE_NOCHECK` as part of their `assert` argument.

Unlike the `MPI_Win_fence` case, these assert values are less likely to be useful. For example, many programs will perform stores to the local window before beginning an exposure epoch with `MPI_Win_post` (eliminating `MPI_MODE_NOSTORE` as a valid assert value). Using `MPI_Get` instead of `MPI_Put` or `MPI_Accumulate` by the origin processes would allow `MPI_MODE_NOPUT` to be used as an `assert` value, but that is not a good reason to prefer `MPI_Get` over `MPI_Put`. The assert value `MPI_MODE_-NOCHECK` requires some outside synchronization to ensure that the conditions for its use are met; these are similar to those needed for a ready-send (such as `MPI_Rsend`).

The info key `no_locks` may be used with a `MPI_Win_create` call if `MPI_Win_-lock` and `MPI_Win_unlock` are never used with the created window object. Just as for programs that use `MPI_Win_fence` to complete RMA operations, this can be an important optimization.

6.12   Summary

This chapter has covered two major topics: passive target RMA and scalable synchronization. The majority of the chapter has focused on passive target RMA: remote access without active cooperation by the target process. This provides a true one-sided operation, compared with the active target RMA introduced in Chapter 5 that relies on all processes, both origin and target, calling `MPI_Win_fence`. The passive target synchronization, using `MPI_Win_lock` and `MPI_Win_unlock` to define an access epoch, is designed to allow the widest portability and performance by an MPI implementation.

However, the looseness of the synchronization (the nonblocking lock) makes other operations more awkward, particularly read-modify-write operations. We showed how to implement one of the most basic read-modify-write operations, a fetch-and-add, in several ways, including one that is relatively simple and another that is scalable but more complex. With a fetch-and-add, many important distributed data structures, such as queues, stacks, and lists, can be implemented. We used our implementation of fetch-and-add in two examples: a distributed array library and a distributed list. The distributed list example also allowed us to compare a shared-memory implementation with MPI RMA; this example will help users who wish to port an application to a distributed-memory system using MPI.

The third form of RMA synchronization defined by the MPI Standard is another form of active target synchronization, but one that identifies the target and origin processes for any RMA operation. This allows an MPI implementation to provide a synchronization mechanism that is as scalable as the application. We illustrated this by revisiting the ghost-point-exchange example introduced in Chapter 5, replacing calls to `MPI_Win_fence` with the scalable synchronization routines `MPI_Win_post`, `MPI_Win_start`, `MPI_Win_complete`, and `MPI_Win_wait`.

7 Dynamic Process Management

In this chapter we describe the MPI approach to the creation of new MPI processes *by* MPI processes. We also describe how separately started MPI applications can establish contact and exchange MPI messages with one another.

7.1 Introduction

The MPI-1 Standard does not say anything about how processes are started. Process startup takes place outside an MPI program, and an MPI process calls `MPI_Comm_size` to find out how many processes were started and calls `MPI_Comm_rank` to find out which one it is. The number of processes is thus fixed no later than when `MPI_Init` returns.

MPI users asked that the MPI Forum revisit this issue for several reasons. The first was that workstation-network users migrating from PVM [24] to MPI were accustomed to using PVM's capabilities for process management. A second reason was that important classes of message-passing applications, such as client-server systems and task-farming jobs, require dynamic process control. A third reason was that with such extensions, it might be possible to write parts of the parallel-computing environment in MPI itself.

This chapter begins by discussing the MPI approach to creating new processes, continuing the discussion of `MPI_Comm_spawn`, begun in Section 2.4, with a new example. We also review communication between groups in an *intercommunicator*, both point to point (defined in MPI-1 but rarely used) and collective (new in MPI-2). Section 7.3 discusses how to connect two MPI programs, using the example of a computational program and a visualization program. The chapter concludes by discussing some of the reasons for the particular design of the MPI dynamic process routines.

7.2 Creating New MPI Processes

The basics of `MPI_Comm_spawn` were introduced in Section 2.4, where we used the parallel copy example to illustrate how to spawn processes from an MPI program. Recall that `MPI_Comm_spawn` creates an intercommunicator containing as its two groups the spawning processes and the spawned processes. In this section we explore `MPI_Comm_spawn` in more detail by revisiting the matrix-vector multiplication program from Chapter 3 of *Using MPI* [32]. This program was presented there as an example of the "master-slave" paradigm. We will adapt it to use a variable

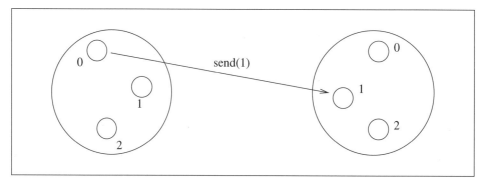

Figure 7.1
Message passing with an intercommunicator

number of slaves, which are not started until after the master decides how many slave processes there should be.

7.2.1 Intercommunicators

Before we plunge into this example, it might be a good idea to review the concept of MPI *intercommunicators*. Intercommunicators are a relatively obscure part of MPI-1, but play a more prominent role in MPI-2, where they turn out to be just what is needed to express some of the new ideas. This is particularly true in the area of dynamic process management. A "normal" MPI communicator is, strictly speaking, an *intracommunicator*. It consists of a context and a group of processes. The distinguishing feature of an *intercommunicator* is that it has associated with it *two* groups of processes, referred to (from the point of view of a specific process) as the *local* group (the group containing the process) and the *remote* group. Processes are identified by rank in group, as usual, but a message sent to a process with a particular rank using an intercommunicator always goes to the process with that rank in the *remote* group. Figure 7.1 shows a message sent from process 0 (in its local group) to process 1. Since it is sent in an intercommunicator, it goes to the process with rank 1 in the remote group. This behavior of point-to-point operations is specified in MPI-1. MPI-1 does not specify the behavior of collective operations on intercommunicators, but MPI-2 does. As in the point-to-point case, communications take place between the two groups. Indeed, we will see an example of an intercommunicator collective operation in our matrix-vector multiplication example.

7.2.2 Matrix-Vector Multiplication Example

Our matrix-vector multiplication example uses the same algorithm employed in Chapter 3 of *Using MPI* [32]. Instead of having all processes started outside the program, however, we will start only the master process and have it start the slaves with `MPI_Comm_spawn`. This means that the most obvious difference between this version and the MPI-1 version is that the master and the slaves are each separate main programs.[1] First let us consider the beginning of the code for the master process, shown in Figure 7.2.

We expect to start this program with

```
mpiexec -n 1 master
```

The program multiplies the matrix `a` by the vector `b` and stores the result in `c`. The parallelism comes from performing the dot products of the rows of `a` with `b` in parallel. We assume that there are more rows of `a` than there are processes, so that each process will do many dot products. For this example, we do *not* assume that all processes execute at the same speed; hence we adopt a *self-scheduling* algorithm for load-balancing purposes. The master process sends rows, one by one, to the slave processes, and when a slave finishes with a row, it sends the result (the dot product) back to the master. If more rows remain to be done, the master sends a row to the slave that just completed a row. From the master's point of view, work is handed out to whichever slave has become idle. From the slave's point of view, it receives a job, works on that job, and sends the result back to the master, simultaneously requesting a new task. The master itself does not compute any dot products. In this way all the slaves are kept busy, even if they work at different speeds.

This algorithm is not a particularly good way to parallelize matrix-vector multiplication, but it demonstrates self-scheduling algorithms well. The algorithm is the same one used in *Using MPI*, but here we do not determine the number of slaves until after the master has started, in order to illustrate both `MPI_Comm_spawn` and the use of `MPI_Bcast` on an intercommunicator, both of which are new in MPI-2. The first part of the master program is shown in Figure 7.2. The only variables new for this version are the intercommunicator `slavecomm`, which will be constructed by `MPI_Comm_spawn`, and the variable `numslaves`, which holds the number of slaves.

In general, a program of this type would do some sort of calculation to determine how many slaves to spawn. As we will see in Section 7.2.5, it can also obtain advice

---

[1] The MPI-1 Standard supports the multiple-instruction multiple-data (MIMD) model as well, but MPI-1 programs are often written using the single-program multiple-data (SPMD) model.

```fortran
! Matrix-vector multiply, with spawning of slaves
PROGRAM main
      use mpi
      integer MAX_ROWS, MAX_COLS
      parameter (MAX_ROWS = 1000, MAX_COLS = 1000)
      double precision a(MAX_ROWS,MAX_COLS), b(MAX_COLS), c(MAX_ROWS)
      double precision buffer(MAX_COLS), ans
      integer slavecomm

      integer ierr, status(MPI_STATUS_SIZE)
      integer i, j, numsent, sender, numslaves
      integer anstype, rows, cols

      call MPI_INIT(ierr)
!     master decides how many slaves to spawn, say 10
      numslaves = 10
      call MPI_COMM_SPAWN('slave', MPI_ARGV_NULL, numslaves, &
                  MPI_INFO_NULL, 0, MPI_COMM_WORLD, &
                  slavecomm, MPI_ERRCODES_IGNORE, ierr)
!     master initializes and then dispatches
      rows   = 100
      cols   = 100
!     initialize a and b
      do 20 j = 1,cols
         b(j) = 1
         do 10 i = 1,rows
            a(i,j) = i
10       continue
20    continue
      numsent = 0
!     send b to each slave
      call MPI_BCAST(b, cols, MPI_DOUBLE_PRECISION, MPI_ROOT, &
                  slavecomm, ierr)
```

Figure 7.2
First part of master for matrix-vector multiplication

from the system on how many slaves it can spawn. To simplify this example, we assume that the master somehow decides to create ten slaves, and so we simply set `numslaves` equal to 10. The call that creates the slaves and the corresponding intercommunicator is

```
call MPI_COMM_SPAWN('slave', MPI_ARGV_NULL, numslaves, &
            MPI_INFO_NULL, 0, MPI_COMM_WORLD, &
            slavecomm, MPI_ERRCODES_IGNORE, ierr)
```

(The Fortran version of) MPI_Comm_spawn has nine arguments. The first is the executable file to be run by the new processes. The second argument is an array of strings to represent the "command line" arguments to the executable. Here, since we are not passing the slaves any command-line arguments, we use the predefined constant MPI_ARGV_NULL. The third argument is the number of slaves to start. Extra information (such as what machines to start the slave processes on), and perhaps even site-specific hints to the job scheduler, can be given in the fourth argument, the info argument. Here, we just pass the predefined constant MPI_INFO_NULL and defer to Section 7.2.5 a fuller discussion of its use with MPI_Comm_spawn. The call to MPI_Comm_spawn is collective (over the communicator specified in the sixth argument), and the first four arguments need not be presented at all of the processes (although they must, of course, be syntactically correct), but will be interpreted only at the "root" process, specified in the fifth argument. Here we specify 0, since there is only one master process. The sixth argument is the communicator over which this call is collective, here MPI_COMM_WORLD.[2]

Next come the output arguments. The seventh argument, here slavecomm, will be set to be the intercommunicator containing both the master (in the local group) and the slaves (in the remote group). The next argument is an array of error codes, one for each new process to be created, but we can (and here do) pass the special constant MPI_ERRCODES_IGNORE instead, to indicate that we are not going to check the individual error codes. The overall error code (the last argument in Fortran or the function value returned in C) can be checked to see whether MPI_Comm_spawn was successful as a whole or not. If it is MPI_SUCCESS, then all processes were successfully created, and all potential communication, both with and among the new processes, is enabled.

The bindings for MPI_Comm_spawn and MPI_Comm_get_parent are shown in Tables 7.1, 7.2, and 7.3. Note that, in the C++ bindings, there are two versions of MPI::Intracomm::Spawn, one with the array_of_errcodes last argument and one

---

[2]Since there is only one process, we could also have used MPI_COMM_SELF.

```
int MPI_Comm_spawn(char *command, char *argv[], int maxprocs,
           MPI_Info info, int root, MPI_Comm comm,
           MPI_Comm *intercomm, int array_of_errcodes[])

int MPI_Comm_get_parent(MPI_Comm *parent)
```

Table 7.1
C bindings for process creation

```
MPI_COMM_SPAWN(command, argv, maxprocs, info, root, comm, intercomm,
           array_of_errcodes, ierror)
           character*(*) command, argv(*)
           integer info, maxprocs, root, comm, intercomm,
               array_of_errcodes(*), ierror

MPI_COMM_GET_PARENT(parent, ierror)
           integer parent, ierror
```

Table 7.2
Fortran bindings for process creation

without. The one without this argument corresponds to calling `MPI_Comm_spawn` with `MPI_ERRCODES_IGNORE` as the last argument in C.

7.2.3 Intercommunicator Collective Operations

Next the master initializes the matrix `a` and the vector `b` and uses the collective operation `MPI_Bcast` to send `b` to the slaves. In MPI-1, collective operations were not defined for intercommunicators such as `slavecomm`, but MPI-2 defines the behavior of collective operations on intercommunicators. For `MPI_Bcast`, the broadcast occurs from the root in the *local* group to all the processes in the *remote* group, which in this case are the slaves. Because there are two groups, the root process indicates itself by using the special value `MPI_ROOT`. The processes receiving the broadcast specify the rank of the root in the other group, just as they would if there were a single group. (Here, where the local group has only one member, the effect is not different from the case in which all processes are in the same (intra)communicator, but in general an intercommunicator `MPI_Bcast` is quite different from an intracommunicator `MPI_Bcast`.) If there is more than one process in the group that contains the root, those processes specify `MPI_PROC_NULL` as the root value. This is illustrated in Figure 7.3.

Note that (at this point) we don't have an intracommunicator containing the mas-

> **MPI::Intercomm MPI::Intracomm::Spawn**(const char* command,
>   const char* argv[], int maxprocs, const MPI::Info& info, int root,
>   int array_of_errcodes[]) const
>
> **MPI::Intercomm MPI::Intracomm::Spawn**(const char* command,
>   const char* argv[], int maxprocs, const MPI::Info& info,
>   int root) const
>
> **MPI::Intercomm MPI::Comm::Get_parent**()

Table 7.3
C++ bindings for process creation

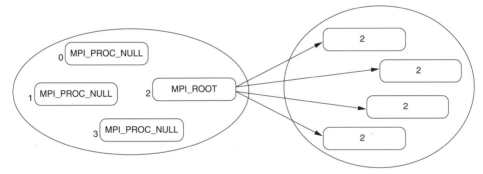

Figure 7.3
Intercommunicator broadcast. The argument used as the `root` field is given inside the box
representing each process. In this example, process 2 in the group on the left is broadcasting to
every process in the group on the right.

ter and the slaves; we could create one with the MPI-1 function `MPI_Intercomm_-`
`merge` as we did in Section 2.4.2, but it will not be necessary in this example.

7.2.4 Intercommunicator Point-to-Point Communication

The rest of the master code is shown in Figure 7.4. It is very similar to the nonspawn
version of the code (Figure 3.7 in *Using MPI* [32]). The major difference is that
the ranks of the slaves go from 0 to `numslaves-1`, since the master is addressing
them, not in `MPI_COMM_WORLD`, but in the remote group of the intercommunicator
`slavecomm`. The master sends all the slaves a row to work with, receives answers
from the slaves, and then sends out new rows until all rows are done. Then it sends
a message with tag 0 to each slave to tell it that the computation is over. Finally,
the master prints the vector `c`, which is the product of `a` and `b`.

```
!      send a row to each slave; tag with row number
       do 40 i = 1,min(numslaves,rows)
          do 30 j = 1,cols
             buffer(j) = a(i,j)
 30       continue
          call MPI_SEND(buffer, cols, MPI_DOUBLE_PRECISION, i-1, &
                        i, slavecomm, ierr)
          numsent = numsent+1
 40    continue
       do 70 i = 1,rows
          call MPI_RECV(ans, 1, MPI_DOUBLE_PRECISION, &
                        MPI_ANY_SOURCE, MPI_ANY_TAG, &
                        slavecomm, status, ierr)
          sender     = status(MPI_SOURCE)
          anstype    = status(MPI_TAG)               ! row is tag value
          c(anstype) = ans
          if (numsent .lt. rows) then                ! send another row
             do 50 j = 1,cols
                buffer(j) = a(numsent+1,j)
 50          continue
             call MPI_SEND(buffer, cols, MPI_DOUBLE_PRECISION, &
                           sender, numsent+1, slavecomm, ierr)
             numsent = numsent+1
          else
             call MPI_SEND(buffer, 0, MPI_DOUBLE_PRECISION, sender, &
                           0, slavecomm, ierr)
          endif
 70    continue

!      print the answer
       do 80 i = 1,rows
          print *, "c(", i, ") = ", c(i)
 80    continue
       call MPI_COMM_FREE(slavecomm, ierr)
       call MPI_FINALIZE(ierr)
END PROGRAM main
```

Figure 7.4
Second part of master for matrix-vector multiply

```fortran
! slave program for matrix-vector multiplication
PROGRAM main
      use mpi
      integer MAX_COLS
      parameter (MAX_COLS = 1000)
      double precision b(MAX_COLS)
      double precision buffer(MAX_COLS), ans

      integer i, ierr, status(MPI_STATUS_SIZE)
      integer row, cols, rows, rank
      integer parentcomm

      call MPI_INIT(ierr)
      call MPI_COMM_GET_PARENT(parentcomm, ierr)
!     the master is now rank 0 in the remote group of the
!     parent intercommunicator.
!     slaves receive b, then compute dot products until
!     done message received
      rows = 100
      cols = 100
      call MPI_BCAST(b, cols, MPI_DOUBLE_PRECISION, 0, &
                     parentcomm, ierr)
      call MPI_COMM_RANK(MPI_COMM_WORLD, rank, ierr)
      if (rank .ge. rows) go to 200    ! skip if more processes than work
 90   call MPI_RECV(buffer, cols, MPI_DOUBLE_PRECISION, 0, &
                    MPI_ANY_TAG, parentcomm, status, ierr)
      if (status(MPI_TAG) .eq. 0) then
         go to 200
      else
         row = status(MPI_TAG)
         ans = 0.0
         do 100 i = 1,cols
            ans = ans+buffer(i)*b(i)
 100     continue
         call MPI_SEND(ans, 1, MPI_DOUBLE_PRECISION, 0, row, &
                       parentcomm, ierr)
         go to 90
      endif
 200  continue
      call MPI_COMM_FREE(parentcomm, ierr)
      call MPI_FINALIZE(ierr)
END PROGRAM main
```

Figure 7.5
Slave part of matrix-vector multiply

The code for the slaves is shown in Figure 7.5. It is very similar to the slave part of the original version (Figure 3.8 in *Using MPI* [32]). The new feature here is that after `MPI_Init`, the slaves can communicate with one another, through their `MPI_COMM_WORLD`, which contains all processes spawned with the same `MPI_Comm_spawn` call, but not with the master. In this example, the slave processes do not communicate with each other; they need communicate only with the master. To obtain a communicator containing the master, the slaves do

```
call MPI_COMM_GET_PARENT(parentcomm, ierr)
```

This returns in `parentcomm` the intercommunicator created by the collective call to `MPI_Comm_spawn` in the master and `MPI_Init` in the slaves. The local group of this communicator (from the slaves' point of view) is the same as the group of their `MPI_COMM_WORLD`. The remote group is the set of processes that collectively called `MPI_Comm_spawn`, which in this case consists of just the master. The slaves address the master as rank 0 in `parentcomm` during the exchange of rows and dot products. When the slaves get the "all done" message (`tag=0`), they call `MPI_Finalize` and exit.

7.2.5   Finding the Number of Available Processes

The MPI Forum spent some time and effort debating whether it was possible to incorporate into the MPI Standard an interface to a job scheduler. It turned out that the variety of schedulers and their interfaces, coupled with the great variety in the types of requests that users wanted to make of their resource managers, made this too difficult. Therefore, MPI's dynamic process management defers to some other possible library any interaction with the scheduler. The one feature remaining from this discussion that did enter the Standard (although only as an optional feature) is `MPI_UNIVERSE_SIZE`, an attribute of `MPI_COMM_WORLD`. The term "optional" here means that an MPI implementation need not provide a value for the attribute; but if such a value is provided, it works as follows. `MPI_UNIVERSE_SIZE` provides to the MPI application information on how many processes can usefully be run. The application can then use this information to determine how many "additional" processes can usefully be spawned. The value of `MPI_UNIVERSE_SIZE`, even if provided, is not a hard limit; rather, it is a "best guess" by the implementation of how many processes could exist.

The implementation is free to determine the value of the attribute `MPI_UNIVERSE_SIZE` however it wishes. It could come from an environment variable set either by the user or by the system. It could come from runtime interaction with a job scheduler, or it could be set by the process manager. One logical approach is to have `MPI_UNIVERSE_SIZE` set by `mpiexec`. That is, in an environment with both a scheduler and a process manager,[3]

```
mpiexec -n 1 -universe_size 10 matvec-master
```

could perform three functions:

- request 10 "slots" from the job scheduler,
- request from the process manager that 1 process running `matvec_master` be started, and
- arrange for the value of `MPI_UNIVERSE_SIZE` to be set to 10.

Then the `matvec_master` program would know that 9 more processes could be started without requiring additional interaction with the scheduler.

Now let us consider the use of `MPI_UNIVERSE_SIZE` with `MPI_Comm_spawn`. The beginning of `matvec_master` modified to use `MPI_UNIVERSE_SIZE` is shown in Figure 7.6. Features of the program not in our earlier `MPI_Comm_spawn` examples are the following:

- It uses `MPI_UNIVERSE_SIZE` to decide how many processes to spawn.
- It checks the error codes from the attempts to spawn processes.

Let us step through this program. We call `MPI_Comm_get_attr` to see whether the attribute `MPI_UNIVERSE_SIZE` has been set. If it has, we spawn as many processes as the value of `MPI_UNIVERSE_SIZE` tells us are available. Since the master process counts as one process, we spawn one less than the value of the attribute itself. On the other hand, if there is no such attribute (`universe_size_flag = 0`), then we take a more conservative approach. We create an `MPI_Info` object and use it to describe a "soft" request for any number of processes between one and ten. (See Section 2.5 for details on `MPI_Info`.) Here we use the predefined info key `soft` and specify a range of numbers of processes using the same form as for the `-soft` argument to `mpiexec`. We also pass an array of error codes to be filled in, and check for success.

Recall that `MPI_Comm_spawn` returns an intercommunicator (`slavecomm` in this case) in which the remote group consists of the newly spawned processes. We use `MPI_Comm_remote_size` to find out the size of this group, which is the number of slaves.

---

[3]The argument `-universe_size` is not a standard argument for `mpiexec`; it is shown here as an example that some implementations may provide. Other possibilities for specifying the value of `MPI_UNIVERSE_SIZE` include an environment variable or configuration parameter.

```
      integer softinfo
      integer (kind=MPI_ADDRESS_KIND) universe_size
      logical universe_size_flag
      integer numslaves, i, errcodes(10)

      call MPI_COMM_GET_ATTR(MPI_COMM_WORLD, MPI_UNIVERSE_SIZE, &
                  universe_size, universe_size_flag, ierr)
      if (universe_size_flag) then
          call MPI_COMM_SPAWN('slave', MPI_ARGV_NULL, universe_size-1,&
                      MPI_INFO_NULL, 0, MPI_COMM_WORLD, &
                      slavecomm, errcodes, ierr)
      else
          call MPI_INFO_CREATE(softinfo, ierr)
          call MPI_INFO_SET(softinfo, 'soft', '1:10', ierr)
          call MPI_COMM_SPAWN('slave', MPI_ARGV_NULL, 10, &
                      softinfo, 0, MPI_COMM_WORLD, &
                      slavecomm, errcodes, ierr)
          call MPI_INFO_FREE(softinfo, ierr)
      endif
      call MPI_COMM_REMOTE_SIZE(slavecomm, numslaves, ierr)
      do i=1, 10
          if (errcodes(i) .ne. MPI_SUCCESS) then
              print *, 'slave ', i, ' did not start'
          endif
      enddo
      print *, 'number of slaves = ', numslaves
```

Figure 7.6
Modification of the master part of the matrix-vector program to use MPI_UNIVERSE_SIZE to specify the number of available processes

In C and C++, the value returned by `MPI_Comm_get_attr` is a pointer to an integer containing the value, rather than the value itself. This is the same as for the other predefined attributes such as `MPI_TAB_UB`. The code for accessing the value of `MPI_UNIVERSE_SIZE` from C follows:

```
int *universe_size_ptr, universe_size_flag;
...
MPI_Comm_get_attr( MPI_COMM_WORLD, MPI_UNIVERSE_SIZE,
                  &universe_size_ptr, &universe_size_flag );
if (universe_size_flag) {
    printf( "Number of processes available is %d\n",
```

```
char            *slave_argv[2];
...
slave_argv[0] = argv[3];
slave_argv[1] = NULL;
MPI_Comm_spawn( "pcp_slave", slave_argv, num_hosts, hostinfo,
                0, MPI_COMM_SELF, &pcpslaves,
                MPI_ERRCODES_IGNORE );
```

Figure 7.7
Passing command-line arguments to spawned processes

```
                *universe_size_ptr );
}
```

7.2.6 Passing Command-Line Arguments to Spawned Programs

In our examples so far, we have used `MPI_ARGV_NULL` to indicated that the spawned programs are called with no command-line arguments. It is often helpful to pass command-line parameters to the spawned programs. For example, in the parallel copy example in Section 2.4.2, instead of using `MPI_Bcast` to send the name of the output file to each slave, we could have started the processes with a single command-line argument containing the name of the output file. The change to the master program (Figure 2.16) is shown in Figure 7.7.

The `argv` argument to `MPI_Comm_spawn` is different from the `argv` parameter in a C/C++ `main` in two ways: it does not contain the name of the program (the value of `argv[0]` in `main`), and it is null terminated (rather than using an `argc` parameter containing the argument count, as `main` does). In Fortran, the code is similar. An array of **character** is used; an entirely blank string indicates the end of the list.

What if we would like to pass separate command-line arguments to each of the new processes? MPI offers a separate function, `MPI_Comm_spawn_multiple`, for this purpose as well as for starting processes that use different executable files. The bindings are shown in Tables 7.4, 7.5, and 7.6. Basically, the first four arguments specifying the command name, argument vector, number of processes, and info have become arrays of size `count`, which is the first argument.

7.3 Connecting MPI Processes

Some applications are naturally constructed from several separate programs. One example used in *Using MPI* [32] and in the MPI Standard is that of a climate

```
int MPI_Comm_spawn_multiple(int count, char *array_of_commands[],
            char **array_of_argv[], int array_of_maxprocs[],
            MPI_Info array_of_info[], int root, MPI_Comm comm,
            MPI_Comm *intercomm, int array_of_errcodes[])
```

Table 7.4
Spawning multiple executables in C

```
MPI_COMM_SPAWN_MULTIPLE(count, array_of_commands, array_of_argv,
            array_of_maxprocs, array_of_info, root, comm, intercomm,
            array_of_errcodes, ierror)
                integer count, array_of_info(*), array_of_maxprocs(*), root,
                    comm, intercomm, array_of_errcodes(*), ierror
                character*(*) array_of_commands(*), array_of_argv(count, *)
```

Table 7.5
Spawning multiple executables in Fortran

```
MPI::Intercomm MPI::Intracomm::Spawn_multiple(int count,
            const char* array_of_commands[], const char** array_of_argv[],
            const int array_of_maxprocs[], const MPI::Info array_of_info[],
            int root, int array_of_errcodes[])
```

Table 7.6
Spawning multiple executables in C++

simulation constructed from two programs: a simulation of the ocean and a simulation of the atmosphere. In fact, this example was used in *Using MPI* to discuss intercommunicators. Another popular example is one that connects a visualization program to a simulation program. We will consider this example below.

One advantage of the approach in this section is that the choice of visualization program can be made at run time; this is different from having the simulation program spawn the visualization program. The approach also can work when complexities of the runtime environment make it difficult to start the visualization process either with `mpiexec` or with `MPI_Comm_spawn`.

Much of discussion in the MPI Standard on connecting MPI processes talks about *clients* and *servers*. While many of the concepts and issues are shared with traditional client/server models, there are also a number of differences. We prefer to think of the MPI model as a *peer-to-peer* model where one process accepts connections and the other process requests the connection. Because the MPI model for connecting processes does not address traditional client/server issues such as fault tolerance, we prefer to avoid the terms "client" and "server."

7.3.1 Visualizing the Computation in an MPI Program

Often when running a simulation, it is useful to be able to visualize the progress of the simulation, perhaps by using three-dimensional graphics to draw the current state of the solution on the mesh being used to approximate the problem. As our example of interconnecting two MPI programs we enhance the Poisson solver described in Chapter 5 to connect with a visualization program.

We modify the Poisson program as follows:

1.   The program creates a port and accepts a connection on that port. A *port* is nothing but a name that another program can use to connect to the program that created the port. As you would expect, the result of connecting to another MPI program is an intercommunicator connecting the two programs.

2.   At each iteration, the Poisson solver sends the current solution to the visualization program using intercommunicator communication operations.

Our first version assumes that the visualization program is actually a single process. In fact, the visualization program is very simple, as is shown in Figure 7.8. At each iteration, the program receives the iteration number, using a point-to-point intercommunicator operation, and the mesh itself, using `MPI_Gatherv` in an intercommunicator collective operation. The code to initialize the arguments needed by `MPI_Gatherv` uses `MPI_Gather` (also in intercommunicator form) to receive the amount of data that each process in the server will send to this program. The actual graphics drawing is done by the routine `DrawMesh`.

The routine `MPI_Comm_connect` establishes the connection to the other program. Because we choose to have the visualization program connect to the computation program, the visualization program is the *client* of the computation program (the processes that call `MPI_Comm_connect` are always the clients). The input arguments to `MPI_Comm_connect` are the port name, an `info` value, the rank of a "lead" or root process, and an intracommunicator. We will discuss the port name below; it is simply a character string, although its value is determined by the MPI implementation. In this version of the example, we read the port name from standard input.

Enhancements to this program could run the visualization routine in a separate thread, allowing the user to rotate, scale, and otherwise interact with the data

```
#include "mpi.h"
#define MAX_PROCS 128
#define MAX_MESH 512*512
int main( int argc, char *argv[] )
{
    MPI_Comm server;
    int      it, i, nprocs, rcounts[MAX_PROCS], rdispls[MAX_PROCS];
    double   mesh[MAX_MESH];
    char     port_name[MPI_MAX_PORT_NAME];

    MPI_Init( 0, 0 );

    gets( port_name );  /* we assume only one process
                            in MPI_COMM_WORLD */
    MPI_Comm_connect( port_name, MPI_INFO_NULL, 0, MPI_COMM_WORLD,
                      &server );
    MPI_Comm_remote_size( server, &nprocs );

    /* Get the number of data values from each process */
    MPI_Gather( MPI_BOTTOM, 0, MPI_DATATYPE_NULL,
                rcounts, 1, MPI_INT, MPI_ROOT, server );
    /* Compute the mesh displacements */
    rdispls[0] = 0;
    for (i=0; i<nprocs-1; i++)
        rdispls[i+1] = rdispls[i] + rcounts[i];

    while (1) {
        MPI_Recv( &it, 1, MPI_INT, 0, 0, server, MPI_STATUS_IGNORE );
        if (it < 0) break;
        MPI_Gatherv( MPI_BOTTOM, 0, MPI_DATATYPE_NULL,
                     mesh, rcounts, rdispls, MPI_DOUBLE,
                     MPI_ROOT, server );
        DrawMesh( mesh );
        }
    MPI_Comm_disconnect( &server );
    MPI_Finalize();
    return 0;
}
```

Figure 7.8
Visualization program

visually, while the code shown here updates the data each time a new iteration becomes available. Of course, the code uses the appropriate facilities (such as a thread mutex) to ensure that the drawing routine always has a consistent data set and not a mixture of several iterations.

7.3.2 Accepting Connections from Other Programs

We must modify the program that computes the approximations to the Poisson problem to accept the connection from the visualization program and send to it the data to be visualized. The changes are shown in Figure 7.9. The first item to note is that these changes are all additions; the original program is unchanged. For example, if the program was using `MPI_COMM_WORLD` before, it continues to use the same communicator for the computational part of the code. The second item to note is that this program is in Fortran, while our visualization client program is in C. MPI-2 provides for language interoperability, including the ability of programs in different languages to send messages to each other.

The changes to the program come in three places. The first place creates a port that the client program to connect to. To do this, we call `MPI_Open_port`, which returns a port name. As usual, an `info` value may be used to request implementation-specific behavior when requesting a port; in this case, we use `MPI_-INFO_NULL` to get the default behavior. A port name is simply a character string, and we print it out. It is this printed value that the client program must provide to `MPI_Comm_connect` and that is read with the `gets` statement in Figure 7.8.

Once the port is open, the program allows another MPI program to connect to it by calling `MPI_Comm_accept`. This is a collective call over all processes in the input communicator (the fourth argument), with the input arguments (such as the port name) valid at the specified `root`, which is process 0 in this case. An `info` argument is provided here as well to allow for implementation-specific customization. This is a blocking collective call that returns an intercommunicator.

The middle part of the code sends data to the client process, starting with information on the decomposition of the data in the computational process and continuing with the iteration count and current result within the iteration loop. These communication operations match the communication calls in the visualization client.

The final part of the program closes the port and disconnects from the client by calling `MPI_Close_port` and `MPI_Comm_disconnect`. The `MPI_Close_port` call frees up port; after the `MPI_Close_port` call, the port name returned by `MPI_-Open_port` is no longer valid.

```
character*(MPI_MAX_PORT_NAME) port_name
integer    client
...
if (myid .eq. 0) then
    call MPI_OPEN_PORT( MPI_INFO_NULL, port_name, ierr )
    print *, port_name
endif
call MPI_COMM_ACCEPT( port_name, MPI_INFO_NULL, 0, &
                      MPI_COMM_WORLD, client, ierr );
! Send the information needed to send the mesh
call MPI_GATHER( mesh_size, 1, MPI_INTEGER, &
                MPI_BOTTOM, 0, MPI_DATATYPE_NULL, &
                0, client, ierr )
....
! For each iteration, send the local part of the mesh
if (myid .eq. 0) then
    call MPI_SEND( it, 1, MPI_INTEGER, 0, 0, client, ierr )
endif
call MPI_GATHERV( mesh, mesh_size, MPI_DOUBLE_PRECISION, &
                MPI_BOTTOM, 0, 0, &
                MPI_DATATYPE_NULL, 0, client, ierr )
...
! Disconnect from client before exiting
if (myid .eq. 0) then
    call MPI_CLOSE_PORT( port_name, ierr )
endif
call MPI_COMM_DISCONNECT( client, ierr )
call MPI_FINALIZE( ierr )
```

Figure 7.9
Modifications to Poisson example to accept connections from the visualization program and to send data to it

```
int MPI_Open_port(MPI_Info info, char *port_name)

int MPI_Close_port(char *port_name)

int MPI_Comm_accept(char *port_name, MPI_Info info, int root,
            MPI_Comm comm, MPI_Comm *newcomm)

int MPI_Comm_connect(char *port_name, MPI_Info info, int root,
            MPI_Comm comm, MPI_Comm *newcomm)

int MPI_Comm_disconnect(MPI_Comm *comm)
```

Table 7.7
C bindings for client/server functions

The call to MPI_Comm_disconnect ensures that all communication on the communicator has completed before returning; this is the difference between this function and MPI_Comm_free.

The bindings for the routines used in these examples are in Tables 7.7, 7.8, and 7.9.

If the server needs to manage multiple connections at once, it must use a separate thread (see Chapter 8) for each MPI_Comm_accept call. The client need not be changed. Using a thread also allows the server to handle the case of no connections, as we will see in the next chapter.

7.3.3   Comparison with Sockets

The MPI routines for connecting two groups of processes follow a simple model that is similar to the Unix sockets model (see [81] for a description of sockets). A comparison with that model illustrates some of the differences as well as the motivation for the design. The correspondences are shown below:

MPI_Open_port. The socket routines socket, bind, and listen provide a similar function. At the end of bind, a port specified by an IP address and a port number is defined. The listen call prepares the port to receive connection requests. One major difference is that the port number is an input value for bind, whereas it is part of the output value (as part of the port_name) for MPI_Open_port.

MPI_Comm_accept. The socket routine accept establishes the connection and returns a new socket.

```
MPI_OPEN_PORT(info, port_name, ierror)
              character*(*) port_name
              integer info, ierror

MPI_CLOSE_PORT(port_name, ierror)
              character*(*) port_name
              integer ierror

MPI_COMM_ACCEPT(port_name, info, root, comm, newcomm, ierror)
              character*(*) port_name
              integer info, root, comm, newcomm, ierror

MPI_COMM_CONNECT(port_name, info, root, comm, newcomm, ierror)
              character*(*) port_name
              integer info, root, comm, newcomm, ierror

MPI_COMM_DISCONNECT(comm, ierror)
              integer comm, ierror
```

Table 7.8
Fortran bindings for client/server

```
void MPI::Open_port(const MPI::Info& info, char* port_name)

void MPI::Close_port(const char* port_name)

MPI::Intercomm MPI::Intracomm::Accept(const char* port_name,
              const MPI::Info& info, int root) const

MPI::Intercomm MPI::Intracomm::Connect(const char* port_name,
              const MPI::Info& info, int root) const

void MPI::Comm::Disconnect()
```

Table 7.9
C++ bindings for client/server functions

`MPI_Comm_connect`. The socket routines `socket` and `connect` are used to connect to a port.

The differences between these approaches are also important. The most important is that the socket interface establishes a connection between two processes (or threads), whereas the MPI interface connects two groups of processes. In addition, the socket interface provides very fine control on the connection mechanism. For example, the socket operations can be placed into a nonblocking mode (with an `fcntl` call on the socket file descriptor). Because Unix file descriptors are used, an application can use `select` or `poll` to manage multiple `listen` (that is, `MPI_-Comm_accept`) operations within a single process (or thread).

Early discussions in the MPI Forum considered nonblocking versions of the dynamic process routines (see [29] for one proposal). However, the Forum decided that nonblocking collective operations introduce too many complexities and instead recommended the use of separate threads that make blocking calls. In fact, it is often preferable to use threads and the blocking versions of the sockets on those Unix systems that support threads, as this provides a simpler programming model.

Other features of the socket interface, such as control over timeouts, can be accomplished through implementation-specific `info` options. For example, an implementation could provide the info key `timeout` with value in milliseconds; passing an info object containing this key to `MPI_Comm_accept` would allow the implementation to timeout the connection attempt.

7.3.4   Moving Data between Groups of Processes

If the data is large, the visualization program itself may need to be parallel (for example, an MPI version of POV-Ray [70]). In this case, we need to send a data structure that is distributed in one way on one group of processes to a different distribution on another group of processes.

For simplicity, we will consider the case of two different one-dimensional decompositions as illustrated in Figure 7.10. Each process on the left must send data to one or more processes on the right. This could be written as a collection of intercommunicator point-to-point operations (using nonblocking send and receive operations to ensure that the operations don't cause deadlock or sequentialization), but we will illustrate an alternative approach using the intercommunicator collective routine `MPI_Alltoallv`.

The routine `MPI_Alltoallv` is a more flexible version of the routine `MPI_-Alltoall`. In the intracommunicator form, each process sends different data to every other process. In the intercommunicator version, each process in one group

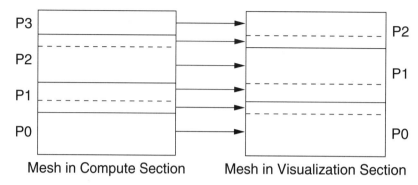

Figure 7.10
Data transfers between the simulation program (4 processes) and the visualization program (3 processes). Solid lines indicate the decomposition of the mesh among processes. Arrows indicate the transfers that take place. Dashed lines show the division of the mesh in terms of the other group of processes.

sends different data to every other process in the other group. In our case, every process is not sending to every other process. For those processes to which no data is being sent, we simply set the `sendcount` for those destinations to zero. The code in Figure 7.11 computes the `sendcounts` and `sdispls` arguments for `MPI_Alltoallv`, where the calling process has rows `s` to `e` of the mesh, and the decomposition on the visualization server is given by the array `m`, where `m(i)` is the number of rows on process `i`.

`MPI_Alltoallv` may be preferable to individual send and receive operations when MPI is being used over a wide-area network. For example, the visualization program may be running on a local graphics workstation while the computational program may be running on a remote supercomputer. Using `MPI_Alltoallv` allows an MPI implementation to better optimize the movement of data between the two systems, because the entire data motion is concisely described by the arguments to `MPI_-Alltoallv`.

7.3.5 Name Publishing

In the example above, the port name is moved between the server and the client by using `print` to print the name onto standard output and `gets` to read the name from standard input. This is completely general but more than a little awkward. Fortunately, MPI-2 provides a partial solution. We can think of the

```
print *, port_name
```

step as *publishing* the port name to the outside world. Similarly, the

```
r_s   = 1
displ = 0
do i=0, viz_numprocs-1
    if (s .ge. r_s + m(i)) then
        sendcounts(i) = 0
        sdispls(i) = 0
    elseif (e .lt. r_s) then
        sendcounts(i) = 0
        sdispls(i) = 0
    else
        sendcounts(i) = min( e - s + 1, r_s + m(i) - s) * nx
        sdispls(i)    = displ
        displ         = displ + sendcounts(i)
    endif
    r_s = r_s + m(i)
enddo
```

Figure 7.11
Code to compute arguments for MPI_Alltoallv

```
gets( port_name );
```

call in the client is asking the user to look up the port name. MPI-2 provides an alternative to printing and reading that is called a *name service*. In the MPI-2 approach, a program may associate a port name with a private name chosen by the programmer. This private name is called the *service name*. A port name is associated with a service name by calling the routine MPI_Publish_name; the association may be removed by calling MPI_Unpublish_name.

A process that needs a particular port name may look it up by passing the service name to MPI_Lookup_name. Since the service name is defined by the programmer rather than the MPI implementation (or runtime system), the service name may be hard-coded into the application.

Figure 7.12 shows the changes that must be made to the visualization and simulation programs to allow them to use the MPI name publishing routines rather than print and gets. The bindings for the name service routines are given in Tables 7.10, 7.11, and 7.12.

Name publishing has a number of limitations. The most important limitation is that since the service names are chosen by the programmer, it is always possible for two programmers to choose the same service name for two different applications. There is no perfect solution to this problem, but a number of approaches

Visualization Program:

```
MPI_Lookup_name( "Poisson", MPI_INFO_NULL, port_name );
MPI_Comm_connect( port_name, MPI_INFO_NULL, 0, MPI_COMM_WORLD,
                  &server );
```

Simulation Program:

```
character*(MPI_MAX_PORT_NAME) port_name
integer    client
...
if (myid .eq. 0) then
    call MPI_OPEN_PORT( MPI_INFO_NULL, port_name, ierr )
    call MPI_PUBLISH_NAME( 'Poisson', MPI_INFO_NULL, &
                           port_name, ierr )
endif
call MPI_COMM_ACCEPT( port_name, MPI_INFO_NULL, 0, &
                      MPI_COMM_WORLD, client, ierr );
...
if (myid .eq. 0) then
    call MPI_UNPUBLISH_NAME( 'Poisson', MPI_INFO_NULL, &
                             port_name, ierr )
    call MPI_CLOSE_PORT( port_name, ierr )
endif
```

Figure 7.12
Code changes to the example in Figures 7.8 and 7.9 to use name publishing

---

int **MPI_Publish_name**(char *service_name, MPI_Info info, char *port_name)

int **MPI_Unpublish_name**(char *service_name, MPI_Info info, char *port_name)

int **MPI_Lookup_name**(char *service_name, MPI_Info info, char *port_name)

Table 7.10
C bindings for name publishing

MPI_PUBLISH_NAME(service_name, info, port_name, ierror)
        integer info, ierror
        character*(*) service_name, port_name

MPI_UNPUBLISH_NAME(service_name, info, port_name, ierror)
        integer info, ierror
        character*(*) service_name, port_name

MPI_LOOKUP_NAME(service_name, info, port_name, ierror)
        character*(*) service_name, port_name
        integer info, ierror

Table 7.11
Fortran bindings for name publishing

---

void MPI::Publish_name(const char* service_name, const MPI::Info& info,
        const char* port_name)

void MPI::Unpublish_name(const char* service_name, const MPI::Info& info,
        const char* port_name)

void MPI::Lookup_name(const char* service_name, const MPI::Info& info,
        char* port_name)

Table 7.12
C++ bindings for name publishing

can be used to reduce the chance for trouble. One approach that is used by commercial distributed-computing systems such as DCE [23] is to provide a central clearing house for service names. The programmer requests a service name and is given a name that is guaranteed to be unique (at least within the domain that the distributed-computing system is running over, which is all that is required). The downsides to this approach are that the names are often long strings of seemingly random characters and that a central registry of names must be maintained, even as the domain of available computers changes. Furthermore, each user of the client and server must acquire their own service names.

A simpler but slightly less robust approach is for the service name to include the user's login name (this allows multiple users to use the same program without having their service names collide). For example, instead of using `"Poisson"` as the service name for the visualization client, we might use the code

```
sprintf( service_name, "Poisson-%s", cuserid( NULL ) );
```

The routine `cuserid` returns the name of user associated with the calling process. There is no direct Fortran equivalent, but it is usually possible to access this information through an implementation-specific way (if necessary, calling a C routine to perform the operation).

Another limitation of the name-service routines is that an MPI implementation is not required to provide a usable name service. That is, the routines `MPI_Publish_-name`, `MPI_Unpublish_name`, and `MPI_Lookup_name` must be provided, but they can return failure for all operations.[4]

7.4   Design of the MPI Dynamic Process Routines

Programmers that are used to the simple Unix command `rsh` or Unix function `fork` can find the MPI approach to dynamic process management complex. This section explains some of the reasons for the MPI approach.

7.4.1   Goals for MPI Dynamic Process Management

The design of the MPI dynamic process routines maintains the properties that have made MPI successful: portability, determinism, scalability, and performance. In addition, it exploits the power of MPI communicators (particularly intercommunicators) to accomplish this with only three new functions: `MPI_Comm_spawn`, and `MPI_Comm_get_parent`.

Portability.   The most basic requirement is that users be able to write portable applications that can run in a variety of job-scheduling/process-management environments. This seemingly simple requirement is in fact one of the most demanding. Job scheduling and process management environments are very different in different systems. For example, many programmers are familiar with clusters of workstations, which offer a wide variety of flexible and powerful options. But many high-performance systems provide fewer features, trading flexibility for performance. For instance, a number of massively parallel processors (MPPs) allow either one process per node (e.g., SGI/Cray T3D and T3E) or one process per node when using the high-performance interconnect (IBM SP). Furthermore, to optimize communication, some high-performance systems take advantage of the fact that the collection

---

[4]By default, errors are fatal; therefore, checking the return value from these routines requires changing the error handler for `MPI_COMM_WORLD`.

of processes is unchanging. Changes to the communication layout are expensive and may require collective operations (this is in fact what a parallel job-startup program does on some MPPs). Finally, the division of labor between a job scheduler and a process starter, while natural, is not universal. The MPI model assumes only that a new collection of processes can be started and connected together and to the parent processes. This capability is close to what most environments, even on MPPs, require to start an MPI-1 job, and the MPI Forum felt that this would be portable.

Determinism. The semantics of dynamic process creation must be carefully designed to avoid race conditions. In MPI, every process is a member of at least one communicator. The collection of processes in a communicator must be unchanging. If it isn't, collective operations (such as `MPI_Allreduce`) no longer have well-defined meanings. Adding processes to an MPI "job" requires the creation of a new communicator. Removing processes requires freeing the communicators, window objects, and MPI file objects that contain the exiting processes. The requirement of determinism dictated the use of communicators and collective operations in creating processes. Note that the "two-party" approach used in many systems that create one process at a time can be implemented in MPI by simply using `MPI_COMM_-SELF` as the communicator for the spawning process and using a soft spawn of one process in `MPI_Comm_spawn`. The MPI approach permits this use, but also allows for scalably spawning large numbers of processes that are provided with efficient interprocess communications.

Scalability and performance. One of the ways in which MPI achieves scalability and performance is through the use of collective operations that concisely describe an operation that involves large numbers of processes. Rather than create new processes through individual requests to a job manager and process creator, MPI allows the programmer to make a single request for a large number of processes that will belong to a single group (one of the two groups in the intercommunicator returned by `MPI_Comm_spawn`).

In summary, when trying to understand the design choices for the MPI dynamic process routines, it is important to think not of what can be done on a few workstations running some variety of Unix but what would be required for a supercomputer that provides only a batch-scheduling interface and only one process per node. The MPI design allows a program to run on either system without change (other than the path name for the program).

7.4.2   What MPI Did Not Standardize

We have noted that several features are dependent on the MPI implementation. The MPI Forum spent a great deal of time discussing these, but in the end concluded that there was no approach that was both general enough to maintain the portability of MPI and powerful enough to provide a useful facility for users of MPI. This was particularly true for the interface to the job scheduler and process manager.

Many job schedulers provide a rich command language for specifying the resources to be used for a job. These may include specific software releases, hardware (cache size or CPU speed), and even priorities (for example, a processor with set A of capabilities or, if that is not available, then one with set B). Some research systems have provided limited subsets of these capabilities, and the MPI Forum considered following their lead. In the end, however, the Forum felt that any specific choice was worse than no choice at all. Instead, the Forum invented the `MPI_Info` argument as a general hook for providing implementation-specific information to `MPI_Comm_-spawn`. This general "hints" mechanism for providing a portable way to specify implementation-specific information was so useful that it was applied to the I/O and RMA routines as well.

Although it is unfortunate that the MPI Forum could not standardize the job-manager and process-startup interface, it is exactly the same situation that users face for file names. While users of Unix systems may feel that file names are standard, there remain important differences with other operating systems. For example, with Windows, valid characters are different, directory-separator character is different, and Unix has no "drive" letter. Even within Unix, different file-system implementations offer different performance and correctness properties; specifying the file name can select completely different file system environments.

8 Using MPI with Threads

Threads form an important programming model that separates a process into a single address space and one or more *threads* of control. Threads provide a natural programming model for symmetric multiprocessors; they are also an effective way to hide latency in high-latency operations. MPI-1 was designed to work well with threads; MPI-2 adds features to improve the ability of MPI implementations to deliver high performance to both single-threaded and multithreaded programs.

We first cover what threads are and why they are useful. Section 8.2 describes how MPI interacts with threads. In Section 8.3, we revisit the `NXTVAL` routine, this time implemented using threads with MPI. Threads are often used to create nonblocking operations from blocking ones; we show how to do this with MPI in Section 8.4. We conclude with some comments on mixed-model programming (MPI and threads together).

8.1 Thread Basics and Issues

Throughout this book we have referred constantly to *processes* as the entities that communicate with one another. A process may be defined loosely as an address space together with a current state consisting of a program counter, register values, and a subroutine call stack. The fact that a process has only one program counter means that it is doing only one thing at a time; we call such a process *single threaded*. Multiple processes may be executed on a single processor through timesharing, so in some sense the processor is doing more than one thing at a time, but the process isn't.

Both vendors and users have experimented with a generalization of this situation in which processes have multiple program counters (with associated register values and stacks) sharing the process's address space. The (program counter, register set, stack) triple is called a *thread* and is very much like a process in its own right except that it does not have an address space of its own.

The motivation for threads is to allow a concurrent programming model within a single process, with very rapid switching of control of the CPU from one thread to another possible because little or no memory management is involved.

Individual threads are not visible outside a process. Therefore, MPI communication among multithreaded processes does not address individual threads; the threads of a process can perform MPI operations on behalf of their processes. Using threads in conjunction with message passing can be extremely convenient, for several reasons:

- Threads provide a natural implementation of nonblocking communication operations. A thread can be created to do a blocking receive operation. As long as this blocks only the thread and not the process, it has the effect of a nonblocking receive. The same applies to sends.
- Threads can increase the convenience and efficiency of the implementation of collective operations.
- Threads are becoming the parallel programming model of choice for "symmetric multiprocessing" shared-memory machines.
- Threads can help improve performance by helping to make highly latent systems more "latency tolerant."

8.1.1   Thread Safety

In order for threads to be used in conjunction with a message-passing library, however, the library must be designed to work well with threads. This property is called *thread safety*. Thread safety means that multiple threads can be executing message-passing library calls without interfering with one another. Thread *unsafety* occurs when the message-passing system is expected to hold certain parts of the process state and it is impossible to hold that process state for more than one thread at a time. For example, some libraries use the concept of "the most recently received message" to avoid passing a status argument stored on the process's stack. That is, user code will look something like

```
recv(msg, type);
src = get_src();
len = get_len();
```

This approach works in the single-threaded case, but in the multithreaded case, several receives may be in progress simultaneously, and when `get_src` is called, it may not be clear for which message the source is supposed to be returned. MPI solves this particular problem by returning the source as part of the status object, which normally resides on the stack of a specific thread. This problem of a resource that is owned by the message-passing library instead of by the user thread can arise in the case of other data structures as well, such as message buffers, error fields, or "current" contexts. MPI has been carefully engineered to be thread safe in its semantics, and implementers are encouraged to provide thread-safe implementations, so that MPI can work hand in hand with thread libraries.

For an application to use MPI with threads, it isn't enough that the implementation of MPI be thread-safe. The thread library must be aware of the MPI implementation to the extent that execution of a blocking operation will cause the current thread to yield control to another thread in the process rather than cause the process to block. When a message arrives, a thread waiting for it should be made runnable again. Furthermore, when a system call is made, the operating system should block only the thread that made the call, not all threads, or much of the flexibility of user-level threads is lost.

The issue of threads has been widely discussed and implemented in slightly different ways by various vendors. Fortunately, the POSIX standard [42], also known as *Pthreads*, seems likely to become the most widely used definition for threads.

Threads are also becoming a widely used programming paradigm for shared-memory multiprocessors, which are now appearing from a number of vendors. MPI can be used to program networks of such machines precisely because it is designed to be thread safe. (A higher-level paradigm for programming with the thread model is *monitors*, discussed in [6].) Threads may also be used by a compiler to provide parallelism with little or no direct involvement by the programmer. The OpenMP [67] programming model is one example of a popular thread-based programming model for shared-memory multiprocessors.

8.1.2   Threads and Processes

Thread systems where the operating system (the kernel) is not involved in managing the individual threads are called *user threads*. User threads tend to be faster than *kernel threads* (that is, the time that it takes to switch between threads within the same process is typically smaller with user threads), but often have the restriction that some system calls will block all threads in the process containing the thread that made the system call, not just the calling thread. Such system calls include `read`, `write`, `recv`, and `send`. This tradeoff in performance versus generality can make it difficult to write truly portable multithreaded programs, since the application cannot assume that the entire process will not be blocked when a thread calls a library routine. The POSIX thread (Pthreads) specification does not specify whether the threads are user or kernel; it is up to the threads implementation.

8.2   MPI and Threads

The MPI-1 Standard was designed to be thread-safe: with the exception of `MPI_-Probe` and `MPI_Iprobe`, there is no global state or notion of "current value" in the MPI specification (see Section 5.2.3 in *Using MPI* [32]). Thread-safe implementations of MPI-1 have been developed [91] and have confirmed that the MPI-1 design is thread-safe. In MPI-2, the I/O routines that contain explicit offsets (e.g., `MPI_-`

`File_read_at`) provide a thread-safe alternative to use of a separate seek operation. In other words, `MPI_File_seek` has the same thread-safety issues as `MPI_Probe`; MPI-2 does, however, provide a thread-safe alternative to using `MPI_File_seek` through the explicit offset versions of the I/O routines.

The MPI-2 Standard benefited from experiences in using threads and building thread-safe MPI implementations. For example, the portability problems experienced by multithreaded applications because of the differences between the capabilities of user and kernel threads led the MPI Forum to require that MPI calls block only the calling thread. This still doesn't address the issue of user versus kernel threads, but if the application uses MPI for all interprocess communication and I/O and makes no explicit system calls, a multithreaded MPI application (assuming that the MPI implementation provides the necessary level of thread support as defined below) is portable, even if the thread system provides only user threads.

The MPI Forum also required that correct MPI programs not attempt to have multiple threads complete the same nonblocking MPI operation. For example, it is invalid to start a nonblocking MPI operation in one thread and then allow several threads to call `MPI_Wait` or `MPI_Test` on the request object. It is permissible, of course, to have one thread start a nonblocking MPI operation and have a different thread complete it, as long as there is no possibility that two threads will try to complete (or test) the same operation. This restriction allows MPI implementations to provide high performance in operations involving request objects because the implementation can rely on the fact that only one (user-defined) thread will ever operate on the request.

Another issue has been the performance tradeoffs between multithreaded and single-threaded code. While having multiple threads enables an application to use multiple processors or to perform alternate work while a high-latency operation—such as I/O—proceeds, multithreaded code also requires operations to guard against inconsistent updates to the same memory location from different threads (see Section 4.3). These additional operations, particularly if they involve software locks or system calls, can be quite expensive. Some vendors have provided both single-threaded and multithreaded libraries, but then an application (and even more so, a library) is faced with the question: have I been linked with the right library? If not, the application will still run but will suffer occasional and mysterious errors.

These experiences are most clearly shown in the new MPI-2 function to initialize an MPI program: `MPI_Init_thread`. This function, in addition to the `argc` and `argv` arguments of `MPI_Init`, requests a level of thread support, and returns the level of thread support that was granted. Here are the kinds of thread support, in order of increasing generality:

---

int **MPI_Init_thread**(int *argc, char ***argv, int required, int *provided)

Table 8.1
C binding for initializing MPI with threads

MPI_INIT_THREAD(required, provided, ierror)
                    integer required, provided, ierror

Table 8.2
Fortran binding for initializing MPI with threads

MPI_THREAD_SINGLE: Only one (user) thread

MPI_THREAD_FUNNELED: Many user threads, but only the main thread may make MPI calls

MPI_THREAD_SERIALIZED: Many user threads may make MPI calls, but only one thread at a time does so (the user must guarantee this)

MPI_THREAD_MULTIPLE: Free for all. Any thread may make MPI calls at any time.

All values are integers and are ordered so that the more general value is greater than all of the more restrictive levels of support.

The bindings for MPI_Init_thread are shown in Tables 8.1, 8.2, and 8.3. An MPI implementation is permitted to return any of these values as the value of provided. For example, an MPI implementation that is not thread safe will always return MPI_THREAD_SINGLE. On the other hand, an MPI implementation could be provided in several different versions, using the value of required to determine which to choose (through dynamic linking of the libraries), and reporting the value provided. This allows the MPI implementer and the MPI user to choose whether to pay any performance penalty that might come with a fully multithreaded MPI implementation.

The function MPI_Init_thread can be used instead of MPI_Init. That is, while an MPI-1 program starts with MPI_Init and ends with MPI_Finalize, an MPI-2 program can start either with MPI_Init or MPI_Init_thread. Regardless of whether MPI_Init or MPI_Init_thread is called, the MPI program must end with a call to MPI_Finalize (there is no "MPI_Finalize_thread"). In addition, the MPI-2 Standard requires that the thread in each process that called MPI_Init or MPI_Init_thread, which MPI calls the *main thread*, also be the (only) thread in that process that calls MPI_Finalize.

---

int **MPI::Init_thread**(int &argc, char **&argv, int required)

int **MPI::Init_thread**(int required)

Table 8.3
C++ bindings for initializing MPI with threads. The returned value is the level of thread
support provided.

Note that the value of **required** does *not* need to have the same value on each
process that is calling `MPI_Init_thread`. An MPI implementation may choose to
give the same value of **provided**, of course. We will see below an example where
different levels of thread support may be chosen.

The most thread-friendly level of support is `MPI_THREAD_MULTIPLE`. When this
level of support is provided, MPI routines may be used in any combination of
threads. Such an MPI implementation is called *thread compliant*.

`MPI_Init` can initialize MPI to any level of thread support; command-line arguments to `mpiexec` or environment variables may affect the level of thread support.

There are no MPI routines to create a thread; that task is left to other tools,
which may be compilers or libraries. In the next section, we show an example where
the new thread is created by using a Pthreads library call. In an OpenMP program,
the compiler may create the additional threads. By leaving the exact method of
thread creation to other standards, MPI ensures that programs may use any thread
approach that is available (as long as it is consistent with the MPI implementation).

8.3 Yet Another Version of NXTVAL

One example that we have used is that of a "next value" routine that increments
a counter and returns the value. In *Using MPI* [32], we used this example in
Section 7.1 to illustrate the use of `MPI_Comm_split`, ready sends, and multiple
completions. In Section 6.5 of this book, we developed a version that used remote
memory access. In this section we consider a solution to the same problem that
uses threads.

Specifically, we will dedicate a thread to providing the counter. This thread will
use a blocking receive to wait for requests for a new value and will simply return
the data with a blocking send.

The code in Figure 8.1 is reasonably simple. Only a few items need mentioning.
The process with rank zero creates the thread in `init_counter`. Any process,
including the one with rank zero, may then call `counter_nxtval` to fetch the current

```
void *counter_routine( MPI_Comm *counter_comm_p )
{
    int incr, ival = 0;
    MPI_Status status;
    while (1) {
        MPI_Recv( &incr, 1, MPI_INT, MPI_ANY_SOURCE, MPI_ANY_TAG,
                    *counter_comm_p, &status );
        if (status.MPI_TAG == 1) return;
        MPI_Send( &ival, 1, MPI_INT, status.MPI_SOURCE, 0,
                    *counter_comm_p );
        ival += incr;
    }
}
/* We discuss how to eliminate this global var in the text */
static pthread_t thread_id;
void init_counter( MPI_Comm comm, MPI_Comm *counter_comm_p )
{
    int rank;
    MPI_Comm_dup( comm, counter_comm_p );
    MPI_Comm_rank( comm, &rank );
    if (rank == 0)
        pthread_create( &thread_id, NULL, counter_routine,
                        counter_comm_p );
}
/* Any process can all this to fetch and increment by value */
void counter_nxtval( MPI_Comm counter_comm, int incr, int *value )
{
    MPI_Send(&incr, 0, MPI_INT, 0, 1, counter_comm);
    MPI_Recv(value, 1, MPI_INT, 0, 0, counter_comm, MPI_STATUS_IGNORE);
}
/* Every process in counter_comm (including rank 0!)
   must call stop counter */
void stop_counter( MPI_Comm *counter_comm_p )
{
    int rank;
    MPI_Barrier( *counter_comm_p );
    MPI_Comm_rank( *counter_comm_p, &rank );
    if (rank == 0) {
        MPI_Send( MPI_BOTTOM, 0, MPI_INT, 0, 1, *counter_comm_p );
        pthread_join( thread_id, NULL );
    }
    MPI_Comm_free( counter_comm_p );
}
```

Figure 8.1
Version of nxtval using threads

value and increment it by the value of `incr`. The `stop_counter` routine uses a `MPI_Barrier` first to ensure that no process is still trying to use the counter. The process with rank zero then sends a message to itself, but this message is received in `counter_routine`, which is running in a separate thread. Receiving that message causes `counter_routine` to exit, thereby terminating that thread. The `pthread_join` call in `stop_counter` causes the process that created the thread to wait until the thread finishes.

This code depends on the MPI guarantee that a blocking MPI call blocks only the calling thread, not all of the threads in the process. Without this requirement, a thread-safe implementation of MPI would have little value. This does require the `MPI_THREAD_MULTIPLE` mode. However, only one process needs this level of thread support. If no other processes are using threads, they could specify `MPI_THREAD_SINGLE` as the required level of thread support.

The variable `thread_id` is global in Figure 8.1. This prevents more than one counter from being active at any time in any single process. However, we all know that global variables are bad. Fortunately, MPI provides a convenient way to attach this variable to the output communicator, `counter_comm_p`, through the use of attributes. Attributes are covered in more detail in *Using MPI* [32] in Section 6.2.1.

8.4 Implementing Nonblocking Collective Operations

The `nxtval` code in Figure 8.1 demonstrates how to implement what is sometimes called an "hrecv" (from the Intel NX library) or "interrupt-driven receive" by using a blocking receive operation and threads. In fact, most nonblocking operations can be viewed as if they were implemented as a blocking operation in a separate thread. One reason that nonblocking collective operations were not included in MPI-2 is that they can be implemented by calling the matching blocking collective operation using a separate thread.[1]

An example of blocking collective operation whose nonblocking version we'd like to have is `MPI_Comm_accept`. Because `MPI_Comm_accept` is not a nonblocking operation, it cannot be cancelled. This means that an MPI program that calls `MPI_Comm_accept` cannot continue until the `MPI_Comm_accept` returns. To handle this,

---

[1] We've brushed under the rug a number of difficulties with nonblocking collective operations, such as what happens if the same process has several outstanding collective operations on the same communicator (which is not valid in MPI) and what a request object would look like. But for many of the purposes for which users wish to use nonblocking collective operations, using a separate thread and the blocking version of the operation is adequate.

```
      integer exit_msg, server
      parameter (exit_msg = -1)
      ...
      call MPI_COMM_CONNECT( port_name, MPI_INFO_NULL, 0, &
                             MPI_COMM_SELF, server, ierr )
      call MPI_BCAST( exit_msg, 1, MPI_INTEGER, MPI_ROOT, &
                      server, ierr )
      call MPI_COMM_DISCONNECT( server, ierr )
```

Figure 8.2
Code to connect and terminate a connection

a program that uses `MPI_Comm_accept` to allow, but not require, another MPI program to attach to it should make a "dummy" connect request to satisfy the `MPI_Comm_accept`. For example, in Section 7.3.2, we showed a program that allowed a visualization program to connect to it to allow the visualization program to draw data as it was being computed.

But what if we do not want to require the visualization program to connect before proceeding with the computation? We can start by placing the `MPI_Comm_-accept` into a separate thread. This allows the program to continue even while the `MPI_Comm_accept` is waiting.

However, the program cannot exit until the `MPI_Comm_accept` completes. The easiest way to handle this situation is to have the same program connect to itself to complete the connection, as shown in Figure 8.2.

To allow for this case, we also change the initial connect and accept code so that the first communication is an integer that indicates either a normal (e.g., visualization client) connection or an exit message. We use an intercommunicator broadcast to ensure that all of the participating processes receive the message.

8.5   Mixed-Model Programming: MPI for SMP Clusters

One of the most popular computer architectures is a cluster of symmetric multiprocessors (SMPs). Another popular architecture is the nonuniform memory-access (NUMA) shared-memory computer. On both of these kinds of architectures, the approach of combining message-passing with shared-memory techniques (such as threads) can provide an effective programming model. This approach is often called *mixed-model* programming.

MPI was designed to encourage mixed-model programming. The thread-safe

int **MPI_Query_thread**(int *provided)
int **MPI_Is_thread_main**(int *flag)

Table 8.4
C routines to discover the level of thread support

MPI_QUERY_THREAD(provided, ierror)   integer provided, ierror

MPI_IS_THREAD_MAIN(flag, ierror)
    logical flag
    integer ierror

Table 8.5
Fortran routines to discover the level of thread support

design has made it relatively easy to use MPI with programs that use either implicit, compiler-based parallelism or explicit, user-programmed parallelism. In this model, the most common MPI thread mode is `MPI_THREAD_FUNNELED`: only one thread performs MPI calls. The other threads are used only for compute tasks. Using MPI with this model is very simple: in fact, it often amounts to nothing more than using a compiler switch to enable the automatic generation by the compiler of multithreaded code for loops. In other cases (e.g., when using OpenMP [67, 68]), a few changes or annotations to the code must be made to enable the thread-based parallelization of loops.

However, if library routines might be called by some of the compute threads, additional care must be exercised. In the `MPI_THREAD_FUNNELED` model, a library routine that is called by a thread may wish to ensure that it be allowed to perform MPI calls. It can discover the level of thread support by calling `MPI_Query_-thread`, which returns the level of thread support that has been provided. If the level is `MPI_THREAD_FUNNELED`, only the "main" thread may make MPI calls. A thread can determine whether it is the main thread by calling `MPI_Is_thread_-main`, which returns a logical value indicating whether the calling thread is the same thread that called `MPI_Init` or `MPI_Init_thread`. The bindings for these calls are given in Tables 8.4, 8.5, and 8.6.

Figure 8.3 shows how a library routine could determine that it has an adequate level of thread support. This code takes advantage of the ordering of the values of the levels of thread support to simplify the tests. Note that `MPI_Query_thread`

---

int MPI::Query_thread()

bool MPI::Is_thread_main()

Table 8.6
C++ routines to discover the level of thread support

```
int thread_level, thread_is_main;

MPI_Query_thread( &thread_level );
MPI_Is_thread_main( &thread_is_main );
if (thread_level > MPI_THREAD_FUNNELED ||
    (thread_level == MPI_THREAD_FUNNELED && thread_is_main)) {
    ... we may make MPI calls
}
else {
    printf( "Error! Routine makes MPI calls\n\
This thread does not support them\n");
    return 1;
}
...
```

Figure 8.3
Code to test for the necessary level of thread support. Note that if the thread_level is
MPI_THREAD_SERIALIZED, the user must ensure that no other thread makes MPI calls when this
library may be making MPI calls.

and MPI_Is_thread_main may be used even when MPI is initialized with MPI_Init
instead of MPI_Init_thread.

Using MPI programs with OpenMP. Some systems for thread-based parallelism, such as OpenMP [67, 68], allow the user to control the number of threads
with environment variables. Unfortunately, MPI does not require that the environment variables (or argc and argv) be propagated to every process by the MPI
implementation. Therefore, instead of using the environment variables directly, you
must specifically set the number of threads to use. Since many MPI implementations start the process with rank 0 in MPI_COMM_WORLD with the user's environment,
the code in Figure 8.4 can be used. The routine omp_get_num_threads will return
the number of threads, in case you wish to check that the requested number of
threads was provided.

```
MPI_Comm_rank( MPI_COMM_WORLD, &rank );
if (rank == 0) {
    nthreads_str = getenv( "OMP_NUM_THREADS" );
    if (nthreads_str)
        nthreads = atoi( nthreads_str );
    else
        nthreads = 1;
}
MPI_Bcast( &nthreads, 1, MPI_INT, 0, MPI_COMM_WORLD );
omp_set_num_threads( nthreads );
```

Figure 8.4
Code to set the number of OpenMP threads from within an MPI program.

9 Advanced Features

In this chapter we consider some advanced features of MPI-2 that are particularly useful to library writers.

9.1 Defining New File Data Representations

We mentioned in Chapter 3 that users can define new file data representations and register them with the MPI implementation. We explain this feature with the help of a simple example.

Let's define a new file data format called `int64` in which integers are of length 8 bytes and stored in little-endian format. Let's assume that we are running the program on a machine in which integers are of length 4 bytes and in big-endian order. In other words, both the size of integers and the byte order are different in the native representation and in the file. For simplicity, we consider only one datatype, namely, integers, and assume that the program uses only integers. Other datatypes can be handled similarly.

We can create this new data format and register it with the MPI implementation using the function `MPI_Register_datarep` as follows:

```
MPI_Register_datarep("int64", read_conv_fn, write_conv_fn,
                     dtype_file_extent_fn, NULL);
```

where `int64` is the name of the new data representation, and `read_conv_fn`, `write_-conv_fn`, and `dtype_file_extent_fn` are pointers to functions that we must provide. The implementation will use `read_conv_fn` and `write_conv_fn` to convert data from file format to native format and vice versa. The implementation will use `dtype_file_extent_fn` to determine the extent of a datatype in the new data representation. The final parameter is an extra-state parameter, which the implementation will pass to the conversion functions and the extent function each time it calls them. This parameter allows the user to pass additional information to those functions. We just pass a null parameter here. After the new data representation is registered in this way, we can use it any time in the rest of the program by passing `int64` as the `datarep` argument to `MPI_File_set_view`.

For the `int64` format, we can define `dtype_file_extent_fn` simply as

```
int dtype_file_extent_fn(MPI_Datatype datatype,
                         MPI_Aint *file_extent,
                         void *extra_state)
{
```

```
        if (datatype == MPI_INT) return 8;
        else return MPI_ERR_TYPE;
}
```

The MPI Standard specifies that the implementation will pass to dtype_file_-extent_fn only basic (predefined) datatypes used by the user. Even if the user uses derived datatypes in the program, the implementation will pass only the constituent basic datatypes of that derived datatype, not the derived datatype itself. For our example, therefore, we need only implement this function to handle the integer datatype. For any other datatype, we return error.

For reading integers stored in a file in int64 format on a machine with 4-byte integers in big-endian order, we can define the read conversion function as follows:

```
int read_conv_fn(void *userbuf, MPI_Datatype datatype,
                 int count, void *filebuf, MPI_Offset position,
                 void *extra_state)
{
    int i;

    if (datatype != MPI_INT) return MPI_ERR_TYPE;
    byte_swap((long long *) filebuf, count);
    for (i=0; i<count; i++)
        ((int *) userbuf)[position + i] =
                            ((long long *) filebuf)[i];
    return MPI_SUCCESS;
}
```

Here we have assumed that long long is an 8-byte integer. The MPI implementation will call this function from within any MPI function that does a file read. Before calling this function, the implementation will read count items of type datatype (integers in this case) from the file and store them contiguously in the buffer filebuf. To read the correct amount of data, the implementation will use dtype_file_extent_fn to determine the extent of an integer in the int64 format. The read conversion function must copy these count integers that are in int64 format in filebuf into native format in userbuf. The data must be stored starting from an offset in userbuf specified by the position parameter. This parameter is provided for the following reason: if there isn't enough memory for the implementation to allocate a filebuf large enough to store all the data to be read, the implementation can allocate a smaller filebuf, read the data in parts, and call read_conv_fn with different values for position each time.

In `read_conv_fn`, we return an error if the datatype passed is not `MPI_INT`, because the Standard specifies that the implementation will pass to this function only the datatypes used by the user. (Unlike for `dtype_file_extent_fn`, the conversion functions will be passed a derived datatype if the user uses a derived datatype.) We implement `read_conv_fn` by first calling a function `byte_swap` that does the byte swapping necessary to convert each 8-byte integer in an array of `n` integers from little-endian to big-endian; the implementation of `byte_swap` is left to the reader.

The write conversion function is implemented similarly. We first copy `count` number of 4-byte integers starting from the offset `position` in `userbuf` into `filebuf` by appropriate type-casting. We then call the byte-swapping routine.

```
int write_conv_fn(void *userbuf, MPI_Datatype datatype,
                  int count, void *filebuf, MPI_Offset position,
                  void *extra_state)
{
    int i;

    if (datatype != MPI_INT) return MPI_ERR_TYPE;
    for (i=0; i<count; i++)
        ((long long *) filebuf)[i] =
                            ((int *) userbuf)[position + i];
    byte_swap((long long *) filebuf, count);
    return MPI_SUCCESS;
}
```

The C, Fortran, and C++ bindings for `MPI_Register_datarep` are given in Tables 9.1, 9.2, and 9.3.

9.2   External Interface Functions

MPI-2 defines a set of functions, called *external interface functions*, that enable users to do certain things that would otherwise require access to the source code of an MPI implementation. These functions include functions for decoding datatypes, creating request objects for new nonblocking operations (called *generalized requests*), filling in the `status` object, and adding new error codes and classes. The external interface functions are useful to library writers. They can be used, for example, to layer the MPI-2 I/O functions on top of any MPI-1 implementation that also supports the MPI-2 external interface functions. Our implementation of the

```
int MPI_Register_datarep(char *datarep,
             MPI_Datarep_conversion_function *read_conversion_fn,
             MPI_Datarep_conversion_function *write_conversion_fn,
             MPI_Datarep_extent_function *dtype_file_extent_fn,
             void *extra_state)

typedef int MPI_Datarep_conversion_function(void *userbuf,
             MPI_Datatype datatype, int count, void *filebuf,
             MPI_Offset position, void *extra_state)

typedef int MPI_Datarep_extent_function(MPI_Datatype datatype,
             MPI_Aint *file_extent, void *extra_state)
```

Table 9.1
C binding for MPI_Register_datarep. MPI_Datarep_conversion_function and
MPI_Datarep_extent_function are not MPI functions; they show the calling sequences for the
callback functions passed to MPI_Register_datarep.

```
MPI_REGISTER_DATAREP(datarep, read_conversion_fn, write_conversion_fn,
             dtype_file_extent_fn, extra_state, ierror)
      character*(*) datarep
      external read_conversion_fn, write_conversion_fn,
          dtype_file_extent_fn
      integer(kind=MPI_ADDRESS_KIND) extra_state
      integer ierror

subroutine READ_CONVERSION_FUNCTION(userbuf, datatype, count,
             filebuf, position, extra_state, ierror)
      <type> userbuf(*), filebuf(*)
      integer count, datatype, ierror
      integer(kind=MPI_OFFSET_KIND) position
      integer(kind=MPI_ADDRESS_KIND) extra_state

subroutine DTYPE_FILE_EXTENT_FN(datatype, extent, extra_state, ierror)
      integer datatype, ierror
      integer(kind=MPI_ADDRESS_KIND) extent, extra_state
```

Table 9.2
Fortran binding for MPI_Register_datarep. read_conversion_function and
dtype_file_extent_fn are not MPI functions; they show the calling sequences for the callback
functions passed to MPI_Register_datarep. write_conversion_function has the same argument
list as read_conversion_function.

---

void MPI::Register_datarep(const char* datarep,

　　　　　MPI::Datarep_conversion_function* read_conversion_fn,

　　　　　MPI::Datarep_conversion_function* write_conversion_fn,

　　　　　MPI::Datarep_extent_function* dtype_file_extent_fn,

　　　　　void* extra_state)

Table 9.3
C++ binding for MPI_Register_datarep. The bindings for the callback functions are similar to the C case in Table 9.1.

MPI-2 I/O functions (ROMIO) uses this feature and therefore works with multiple MPI-1 implementations [88].

9.2.1   Decoding Datatypes

An MPI datatype is an opaque object that describes data layout. In many cases, such as for layering the MPI-2 I/O functions, it is necessary to know what a datatype represents. With purely MPI-1 functionality it is not possible to do so unless one has access to the internal representation of datatypes in the implementation. Such an approach is clearly nonportable. MPI-2, therefore, has defined a mechanism by which users can portably decode a datatype. Two functions are provided for this purpose: MPI_Type_get_envelope and MPI_Type_get_contents. To see how these functions can be used, let's write a simple program to determine whether a given datatype is a derived datatype of type hvector and, if so, print the count, blocklength, and stride that was used to create this hvector type. This program is shown in Figure 9.1.

We first call the function MPI_Type_get_envelope to determine whether the given datatype is of type hvector. The first argument to this function is the datatype itself. The function returns in the last argument a constant, called **combiner**, that indicates the kind of datatype. For example, it returns MPI_COMBINER_NAMED if the datatype is a predefined (basic) datatype, MPI_COMBINER_INDEXED if it is an indexed datatype, and so on. For derived datatypes, however, it is not sufficient just to know the kind of datatype; we also need to know how that derived datatype was constructed. The three arguments, **nints**, **nadds**, and **ntypes**, are output parameters that help us in this regard. **nints** tells us how many integer parameters were used in the constructor function that created **datatype**, **nadds** tells us how many address-sized parameters were used, and **ntypes** tells us how many datatypes were used. We use these values to allocate buffers of the right size and pass them to the function MPI_Type_get_contents in order to retrieve all the parameters that

```
#include "mpi.h"
#include <stdio.h>
#include <stdlib.h>

void is_type_hvector(MPI_Datatype datatype)
{
    int nints, nadds, ntypes, combiner, *ints;
    MPI_Aint *adds;
    MPI_Datatype *types;

    MPI_Type_get_envelope(datatype, &nints, &nadds, &ntypes,
                          &combiner);

    if (combiner != MPI_COMBINER_HVECTOR)
        printf("not type_hvector\n");
    else {
        printf("is type_hvector\n");
        ints = (int *) malloc(nints*sizeof(int));
        adds = (MPI_Aint *) malloc(nadds*sizeof(MPI_Aint));
        types = (MPI_Datatype *) malloc(ntypes*sizeof(MPI_Datatype));

        MPI_Type_get_contents(datatype, nints, nadds, ntypes,
                              ints, adds, types);
        printf("count = %d, blocklength = %d, stride = %ld\n",
               ints[0], ints[1], adds[0]);
        free(ints);
        free(adds);
        free(types);
    }
}
```

Figure 9.1
Code that checks if a given datatype is of type hvector and, if so, prints the count, blocklength, and stride

> int **MPI_Type_get_envelope**(MPI_Datatype datatype, int *num_integers,
>   int *num_addresses, int *num_datatypes, int *combiner)
>
> int **MPI_Type_get_contents**(MPI_Datatype datatype, int max_integers,
>   int max_addresses, int max_datatypes, int array_of_integers[],
>   MPI_Aint array_of_addresses[], MPI_Datatype array_of_datatypes[])

Table 9.4
C bindings for `MPI_Type_get_envelope` and `MPI_Type_get_contents`

were used to create `datatype`.

For an hvector datatype in our example program, `MPI_Type_get_envelope` returns `combiner=MPI_COMBINER_HVECTOR`, `nints=2`, `nadds=1`, and `ntypes=1`. We allocate three arrays, called `ints`, `adds`, and `types`, of sizes `nints`, `nadds`, and `ntypes`, respectively. We next call `MPI_Type_get_contents` with `datatype` as the first parameter; then the three values `nints`, `nadds`, and `ntypes`; and finally the three arrays `ints`, `adds`, and `types`. The implementation will fill these arrays with the parameters that were used in the construction of `datatype`. For each kind of derived datatype (contiguous, vector, indexed, etc.), the MPI Standard specifies exactly how these arrays are filled. For an hvector datatype, `ints[0]` and `ints[1]` contain the count and blocklength that were passed to the hvector constructor function, `adds[0]` contains the stride, and `types[0]` contains a datatype equivalent to the datatype passed to the hvector constructor.

We can recursively call `MPI_Type_get_envelope` and `MPI_Type_get_contents` on the returned datatype until we reach a basic datatype. In this way, recursively constructed datatypes can be recursively decoded.

We note that `MPI_Type_get_contents` must be called only for derived datatypes. It is erroneous to call this function for a basic datatype, and, in fact, there is no reason to do so. One can determine the type of a basic datatype by simply doing a comparison check, such as "if (datatype == MPI_INT)." One cannot use a C `switch` statement, however, because `MPI_INT`, `MPI_DOUBLE`, and so forth are not necessarily compile-time constants.

C, Fortran, and C++ bindings for the datatype decoding functions are given in Tables 9.4, 9.5, and 9.6.

9.2.2 Generalized Requests

MPI enables users to define new nonblocking operations, create `MPI_Request` objects for them, and use any of the usual MPI functions, such as `MPI_Test`, `MPI_`-

---

MPI_TYPE_GET_ENVELOPE(datatype, num_integers, num_addresses,
              num_datatypes, combiner, ierror)
       integer datatype, num_integers, num_addresses, num_datatypes,
              combiner, ierror

MPI_TYPE_GET_CONTENTS(datatype, max_integers, max_addresses,
              max_datatypes, array_of_integers, array_of_addresses,
              array_of_datatypes, ierror)
       integer datatype, max_integers, max_addresses, max_datatypes,
              array_of_integers(*), array_of_datatypes(*), ierror
       integer(kind=MPI_ADDRESS_KIND) array_of_addresses(*)

Table 9.5
Fortran bindings for `MPI_Type_get_envelope` and `MPI_Type_get_contents`

---

void MPI::Datatype::Get_envelope(int& num_integers, int& num_addresses,
              int& num_datatypes, int& combiner) const

void MPI::Datatype::Get_contents(int max_integers, int max_addresses,
              int max_datatypes, int array_of_integers[],
              MPI::Aint array_of_addresses[],
              MPI::Datatype array_of_datatypes[]) const

Table 9.6
C++ bindings for `MPI_Type_get_envelope` and `MPI_Type_get_contents`

`Wait`, or their variants, to test or wait for the completion of these operations. Such requests are called *generalized requests*.

To understand how generalized requests can be used, let's consider the example of implementing the nonblocking write function `MPI_File_iwrite` on top of its blocking version, `MPI_File_write`, using a thread. We have split the code into two figures: Figure 9.2 contains the function `MPI_File_iwrite`, and Figure 9.3 contains other functions used in Figure 9.2.

Implementing `MPI_File_iwrite`. In the implementation of `MPI_File_iwrite` we first allocate a structure called **params** and fill it with various parameters that we want to pass to the thread function `write_thread` and to the callback functions associated with the generalized request (explained below). We directly fill into this structure the parameters `fh`, `buf`, and `count` that were passed to `MPI_File_iwrite`. We do not store the original datatype directly because the user may free the data-

```
#include "mpi.h"
#include <pthread.h>

typedef struct {
    MPI_File fh;
    void *buf;
    int count;
    MPI_Datatype *datatype;
    MPI_Request *request;
    MPI_Status *status;
} params_struct;

void *write_thread(void *ptr);

int MPI_File_iwrite(MPI_File fh, void *buf, int count,
                    MPI_Datatype datatype, MPI_Request *request)
{
    pthread_t thread;
    params_struct *params;
    MPI_Status *status;

    status = (MPI_Status *) malloc(sizeof(MPI_Status));
    params = (params_struct *) malloc(sizeof(params_struct));
    params->fh = fh;
    params->buf = buf;
    params->count = count;
    params->status = status;
    MPI_Type_dup(datatype, params->datatype);

    MPI_Grequest_start(query_fn, free_fn, cancel_fn,
                       (void *) params, request);
    params->request = request;
    pthread_create(&thread, NULL, write_thread, (void *) params);
    return MPI_SUCCESS;
}
```

Figure 9.2
Implementing MPI_File_iwrite on top of MPI_File_write using generalized requests and threads.
The functions write_thread, query_fn, free_fn, and cancel_fn are defined in Figure 9.3.

```
void *write_thread(void *ptr)
{
    params_struct *params;

    params = (params_struct *) ptr;
    MPI_File_write(params->fh, params->buf, params->count,
                   *(params->datatype), params->status);
    MPI_Grequest_complete(*(params->request));
    return 0;
}

int query_fn(void *extra_state, MPI_Status *status)
{
    params_struct *params;
    int count;

    params = (params_struct *) extra_state;
    MPI_Get_elements(params->status, *(params->datatype), &count);
    MPI_Status_set_elements(status, *(params->datatype), count);
    MPI_Status_set_cancelled(status, 0);
    return MPI_SUCCESS;
}

int free_fn(void *extra_state)
{
    free(((params_struct *) extra_state)->status);
    MPI_Type_free(((params_struct *) extra_state)->datatype);
    free(extra_state);
    return MPI_SUCCESS;
}

int cancel_fn(void *extra_state, int complete)
{
    return MPI_SUCCESS;
}
```

Figure 9.3
Definitions of functions used in the code in Figure 9.2

type immediately after MPI_File_iwrite returns.[1] We instead create a duplicate of the datatype using MPI_Type_dup and store this duplicate. We also dynamically allocate a status object and store a pointer to it in the params structure. We do so because we need to pass this status object around the various callback functions: we will use it as the status argument to MPI_File_write, and we will query its contents in order to fill the corresponding status object for the generalized request. The status object, therefore, must remain allocated until the generalized request is freed.

The function to create a generalized request is MPI_Grequest_start. The name is somewhat misleading: this function does not actually start any operation; it just creates a new request object that can be associated with the new nonblocking operation being defined. We must start the nonblocking operation separately, and we do so by using the POSIX [42] function pthread_create, which creates a new thread.[2]

The first three arguments to MPI_Grequest_start are callback functions that we must provide. The MPI implementation will use these callback functions when MPI_Test, MPI_Wait, MPI_Cancel, and other such MPI functions are called on the generalized request. We explain below how we have implemented these callback functions. The fourth argument to MPI_Grequest_start is an extra-state argument, which the implementation does not use itself but simply passes to the callback functions each time they are called. We pass the params structure as this argument. The implementation returns a request object, called *generalized request*, as the fifth argument. To the user, this generalized request is like any other request object returned by a nonblocking MPI function. Any of the usual functions, such as MPI_-Test or MPI_Wait, can be called on this object. The implementation will invoke the callback functions to implement test, wait, and other operations on the generalized request.

We start the nonblocking write with a call to pthread_create, which creates a new thread within the process. The ID of the newly created thread is returned in the first argument. The second argument specifies the attributes for the new thread; we just pass a null argument, which means that the default thread attributes will be used. The third argument specifies the function that the thread will execute. In this

---

[1]MPI allows the user to free an MPI object after the routine that begins a nonblocking operation; the MPI implementation internally retains all necessary information about the object until the nonblocking operation completes.

[2]Note that if we used the thread to call a blocking system routine, such as write, we would need to ensure that the thread was a kernel thread, as discussed in Chapter 8. Since we will use an MPI call for the I/O, MPI guarantees that calling the MPI blocking routine will block only the thread, not the process.

example, the function is `write_thread`. The final argument is the parameter that the thread will pass to the function `write_thread`; we pass the `params` structure as this argument. Since `write_thread` is run as a separate thread, `pthread_create` returns without waiting for `write_thread` to complete. As a result, the function `MPI_File_iwrite` returns with the write operation initiated but not completed, that is, as a nonblocking write operation.

• `write_thread`. In the function `write_thread`, we simply call the blocking version (`MPI_File_write`) of the nonblocking function being implemented. The parameters passed to this function are extracted from the `params` structure. Since this is a blocking function, it returns only after the write has completed. After it returns, we call the function `MPI_Grequest_complete` to inform the implementation that the operation associated with the generalized request has completed. Only after `MPI_Grequest_complete` has been called will the implementation return `flag=true` when the user calls `MPI_Test` on the request. Similarly, `MPI_Wait` will return only after `MPI_Grequest_complete` has been called.

Let's now see how we have implemented the three callback functions passed to `MPI_Grequest_start`.

• `query_fn`. The MPI implementation will call `query_fn` to fill the status object for the request. This will occur, for example, when `MPI_Test` or `MPI_Wait` are called on the request. The implementation will pass to `query_fn` the `params` structure that we passed as the `extra_state` argument to `MPI_Grequest_start`. The second argument passed to `query_fn` is a status object that we must fill. To fill the status object, we use the functions `MPI_Status_set_elements` and `MPI_Status_set_cancelled`, which also are external interface functions defined in MPI-2.

Recall that the `params` structure contains a status object that was filled by `MPI_File_write` in the function `write_thread`. We use the MPI-1 function `MPI_Get_elements` to retrieve the number of basic elements that were written by `MPI_File_write`. We then use `MPI_Status_set_elements` to enter the same value in the status object passed by the MPI implementation to `query_fn`. Note that there is no function like `MPI_Status_set_count` in MPI for setting the value to be returned when `MPI_Get_count` is called on the status object. This is because the implementation can calculate the count from the number of basic elements that we have specified using `MPI_Status_set_elements`.

We also need to specify in the status object if the request had been successfully cancelled in response to an `MPI_Cancel` called by the user. The user can check whether the cancellation was successful by using the function `MPI_Test_cancelled`.

In this simple example, we do not support cancellation of requests; therefore, we simply pass 0 as the second argument to MPI_Status_set_cancelled.

- **free_fn.** The MPI implementation will invoke the callback function free_fn to free all resources allocated by the user for implementing the generalized request. free_fn will be invoked when the generalized request is freed, for example, with MPI_Test, MPI_Wait, or MPI_Request_free. The implementation also passes to free_fn the extra_state argument (params structure) that we passed to MPI_-Grequest_start. In the free_fn, we free the data structures that we allocated in the implementation of MPI_File_iwrite, namely, the status object and the duplicated datatype stored in the params structure and then the params structure itself.

- **cancel_fn.** The MPI implementation will invoke the callback function cancel_-fn when the user attempts to cancel the nonblocking operation using MPI_Cancel. The implementation will pass complete=true to cancel_fn if MPI_Grequest_-complete has already been called on the request (by the separate thread executing the function write_thread); otherwise, it will pass complete=false. This lets us know whether the nonblocking operation has already completed and therefore cannot be cancelled. In this simple example, however, we do not support cancellation anyway. Therefore, we simply return MPI_SUCCESS.

Note that in order to know whether the request was successfully cancelled, the user must call MPI_Test_cancelled. Calling MPI_Test_cancelled will cause the implementation to invoke the query_fn in which we set the cancelled field of the status object to 0, indicating that the request was not cancelled.

We stress the fact that the mechanism for generalized requests in MPI does *not* start nonblocking operations, nor does it cause them to progress or complete. The user must use some other mechanism (for example, threads) to take care of initiation, progress, and completion of the operation. MPI needs to be informed only of the completion of the generalized request (by calling MPI_Grequest_complete).

C, Fortran, and C++ bindings for the MPI functions for generalized requests and for filling the status object are given in Tables 9.7, 9.8, and 9.9.

9.2.3   Adding New Error Codes and Classes

A layered library, such as an implementation of the MPI-2 I/O functions on top of an MPI-1 implementation, may need to add new error codes and classes to the ones already defined by the MPI implementation. These would allow the user to call the usual MPI-1 functions on error code and classes, namely, MPI_Error_class to

---

int **MPI_Grequest_start**(MPI_Grequest_query_function *query_fn,
                MPI_Grequest_free_function *free_fn,
                MPI_Grequest_cancel_function *cancel_fn, void *extra_state,
                MPI_Request *request)

typedef int **MPI_Grequest_query_function**(void *extra_state,MPI_Status *status)

typedef int **MPI_Grequest_free_function**(void *extra_state)

typedef int **MPI_Grequest_cancel_function**(void *extra_state, int complete)

int **MPI_Grequest_complete**(MPI_Request request)

int **MPI_Status_set_elements**(MPI_Status *status, MPI_Datatype datatype,
                int count)

int **MPI_Status_set_cancelled**(MPI_Status *status, int flag)

Table 9.7
C bindings for the MPI functions for generalized requests and for filling the status object.
MPI_Grequest_query_function, MPI_Grequest_free_function, and
MPI_Grequest_cancel_function are not MPI functions; they show the calling sequences for the
callback functions passed to MPI_Grequest_start.

determine the error class to which an error code belongs and MPI_Error_string to
retrieve a text string associated with the error code. MPI provides three functions
for adding new error codes and classes: MPI_Add_error_class, MPI_Add_error_-
code, and MPI_Add_error_string. As an example, let's see how a layered library
of the MPI-2 I/O functionality can add the I/O error class MPI_ERR_AMODE, an
error code associated with this class, and the corresponding error strings to the
MPI implementation. The program fragment is shown in Figure 9.4.

Note that an error class indicates a particular kind of error in general. Multiple
error codes, corresponding to more specific errors, can be associated with an error
class. In this example, we define a new error class, MPI_ERR_AMODE, and a specific
error code, MPIO_ERR_AMODE_COMB, associated with this class. We use MPIO_, and
not MPI_, for the error code because error codes are not predefined in MPI; only
error classes are. We have defined the error code and class as external variables
because they need to be used in other parts of the layered I/O library.

We use the function MPI_Add_error_class to create a new error class called
MPI_ERR_AMODE. The MPI implementation assigns a value to the new error class;
we cannot directly assign a value to it ourselves. We use the function MPI_Add_-

MPI_GREQUEST_START(query_fn, free_fn, cancel_fn, extra_state, request, ierror)
          integer request, ierror
          external query_fn, free_fn, cancel_fn
          integer (kind=MPI_ADDRESS_KIND) extra_state

subroutine QUERY_FN(extra_state, status, ierror)
          integer status(MPI_STATUS_SIZE), ierror
          integer(kind=MPI_ADDRESS_KIND) extra_state

subroutine FREE_FN(extra_state,ierror)
          integer ierror
          integer(kind=MPI_ADDRESS_KIND) extra_state

subroutine CANCEL_FN(extra_state, complete, ierror)
          integer ierror
          integer(kind=MPI_ADDRESS_KIND) extra_state
          logical complete

MPI_GREQUEST_COMPLETE(request, ierror)
          integer request, ierror

MPI_STATUS_SET_ELEMENTS(status, datatype, count, ierror)
          integer status(MPI_STATUS_SIZE), datatype, count, ierror

MPI_STATUS_SET_CANCELLED(status, flag, ierror)
          integer status(MPI_STATUS_SIZE), ierror
          logical flag

Table 9.8
Fortran bindings for MPI_Grequest_start and MPI_Grequest_complete. query_fn, free_fn, and cancel_fn are not MPI functions; they show the calling sequences for the callback functions passed to MPI_Grequest_start.

MPI::Grequest MPI::Grequest::Start(
　　　　　　const MPI::Grequest::Query_function query_fn,
　　　　　　const MPI::Grequest::Free_function free_fn,
　　　　　　const MPI::Grequest::Cancel_function cancel_fn, void **extra_state)**

void MPI::Grequest::Complete()

void MPI::Status::Set_elements(const MPI::Datatype& datatype, int count)

void MPI::Status::Set_cancelled(bool flag)

Table 9.9
C++ bindings for `MPI_Grequest_start` and `MPI_Grequest_complete`. The bindings for the callback functions are similar to the C case in Table 9.7.

```
extern int MPI_ERR_AMODE;          /* error class */
extern int MPIO_ERR_AMODE_COMB;    /* error code */

MPI_Add_error_class(&MPI_ERR_AMODE);
MPI_Add_error_code(MPI_ERR_AMODE, &MPIO_ERR_AMODE_COMB);
MPI_Add_error_string(MPI_ERR_AMODE,
  "Error related to the amode passed to MPI_File_open");
MPI_Add_error_string(MPIO_ERR_AMODE_COMB,
  "MPI_MODE_RDWR and MPI_MODE_RDONLY cannot be specified together");
```

Figure 9.4
Adding new error codes and classes to an MPI implementation. In this example, a layered library of the MPI-2 I/O functionality adds the error class MPI_ERR_AMODE, an error code associated with this class, and the corresponding error strings to the MPI implementation.

error_code to create a new error code, MPIO_ERR_AMODE_COMB, associated with the error class MPI_ERR_AMODE. The implementation assigns a value to this error code. Next we use the function MPI_Add_error_string to associate a text string with the new error class and error code. Note that the string associated with the error class indicates a general error about amode, whereas the string associated with the error code indicates a very specific error. After the new error code and class have been added in this fashion, users can use the functions MPI_Error_class and MPI_Error_string on the new error code and class.

C, Fortran, and C++ bindings for MPI_Add_error_class, MPI_Add_error_code, and MPI_Add_error_string are given in Tables 9.10, 9.11, and 9.12.

---

int **MPI_Add_error_class**(int *errorclass)

int **MPI_Add_error_code**(int errorclass, int *errorcode)

int **MPI_Add_error_string**(int errorcode, char *string)

Table 9.10
C bindings for the functions for adding new error codes and classes

---

MPI_ADD_ERROR_CLASS(errorclass, ierror)
        integer errorclass, ierror

MPI_ADD_ERROR_CODE(errorclass, errorcode, ierror)
        integer errorclass, errorcode, ierror

MPI_ADD_ERROR_STRING(errorcode, string, ierror)
        integer errorcode, ierror
        character*(*) string

Table 9.11
Fortran bindings for the functions for adding new error codes and classes

---

int **MPI::Add_error_class**()

int **MPI::Add_error_code**(int errorclass)

void **MPI::Add_error_string**(int errorcode, const char* string)

Table 9.12
C++ bindings for the functions for adding new error codes and classes

9.3   Mixed-Language Programming

Library writers often write a library in one language (for example, C) and provide interfaces to it (called wrappers) from other languages (for example, Fortran and C++). MPI provides features that make it possible for a program written in one language to call MPI functions implemented in another language. The three languages that MPI supports are C, Fortran, and C++. MPI also allows programs written in different languages to send messages to one another; we considered such an example in Chapter 7.

Let us consider the example of implementing the Fortran interface for the MPI function MPI_File_write on top of its C implementation. The code is shown in

```
#include "mpi.h"

void mpi_file_write_(MPI_Fint *fh, void *buf, int *count,
                     MPI_Fint *datatype, MPI_Fint *status,
                     MPI_Fint *err)
{
    MPI_File fh_c;
    MPI_Datatype datatype_c;
    MPI_Status status_c;

    fh_c = MPI_File_f2c(*fh);
    datatype_c = MPI_Type_f2c(*datatype);
    *err = (MPI_Fint) MPI_File_write(fh_c, buf, *count, datatype_c,
                                     &status_c);
    MPI_Status_c2f(&status_c, status);
}
```

Figure 9.5
Implementing the Fortran interface for MPI_File_write

Figure 9.5. When a user compiles a Fortran program containing a call to the
"external" function MPI_File_write, the compiler creates an object file in which
this function is named according to some convention followed by the compiler. For
example, some compilers convert the function name to all lower-case letters and
append an underscore at the end, some compilers add a double underscore at the
end, some don't add an underscore, and some convert the function name to all
capital letters. For the Fortran program to link correctly, we must define the name
of the C wrapper function according to the convention followed by the Fortran
compiler. Let's assume that the Fortran compiler converts the function name to
lower case and adds an underscore. Therefore, we name the wrapper function
mpi_file_write_.

The argument list to this function takes into account the fact that parameters to
functions in Fortran are passed by reference (as addresses) and that handles to MPI
objects in Fortran are defined to be of type integer. Since an integer in Fortran
may not be of the same size as an integer in C, MPI provides a datatype called
MPI_Fint in C and C++, which represents an integer of the same size as a Fortran
integer. Therefore, all arguments to mpi_file_write_ other than the user's buffer
are of type MPI_Fint*.

Before we can call the C function MPI_File_write, the Fortran handles to MPI
objects must be converted to C handles. MPI provides handle conversion functions

MPI_File **MPI_File_f2c**(MPI_Fint file)

MPI_Datatype **MPI_Type_f2c**(MPI_Fint datatype)

int **MPI_Status_c2f**(MPI_Status *c_status, MPI_Fint *f_status)

Table 9.13
Bindings for the conversion functions used in Figure 9.5

to convert from C handles to Fortran handles and vice versa. We use MPI_File_f2c to convert the Fortran file handle to a C file handle and MPI_Type_f2c to convert the Fortran datatype handle to a C datatype handle. Then we call the C function MPI_File_write and pass it the C file handle and the C datatype. Since status is an output parameter, we define a new C status object and pass it to the function. After the function returns, we call MPI_Status_c2f, which copies all the information contained in the C status object into the Fortran status object passed by the user. Note that MPI_Status_c2f is slightly different from handle conversion functions such as MPI_File_c2f, because status objects are explicitly allocated by the user and are not system objects. Handle conversion functions merely convert handles between languages, whereas MPI_Status_c2f actually copies all the information contained in a C status object (a structure of type MPI_Status) into a user-supplied Fortran status object (an integer array of size MPI_STATUS_SIZE).

The MPI Standard specifies that datatypes defined in any language can be used in any other language after the handles have been converted appropriately using MPI_Type_f2c or MPI_Type_c2f (see Section 2.2.6 of [27]). For example, if the Fortran call to MPI_File_write specifies the datatype MPI_COMPLEX, the Fortran wrapper function can pass this datatype to the C function MPI_File_write after handle conversion with MPI_Type_f2c.

Similar handle conversion functions are provided for all other MPI objects, namely, groups, communicators, requests, window objects, info, and op. All handle conversion functions are defined in C only; they do not have Fortran and C++ bindings. Handles can be passed from C to C++ by using overloaded C++ operators called from C++ code. No provision exists in MPI for direct access to C++ objects from C and for direct access to C or C++ objects from Fortran.

The bindings for the conversion functions used in Figure 9.5 are given in Table 9.13.

9.4 Attribute Caching

MPI allows users to cache user-defined information on certain MPI objects, such as
communicators, datatypes, and windows. This feature of MPI is particularly useful
to library writers. MPI-1 supports this feature on communicators only. MPI-2
extended attribute caching to datatypes and windows. Let us consider an example
in which a library needs to decode a derived datatype and create a "flattened"
version of the datatype consisting of a list of offsets and lengths for use later in
the program. Flattening of datatypes is needed, for example, in a layered library
that implements the MPI-2 I/O functionality. Storing this flattened information
on the datatype itself by using attribute caching is very handy here because of the
following reasons:

- The flattened information can be easily accessed whenever the datatype is passed
to the library.
- When the user frees the datatype using `MPI_Type_free`, the MPI implementation
also frees the flattened information using the delete function that was provided
when the flattened information was cached as an attribute on the datatype. If the
flattened information is instead stored in some other way, such as in a table or list
indexed by the datatype handle, one cannot ensure that the flattened information
will be freed when the user frees the datatype. If the flattened information is not
freed when the user frees the datatype and if the MPI implementation reuses the
same datatype handle for a newly created derived datatype, there is a danger of the
library using the old flattened information for the new datatype. Attribute caching
eliminates this problem.

Figures 9.6 and 9.7 show the code for caching a flattened version of a datatype as
an attribute on the datatype. To store the flattened information, we use a structure
of type `flat_struct`, which contains an array of offsets, an array of lengths, the
number of entries (n) in these two arrays, and a reference count to avoid creating
multiple copies of this structure when the datatype is duplicated using `MPI_Type_-`
`dup`. We do not show the actual code for flattening a datatype; it can be written
along the lines of Figure 9.1 by using the functions `MPI_Type_get_envelope` and
`MPI_Type_get_contents` recursively.

We use the function `MPI_Type_create_keyval` to create a new attribute key that,
together with an associated value, can be cached on a datatype. The first two
parameters to `MPI_Type_create_keyval` are callback functions—a copy function
and a delete function—that we must provide. They are described below. MPI
returns in the third argument a key that we can use to cache an attribute value

```
#include "mpi.h"

typedef struct {
    MPI_Aint *offsets;
    int *lengths;
    int n; /*no. of entries in the offsets and lengths arrays*/
    int ref_count; /* reference count */
} flat_struct;

void Flatten_datatype(MPI_Datatype datatype)
{
    flat_struct *flat_dtype;
    int key;

    flat_dtype = (flat_struct *) malloc(sizeof(flat_struct));
    flat_dtype->ref_count = 1;

    /* code for allocating memory for the arrays "offsets" and
        "lengths" and for flattening the datatype and filling in the
        offsets and lengths arrays goes here */

    MPI_Type_create_keyval(Copy_fn, Delete_fn, &key, (void *) 0);
    MPI_Type_set_attr(datatype, key, flat_dtype);
}
```

Figure 9.6

Using attribute caching on datatypes to cache a flattened version of a datatype on the datatype itself. The copy and delete functions for the attribute key are defined in Figure 9.7.

on the datatype. The fourth argument is an extra-state argument, which MPI will simply pass on to the callback functions. We use the function MPI_Type_set_attr to store this key on the datatype and associate the flattened datatype as the value of this key. Attribute values are address-sized integers; therefore, we store a pointer to the flattened datatype as the attribute value.

The copy and delete callback functions for the attribute key are defined in Figure 9.7. MPI will call the copy function when the datatype is duplicated using MPI_Type_dup. In the copy function, we merely increment the reference count by one. We also set the flag parameter to 1 to indicate that we want this attribute to be cached on the duplicated datatype. If flag is set to 0, the attribute will be deleted from the duplicated datatype. In the attr_val_out parameter, we must return the attribute value associated with this key on the duplicated datatype. In

```
int Copy_fn(MPI_Datatype datatype, int key, void *extra_state,
            void *attr_val_in, void *attr_val_out, int *flag)
{
    ((flat_struct *) attr_val_in)->ref_count += 1;
    *((flat_struct **) attr_val_out) = (flat_struct *) attr_val_in;
    *flag = 1;
    return MPI_SUCCESS;
}

int Delete_fn(MPI_Datatype datatype, int key, void *attr_val,
              void *extra_state)
{
    flat_struct *flat_dtype;

    flat_dtype = (flat_struct *) attr_val;
    flat_dtype->ref_count -= 1;
    if (flat_dtype->ref_count == 0) {
        free(flat_dtype->offsets);
        free(flat_dtype->lengths);
        free(flat_dtype);
    }
    return MPI_SUCCESS;
}
```

Figure 9.7
Definitions of the copy and delete functions used in Figure 9.6

this case, the value is the same as the value on the original datatype, namely, a pointer to the flattened datatype structure, which MPI passes in the attr_val_in parameter.

Although both attr_val_in and attr_val_out are of type void*, they are defined differently. attr_val_in is the value itself, which is an address-sized variable and therefore of type void*. attr_val_out, however, is an output parameter; MPI will pass the address of the new attribute value as this parameter. attr_val_out is therefore an address of an address-sized variable, which is also defined as void*. Since attr_val_out is the address of the new attribute value and attr_val_in is the input value itself, we *cannot* simply do

```
attr_val_out = attr_val_in;
```

Instead we do

```
*((flat_struct **) attr_val_out) = (flat_struct *) attr_val_in;
```

---

int **MPI_Type_create_keyval**(MPI_Type_copy_attr_function *type_copy_attr_fn,
                MPI_Type_delete_attr_function *type_delete_attr_fn,
                int *type_keyval, void *extra_state)

typedef int **MPI_Type_copy_attr_function**(MPI_Datatype oldtype,int type_keyval,
                void *extra_state, void *attribute_val_in,void *attribute_val_out,
                int *flag)

typedef int **MPI_Type_delete_attr_function**(MPI_Datatype type, int type_keyval,
                void *attribute_val, void *extra_state)

int **MPI_Type_set_attr**(MPI_Datatype type, int type_keyval, void *attribute_val)

Table 9.14
C bindings for the attribute caching functions used in Section 9.4. MPI_Type_copy_attr_function
and MPI_Type_delete_attr_function are not MPI functions; they show the calling sequences for
the callback functions passed to MPI_Type_create_keyval.

MPI will call the delete function when the datatype is freed using MPI_Type_free.
In the delete function, we decrement the reference count. If the count is zero after
decrementing, we free the memory allocated for the flattened datatype.

C, Fortran, and C++ bindings for the attribute caching functions used in this
example are given in Tables 9.14, 9.15, and 9.16.

For cases where no special copy or delete functions are needed, MPI provides
"do-nothing" functions. These are MPI_COMM_NULL_COPY_FN and MPI_COMM_NULL_-
DELETE_FN for communicator attributes, MPI_TYPE_NULL_COPY_FN and MPI_TYPE_-
NULL_DELETE_FN for datatype attributes, and MPI_WIN_NULL_COPY_FN and MPI_-
WIN_NULL_DELETE_FN for window object attributes.

9.5 Error Handling

In this section we describe MPI's support for handling errors in programs.

9.5.1 Error Handlers

MPI associates an error handler function with each communicator, window object,
and file handle. If an error occurs in an MPI function, the implementation will
invoke the associated error handler. The default error handler for communicators
and window objects is MPI_ERRORS_ARE_FATAL, whereas for file handles it is MPI_-
ERRORS_RETURN. In other words, if the default error handlers are set and an error

MPI_TYPE_CREATE_KEYVAL(type_copy_attr_fn, type_delete_attr_fn,
            type_keyval, extra_state, ierror)
            external type_copy_attr_fn, type_delete_attr_fn
            integer type_keyval, ierror
            integer(kind=MPI_ADDRESS_KIND) extra_state

subroutine TYPE_COPY_ATTR_FN(oldtype, type_keyval, extra_state,
            attribute_val_in, attribute_val_out, flag, ierror)
            integer oldtype, type_keyval, ierror
            integer(kind=MPI_ADDRESS_KIND) extra_state, attribute_val_in,
                attribute_val_out
            logical flag

subroutine TYPE_DELETE_ATTR_FN(type, type_keyval, attribute_val,
            extra_state, ierror)
            integer type, type_keyval, ierror
            integer(kind=MPI_ADDRESS_KIND) attribute_val, extra_state

MPI_TYPE_SET_ATTR(type, type_keyval, attribute_val, ierror)
            integer type, type_keyval, ierror
            integer(kind=MPI_ADDRESS_KIND) attribute_val

Table 9.15
Fortran bindings for the attribute caching functions used in Section 9.4. `type_copy_attr_fn` and
`type_delete_attr_fn` are not MPI functions; they show the calling sequences for the callback
functions passed to `MPI_Type_create_keyval`.

int MPI::Datatype::Create_keyval(
            MPI::Datatype::Copy_attr_function* type_copy_attr_fn,
            MPI::Datatype::Delete_attr_function* type_delete_attr_fn,
            void* extra_state)

void MPI::Datatype::Set_attr(int type_keyval, const void* attribute_val)

Table 9.16
C++ bindings for the attribute caching functions used in Section 9.4. The bindings for the
callback functions are similar to the C case in Table 9.14.

occurs in a non-I/O function, the program will abort, whereas if an error occurs in an I/O function, the implementation will *try to* continue execution by returning an appropriate error code.

MPI provides functions to create a new error handler, to associate it with a communicator, window object, or file handle, and to explicitly invoke an error handler. Let's consider the case of file handles. The function for creating a new error handler that can be associated with a file handle is `MPI_File_create_errhandler`; the function for associating an error handler with a file handle is `MPI_File_set_errhandler`; and the function for explicitly invoking the error handler associated with a file handle is `MPI_File_call_errhandler`. Similar functions exist for communicators and window objects.

The default error handler for all files can be changed by calling `MPI_File_set_errhandler` with a null file handle, `MPI_FILE_NULL`, before any file is opened in the program. This method (of passing a null handle), however, cannot be used for communicators and window objects. The default error handler for all communicators can be changed by changing the error handler associated with `MPI_COMM_WORLD` immediately after MPI is initialized. Newly created communicators will inherit the new error handler from the "parent" communicator. There is no way to change the default error handler for all window objects; it must be changed explicitly for each window object by using `MPI_Win_set_errhandler`.

9.5.2 Error Codes and Classes

Almost all MPI functions in C and Fortran return an error code. In C, the error code is the return value of the MPI function; in Fortran, it is the `ierror` argument to the function. If the function returns successfully, the error code is set to `MPI_SUCCESS`; if not, an implementation-defined error code is returned. Error codes can be mapped onto standard MPI error classes by using the function `MPI_Error_class`. The function `MPI_Error_string` can be used to obtain a text string corresponding to the error code. The error classes defined in MPI for I/O and remote memory operations are listed in Tables 9.17 and 9.18, respectively. Other error classes defined in MPI-2—for dynamic process management, info functions, and some miscellaneous functions—are listed in Table 9.19. The error classes defined in MPI-1 are given in Chapter 7 of *Using MPI* [32].

For example, consider the following program fragment. For demonstration purposes, we use both methods of printing an error message: via error classes and via error strings.

```
errcode = MPI_File_open(MPI_COMM_WORLD, "/pfs/datafile",
```

```
                                MPI_MODE_RDONLY, MPI_INFO_NULL, &fh);
    if (errcode != MPI_SUCCESS) {
        MPI_Error_class(errcode, &errclass);
        if (errclass == MPI_ERR_NO_SUCH_FILE)
            printf("File does not exist\n");
        else {
            MPI_Error_string(errcode, str, &len);
            printf("%s\n", str);
        }
    }
```

The C++ functions do not return error codes. If an error occurs in non-I/O functions, the default error handler `MPI::ERRORS_ARE_FATAL` causes the program to abort. In the case of errors in I/O functions, the default I/O error handler `MPI::ERRORS_RETURN` simply returns control to the calling function; there is no provision for the user to retrieve the error code. To catch errors, users must change the error handler to `MPI::ERRORS_THROW_EXCEPTIONS`, which uses the C++ exception mechanism to signal an error by throwing an `MPI::Exception` object.

9.6   Topics Not Covered in This Book

MPI-2 has additional routines that we have not covered in this book. They include the following.

- Routines to add and retrieve printable names to MPI objects:
`MPI_Comm_set_name`, `MPI_Comm_get_name`, `MPI_Win_set_name`,
`MPI_Win_set_name`, `MPI_Type_set_name`, and `MPI_Win_get_name`.
- A routine to create an MPI connection out of an existing non-MPI connection:
`MPI_Comm_Join`
- Additional routines for I/O, including: `MPI_File_get_amode`,
`MPI_File_get_atomicity`, `MPI_File_get_byte_offset`, `MPI_File_get_group`,
`MPI_File_get_position`, `MPI_File_get_position_shared`,
`MPI_File_get_view`, `MPI_File_iread_at`, `MPI_File_preallocate`,
`MPI_File_read_all_begin`, `MPI_File_read_all_end`,
`MPI_File_read_at_all_begin`, `MPI_File_read_at_all_end`,
`MPI_File_set_size`, `MPI_File_write_at_all_begin`,
`MPI_File_write_at_all_end`, `MPI_File_write_ordered_begin`, and
`MPI_File_write_ordered_end`.

`MPI_ERR_FILE`	Invalid file handle
`MPI_ERR_NOT_SAME`	Collective argument not identical on all processes or collective routines called in a different order by different processes
`MPI_ERR_AMODE`	Error related to the `amode` passed to `MPI_File_open`
`MPI_ERR_UNSUPPORTED_DATAREP`	Unsupported `datarep` passed to `MPI_File_set_view`
`MPI_ERR_UNSUPPORTED_OPERATION`	Unsupported operation, such as seeking on a file that supports sequential access only
`MPI_ERR_NO_SUCH_FILE`	File does not exist
`MPI_ERR_FILE_EXISTS`	File exists
`MPI_ERR_BAD_FILE`	Invalid file name (e.g., path name too long)
`MPI_ERR_ACCESS`	Permission denied
`MPI_ERR_NO_SPACE`	Not enough space
`MPI_ERR_QUOTA`	Quota exceeded
`MPI_ERR_READ_ONLY`	Read-only file or file system
`MPI_ERR_FILE_IN_USE`	File operation could not be completed because the file is currently open by some process
`MPI_ERR_DUP_DATAREP`	Conversion functions could not be registered because a data representation identifier that was already defined was passed to `MPI_Register_datarep`
`MPI_ERR_CONVERSION`	An error occurred in a user-supplied data conversion function
`MPI_ERR_IO`	Other I/O error

Table 9.17
Error classes for I/O

`MPI_ERR_WIN`	Invalid `win` argument
`MPI_ERR_BASE`	Invalid `base` argument
`MPI_ERR_SIZE`	Invalid `size` argument
`MPI_ERR_DISP`	Invalid `disp` argument
`MPI_ERR_LOCKTYPE`	Invalid `locktype` argument
`MPI_ERR_ASSERT`	Invalid `assert` argument
`MPI_ERR_RMA_CONFLICT`	Conflicting accesses to window
`MPI_ERR_RMA_SYNC`	Wrong synchronization of RMA calls

Table 9.18
Error classes for RMA operations

Dynamic Process Management

MPI_ERR_SPAWN	Unable to spawn specified number of processes
MPI_ERR_PORT	Named port does not exist or has been closed
MPI_ERR_SERVICE	An attempt to unpublish a name that has not been published or has already been unpublished
MPI_ERR_NAME	Service name has not been published

Info Functions

MPI_ERR_INFO_KEY	Size of info key exceeds MPI_MAX_INFO_KEY
MPI_ERR_INFO_VALUE	Size of info value exceeds MPI_MAX_INFO_VAL
MPI_ERR_INFO_NOKEY	Key not defined in info object

Miscellaneous

MPI_ERR_KEYVAL	Invalid attribute key
MPI_ERR_NO_MEM	Out of memory in MPI_Alloc_mem

Table 9.19
Other error classes defined in MPI-2

- Additional routines for manipulating info objects: MPI_Info_delete, MPI_Info_dup, and MPI_Info_get_valuelen.
- Routines to pack and unpack from a specified external data representation: MPI_Pack_external and MPI_Unpack_external.

Although these routines did not find a natural place in our book, they may be just what you need. For example, the routines for naming MPI objects can allow an MPI-aware debugger to print more detailed information about an MPI object. We encourage you to consider these routines when developing an application.

10 Conclusions

In this chapter we summarize our journey through the new types of parallel programs that are enabled by MPI-2, comment on the current status of MPI-2 implementations, and speculate on future directions for MPI.

10.1 New Classes of Parallel Programs

By providing a standard message-passing interface, MPI-1 made it possible for the parallel programs of its time to become portable. Many message-passing programs, particularly in the area of scientific computing, were already in production use. Over a relatively short period, most of them were converted to MPI and thus achieved portability. New message-passing applications were developed that used MPI from the very beginning.

MPI confers portability in both "space" and "time." An MPI application can be run on multiple parallel computers or developed on one and run in production mode on another (space portability). Perhaps even more important, an MPI application can be moved from one generation of machines to the next (time portability). This property has proven to be extremely important as the set of parallel computer vendors and types of parallel machines have undergone rapid change.

The MPI-2 Standard greatly extends the range of programs that can be written portably from their inception. Programs that require high-performance I/O, programs with dynamically changing numbers of processes, programs that use loose synchronization and remote memory access, and libraries that extend MPI itself are all starting to be written, and, because of MPI, they can be written portably.

10.2 MPI-2 Implementation Status

MPI-2 is larger and more complex than MPI-1, and implementation is proceeding more slowly. Nonetheless, as this book is being written (in the summer of 1999), one complete MPI-2 implementation already exists and several others are under development.

10.2.1 Vendor Implementations

Fujitsu offers a complete MPI-2 implementation, done by PALLAS. Compaq (formerly Digital), Fujitsu, HP, IBM, NEC, SGI, Sun, and others are in the process of providing MPI-2 functionality, in most cases starting with parallel I/O. The current release of HP's MPI includes some of the remote memory access functions, as

well the MPI-2 thread functions and multithreading of MPI calls. The Edinburgh
Parallel Computing Center has developed a nearly complete implementation of the
remote-memory functions for the Cray/SGI T3D [9]. Compaq has demonstrated
one-sided operations but has not yet released them. We expect to see more and
more parts of MPI-2 appear in each of these companies' MPI products as time goes
by.

10.2.2 Free, Portable Implementations

The most widely used publicly available MPI implementations are LAM [7] and
MPICH [30]. These MPI implementations are particularly popular on heterogeneous workstation networks and "Beowulf" clusters, where no vendor implementation is available. MPICH is also used on massively parallel processors where it
competes with vendor MPI implementations.

Both LAM and MPICH are moving in the direction of MPI-2. Both already
offer the parallel I/O part of MPI-2 (see Section 10.2.3) and the C++ bindings for
MPI-1. LAM also has the dynamic process management functionality and part of
the remote memory operations. As of this writing, MPICH is undergoing an internal
redesign (see Appendix B of *Using MPI* [32]) in preparation for the addition of full
MPI-2 functionality.

10.2.3 Layering

For some areas of MPI-2, it is possible for a third party to supply part of the MPI
library in such a way that it uses any underlying MPI-1 implementation. We discussed this approach in Chapter 9 for implementing the MPI-2 I/O functionality.
This approach has been used in at least three different implementations of the MPI-2
I/O functions: our portable implementation, ROMIO [88]; the portable implementation PMPIO from NASA Ames Research Center [22]; and the implementation
on top of HPSS from Lawrence Livermore National Laboratory [45]. A group at
the University of Notre Dame has implemented the MPI-1 C++ bindings [66] as
wrappers for the C versions of the MPI-1 functions.

10.3 Where Does MPI Go from Here?

It is not known yet whether there will be an "MPI-3." Standardizing the basic
message-passing operations (MPI-1) has been a great success. The benefits of
standardizing the significant extensions to the message-passing model represented
by MPI-2 have yet to be realized. More experience is needed with the development

of applications that utilize the wide range of capabilities provided by MPI-2. We can expect these applications to appear as more and more MPI-2 implementations are released.

MPI-2 is certainly not the end of the line. As parallel computing hardware and software environments continue to evolve, the need for standardization in a number of areas will become apparent. Indeed, the most important benefit of MPI may turn out to be that it has raised expectations among application developers that vendors, users, and computer scientists can truly cooperate in the development of community standards that provide portability in both space and time. There are many areas where such cooperation would benefit the entire community. In some of these areas efforts are already under way. Others remain research areas with standardization still premature but possible in the future. In this section we briefly discuss some of these areas. Discussions that took place in the MPI Forum on several of these topics can be found in the MPI Forum's "Journal of Development," where ideas that were considered noteworthy but not ready for standardization were recorded [57].

10.3.1   More Remote Memory Operations

The MPI Forum debated a much larger list of RMA operations than the set that was eventually voted into the Standard. As discussed in Chapter 6, experience may show that the Forum's drive for economy went too far, and some of the operations that were voted out should have remained in. One test that should be applied to potential MPI-style remote-memory operations is that it should be straightforward to translate existing successful remote memory access libraries to their MPI counterparts. Examples are the Cray shmem library [18] and the Global Arrays library [63]. MPI remote memory operations should also make it easy to implement concepts, such as *monitors* [40], that have proven useful from the theoretical as well as practical point of view for managing shared data.

10.3.2   More on Threads

The MPI Forum also considered a more far-ranging set of functions for specifying explicit multithreading algorithms before settling on the narrow set of functions described in Chapter 8. As experience grows with multithreading and as both hardware and software environments provide more support for efficient multithreading, MPI may need to be extended in order to express algorithms that blend explicit (as opposed to automatic or compiler-directed) multithreading with MPI message-passing and remote-memory operations. Such an integrated environment would form a solid foundation for the next round of research on and experimentation with advanced programming models.

10.3.3   More Language Bindings

Java is here to stay as a major programming language. Its use as a language for scientific applications is just beginning, but there is already an effort, called the Java Grande Forum [44], to improve Java's performance and usability for scientific applications. Part of this effort is to propose a set of Java bindings for MPI [11]. While much of the C++ binding effort in MPI-2 can be carried over to Java, the new language presents its own set of problems (and opportunities!) with respect to MPI.

As parallel computing begins to be applied more and more in the business community, even as a way of speeding up old application systems, there may be interest in a COBOL binding.

10.3.4   Interoperability of MPI Implementations

One feature that users asked for soon after multiple MPI implementations appeared was *interoperability*, the ability for different MPI implementations to communicate. Such a system would enable a single application to run on multiple parallel computers, using a different MPI implementation on each. Now nearing completion is an effort, called IMPI (Interoperable MPI), to define the necessary protocols so that an MPI implementation can communicate with other similarly enabled MPI implementations. A draft of the protocol specification is available [14].

10.3.5   Real-Time MPI

During the MPI-2 Forum meetings, one group discussed the restrictions and extensions that would be necessary to adapt MPI for a number of different types of real-time environments. These deliberations were unfinished at the time the MPI-2 Standard was published, but the group continued to meet afterwards, calling itself the "MPI/RT Forum" [61]. The MPI/RT Forum has produced several versions of the MPI/RT specification [72].

10.4   Final Words

In this book we have illustrated and discussed the features of MPI-2. These features extend the programming model provided by MPI-1 and position MPI as a standard for new kinds of parallel programs. Throughout the book we have taken the opportunity to discuss some of the subtler issues of the message-passing model and its extensions. We hope users find this guide helpful in their development of advanced MPI applications.

A Summary of MPI-2 Routines and Their Arguments

This Appendix contains the bindings for the MPI-2 routines in C, Fortran, and C++.

A.1 C Routines

This section describes the C routines from [58].

```
int MPI_Accumulate(void *origin_addr, int origin_count,
        MPI_Datatype origin_datatype, int target_rank,
        MPI_Aint target_disp, int target_count,
        MPI_Datatype target_datatype, MPI_Op op, MPI_Win win)
```
Accumulates data in the window of the target process using the specified operation

```
int MPI_Add_error_class(int *errorclass)
```
Creates a new error class and returns its value

```
int MPI_Add_error_code(int errorclass, int *error)
```
Creates a new error code associated with the specified error class and returns its value

```
int MPI_Add_error_string(int errorcode, char *string)
```
Associates an error string with an error code or class

```
int MPI_Alloc_mem(MPI_Aint size, MPI_Info info, void *baseptr)
```
Allocates memory that may be used for (potentially faster) RMA and message-passing operations

```
int MPI_Alltoallw(void *sendbuf, int sendcounts[], int sdispls[],
        MPI_Datatype sendtypes[], void *recvbuf, int recvcounts[],
        int rdispls[], MPI_Datatype recvtypes[], MPI_Comm comm)
```
Sends data from all to all processes, with variable counts, displacements, and datatypes

```
int MPI_Close_port(char *port_name)
```
Releases the network address represented by the specified port name

```
int MPI_Comm_accept(char *port_name, MPI_Info info, int root,
        MPI_Comm comm, MPI_Comm *newcomm)
```
Establishes communication with a client

```
MPI_Fint MPI_Comm_c2f(MPI_Comm comm)
```
Converts a C communicator handle to a Fortran communicator handle

```
int MPI_Comm_call_errhandler(MPI_Comm comm, int error)
```
Invokes the error handler associated with a communicator

`int MPI_Comm_connect(char *port_name, MPI_Info info, int root,`
`        MPI_Comm comm, MPI_Comm *newcomm)`
Establishes communication with a server

`int MPI_Comm_create_errhandler(MPI_Comm_errhandler_fn *function,`
`        MPI_Errhandler *errhandler)`
Creates an error handler that can be attached to communicators

`int MPI_Comm_create_keyval(MPI_Comm_copy_attr_function *comm_copy_-`
`        attr_fn, MPI_Comm_delete_attr_function *comm_delete_attr_fn,`
`        int *comm_keyval, void *extra_state)`
Creates a new attribute key that can be cached on communicators

`int MPI_Comm_delete_attr(MPI_Comm comm, int comm_keyval)` *Deletes an attribute key cached on a communicator*
`int MPI_Comm_disconnect(MPI_Comm *comm)` *Waits for all pending communication in the communicator to complete and then frees the communicator*
`MPI_Comm MPI_Comm_f2c(MPI_Fint comm)` *Converts a Fortran communicator handle to a C communicator handle*
`int MPI_Comm_free_keyval(int *comm_keyval)` *Frees an attribute key created with* `MPI_Comm_create_keyval`

`int MPI_Comm_get_attr(MPI_Comm comm, int comm_keyval, void`
`        *attribute_val, int *flag)`
Returns the value associated with an attribute key cached on a communicator

`int MPI_Comm_get_errhandler(MPI_Comm comm,`
`        MPI_Errhandler *errhandler)`
Returns the error handler currently associated with a communicator

`int MPI_Comm_get_name(MPI_Comm comm, char *comm_name, int *resultlen)` *Returns the name associated with a communicator*
`int MPI_Comm_get_parent(MPI_Comm *parent)` *Returns the parent intercommunicator of a spawned process*
`int MPI_Comm_join(int fd, MPI_Comm *intercomm)` *Creates an intercommunicator from the union of two MPI processes that are connected by a socket*

`int MPI_Comm_set_attr(MPI_Comm comm, int comm_keyval, void`
`        *attribute_val)`
Sets the value for an attribute key cached on a communicator

```
int MPI_Comm_set_errhandler(MPI_Comm comm, MPI_Errhandler errhandler)
```
Attaches a new error handler to a communicator

```
int MPI_Comm_set_name(MPI_Comm comm, char *comm_name)
```
Associates a name with a communicator

```
int MPI_Comm_spawn(char *command, char *argv[], int maxprocs,
        MPI_Info info, int root, MPI_Comm comm,
        MPI_Comm *intercomm, int array_of_errcodes[])
```
Spawns new processes running an MPI program

```
int MPI_Comm_spawn_multiple(int count, char *array_of_commands[],
        char **array_of_argv[], int array_of_maxprocs[],
        MPI_Info array_of_info[], int root, MPI_Comm comm,
        MPI_Comm *intercomm, int array_of_errcodes[])
```
Spawns new processes running different MPI programs

```
int MPI_Exscan(void *sendbuf, void *recvbuf, int count,
        MPI_Datatype datatype, MPI_Op op, MPI_Comm comm)
```
Performs a prefix reduction

```
MPI_Fint MPI_File_c2f(MPI_File file)
```
Converts a C file handle to a Fortran file handle

```
int MPI_File_call_errhandler(MPI_File fh, int error)
```
Invokes the error handler associated with a file

```
int MPI_File_close(MPI_File *fh)
```
Closes a file

```
int MPI_File_create_errhandler(MPI_File_errhandler_fn *function,
        MPI_Errhandler *errhandler)
```
Creates an error handler that can be attached to files

```
int MPI_File_delete(char *filename, MPI_Info info)
```
Deletes a file

```
MPI_File MPI_File_f2c(MPI_Fint file)
```
Converts a Fortran file handle to a C file handle

```
int MPI_File_get_amode(MPI_File fh, int *amode)
```
Returns the access mode of a file

```
int MPI_File_get_atomicity(MPI_File fh, int *flag)
```
Returns the current setting for atomicity of file accesses

```
int MPI_File_get_byte_offset(MPI_File fh, MPI_Offset offset,
        MPI_Offset *disp)
```
Converts a view-relative file offset into an absolute byte offset

int MPI_File_get_errhandler(MPI_File file,   MPI_Errhandler *errhandler) *Returns the error handler associated with a file*
int MPI_File_get_group(MPI_File fh, MPI_Group *group) *Returns a duplicate of the group of the communicator used to open a file*
int MPI_File_get_info(MPI_File fh, MPI_Info *info_used) *Returns a new info object containing the hints currently associated with a file*
int MPI_File_get_position(MPI_File fh, MPI_Offset *offset) *Returns the current location of the individual file pointer*
int MPI_File_get_position_shared(MPI_File fh, MPI_Offset *offset) *Returns the current location of the shared file pointer*
int MPI_File_get_size(MPI_File fh, MPI_Offset *size) *Returns the size of a file in bytes*
int MPI_File_get_type_extent(MPI_File fh, MPI_Datatype datatype,   MPI_Aint *extent) *Returns the extent of a datatype in the file data representation*
int MPI_File_get_view(MPI_File fh, MPI_Offset *disp,   MPI_Datatype *etype, MPI_Datatype *filetype, char *datarep) *Returns the current file view*
int MPI_File_iread(MPI_File fh, void *buf, int count,   MPI_Datatype datatype, MPI_Request *request) *Starts a nonblocking file read from the current location of the individual file pointer*
int MPI_File_iread_at(MPI_File fh, MPI_Offset offset, void *buf,   int count, MPI_Datatype datatype, MPI_Request *request) *Starts a nonblocking file read from the specified offset*
int MPI_File_iread_shared(MPI_File fh, void *buf, int count,   MPI_Datatype datatype, MPI_Request *request) *Starts a nonblocking file read from the current location of the shared file pointer*
int MPI_File_iwrite(MPI_File fh, void *buf, int count,   MPI_Datatype datatype, MPI_Request *request) *Starts a nonblocking file write from the current location of the individual file pointer*
int MPI_File_iwrite_at(MPI_File fh, MPI_Offset offset, void *buf,   int count, MPI_Datatype datatype, MPI_Request *request) *Starts a nonblocking file write from the specified offset*

```
int MPI_File_iwrite_shared(MPI_File fh, void *buf, int count,
        MPI_Datatype datatype, MPI_Request *request)
```
Starts a nonblocking file write from the current location of the shared file pointer

```
int MPI_File_open(MPI_Comm comm, char *filename, int amode,
        MPI_Info info, MPI_File *fh)
```
Opens a file

```
int MPI_File_preallocate(MPI_File fh, MPI_Offset size)
```
Preallocates disk space for a file

```
int MPI_File_read(MPI_File fh, void *buf, int count,
        MPI_Datatype datatype, MPI_Status *status)
```
Reads from the current location of the individual file pointer

```
int MPI_File_read_all(MPI_File fh, void *buf, int count,
        MPI_Datatype datatype, MPI_Status *status)
```
Collective read from the current location of the individual file pointer

```
int MPI_File_read_all_begin(MPI_File fh, void *buf, int count,
        MPI_Datatype datatype)
```
Starts a split collective read from the current location of the individual file pointer

```
int MPI_File_read_all_end(MPI_File fh, void *buf, MPI_Status *status)
```
Completes a split collective read started with MPI_File_read_all_begin

```
int MPI_File_read_at(MPI_File fh, MPI_Offset offset, void *buf,
        int count, MPI_Datatype datatype, MPI_Status *status)
```
Reads from the specified file offset

```
int MPI_File_read_at_all(MPI_File fh, MPI_Offset offset, void *buf,
        int count, MPI_Datatype datatype, MPI_Status *status)
```
Collective read from the specified file offset

```
int MPI_File_read_at_all_begin(MPI_File fh, MPI_Offset offset,
        void *buf, int count, MPI_Datatype datatype)
```
Starts a split collective read from the specified file offset

```
int MPI_File_read_at_all_end(MPI_File fh, void *buf,
        MPI_Status *status)
```
Completes a split collective read started with MPI_File_read_at_all_begin

```
int MPI_File_read_ordered(MPI_File fh, void *buf, int count,
        MPI_Datatype datatype, MPI_Status *status)
```
Collective read using the shared file pointer

```
int MPI_File_read_ordered_begin(MPI_File fh, void *buf, int count,
        MPI_Datatype datatype)
```
Starts a split collective read using the shared file pointer

```
int MPI_File_read_ordered_end(MPI_File fh, void *buf,
        MPI_Status *status)
```
Completes a split collective read started with MPI_File_read_ordered_begin

```
int MPI_File_read_shared(MPI_File fh, void *buf, int count,
        MPI_Datatype datatype, MPI_Status *status)
```
Reads from the current location of the shared file pointer

```
int MPI_File_seek(MPI_File fh, MPI_Offset offset, int whence)
```
Moves the individual file pointer

```
int MPI_File_seek_shared(MPI_File fh, MPI_Offset offset, int whence)
```
Moves the shared file pointer

```
int MPI_File_set_atomicity(MPI_File fh, int flag)
```
Sets atomicity of file accesses

```
int MPI_File_set_errhandler(MPI_File file, MPI_Errhandler errhandler)
```
Attaches a new error handler to a file

```
int MPI_File_set_info(MPI_File fh, MPI_Info info)
```
Sets new values for the hints associated with a file

```
int MPI_File_set_size(MPI_File fh, MPI_Offset size)
```
Sets the file size

```
int MPI_File_set_view(MPI_File fh, MPI_Offset disp,
        MPI_Datatype etype, MPI_Datatype filetype, char *datarep,
        MPI_Info info)
```
Sets the file view

```
int MPI_File_sync(MPI_File fh)
```
Synchronizes any cached file data with that on the storage device

```
int MPI_File_write(MPI_File fh, void *buf, int count,
        MPI_Datatype datatype, MPI_Status *status)
```
Writes from the current location of the individual file pointer

```
int MPI_File_write_all(MPI_File fh, void *buf, int count,
        MPI_Datatype datatype, MPI_Status *status)
```
Collective write from the current location of the individual file pointer

```
int MPI_File_write_all_begin(MPI_File fh, void *buf, int count,
        MPI_Datatype datatype)
```
Starts a split collective write from the current location of the individual file pointer

```
int MPI_File_write_all_end(MPI_File fh, void *buf, MPI_Status *status)
```
Completes a split collective write started with MPI_File_write_all_begin

```
int MPI_File_write_at(MPI_File fh, MPI_Offset offset, void *buf,
          int count, MPI_Datatype datatype, MPI_Status *status)
```
Writes from the specified file offset

```
int MPI_File_write_at_all(MPI_File fh, MPI_Offset offset, void *buf,
          int count, MPI_Datatype datatype, MPI_Status *status)
```
Collective write from the specified file offset

```
int MPI_File_write_at_all_begin(MPI_File fh, MPI_Offset offset,
          void *buf, int count, MPI_Datatype datatype)
```
Starts a split collective write from the specified file offset

```
int MPI_File_write_at_all_end(MPI_File fh, void *buf,
          MPI_Status *status)
```
Completes a split collective write started with MPI_File_write_at_all_begin

```
int MPI_File_write_ordered(MPI_File fh, void *buf, int count,
          MPI_Datatype datatype, MPI_Status *status)
```
Collective write using the shared file pointer

```
int MPI_File_write_ordered_begin(MPI_File fh, void *buf, int count,
          MPI_Datatype datatype)
```
Starts a split collective write using the shared file pointer

```
int MPI_File_write_ordered_end(MPI_File fh, void *buf,
          MPI_Status *status)
```
Completes a split collective write started with MPI_File_write_ordered_begin

```
int MPI_File_write_shared(MPI_File fh, void *buf, int count,
          MPI_Datatype datatype, MPI_Status *status)
```
Writes from the current location of the shared file pointer

```
int MPI_Finalized(int *flag)
```
Indicates whether MPI_Finalize *has completed*

```
int MPI_Free_mem(void *base)
```
Frees memory allocated with MPI_Alloc_mem

```
int MPI_Get(void *origin_addr, int origin_count,
          MPI_Datatype origin_datatype, int target_rank,
          MPI_Aint target_disp, int target_count,
          MPI_Datatype target_datatype, MPI_Win win)
```
Starts a one-sided receive operation

`int MPI_Get_address(void *location, MPI_Aint *address)`
Returns the address of a location in memory
`int MPI_Grequest_complete(MPI_Request request)`
Informs MPI that the operations represented by a generalized request are complete

`int MPI_Grequest_start(MPI_Grequest_query_function *query_fn,`
`        MPI_Grequest_free_function *free_fn,`
`        MPI_Grequest_cancel_function *cancel_fn, void *extra_state,`
`        MPI_Request *request)`

Creates a new generalized request object
`MPI_Fint MPI_Group_c2f(MPI_Group group)`
Converts a C group handle to a Fortran group handle
`MPI_Group MPI_Group_f2c(MPI_Fint group)`
Converts a Fortran group handle to a C group handle
`MPI_Fint MPI_Info_c2f(MPI_Info info)`
Converts a C info handle to a Fortran info handle
`int MPI_Info_create(MPI_Info *info)`
Creates a new info object
`int MPI_Info_delete(MPI_Info info, char *key)`
Deletes a (key,value) pair from an info object
`int MPI_Info_dup(MPI_Info info, MPI_Info *newinfo)`
Returns a duplicate of an info object
`MPI_Info MPI_Info_f2c(MPI_Fint info)`
Converts a Fortran info handle to a C info handle
`int MPI_Info_free(MPI_Info *info)`
Frees an info object
`int MPI_Info_get(MPI_Info info, char *key, int valuelen, char *value,` `        int *flag)`
Returns the value associated with an info key
`int MPI_Info_get_nkeys(MPI_Info info, int *nkeys)`
Returns the number of keys currently defined in the info object
`int MPI_Info_get_nthkey(MPI_Info info, int n, char *key)`
Returns the nth key defined in the info object
`int MPI_Info_get_valuelen(MPI_Info info, char *key, int *valuelen,` `        int *flag)`
Returns the length of the value string associated with an info key

`int MPI_Info_set(MPI_Info info, char *key, char *value)`   *Adds a (key,value) pair to an info object*

`int MPI_Init_thread(int *argc, char *((*argv)[]), int required,`
 `        int *provided)`
 Initializes MPI and initializes the MPI thread environment

`int MPI_Is_thread_main(int *flag)`   *Indicates whether the thread calling this function is the main thread*

`int MPI_Lookup_name(char *service_name, MPI_Info info,`
 `        char *port_name)`
 Returns the port name associated with a service name

`MPI_Fint MPI_Op_c2f(MPI_Op op)`   *Converts a C op handle to a Fortran op handle*
`MPI_Op MPI_Op_f2c(MPI_Fint op)`   *Converts a Fortran op handle to a C op handle*
`int MPI_Open_port(MPI_Info info, char *port_name)`   *Establishes a network address at which the server will be able to accept connections from clients*

`int MPI_Pack_external(char *datarep, void *inbuf, int incount,`
 `        MPI_Datatype datatype, void *outbuf, MPI_Aint outsize,`
 `        MPI_Aint *position)`
 Packs data into a contiguous buffer in external32 format

`int MPI_Pack_external_size(char *datarep, int incount,`
 `        MPI_Datatype datatype, MPI_Aint *size)`
 Returns the amount of space needed to pack a datatype in external32 format

`int MPI_Publish_name(char *service_name, MPI_Info info,`
 `        char *port_name)`
 Publishes a (port_name, service_name) pair

`int MPI_Put(void *origin_addr, int origin_count,`
 `        MPI_Datatype origin_datatype, int target_rank,`
 `        MPI_Aint target_disp, int target_count,`
 `        MPI_Datatype target_datatype, MPI_Win win)`
 Starts a one-sided send operation

`int MPI_Query_thread(int *provided)`   *Returns the current level of thread support*

int MPI_Register_datarep(char *datarep,
        MPI_Datarep_conversion_function *read_conversion_fn,
        MPI_Datarep_conversion_function *write_conversion_fn,
        MPI_Datarep_extent_function *dtype_file_extent_fn,
        void *extra_state)
Adds a new file data representation to MPI

MPI_Fint MPI_Request_c2f(MPI_Request request) *Converts a C request handle to a Fortran request handle*
MPI_Request MPI_Request_f2c(MPI_Fint request) *Converts a Fortran request handle to a C request handle*
int MPI_Request_get_status(MPI_Request request, int *flag,   MPI_Status *status) *Tests completion of a nonblocking operation but does not free the request object if complete*
int MPI_Status_c2f(MPI_Status *c_status, MPI_Fint *f_status) *Converts a C status object to a Fortran status object*
int MPI_Status_f2c(MPI_Fint *f_status, MPI_Status *c_status) *Converts a Fortran status object to a C status object*
int MPI_Status_set_cancelled(MPI_Status *status, int flag) *Sets the value to be returned by* MPI_Test_cancelled
int MPI_Status_set_elements(MPI_Status *status,   MPI_Datatype datatype, int count) *Sets the value to be returned by* MPI_Get_elements
MPI_Fint MPI_Type_c2f(MPI_Datatype datatype) *Converts a C datatype handle to a Fortran datatype handle*

int MPI_Type_create_darray(int size, int rank, int ndims,
        int array_of_gsizes[], int array_of_distribs[],
        int array_of_dargs[], int array_of_psizes[], int order,
        MPI_Datatype oldtype, MPI_Datatype *newtype)
Creates a distributed array datatype

int MPI_Type_create_f90_complex(int p, int r, MPI_Datatype *newtype) *Returns a predefined MPI datatype that matches a Fortran 90* complex *variable with the specified precision and decimal exponent range*
int MPI_Type_create_f90_integer(int r, MPI_Datatype *newtype) *Returns a predefined MPI datatype that matches a Fortran 90* integer *variable with the specified number of decimal digits*

`int MPI_Type_create_f90_real(int p, int r, MPI_Datatype *newtype)` *Returns a predefined MPI datatype that matches a Fortran 90 real variable with the specified precision and decimal exponent range*

`int MPI_Type_create_hindexed(int count, int array_of_blocklengths[],`
        `MPI_Aint array_of_displacements[], MPI_Datatype oldtype,`
        `MPI_Datatype *newtype)`
Creates an indexed datatype with offsets in bytes

`int MPI_Type_create_hvector(int count, int blocklength,`
        `MPI_Aint stride, MPI_Datatype oldtype,`
        `MPI_Datatype *newtype)`
Creates a vector (strided) datatype with offset in bytes

`int MPI_Type_create_indexed_block(int count, int blocklength,`
        `int array_of_displacements[], MPI_Datatype oldtype,`
        `MPI_Datatype *newtype)`
Creates an indexed datatype with constant blocklength

`int MPI_Type_create_keyval(`
        `MPI_Type_copy_attr_function *type_copy_attr_fn,`
        `MPI_Type_delete_attr_function *type_delete_attr_fn,`
        `int *type_keyval, void *extra_state)`
Creates a new attribute key that can be cached on datatypes

`int MPI_Type_create_resized(MPI_Datatype oldtype, MPI_Aint lb,`
        `MPI_Aint extent, MPI_Datatype *newtype)`
Returns a new datatype with the specified lower bound and extent

`int MPI_Type_create_struct(int count, int array_of_blocklengths[],`
        `MPI_Aint array_of_displacements[],`
        `MPI_Datatype array_of_types[], MPI_Datatype *newtype)`
Creates a struct datatype

`int MPI_Type_create_subarray(int ndims, int array_of_sizes[],`
        `int array_of_subsizes[], int array_of_starts[], int order,`
        `MPI_Datatype oldtype, MPI_Datatype *newtype)`
Creates a subarray datatype

`int MPI_Type_delete_attr(MPI_Datatype type, int type_keyval)` *Deletes an attribute key cached on a datatype*
`int MPI_Type_dup(MPI_Datatype type, MPI_Datatype *newtype)` *Returns a duplicate of a datatype*

`MPI_Datatype MPI_Type_f2c(MPI_Fint datatype)` *Converts a Fortran datatype handle to a C datatype handle*
`int MPI_Type_free_keyval(int *type_keyval)` *Frees an attribute key created with* `MPI_Type_create_keyval`

`int MPI_Type_get_attr(MPI_Datatype type, int type_keyval,`
`        void *attribute_val, int *flag)`
Returns the value associated with an attribute key cached on a datatype

`int MPI_Type_get_contents(MPI_Datatype datatype, int max_integers,`
`        int max_addresses, int max_datatypes,`
`        int array_of_integers[], MPI_Aint array_of_addresses[],`
`        MPI_Datatype array_of_datatypes[])`
Returns the values of the parameters used to construct a derived datatype

`int MPI_Type_get_envelope(MPI_Datatype datatype, int *num_integers,`
`        int *num_addresses, int *num_datatypes, int *combiner)`
Returns the type of datatype and the number and type of arguments used to create the datatype

`int MPI_Type_get_extent(MPI_Datatype datatype, MPI_Aint *lb,`
`        MPI_Aint *extent)`
Returns the lower bound and extent of a datatype

`int MPI_Type_get_name(MPI_Datatype type, char *type_name,`
`        int *resultlen)`
Returns the name associated with a datatype

`int MPI_Type_get_true_extent(MPI_Datatype datatype, MPI_Aint *true_lb,`
`        MPI_Aint *true_extent)`
Returns the true extent of a datatype

`int MPI_Type_match_size(int typeclass, int size, MPI_Datatype *type)` *Returns an MPI datatype matching a local variable of specified type and size*

`int MPI_Type_set_attr(MPI_Datatype type, int type_keyval,`
`        void *attribute_val)`
Sets the value for an attribute key cached on a datatype

`int MPI_Type_set_name(MPI_Datatype type, char *type_name)` *Associates a name with a datatype*

`int MPI_Unpack_external(char *datarep, void *inbuf, MPI_Aint insize,`
`        MPI_Aint *position, void *outbuf, int outcount,`
`        MPI_Datatype datatype)`
Unpacks data stored contiguously in external32 format

`int MPI_Unpublish_name(char *service_name, MPI_Info info,`
`        char *port_name)`
Unpublishes a previously published service name

`MPI_Fint MPI_Win_c2f(MPI_Win win)` *Converts a C window object handle to a Fortran window object handle*
`int MPI_Win_call_errhandler(MPI_Win win, int error)` *Invokes the error handler associated with a window object*
`int MPI_Win_complete(MPI_Win win)` *Completes an RMA access epoch started with* `MPI_Win_start`

`int MPI_Win_create(void *base, MPI_Aint size, int disp_unit,`
`        MPI_Info info, MPI_Comm comm, MPI_Win *win)`
Creates a new window object

`int MPI_Win_create_errhandler(MPI_Win_errhandler_fn *function,`
`        MPI_Errhandler *errhandler)`
Creates an error handler that can be attached to window objects

`int MPI_Win_create_keyval(MPI_Win_copy_attr_function *win_copy_attr_fn,`
`        MPI_Win_delete_attr_function *win_delete_attr_fn,`
`        int *win_keyval, void *extra_state)`
Creates a new attribute key that can be cached on window objects

`int MPI_Win_delete_attr(MPI_Win win, int win_keyval)` *Deletes an attribute key cached on a window object*
`MPI_Win MPI_Win_f2c(MPI_Fint win)` *Converts a Fortran window object handle to a C window object handle*
`int MPI_Win_fence(int assert, MPI_Win win)` *Synchronizes RMA operations on a window object*
`int MPI_Win_free(MPI_Win *win)` *Frees a window object*
`int MPI_Win_free_keyval(int *win_keyval)` *Frees an attribute key created with* `MPI_Win_create_keyval`

`int MPI_Win_get_attr(MPI_Win win, int win_keyval, void *attribute_val,`
`        int *flag)`
Returns the value associated with an attribute key cached on a window object

`int MPI_Win_get_errhandler(MPI_Win win, MPI_Errhandler *errhandler)` *Returns the error handler associated with a window object*

int MPI_Win_get_group(MPI_Win win, MPI_Group *group)
Returns a duplicate of the group of the communicator used to create a window object

int MPI_Win_get_name(MPI_Win win, char *win_name, int *resultlen)
Returns the name associated with a window object

int MPI_Win_lock(int lock_type, int rank, int assert, MPI_Win win)
Starts an RMA access epoch enabling RMA operations only on the window at the specified process

int MPI_Win_post(MPI_Group group, int assert, MPI_Win win)
Starts an RMA exposure epoch for the local window associated with a window object

int MPI_Win_set_attr(MPI_Win win, int win_keyval, void *attribute_val)
Sets the value for an attribute key cached on a window object

int MPI_Win_set_errhandler(MPI_Win win, MPI_Errhandler errhandler)
Attaches a new error handler to a window object

int MPI_Win_set_name(MPI_Win win, char *win_name)
Associates a name with a window object

int MPI_Win_start(MPI_Group group, int assert, MPI_Win win)
Starts an RMA access epoch, enabling access only on windows at processes in the specified group

int MPI_Win_test(MPI_Win win, int *flag)
Tests whether RMA operations on the window object exposed with MPI_Win_post have completed

int MPI_Win_unlock(int rank, MPI_Win win)
Completes an RMA access epoch started with MPI_Win_lock

int MPI_Win_wait(MPI_Win win)
Completes an RMA exposure epoch started with MPI_Win_post

A.2   Fortran Routines

This section describes the Fortran routines from [58].

```
MPI_Accumulate(origin_addr, origin_count, origin_datatype,
        target_rank, target_disp, target_count, target_datatype, op,
        win, ierror)
<type> origin_addr(*)
integer(kind=MPI_ADDRESS_KIND) target_disp
integer origin_count, origin_datatype,target_rank, target_count,
target_datatype, op, win, ierror
```
Accumulates data in the window of the target process using the specified operation

```
MPI_Add_error_class(errorclass, ierror)
integer errorclass, ierror
```
Creates a new error class and returns its value

```
MPI_Add_error_code(errorclass, errorcode, ierror)
integer errorclass, errorcode, ierror
```
Creates a new error code associated with the specified error class and returns its value

```
MPI_Add_error_string(errorcode, string, ierror)
integer errorcode, ierror
character*(*) string
```
Associates an error string with an error code or class

```
MPI_Alloc_mem(size, info, baseptr, ierror)
integer info, ierror
integer(kind=MPI_ADDRESS_KIND) size, baseptr
```
Allocates memory that may be used for (potentially faster) RMA and message-passing operations

```
MPI_Alltoallw(sendbuf, sendcounts, sdispls, sendtypes, recvbuf,
        recvcounts, rdispls, recvtypes, comm, ierror)
<type> sendbuf(*), recvbuf(*)
integer sendcounts(*), sdispls(*), sendtypes(*), recvcounts(*),
rdispls(*), recvtypes(*), comm, ierror
```
Sends data from all to all processes, with variable counts, displacements, and data-types

```
MPI_Close_port(port_name, ierror)
character*(*) port_name
integer ierror
```
Releases the network address represented by the specified port name

```
MPI_Comm_accept(port_name, info, root, comm, newcomm, ierror)
character*(*) port_name
integer info, root, comm, newcomm, ierror
```
Establishes communication with a client

```
MPI_Comm_call_errhandler(comm, errorcode, ierror)
integer comm, errorcode, ierror
```
Invokes the error handler associated with a communicator

```
MPI_Comm_connect(port_name, info, root, comm, newcomm, ierror)
character*(*) port_name
integer info, root, comm, newcomm, ierror
```
Establishes communication with a server

```
MPI_Comm_create_errhandler(function, errhandler, ierror)
external function
integer errhandler, ierror
```
Creates an error handler that can be attached to communicators

```
MPI_Comm_create_keyval(comm_copy_attr_fn, comm_delete_attr_fn,
          comm_keyval, extra_state, ierror)
external comm_copy_attr_fn, comm_delete_attr_fn
integer comm_keyval, ierror
integer(kind=MPI_ADDRESS_KIND) extra_state
```
Creates a new attribute key that can be cached on communicators

```
MPI_Comm_delete_attr(comm, comm_keyval, ierror)
integer comm, comm_keyval, ierror
```
Deletes an attribute key cached on a communicator

```
MPI_Comm_disconnect(comm, ierror)
integer comm, ierror
```
Waits for all pending communication in the communicator to complete and then frees the communicator

```
MPI_Comm_free_keyval(comm_keyval, ierror)
integer comm_keyval, ierror
```
Frees an attribute key created with MPI_Comm_create_keyval

MPI_Comm_get_attr(comm, comm_keyval, attribute_val, flag, ierror) integer comm, comm_keyval, ierror integer(kind=MPI_ADDRESS_KIND) attribute_val logical flag *Returns the value associated with an attribute key cached on a communicator*
MPI_Comm_get_errhandler(comm, errhandler, ierror) integer comm, errhandler, ierror *Returns the error handler currently associated with a communicator*
MPI_Comm_get_name(comm, comm_name, resultlen, ierror) integer comm, resultlen, ierror character*(*) comm_name *Returns the name associated with a communicator*
MPI_Comm_get_parent(parent, ierror) integer parent, ierror *Returns the parent intercommunicator of a spawned process*
MPI_Comm_join(fd, intercomm, ierror) integer fd, intercomm, ierror *Creates an intercommunicator from the union of two MPI processes that are connected by a socket*
MPI_Comm_set_attr(comm, comm_keyval, attribute_val, ierror) integer comm, comm_keyval, ierror integer(kind=MPI_ADDRESS_KIND) attribute_val
MPI_Comm_set_errhandler(comm, errhandler, ierror) integer comm, errhandler, ierror *Sets the value for an attribute key cached on a communicator*
MPI_Comm_set_name(comm, comm_name, ierror) integer comm, ierror character*(*) comm_name *Associates a name with a communicator*
MPI_Comm_spawn(command, argv, maxprocs, info, root, comm, intercomm,   array_of_errcodes, ierror) character*(*) command, argv(*) integer info, maxprocs, root, comm, intercomm, array_of_errcodes(*), ierror *Spawns new processes running an MPI program*

MPI_Comm_spawn_multiple(count, array_of_commands, array_of_argv,
        array_of_maxprocs, array_of_info, root, comm, intercomm,
        array_of_errcodes, ierror)
integer count, array_of_info(*), array_of_maxprocs(*), root, comm,
intercomm, array_of_errcodes(*), ierror
character*(*) array_of_commands(*), array_of_argv(count,*)
Spawns new processes running different MPI programs

MPI_Exscan(sendbuf, recvbuf, count, datatype, op, comm, ierror)
<type> sendbuf(*), recvbuf(*)
integer count, datatype, op, comm, ierror
Performs a prefix reduction

MPI_File_call_errhandler(fh, errorcode, ierror)
integer fh, errorcode, ierror
Invokes the error handler associated with a file

MPI_File_close(fh, ierror)
integer fh, ierror
Closes a file

MPI_File_create_errhandler(function, errhandler, ierror)
external function
integer errhandler, ierror
Creates an error handler that can be attached to files

MPI_File_delete(filename, info, ierror)
character*(*) filename
integer info, ierror
Deletes a file

MPI_File_get_amode(fh, amode, ierror)
integer fh, amode, ierror
Returns the access mode of a file

MPI_File_get_atomicity(fh, flag, ierror)
integer fh, ierror
logical flag
Returns the current setting for atomicity of file accesses

MPI_File_get_byte_offset(fh, offset, disp, ierror)
integer fh, ierror
integer(kind=MPI_OFFSET_KIND) offset, disp
Converts a view-relative file offset into an absolute byte offset

MPI_File_get_errhandler(file, errhandler, ierror)
integer file, errhandler, ierror
Returns the error handler associated with a file

MPI_File_get_group(fh, group, ierror)
integer fh, group, ierror
Returns a duplicate of the group of the communicator used to open a file

MPI_File_get_info(fh, info_used, ierror)
integer fh, info_used, ierror
Returns a new info object containing the hints currently associated with a file

MPI_File_get_position(fh, offset, ierror)
integer fh, ierror
integer(kind=MPI_OFFSET_KIND) offset
Returns the current location of the individual file pointer

MPI_File_get_position_shared(fh, offset, ierror)
integer fh, ierror
integer(kind=MPI_OFFSET_KIND) offset
Returns the current location of the shared file pointer

MPI_File_get_size(fh, size, ierror)
integer fh, ierror
integer(kind=MPI_OFFSET_KIND) size
Returns the size of a file in bytes

MPI_File_get_type_extent(fh, datatype, extent, ierror)
integer fh, datatype, ierror
integer(kind=MPI_ADDRESS_KIND) extent
Returns the extent of a datatype in the file data representation

MPI_File_get_view(fh, disp, etype, filetype, datarep, ierror)
integer fh, etype, filetype, ierror
character*(*) datarep, integer(kind=MPI_OFFSET_KIND) disp
Returns the current file view

MPI_File_iread(fh, buf, count, datatype, request, ierror)
<type> buf(*)
integer fh, count, datatype, request, ierror
Starts a nonblocking file read from the current location of the individual file pointer

MPI_File_iread_at(fh, offset, buf, count, datatype, request, ierror) \<type\> buf(*) integer fh, count, datatype, request, ierror integer(kind=MPI_OFFSET_KIND) offset *Starts a nonblocking file read from the specified offset*
MPI_File_iread_shared(fh, buf, count, datatype, request, ierror) \<type\> buf(*) integer fh, count, datatype, request, ierror *Starts a nonblocking file read from the current location of the shared file pointer*
MPI_File_iwrite(fh, buf, count, datatype, request, ierror) \<type\> buf(*) integer fh, count, datatype, request, ierror *Starts a nonblocking file write from the current location of the individual file pointer*
MPI_File_iwrite_at(fh, offset, buf, count, datatype, request, ierror) \<type\> buf(*) integer fh, count, datatype, request, ierror integer(kind=MPI_OFFSET_KIND) offset *Starts a nonblocking file write from the specified offset*
MPI_File_iwrite_shared(fh, buf, count, datatype, request, ierror) \<type\> buf(*) integer fh, count, datatype, request, ierror *Starts a nonblocking file write from the current location of the shared file pointer*
MPI_File_open(comm, filename, amode, info, fh, ierror) character*(*) filename integer comm, amode, info, fh, ierror *Opens a file*
MPI_File_preallocate(fh, size, ierror) integer fh, ierror integer(kind=MPI_OFFSET_KIND) size *Preallocates disk space for a file*
MPI_File_read(fh, buf, count, datatype, status, ierror) \<type\> buf(*) integer fh, count, datatype, status(MPI_STATUS_SIZE), ierror *Reads from the current location of the individual file pointer*

```
MPI_File_read_all(fh, buf, count, datatype, status, ierror)
<type> buf(*)
integer fh, count, datatype, status(MPI_STATUS_SIZE), ierror
```
Collective read from the current location of the individual file pointer

```
MPI_File_read_all_begin(fh, buf, count, datatype, ierror)
<type> buf(*)
integer fh, count, datatype, ierror
```
Starts a split collective read from the current location of the individual file pointer

```
MPI_File_read_all_end(fh, buf, status, ierror)
<type> buf(*)
integer fh, status(MPI_STATUS_SIZE), ierror
```
Completes a split collective read started with MPI_File_read_all_begin

```
MPI_File_read_at(fh, offset, buf, count, datatype, status, ierror)
<type> buf(*)
integer fh, count, datatype, status(MPI_STATUS_SIZE), ierror
integer(kind=MPI_OFFSET_KIND) offset
```
Reads from the specified file offset

```
MPI_File_read_at_all(fh, offset, buf, count, datatype, status,
          ierror)
<type> buf(*)
integer fh, count, datatype, status(MPI_STATUS_SIZE), ierror
integer(kind=MPI_OFFSET_KIND) offset
```
Collective read from the specified file offset

```
MPI_File_read_at_all_begin(fh, offset, buf, count, datatype, ierror)
<type> buf(*)
integer fh, count, datatype, ierror
integer(kind=MPI_OFFSET_KIND) offset
```
Starts a split collective read from the specified file offset

```
MPI_File_read_at_all_end(fh, buf, status, ierror)
<type> buf(*)
integer fh, status(MPI_STATUS_SIZE), ierror
```
Completes a split collective read started with MPI_File_read_at_all_begin

```
MPI_File_read_ordered(fh, buf, count, datatype, status, ierror)
<type> buf(*)
integer fh, count, datatype, status(MPI_STATUS_SIZE), ierror
```
Collective read using the shared file pointer

```
MPI_File_read_ordered_begin(fh, buf, count, datatype, ierror)
<type> buf(*)
integer fh, count, datatype, ierror
```
Starts a split collective read using the shared file pointer

```
MPI_File_read_ordered_end(fh, buf, status, ierror)
<type> buf(*)
integer fh, status(MPI_STATUS_SIZE), ierror
```
Completes a split collective read started with MPI_File_read_ordered_begin

```
MPI_File_read_shared(fh, buf, count, datatype, status, ierror)
<type> buf(*)
integer fh, count, datatype, status(MPI_STATUS_SIZE), ierror
```
Reads from the current location of the shared file pointer

```
MPI_File_seek(fh, offset, whence, ierror)
integer fh, whence, ierror
integer(kind=MPI_OFFSET_KIND) offset
```
Moves the individual file pointer

```
MPI_File_seek_shared(fh, offset, whence, ierror)
integer fh, whence, ierror
integer(kind=MPI_OFFSET_KIND) offset
```
Moves the shared file pointer

```
MPI_File_set_atomicity(fh, flag, ierror)
integer fh, ierror
logical flag
```
Sets atomicity of file accesses

```
MPI_File_set_errhandler(file, errhandler, ierror)
integer file, errhandler, ierror
```
Attaches a new error handler to a file

```
MPI_File_set_info(fh, info, ierror)
integer fh, info, ierror
```
Sets new values for the hints associated with a file

```
MPI_File_set_size(fh, size, ierror)
integer fh, ierror
integer(kind=MPI_OFFSET_KIND) size
```
Sets the file size

```
MPI_File_set_view(fh, disp, etype, filetype, datarep, info, ierror)
integer fh, etype, filetype, info, ierror
character*(*) datarep
integer(kind=MPI_OFFSET_KIND) disp
```
Sets the file view

```
MPI_File_sync(fh, ierror)
integer fh, ierror
```
Synchronizes file data with that on the storage device

```
MPI_File_write(fh, buf, count, datatype, status, ierror)
<type> buf(*)
integer fh, count, datatype, status(MPI_STATUS_SIZE), ierror
```
Writes from the current location of the individual file pointer

---

```
MPI_File_write_all(fh, buf, count, datatype, status, ierror)
<type> buf(*)
integer fh, count, datatype, status(MPI_STATUS_SIZE), ierror
```
Collective write from the current location of the individual file pointer

---

```
MPI_File_write_all_begin(fh, buf, count, datatype, ierror)
<type> buf(*)
integer fh, count, datatype, ierror
```
Starts a split collective write from the current location of the individual file pointer

---

```
MPI_File_write_all_end(fh, buf, status, ierror)
<type> buf(*)
integer fh, status(MPI_STATUS_SIZE), ierror
```
Completes a split collective write started with MPI_File_write_all_begin

---

```
MPI_File_write_at(fh, offset, buf, count, datatype, status, ierror)
<type> buf(*)
integer fh, count, datatype, status(MPI_STATUS_SIZE), ierror
integer(kind=MPI_OFFSET_KIND) offset
```
Writes from the specified file offset

```
MPI_File_write_at_all(fh, offset, buf, count, datatype, status,
          ierror)
<type> buf(*)
integer fh, count, datatype, status(MPI_STATUS_SIZE), ierror
integer(kind=MPI_OFFSET_KIND) offset
```
Collective write from the specified file offset

`MPI_File_write_at_all_begin(fh, offset, buf, count, datatype, ierror)`
`<type> buf(*)`
`integer fh, count, datatype, ierror`
`integer(kind=MPI_OFFSET_KIND) offset`
Starts a split collective write from the specified file offset

`MPI_File_write_at_all_end(fh, buf, status, ierror)`
`<type> buf(*)`
`integer fh, status(MPI_STATUS_SIZE), ierror`
Completes a split collective write started with `MPI_File_write_at_all_begin`

`MPI_File_write_ordered(fh, buf, count, datatype, status, ierror)`
`<type> buf(*)`
`integer fh, count, datatype, status(MPI_STATUS_SIZE), ierror`
Collective write using the shared file pointer

`MPI_File_write_ordered_begin(fh, buf, count, datatype, ierror)`
`<type> buf(*)`
`integer fh, count, datatype, ierror`
Starts a split collective write using the shared file pointer

`MPI_File_write_ordered_end(fh, buf, status, ierror)`
`<type> buf(*)`
`integer fh, status(MPI_STATUS_SIZE), ierror`
Completes a split collective write started with `MPI_File_write_ordered_begin`

`MPI_File_write_shared(fh, buf, count, datatype, status, ierror)`
`<type> buf(*)`
`integer fh, count, datatype, status(MPI_STATUS_SIZE), ierror`
Writes from the current location of the shared file pointer

`MPI_Finalized(flag, ierror)`
`logical flag`
`integer ierror`
Indicates whether `MPI_Finalize` *has completed*

`MPI_Free_mem(base, ierror)`
`<type> base(*)`
`integer ierror`
Frees memory allocated with `MPI_Alloc_mem`

`MPI_Get(origin_addr, origin_count, origin_datatype, target_rank,`
`        target_disp, target_count, target_datatype, win, ierror)`
`<type> origin_addr(*)`
`integer(kind=MPI_ADDRESS_KIND) target_disp`
`integer origin_count, origin_datatype, target_rank, target_count,`
`target_datatype, win, ierror`
Starts a one-sided receive operation

`MPI_Get_address(location, address, ierror)`
`<type> location(*)`
`integer ierror`
`integer(kind=MPI_ADDRESS_KIND) address`
Returns the address of a location in memory

`MPI_Grequest_complete(request, ierror)`
`integer request, ierror`
Informs MPI that the operations represented by a generalized request are complete

`MPI_Grequest_start(query_fn, free_fn, cancel_fn, extra_state, request,`
`        ierror)`
`integer request, ierror`
`external query_fn, free_fn, cancel_fn`
`integer (kind=MPI_ADDRESS_KIND) extra_state`
Creates a new generalized request object

`MPI_Info_create(info, ierror)`
`integer info, ierror`
Creates a new info object

`MPI_Info_delete(info, key, ierror)`
`integer info, ierror`
`character*(*) key`
Deletes a (key,value) pair from an info object

`MPI_Info_dup(info, newinfo, ierror)`
`integer info, newinfo, ierror`
Returns a duplicate of an info object

`MPI_Info_free(info, ierror)`
`integer info, ierror`
Frees an info object

```
MPI_Info_get(info, key, valuelen, value, flag, ierror)
integer info, valuelen, ierror
character*(*) key, value
logical flag
```
Returns the value associated with an info key

```
MPI_Info_get_nkeys(info, nkeys, ierror)
integer info, nkeys, ierror
```
Returns the number of keys currently defined in the info object

```
MPI_Info_get_nthkey(info, n, key, ierror)
integer info, n, ierror
character*(*) key
```
Returns the nth key defined in the info object

```
MPI_Info_get_valuelen(info, key, valuelen, flag, ierror)
integer info, valuelen, ierror
logical flag
character*(*) key
```
Returns the length of the value string associated with an info key

```
MPI_Info_set(info, key, value, ierror)
integer info, ierror
character*(*) key, value
```
Adds a (key,value) pair to an info object

```
MPI_Init_thread(required, provided, ierror)
integer required, provided, ierror
```
Initializes MPI and initializes the MPI thread environment

```
MPI_Is_thread_main(flag, ierror)
logical flag
integer ierror
```
Indicates whether the thread calling this function is the main thread

```
MPI_Lookup_name(service_name, info, port_name, ierror)
character*(*) service_name, port_name
integer info, ierror
```
Returns the port name associated with a service name

```
MPI_Open_port(info, port_name, ierror)
character*(*) port_name
integer info, ierror
```
Establishes a network address at which the server will be able to accept connections from clients

```
MPI_Pack_external(datarep, inbuf, incount, datatype, outbuf, outsize,
          position, ierror)
integer incount, datatype, ierror
integer(kind=MPI_ADDRESS_KIND) outsize, position
character*(*) datarep
<type> inbuf(*), outbuf(*)
```
Packs data into a contiguous buffer in external32 format

```
MPI_Pack_external_size(datarep, incount, datatype, size, ierror)
integer incount, datatype, ierror
integer(kind=MPI_ADDRESS_KIND) size
character*(*) datarep
```
Returns the amount of space needed to pack a datatype in external32 format

```
MPI_Publish_name(service_name, info, port_name, ierror)
integer info, ierror
character*(*) service_name, port_name
```
Publishes a (port_name, service_name) pair

```
MPI_Put(origin_addr, origin_count, origin_datatype, target_rank,
          target_disp, target_count, target_datatype, win, ierror)
<type> origin_addr(*)
integer(kind=MPI_ADDRESS_KIND) target_disp
integer origin_count, origin_datatype, target_rank, target_count,
target_datatype, win, ierror
```
Starts a one-sided send operation

```
MPI_Query_thread(provided, ierror)
integer provided, ierror
```
Returns the current level of thread support

`MPI_Register_datarep(datarep, read_conversion_fn, write_conversion_fn,`
　　　`dtype_file_extent_fn, extra_state, ierror)`
`character*(*) datarep`
`external read_conversion_fn, write_conversion_fn, dtype_file_extent_fn`
`integer(kind=MPI_ADDRESS_KIND) extra_state`
`integer ierror`
Adds a new file data representation to MPI

`MPI_Request_get_status( request, flag, status, ierror)`
`integer request, status(MPI_STATUS_SIZE), ierror`
`logical flag`
Tests completion of a nonblocking operation but does not free the request object if complete

`MPI_Sizeof(x, size, ierror)`
`<type> x`
`integer size, ierror`
Returns the size in bytes of the machine representation of a variable

`MPI_Status_set_cancelled(status, flag, ierror)`
`integer status(MPI_STATUS_SIZE), ierror`
`logical flag`
Sets the value to be returned by `MPI_Test_cancelled`

`MPI_Status_set_elements(status, datatype, count, ierror)`
`integer status(MPI_STATUS_SIZE), datatype, count, ierror`
Sets the value to be returned by `MPI_Get_elements`

`MPI_Type_create_darray(size, rank, ndims, array_of_gsizes,`
　　　`array_of_distribs, array_of_dargs, array_of_psizes, order,`
　　　`oldtype, newtype, ierror)`
`integer size, rank, ndims, array_of_gsizes(*), array_of_distribs(*),`
`array_of_dargs(*), array_of_psizes(*), order, oldtype, newtype,`
`ierror`
Creates a distributed array datatype

`MPI_Type_create_f90_complex(p, r, newtype, ierror)`
`integer p, r, newtype, ierror`
Returns a predefined MPI datatype that matches a Fortran 90 `complex` *variable with the specified precision and decimal exponent range*

MPI_Type_create_f90_integer(r, newtype, ierror)
integer r, newtype, ierror
Returns a predefined MPI datatype that matches a Fortran 90 integer *variable with the specified number of decimal digits*

MPI_Type_create_f90_real(p, r, newtype, ierror)
integer p, r, newtype, ierror
Returns a predefined MPI datatype that matches a Fortran 90 real *variable with the specified precision and decimal exponent range*

MPI_Type_create_hindexed(count, array_of_blocklengths,
          array_of_displacements, oldtype, newtype, ierror)
integer count, array_of_blocklengths(*), oldtype, newtype, ierror
integer(kind=MPI_ADDRESS_KIND) array_of_displacements(*)
Creates an indexed datatype with offsets in bytes

MPI_Type_create_hvector(count, blocklength, stide, oldtype, newtype,
          ierror)
integer count, blocklength, oldtype, newtype, ierror
integer(kind=MPI_ADDRESS_KIND) stride
Creates a vector (strided) datatype with offset in bytes

MPI_Type_create_indexed_block(count, blocklength,
          array_of_displacements, oldtype, newtype, ierror)
integer count, blocklength, array_of_displacements(*), oldtype,
newtype, ierror
Creates an indexed datatype with constant blocklength

MPI_Type_create_keyval(type_copy_attr_fn, type_delete_attr_fn,
          type_keyval, extra_state, ierror)
external type_copy_attr_fn, type_delete_attr_fn
integer type_keyval, ierror
integer(kind=MPI_ADDRESS_KIND) extra_state
Creates a new attribute key that can be cached on datatypes

MPI_Type_create_resized(oldtype, lb, extent, newtype, ierror)
integer oldtype, newtype, ierror
integer(kind=MPI_ADDRESS_KIND) lb, extent
Returns a new datatype with the specified lower bound and extent

`MPI_Type_create_struct(count, array_of_blocklengths,`
`        array_of_displacements, array_of_types, newtype, ierror)`
`integer count, array_of_blocklengths(*), array_of_types(*), newtype,`
`ierror`
`integer(kind=MPI_ADDRESS_KIND) array_of_displacements(*)`
Creates a struct datatype

`MPI_Type_create_subarray(ndims, array_of_sizes, array_of_subsizes,`
`        array_of_starts, order, oldtype, newtype, ierror)`
`integer ndims, array_of_sizes(*), array_of_subsizes(*),`
`array_of_starts(*), order, oldtype, newtype, ierror`
Creates a subarray datatype

`MPI_Type_delete_attr(type, type_keyval, ierror)`
`integer type, type_keyval, ierror`
Deletes an attribute key cached on a datatype

`MPI_Type_dup(type, newtype, ierror)`
`integer type, newtype, ierror`
Returns a duplicate of a datatype

`MPI_Type_free_keyval(type_keyval, ierror)`
`integer type_keyval, ierror`
Frees an attribute key created with `MPI_Type_create_keyval`

`MPI_Type_get_attr(type, type_keyval, attribute_val, flag, ierror)`
`integer type, type_keyval, ierror`
`integer(kind=MPI_ADDRESS_KIND) attribute_val`
`logical flag`
Returns the value associated with an attribute key cached on a datatype

`MPI_Type_get_contents(datatype, max_integers, max_addresses,`
`        max_datatypes, array_of_integers, array_of_addresses,`
`        array_of_datatypes, ierror)`
`integer datatype, max_integers, max_addresses, max_datatypes,`
`array_of_integers(*), array_of_datatypes(*), ierror`
`integer(kind=MPI_ADDRESS_KIND) array_of_addresses(*)`
Returns the values of the parameters used to construct a derived datatype

MPI_Type_get_envelope(datatype, num_integers, num_addresses,
          num_datatypes, combiner, ierror)
integer datatype, num_integers, num_addresses, num_datatypes,
combiner, ierror
Returns the type of datatype and the number and type of arguments used to create
the datatype

MPI_Type_get_extent(datatype, lb, extent, ierror)
integer datatype, ierror
integer(kind=MPI_ADDRESS_KIND) lb, extent
Returns the lower bound and extent of a datatype

MPI_Type_get_name(type, type_name, resultlen, ierror)
integer type, resultlen, ierror
character*(*) type_name
Returns the name associated with a datatype

MPI_Type_get_true_extent(datatype, true_lb, true_extent, ierror)
integer datatype, ierror
integer(kind=MPI_ADDRESS_KIND) true_lb, true_extent
Returns the true extent of a datatype

MPI_Type_match_size(typeclass, size, type, ierror)
integer typeclass, size, type, ierror
Returns an MPI datatype matching a local variable of specified type and size

---

MPI_Type_set_attr(type, type_keyval, attribute_val, ierror)
integer type, type_keyval, ierror
integer(kind=MPI_ADDRESS_KIND) attribute_val
Sets the value for an attribute key cached on a datatype

MPI_Type_set_name(type, type_name, ierror)
integer type, ierror
character*(*) type_name
Associates a name with a datatype

MPI_Unpack_external(datarep, inbuf, insize, position, outbuf,
          outcount, datatype, ierror)
integer outcount, datatype, ierror
integer(kind=MPI_ADDRESS_KIND) insize, position
character*(*) datarep
<type> inbuf(*), outbuf(*)
Unpacks data stored contiguously in external32 format

```
MPI_Unpublish_name(service_name, info, port_name, ierror)
integer info, ierror
character*(*) service_name, port_name
```
Unpublishes a previously published service name

```
MPI_Win_call_errhandler(win, errorcode, ierror)
integer win, errorcode, ierror
```
Invokes the error handler associated with a window object

```
MPI_Win_complete(win, ierror)
integer win, ierror
```
Completes an RMA access epoch started with MPI_Win_start

```
MPI_Win_create(base, size, disp_unit, info, comm, win, ierror)
<type> base(*)
integer(kind=MPI_ADDRESS_KIND) size
integer disp_unit, info, comm, win, ierror
```
Creates a new window object

```
MPI_Win_create_errhandler(function, errhandler, ierror)
external function
integer errhandler, ierror
```
Creates an error handler that can be attached to window objects

```
MPI_Win_create_keyval(win_copy_attr_fn, win_delete_attr_fn, win_keyval,
          extra_state, ierror)
external win_copy_attr_fn, win_delete_attr_fn
integer win_keyval, ierror
integer(kind=MPI_ADDRESS_KIND) extra_state
```
Creates a new attribute key that can be cached on window objects

```
MPI_Win_delete_attr(win, win_keyval, ierror)
integer win, win_keyval, ierror
```
Deletes an attribute key cached on a window object

```
MPI_Win_fence(assert, win, ierror)
integer assert, win, ierror
```
Synchronizes RMA operations on a window object

```
MPI_Win_free(win, ierror)
integer win, ierror
```
Frees a window object

`MPI_Win_free_keyval(win_keyval, ierror)`
`integer win_keyval, ierror`
Frees an attribute key created with `MPI_Win_create_keyval`

`MPI_Win_get_attr(win, win_keyval, attribute_val, flag, ierror)`
`integer win, win_keyval, ierror`
`integer(kind=MPI_ADDRESS_KIND) attribute_val`
`logical flag`
Returns the value associated with an attribute key cached on a window object

`MPI_Win_get_errhandler(win, errhandler, ierror)`
`integer win, errhandler, ierror`
Returns the error handler associated with a window object

`MPI_Win_get_group(win, group, ierror)`
`integer win, group, ierror`
Returns a duplicate of the group of the communicator used to create a window object

`MPI_Win_get_name(win, win_name, resultlen, ierror)`
`integer win, resultlen, ierror`
`character*(*) win_name`
Returns the name associated with a window object

`MPI_Win_lock(lock_type, rank, assert, win, ierror)`
`integer lock_type, rank, assert, win, ierror`
Starts an RMA access epoch enabling RMA operations only on the window at the specified process

`MPI_Win_post(group, assert, win, ierror)`
`integer group, assert, win, ierror`
Starts an RMA exposure epoch for the local window associated with a window object

`MPI_Win_set_attr(win, win_keyval, attribute_val, ierror)`
`integer win, win_keyval, ierror`
`integer(kind=MPI_ADDRESS_KIND) attribute_val`
Sets the value for an attribute key cached on a window object

`MPI_Win_set_errhandler(win, errhandler, ierror)`
`integer win, errhandler, ierror`
Attaches a new error handler to a window object

```
MPI_Win_set_name(win, win_name, ierror)
integer win, ierror
character*(*) win_name
```
Associates a name with a window object

```
MPI_Win_start(group, assert, win, ierror)
integer group, assert, win, ierror
```
Starts an RMA access epoch, enabling access only on windows at processes in the specified group

```
MPI_Win_test(win, flag, ierror)
integer win, ierror
logical flag
```
Tests whether RMA operations on the window object exposed with MPI_Win_post *have completed*

```
MPI_Win_unlock(rank, win, ierror)
integer rank, win, ierror
```
Completes an RMA access epoch started with MPI_Win_lock

```
MPI_Win_wait(win, ierror)
integer win, ierror
```
Completes an RMA exposure epoch started with MPI_Win_post

A.3   C++ Routines

This section describes the C++ routines from [58]. To save space, the MPI:: namespace identifier is not shown.

```
Intercomm Intracomm::Accept(const char* port_name, const Info& info,
        int root) const
```
Establishes communication with a client

```
void Win::Accumulate(const void* origin_addr, int origin_count,
        const Datatype& origin_datatype, int target_rank,
        Aint target_disp, int target_count,
        const Datatype& target_datatype, const Op& op) const
```
Accumulates data in the window of the target process using the specified operation

```
int Add_error_class()
```
Creates a new error class and returns its value

int Add_error_code(int errorclass)
Creates a new error code associated with the specified error class and returns its value

void Add_error_string(int errorcode, const char* string)
Associates an error string with an error code or class

void* Alloc_mem(Aint size, const Info& info)
Allocates memory that may be used for (potentially faster) RMA and message-passing operations

void Comm::Alltoallw(const void* sendbuf, const int sendcounts[],
const int sdispls[], const Datatype sendtypes[],
void* recvbuf, const int recvcounts[], const int rdispls[],
const Datatype recvtypes[]) const
Sends data from all to all processes, with variable counts, displacements, and data-types

void Comm::Call_errhandler(int errorcode) const
Invokes the error handler associated with a communicator

void File::Call_errhandler(int errorcode) const
Invokes the error handler associated with a file

void Win::Call_errhandler(int errorcode) const
Invokes the error handler associated with a window object

void Close_port(const char* port_name)
Releases the network address represented by the specified port name

void File::Close()
Closes a file

void Grequest::Complete()
Informs MPI that the operations represented by a generalized request are complete

void Win::Complete() const
Completes an RMA access epoch started with MPI_Win_start

Intercomm Intracomm::Connect(const char* port_name,
const Info& info, int root) const
Establishes communication with a server

Info Info::Create()
Creates a new info object

Win Win::Create(const void* base, Aint size, int disp_unit,
const Info& info, const Intracomm& comm)
Creates a new window object

`Datatype Datatype::Create_darray(int size, int rank, int ndims,`
`        const int array_of_gsizes[], const int array_of_distribs[],`
`        const int array_of_dargs[], const int array_of_psizes[],`
`        int order) const`
Creates a distributed array datatype

`Errhandler Comm::Create_errhandler(Comm::Errhandler_fn* function)` *Creates an error handler that can be attached to communicators*
`Errhandler File::Create_errhandler(File::Errhandler_fn* function)` *Creates an error handler that can be attached to files*
`Errhandler Win::Create_errhandler(Win::Errhandler_fn* function)` *Creates an error handler that can be attached to window objects*
`Datatype Datatype::Create_f90_complex(int p, int r) const` *Returns a predefined MPI datatype that matches a Fortran 90* complex *variable* *with the specified precision and decimal exponent range*
`Datatype Datatype::Create_f90_integer(int r) const` *Returns a predefined MPI datatype that matches a Fortran 90* integer *variable* *with the specified number of decimal digits*
`Datatype Datatype::Create_f90_real(int p, int r) const` *Returns a predefined MPI datatype that matches a Fortran 90* real *variable with* *the specified precision and decimal exponent range*

`Datatype Datatype::Create_hindexed(int count,`
`        const int array_of_blocklengths[],`
`        const Aint array_of_displacements[]) const`
Creates an indexed datatype with offsets in bytes

`Datatype Datatype::Create_hvector(int count, int blocklength,`
`        Aint stride) const`
Creates a vector (strided) datatype with offset in bytes

`Datatype Datatype::Create_indexed_block(int count, int blocklength,`
`        const int array_of_displacements[]) const`
Creates an indexed datatype with constant blocklength

`int Comm::Create_keyval(Comm::Copy_attr_function* comm_copy_attr_fn,`
`        Comm::Delete_attr_function* comm_delete_attr_fn,`
`        void* extra_state)`
Creates a new attribute key that can be cached on communicators

```
int Datatype::Create_keyval(
        Datatype::Copy_attr_function* type_copy_attr_fn,
        Datatype::Delete_attr_function* type_delete_attr_fn,
        void* extra_state)
```
Creates a new attribute key that can be cached on datatypes

```
int Win::Create_keyval(Win::Copy_attr_function* win_copy_attr_fn,
        Win::Delete_attr_function* win_delete_attr_fn,
        void* extra_state)
```
Creates a new attribute key that can be cached on window objects

```
Datatype Datatype::Create_struct(int count,
        const int array_of_blocklengths[],
        const Aint array_of_displacements[], const Datatype
        array_of_types[])
```
Creates a struct datatype

```
Datatype Datatype::Create_subarray(int ndims,
        const int array_of_sizes[], const int array_of_subsizes[],
        const int array_of_starts[], int order) const
```
Creates a subarray datatype

```
void File::Delete(const char* filename, const Info& info)
```
Deletes a file

```
void Info::Delete(const char* key)
```
Deletes a (key,value) pair from an info object

```
void Comm::Delete_attr(int comm_keyval)
```
Deletes an attribute key cached on a communicator

```
void Datatype::Delete_attr(int type_keyval)
```
Deletes an attribute key cached on a datatype

```
void Win::Delete_attr(int win_keyval)
```
Deletes an attribute key cached on a window object

```
void Comm::Disconnect()
```
Waits for all pending communication in the communicator to complete and then frees the communicator

```
Datatype Datatype::Dup() const
```
Returns a duplicate of a datatype

```
Info Info::Dup() const
```
Returns a duplicate of an info object

`void Intracomm::Exscan(const void* sendbuf, void* recvbuf,`
`           int count, const Datatype& datatype, const Op& op) const`
Performs a prefix reduction

`void Win::Fence(int assert) const` *Synchronizes RMA operations on a window object*
`void Info::Free()` *Frees an info object*
`void Win::Free()` *Frees a window object*
`void Comm::Free_keyval(int& comm_keyval)` *Frees an attribute key created with* `MPI_Comm_create_keyval`
`void Datatype::Free_keyval(int& type_keyval)` *Frees an attribute key created with* `MPI_Type_create_keyval`
`void Win::Free_keyval(int& win_keyval)` *Frees an attribute key created with* `MPI_Win_create_keyval`
`void Free_mem(void *base)` *Frees memory allocated with* `MPI_Alloc_mem`
`bool Info::Get(const char* key, int valuelen, char* value) const` *Returns the value associated with an info key*

`void Win::Get(void *origin_addr, int origin_count,`
`           const Datatype& origin_datatype, int target_rank,`
`           Aint target_disp, int target_count,`
`           const Datatype& target_datatype) const`
Starts a one-sided receive operation

`Aint Get_address(void* location)` *Returns the address of a location in memory*
`int File::Get_amode() const` *Returns the access mode of a file*
`bool File::Get_atomicity() const` *Returns the current setting for atomicity of file accesses*
`bool Comm::Get_attr(int comm_keyval, void* attribute_val) const` *Returns the value associated with an attribute key cached on a communicator*
`bool Datatype::Get_attr(int type_keyval, void* attribute_val) const` *Returns the value associated with an attribute key cached on a datatype*

`bool Win::Get_attr(const Win& win, int win_keyval,`
`        void* attribute_val) const`
Returns the value associated with an attribute key cached on a window object

`Offset File::Get_byte_offset(const Offset disp) const` *Converts a view-relative file offset into an absolute byte offset*

`void Datatype::Get_contents(int max_integers, int max_addresses,`
`        int max_datatypes, int array_of_integers[],`
`        Aint array_of_addresses[], Datatype array_of_datatypes[])`
`        const`
Returns the values of the parameters used to construct a derived datatype

`void Datatype::Get_envelope(int& num_integers, int& num_addresses,`
`        int& num_datatypes, int& combiner) const`
Returns the type of datatype and the number and type of arguments used to create the datatype

`Errhandler Comm::Get_errhandler() const` *Returns the error handler currently associated with a communicator*
`Errhandler File::Get_errhandler() const` *Returns the error handler currently associated with a file*
`Errhandler Win::Get_errhandler() const` *Returns the error handler currently associated with a window object*
`void Datatype::Get_extent(Aint& lb, Aint& extent) const` *Returns the lower bound and extent of a datatype*
`Group File::Get_group() const` *Returns a duplicate of the group of the communicator used to open a file*
`Group Win::Get_group() const` *Returns a duplicate of the group of the communicator used to create a window object*
`Info File::Get_info() const` *Returns a new info object containing the hints currently associated with a file*
`void Comm::Get_name(char* comm_name, int& resultlen) const` *Returns the name associated with a communicator*
`void Datatype::Get_name(char* type_name, int& resultlen) const` *Returns the name associated with a datatype*
`void Win::Get_name(char* win_name, int& resultlen) const` *Returns the name associated with a window object*

`int Info::Get_nkeys() const` *Returns the number of keys currently defined in the info object*
`void Info::Get_nthkey(int n, char* key) const` *Returns the nth key defined in the info object*
`Intercomm Comm::Get_parent()` *Returns the parent intercommunicator of a spawned process*
`Offset File::Get_position() const` *Returns the current location of the individual file pointer*
`Offset File::Get_position_shared() const` *Returns the current location of the shared file pointer*
`Offset File::Get_size() const` *Returns the size of a file in bytes*
`bool Request::Get_status() const` *Tests completion of a nonblocking operation but does not free the request object if complete*
`bool Request::Get_status(Status& status) const` *Tests completion of a nonblocking operation but does not free the request object if complete*

`void Datatype::Get_true_extent(Aint& true_lb, Aint& true_extent)`
`         const`
Returns the true extent of a datatype

`Aint File::Get_type_extent(const Datatype& datatype) const` *Returns the extent of a datatype in the file data representation*
`bool Info::Get_valuelen(const char* key, int& valuelen) const` *Returns the length of the value string associated with an info key*

`void File::Get_view(Offset& disp, Datatype& etype,`
`        Datatype& filetype, char* datarep) const`
Returns the current file view

`int Init_thread(int required)` *Initializes MPI and initializes the MPI thread environment*
`int Init_thread(int& argc, char**& argv, int required)` *Initializes MPI and initializes the MPI thread environment*
`Request File::Iread(void* buf, int count, const Datatype& datatype)` *Starts a nonblocking file read from the current location of the individual file pointer*

`Request File::Iread_at(Offset offset, void* buf, int count,`
          `const Datatype& datatype)`
Starts a nonblocking file read from the specified offset

`Request File::Iread_shared(void* buf, int count,`
          `const Datatype& datatype)`
Starts a nonblocking file read from the current location of the shared file pointer

`bool Is_finalized()` *Indicates whether* `MPI_Finalize` *has completed*
`bool Is_thread_main()` *Indicates whether the thread calling this function is the main thread*

`Request File::Iwrite(const void* buf, int count,`
          `const Datatype& datatype)`
Starts a nonblocking file write from the current location of the individual file pointer

`Request File::Iwrite_at(Offset offset, const void* buf, int count,`
          `const Datatype& datatype)`
Starts a nonblocking file write from the specified offset

`Request File::Iwrite_shared(const void* buf, int count,`
          `const Datatype& datatype)`
Starts a nonblocking file write from the current location of the shared file pointer

`Intercomm Comm::Join(const int fd)` *Creates an intercommunicator from the union of two MPI processes that are connected by a socket*
`void Win::Lock(int lock_type, int rank, int assert) const` *Starts an RMA access epoch enabling RMA operations only on the window at the specified process*

`void Lookup_name(const char* service_name, const Info& info,`
          `char* port_name)`
Returns the port name associated with a service name

`void Open_port(const Info& info, char* port_name)` *Establishes a network address at which the server will be able to accept connections from clients*

`File File::Open(const Intracomm& comm, const char* filename,`
          `int amode, const Info& info)`
Opens a file

```
void Datatype::Pack_external(const char* datarep, const void* inbuf,
          int incount, void* outbuf, Aint outsize, Aint& position)
          const
```
Packs data into a contiguous buffer in external32 format

```
Aint Datatype::Pack_external_size(const char* datarep, int incount)
          const
```
Returns the amount of space needed to pack a datatype in external32 format

```
void Win::Post(const Group& group, int assert) const
```
Starts an RMA exposure epoch for the local window associated with a window object

```
void File::Preallocate(Offset size)
```
Preallocates disk space for a file

```
void Publish_name(const char* service_name, const Info& info,
          const char* port_name)
```
Publishes a (port_name, service_name) pair

```
void Win::Put(const void* origin_addr, int origin_count,
          const Datatype& origin_datatype, int target_rank,
          Aint target_disp, int target_count,
          const Datatype& target_datatype) const
```
Starts a one-sided send operation

```
int Query_thread()
```
Returns the current level of thread support

```
void File::Read(void* buf, int count, const Datatype& datatype)
```
Reads from the current location of the individual file pointer

```
void File::Read(void* buf, int count, const Datatype& datatype,
          Status& status)
```
Reads from the current location of the individual file pointer

```
void File::Read_all(void* buf, int count, const Datatype& datatype)
```
Collective read from the current location of the individual file pointer

```
void File::Read_all(void* buf, int count, const Datatype& datatype,
          Status& status)
```
Collective read from the current location of the individual file pointer

```
void File::Read_all_begin(void* buf, int count,
          const Datatype& datatype)
```
Starts a split collective read from the current location of the individual file pointer

```
void File::Read_all_end(void* buf)
```
Completes a split collective read started with MPI_File_read_all_begin

```
void File::Read_all_end(void* buf, Status& status)
```
Completes a split collective read started with MPI_File_read_all_begin

```
void File::Read_at(Offset offset, void* buf, int count,
        const Datatype& datatype)
```
Reads from the specified file offset

```
void File::Read_at(Offset offset, void* buf, int count,
        const Datatype& datatype, Status& status)
```
Reads from the specified file offset

```
void File::Read_at_all(Offset offset, void* buf, int count,
        const Datatype& datatype)
```
Collective read from the specified file offset

```
void File::Read_at_all(Offset offset, void* buf, int count,
        const Datatype& datatype, Status& status)
```
Collective read from the specified file offset

```
void File::Read_at_all_begin(Offset offset, void* buf, int count,
        const Datatype& datatype)
```
Starts a split collective read from the specified file offset

```
void File::Read_at_all_end(void* buf)
```
Completes a split collective read started with MPI_File_read_at_all_begin

```
void File::Read_at_all_end(void* buf, Status& status)
```
Completes a split collective read started with MPI_File_read_at_all_begin

```
void File::Read_ordered(void* buf, int count,
        const Datatype& datatype)
```
Collective read using the shared file pointer

```
void File::Read_ordered(void* buf, int count,
        const Datatype& datatype, Status& status)
```
Collective read using the shared file pointer

```
void File::Read_ordered_begin(void* buf, int count,
        const Datatype& datatype)
```
Starts a split collective read using the shared file pointer

```
void File::Read_ordered_end(void* buf)
```
Completes a split collective read started with MPI_File_read_ordered_begin

```
void File::Read_ordered_end(void* buf, Status& status)
```
Completes a split collective read started with MPI_File_read_ordered_begin

`void File::Read_shared(void* buf, int count,`
`        const Datatype& datatype)`
Reads from the current location of the shared file pointer

`void File::Read_shared(void* buf, int count,`
`        const Datatype& datatype, Status& status)`
Reads from the current location of the shared file pointer

`void Register_datarep(const char* datarep,`
`        Datarep_conversion_function* read_conversion_fn,`
`        Datarep_conversion_function* write_conversion_fn,`
`        Datarep_extent_function* dtype_file_extent_fn,`
`        void* extra_state)`
Adds a new file data representation to MPI

`Datatype Datatype::Resized(const Aint lb, const Aint extent) const` *Returns a new datatype with the specified lower bound and extent*
`void File::Seek(Offset offset, int whence)` *Moves the individual file pointer*
`void File::Seek_shared(Offset offset, int whence)` *Moves the shared file pointer*
`void Info::Set(const char* key, const char* value)` *Adds a (key,value) pair to an info object*
`void File::Set_atomicity(bool flag)` *Sets atomicity of file accesses*

`void Comm::Set_attr(int comm_keyval, const void* attribute_val)`
`        const`
Sets the value for an attribute key cached on a communicator

`void Datatype::Set_attr(int type_keyval, const void* attribute_val)` *Sets the value for an attribute key cached on a datatype*
`void Win::Set_attr(int win_keyval, const void* attribute_val)` *Sets the value for an attribute key cached on a window object*
`void Status::Set_cancelled(bool flag)` *Sets the value to be returned by* `MPI_Test_cancelled`
`void Status::Set_elements(const Datatype& datatype, int count)` *Sets the value to be returned by* `MPI_Get_elements`
`void Comm::Set_errhandler(const Errhandler& errhandler)` *Attaches a new error handler to a communicator*

`void File::Set_errhandler(const Errhandler& errhandler)`   *Attaches a new error handler to a file*
`void Win::Set_errhandler(const Errhandler& errhandler)`   *Attaches a new error handler to a window object*
`void File::Set_info(const Info& info)`   *Sets new values for the hints associated with a file*
`void Comm::Set_name(const char* comm_name)`   *Associates a name with a communicator*
`void Datatype::Set_name(const char* type_name)`   *Associates a name with a datatype*
`void Win::Set_name(const char* win_name)`   *Associates a name with a window object*
`void File::Set_size(Offset size)`   *Sets the file size*

`void File::Set_view(Offset disp, const Datatype& etype,`
 `        const Datatype& filetype, const char* datarep,`
 `        const Info& info)`
 Sets the file view

`Intercomm Intracomm::Spawn(const char* command, const char* argv[],`
 `        int maxprocs, const Info& info, int root) const`
 Spawns new processes running an MPI program

`Intercomm Intracomm::Spawn(const char* command, const char* argv[],`
 `        int maxprocs, const Info& info, int root,`
 `        int array_of_errcodes[]) const`
 Spawns new processes running an MPI program

`Intercomm Intracomm::Spawn_multiple(int count,`
 `        const char* array_of_commands[],`
 `        const char** array_of_argv[],`
 `        const int array_of_maxprocs[], const Info array_of_info[],`
 `        int root)`
 Spawns new processes running different MPI programs

`Intercomm Intracomm::Spawn_multiple(int count,`
`        const char* array_of_commands[],`
`        const char** array_of_argv[],`
`        const int array_of_maxprocs[], const Info array_of_info[],`
`        int root, int array_of_errcodes[])`
Spawns new processes running different MPI programs

`Grequest Grequest::Start(const Grequest::Query_function query_fn,`
`        const Grequest::Free_function free_fn,`
`        const Grequest::Cancel_function cancel_fn, void`
`        *extra_state)`
Creates a new generalized request object

`void Win::Start(const Group& group, int assert) const` *Starts an RMA access epoch, enabling access only on windows at processes in the specified group*
`void File::Sync()` *Synchronizes any cached file data with that on the storage device*
`bool Win::Test() const` *Tests whether RMA operations on the window object exposed with* `MPI_Win_post` *have completed*
`void Win::Unlock(int rank) const` *Completes an RMA access epoch started with* `MPI_Win_lock`

`void Datatype::Unpack_external(const char* datarep,`
`        const void* inbuf, Aint insize, Aint& position,`
`        void* outbuf, int outcount) const`
Unpacks data stored contiguously in external32 format

`void Unpublish_name(const char* service_name, const Info& info,`
`        const char* port_name)`
Unpublishes a previously published service name

`void Win::Wait() const` *Completes an RMA exposure epoch started with* `MPI_Win_post`

`void File::Write(const void* buf, int count,`
`        const Datatype& datatype)`
Writes from the current location of the individual file pointer

`void File::Write(const void* buf, int count,`
`        const Datatype& datatype, Status& status)`
Writes from the current location of the individual file pointer

```
void File::Write_all(const void* buf, int count,
        const Datatype& datatype)
```
Collective write from the current location of the individual file pointer

```
void File::Write_all(const void* buf, int count,
        const Datatype& datatype, Status& status)
```
Collective write from the current location of the individual file pointer

```
void File::Write_all_begin(const void* buf, int count,
        const Datatype& datatype)
```
Starts a split collective write from the current location of the individual file pointer

```
void File::Write_all_end(const void* buf)
```
Completes a split collective write started with MPI_File_write_all_begin

```
void File::Write_all_end(const void* buf, Status& status)
```
Completes a split collective write started with MPI_File_write_all_begin

```
void File::Write_at(Offset offset, const void* buf, int count,
        const Datatype& datatype)
```
Writes from the specified file offset

```
void File::Write_at(Offset offset, const void* buf, int count,
        const Datatype& datatype, Status& status)
```
Writes from the specified file offset

```
void File::Write_at_all(Offset offset, const void* buf, int count,
        const Datatype& datatype)
```
Collective write from the specified file offset

```
void File::Write_at_all(Offset offset, const void* buf, int count,
        const Datatype& datatype, Status& status)
```
Collective write from the specified file offset

```
void File::Write_at_all_begin(Offset offset, const void* buf,
        int count, const Datatype& datatype)
```
Starts a split collective write from the specified file offset

```
void File::Write_at_all_end(const void* buf)
```
Completes a split collective write started with MPI_File_write_at_all_begin

```
void File::Write_at_all_end(const void* buf, Status& status)
```
Completes a split collective write started with MPI_File_write_at_all_begin

```
void File::Write_ordered(const void* buf, int count,
        const Datatype& datatype)
```
Collective write using the shared file pointer

void File::Write_ordered(const void* buf, int count,   const Datatype& datatype, Status& status) *Collective write using the shared file pointer*
void File::Write_ordered_begin(const void* buf, int count,   const Datatype& datatype) *Starts a split collective write using the shared file pointer*
void File::Write_ordered_end(const void* buf) *Completes a split collective write started with* MPI_File_write_ordered_begin
void File::Write_ordered_end(const void* buf, Status& status) *Completes a split collective write started with* MPI_File_write_ordered_begin
void File::Write_shared(const void* buf, int count,   const Datatype& datatype) *Writes from the current location of the shared file pointer*
void File::Write_shared(const void* buf, int count,   const Datatype& datatype, Status& status) *Writes from the current location of the shared file pointer*

B MPI Resources on the World Wide Web

Here we describe how to get access to MPI-related material on the Internet.

MPI home pages. Many MPI "home pages" exist on the World Wide Web. The most important is the MPI Forum's home page, `http://www.mpi-forum.org`. The page at `http://www.mcs.anl.gov/mpi` contains links to other home pages as well as links to tools, tutorials, implementations, and documentation on MPI.

Examples of MPI programs. All of the examples used in this book are available on the Web at `http://www.mcs.anl.gov/mpi/usingmpi2` or by anonymous `ftp` from `ftp.mcs.anl.gov` in directory `pub/mpi/using2/examples`. This directory is organized by book chapter. The file 'README' lists the files by chapter. A Unix 'tar' file (compressed) containing all the examples is available in 'examples.tar.gz'. Instructions for unpacking this file are in the 'README' file.

MPI implementations. The MPICH implementation, written by the authors of this book and others, is freely available and may be downloaded from the Web at `http://www.mcs.anl.gov/mpi/mpich` or by anonymous ftp from `ftp.mcs.anl.gov`. The 'README' file in directory 'pub/mpi' describes how to fetch and install the most recent version of MPICH. The MPICH distribution includes examples and test programs, as well as performance-measurement programs. Most of the test and performance programs may be used with any MPI implementation.

A list of implementations is maintained at `http://www.mpi.nd.edu/MPI`; this includes both freely available and commercial implementations.

The MPI Standard. The MPI Standard is available, in both PostScript and HTML forms, on the Web at `http://www.mpi-forum.org`. Errata for both MPI-1 and MPI-2 are also available there. In addition, archives of the MPI Forum, including e-mail discussions, meeting notes, and voting records, can be viewed there.

Discussion on MPI. A newsgroup, `comp.parallel.mpi`, is devoted to discussion of all aspects of MPI. Discussion of MPI-related issues also sometimes occurs in the more general group `comp.parallel`, devoted to parallel computers and computation.

A "frequently asked questions" (FAQ) page is available at

   `http://www.erc.msstate.edu/mpi/mpi-faq.html`

A great deal of information on parallel-programming projects and tools is available on the Web. We encourage you to investigate other sites on the Web for other resources on MPI and parallel computing.

C Surprises, Questions, and Problems in MPI

This appendix describes some issues that have arisen since the MPI-2 Standard was completed. Most of these are relatively obscure but have been discovered (in most cases) by someone trying to use or implement MPI. We begin with the clear oversights, continue with features that have ambiguous or awkward definitions, and conclude with some common misunderstandings.

For the current status on these issues, check `http://www.mpi-forum.org/docs/` for the errata for MPI-2.

C.1 No `MPI_Errhandler_f2c` and `MPI_Errhandler_c2f`

The MPI Forum, when describing the functions to convert opaque handles between C and Fortran, overlooked error handlers. In MPI 2.0, there is no `MPI_Errhandler_f2c` or `MPI_Errhandler_c2f`. This should be corrected by the MPI Forum.

C.2 No `MPI_LONG_LONG` in C

The MPI Standard specifies an `MPI_LONG_LONG_INT` type but no `MPI_LONG_LONG`. To make matters more confusing, in MPI-2.0, the `unsigned long long` type was added with MPI name `MPI_UNSIGNED_LONG_LONG`. Many MPI implementations support both `MPI_LONG_LONG` and `MPI_LONG_LONG_INT`, but as of MPI-2.0, the only standard-conforming MPI datatype for a `long long` is `MPI_LONG_LONG_INT`.

C.3 `MPI_PROC_NULL` in RMA

The value `MPI_PROC_NULL` may be used in point-to-point communications as a sort of no-op: the call is allowed, but no data is sent (in a send) or received (in a receive). The remote memory access routines do not specifically say whether `MPI_PROC_NULL` is valid for `MPI_Put`, `MPI_Get`, or `MPI_Accumulate`. E-mail discussions have supported the interpretation that `MPI_PROC_NULL` is allowed, but as of this writing, no final decision has been taken.

C.4 `MPI_Offset` Argument for Derived Datatype Constructors

Since many systems support file sizes larger than the memory-address space (for example, 64-bit file sizes but 32-bit memory addresses), file offsets, displacements, and so forth, in MPI are of type `MPI_Offset` rather than `MPI_Aint`. However, in all derived-datatype constructor functions that take byte displacements as arguments, the displacement is of type `MPI_Aint`. Even the new datatype constructor functions defined in MPI-2—`MPI_Type_create_hindexed`, `MPI_Type_create_hvector`, and `MPI_Type_create_struct`—take displacements of type `MPI_Aint`. This means that on systems where `MPI_Offset` is larger than `MPI_Aint`, it is not possible to create a "large" derived datatype of type hindexed, hvector, or struct to describe the data layout in a "large" file.

Most applications, however, should still be able to access large files either by using smaller derived datatypes to "tile" the file (since the file view is defined in terms of a tiling) or by not using derived datatypes at all. The real solution is that the MPI Forum must change the bindings of the datatype constructors to use `MPI_Offset` instead of `MPI_Aint`.

C.5   Use of `MPI_Info_set`

One vendor has interpreted the MPI-2 Standard as restricting the valid keys in `MPI_Info_set` to those defined by the vendor. Unrecognized keys are ignored. The advantage of this approach is that it allows the user to determine from within a program which info keys the implementation supports. The disadvantage with this interpretation is that `MPI_Info` cannot be used to hold key/value pairs for other parts of the code, including layered software. For example, a library might use the MPI profiling interface to provide a replacement for `MPI_File_set_view` that looked at the info value for a key `profiling:trace-file-views` before calling `PMPI_File_set_view`. With the interpretation that only keys defined by the MPI implementation may be set with `MPI_Info_set`, info cannot be used by layered software.

C.6   Values for C++ Versions of MPI Constants

The MPI Forum, in an attempt to provide a more "C++ flavor" to the C++ bindings, defined versions of the MPI constants, such as `MPI_SEEK_SET`, as part of the MPI namespace: `MPI::SEEK_SET`. This seemed like a good idea at the time, but it has a serious problem. In C++, preprocessor definitions are independent of namespaces. Even if a module carefully uses namespaces, another include file can use `#define` to redefine a name. For example, `SEEK_SET` is defined in the header file `<stdio.h>`. This means that `MPI::SEEK_SET` cannot be used in a program that has included `<stdio.h>`, unless the application has been careful to `#undef SEEK_SET` before trying to use `MPI::SEEK_SET`.

At the time this book was being written, the MPI Forum was still discussing how to work around this problem. Fundamentally, the problem is that the C++ preprocessor ignores namespaces, so a real fix would require a change to C++ (or to all C and C++ header files), not MPI. That isn't going to happen, so the MPI Forum will need to select an alternative that is less likely to cause problems, such as using mixed case (e.g., `Seek_set`) or lower case for the MPI C++ constants. To find out how this is resolved, check the errata page at `http://www.mpi-forum.org`.

C.7   Lack of Ordering for RMA

As mentioned before in Section 6.5, all the RMA operations are nonblocking and unordered. That is, even between a pair of processes, RMA operations need not complete in the order in which they were issued.

C.8   Thread Scoping Not Communicator Based

The components of truly modular software should be able to operate correctly independent of the other components in an application. In particular, it shouldn't be necessary for `MPI_Init_thread` to set the limits of thread availability; this could be done on a communicator-by-communicator basis, particularly since MPI uses communicators to separate all other operations (for example, messages on different communicators are noninterfering).

Nonetheless, in this area, MPI is still ahead of many other systems. For example, in one vendor's thread implementation, two libraries are provided: one with working mutual-exclusion routines and one where the mutual exclusion routines are provided, but as no-ops. That is, a multithreaded program can call the mutual-exclusion routines, but they won't actually provide for mutual exclusion. To make matters worse, the broken library is the one that the user will get by default (that is, without using special options). There is no easy and efficient way for an application to discover at run time whether the user has correctly linked with the working versions of mutual exclusion. At least in the MPI case, `MPI_Query_thread` will tell a library routine what level of thread support is present.

C.9   Confusion Caused by MPI Routine Names

In addition to routines that we have already mentioned (such as `MPI_Win_lock`), there are two sets of routines whose names frequently mislead MPI users. These are the "immediate" routines, for example, `MPI_Isend`, and the "test" routines, for example, `MPI_Test`.

The word "immediate," when applied to an MPI routine name for the "I" in names such as `MPI_Isend` and `MPI_Irecv`, does not mean that the operation is "immediate" in the sense of "takes no time." Rather, it means that the operation is nonblocking, and the completion of the routine is independent of any other process. But the routine could still take a significant amount of time.

For example, consider an `MPI_Isend` with a modest-sized message to send. If the MPI implementation is sure that the message can be delivered to the destination without requiring the destination process to take any action, perhaps because the MPI implementation is keeping careful track of available buffer space, then the `MPI_Isend` might not return until the message has been delivered.

The other misleading name is "test." In MPI, "test" really means "test and complete if possible." As a result, a test operation such as `MPI_Test` can also take a significant amount of time. For example, consider the `MPI_Isend` case again, but this time the message is too large to be delivered until the destination process sends an ok-to-send message. If a call to `MPI_Test` on the request for that send occurs after the ok-to-send is received, the `MPI_Test` may not return until the message has been delivered. This can take a significant amount of time; the `MPI_Test` call is only nonblocking, not instantaneous.

D Standardizing External Startup with mpiexec

MPI-1 said nothing about how MPI programs were started. Hence, although MPI programs themselves were portable, scripts that invoked MPI programs were not. Several implementations used the name mpirun for a script or program that started MPI applications. This, however, only made things worse, because their arguments were not compatible, and users encountered the problem of accidentally trying to launch an application linked with one MPI implementation with the mpirun of another implementation. The MPI Forum responded with a standard definition for a launching command called mpiexec, first introduced in Chapter 2 of this book. This feature is not *required* of an MPI implementation in order for the implementation to claim conformance with the Standard, but if such a command exists it is expected to take the form defined by the Standard. Therefore, scripts that use mpiexec can be portable at least among those MPI implementations that implement it. The syntax of mpiexec is shown in Table D.1. Let us consider the example program pmandel for parallel Mandelbrot calculation and display that is described in Chapter 5 of *Using MPI* [32] and distributed with MPICH. The simplest way to start pmandel, assuming that we wish to run it with ten processes altogether, is

```
mpiexec -n 10 pmandel
```

It is also possible to pass command-line arguments to the program as follows:

```
mpiexec -n 10 pmandel -i cool.points -loop
```

or

```
mpiexec -n 10 pmandel -rmin -2 -rmax 2 -imin -2 -imax 2 +zoom
```

Note that MPI does not guarantee that command-line arguments will be propagated to all processes, although some implementations do provide this service. The most portable way to propagate command-line arguments is for process 0 to use MPI_-Bcast to forward them to the other processes.

```
mpiexec -n <numprocs> -soft <exp> -host <name> -arch <name>
        -wdir <dirname> -path <pathname> -file <filename>
        progname <program args>
```

Table D.1
Options for mpiexec

The other possible arguments to `mpiexec` (before the program name) are optional,[1] both for users and for implementers, although if an implementation recognizes them, they must have the meanings specified in the Standard. Some of the arguments can be thought of as part of an interface to a job scheduler that allocates resources. We can specify that all processes be run on a specific machine, for example `big-iron`, with

```
mpiexec -n 10 -host big-iron pmandel
```

If we don't care which host or hosts the program runs on but need to request a given computer architecture or operating system (because the program was compiled for that environment), we can specify something like

```
mpiexec -n 10 -arch sparc-solaris pmandel
```

and expect `mpiexec` to perform such scheduling as necessary to find us ten Solaris workstations to run on.

Perhaps our application can usefully be run on various numbers of processes, depending on what is available. For example, suppose that we wish to run `pmandel` on any number of processes up to ten. Since the `pmandel` application requires at least two processes for its master-slave algorithm, we need at least two processes, but we are willing to accept any number up to the maximum of ten. We would use

```
mpiexec -n 10 -soft 2:10 pmandel
```

The `-soft` argument can be followed by several types of expression. For example,

```
mpiexec -n 1000 -soft 2:1000:2 pmandel
```

specifies an even number of processes (the third number is the stride, with a default value of one when the third value is omitted), and

```
mpiexec -n 1024 -soft 2,4,8,16,32,64,128,256,512,1024 pmandel
```

specifies a power of two as the number of processes, as some algorithms require.

Two other arguments are directed at the process manager rather than the job scheduler. The `-path` argument tells the process manager where to look for the executable to run, and `-wdir` tells the process manager to set the new process's working directory. This is particularly important if the program is going to perform file I/O. Thus

---

[1]Even specifying the number of processes is optional; it may be taken from an environment variable, or default to one, or be defined in any other way by the implementation.

```
mpiexec -n 10 -path /home/me/mpich/examples \
               -wdir /home/me/logfiles pmandel
```

tells `mpiexec` to look for `pmandel` in `/home/me/mpich/examples` and make `/home/me/logfiles` its working directory while running, presumably because it is going to write some logfiles.

Finally, there is a "catchall" argument, `-file`, to provide any further capabilities the implementation wishes to offer that are not covered by these arguments, such as memory requirements to be given to the job scheduler. The `-file` argument specifies a file name that contains information for `mpiexec` that is specific to each particular implementation of MPI. For example, if we say

```
mpiexec -n pmandel -file hosts pmandel
```

for MPICH, then `mpiexec` will look in file 'hosts' for a list of machines to run on.

D.1   Starting Multiple Executables with `mpiexec`

The `mpiexec` command, as described above, starts the same executable on some number of hosts, with each having the same working directory. Only one set of program arguments can be specified. Since MPI programs need not be SPMD (that is, different processes can be executing different programs), we need a way to start multiple executables. This is also necessary when different processes are executing on different architectures (MPI programs can be heterogeneous). Even if we wish to start all processes with same program, we may want to pass them different arguments. One form of `mpiexec` for these cases uses colons to separate sets of arguments. Thus

```
mpiexec -n 5 ocean : -n 10 atmos
```

starts five copies of `ocean` and ten of `atmos`, and

```
mpiexec fasta infile1 : fasta infile2 : fasta infile3
```

starts three processes running `fasta`, each with a different first argument.

Finally,

```
mpiexec -configfile myfile
```

causes `mpiexec` to look in 'myfile' for the command lines. For example, 'myfile' might contain

```
-n 5 -arch solaris-i86 ocean
-n 10 -arch irix-02 atmos
```

This is needed if the parameters to the commands include colons.

D.2   Another Way for MPI Processes to Start

Sometimes an application may not know until run time that it should be parallel
at all. However, it may be difficult, if not impossible, to start MPI processes
with `mpiexec`. For example, another application may be responsible for deciding
whether this application should "become parallel." For such cases, the MPI-2
Standard recommends (but does not mandate) that any process, no matter how it
is started, be able to *become* an MPI process (with an `MPI_COMM_WORLD` consisting
only of itself) by simply calling `MPI_Init`. Then it could use the functions described
in Chapter 7 to create or attach to other MPI processes. This capability is called
singleton MPI_Init in the Standard (see Section 3.5.2 in [27] and 5.5.2 in [58]).

Why is this feature not a strict requirement in the MPI Standard? The Forum
considered that it would be too great a restriction on implementers to require it.
Most MPI-1 implementations require some sort of MPI "environment" to exist
before even the first process is started. For example, there may need to be a
daemon running on each host where MPI processes are to run. In this case, when
a process not started by the daemon calls `MPI_Init`, it is allowed to fail, but the
Standard encourages that `MPI_Init` itself start the daemon if possible and otherwise
set up the MPI environment. This method may be much slower that starting MPI
programs with either `mpiexec` or `MPI_Comm_spawn`.

References

[1] Jeanne C. Adams, Walter S. Brainerd, Jeanne T. Martin, Brian T. Smith, and Jerrold L. Wagener. *Fortran 95 Handbook*. MIT Press, Cambridge, MA, 1997.

[2] F. Andre, D. Herman, and J.-P. Verjus. *Synchronization of Parallel Programs*. Scientific Computing Series. MIT Press, Cambridge, MA, 1985.

[3] Satish Balay, William D. Gropp, Lois Curfman McInnes, and Barry F. Smith. PETSc home page. http://www.mcs.anl.gov/petsc, 1999.

[4] Sandra Johnson Baylor and C. Eric Wu. Parallel I/O workload characteristics using Vesta. In R. Jain, J. Werth, and J. Browne, editors, *Input/Output in Parallel and Distributed Computer Systems*, chapter 7, pages 167–185. Kluwer Academic Publishers, 1996.

[5] Rajesh Bordawekar, Juan Miguel del Rosario, and Alok Choudhary. Design and evaluation of primitives for parallel I/O. In *Proceedings of Supercomputing '93*, pages 452–461. IEEE Computer Society Press, November 1993.

[6] James Boyle, Ralph Butler, Terrence Disz, Barnett Glickfeld, Ewing Lusk, Ross Overbeek, James Patterson, and Rick Stevens. *Portable Programs for Parallel Processors*. Holt, Rinehart, and Winston, New York, NY, 1987.

[7] Greg Burns, Raja Daoud, and James Vaigl. LAM: An open cluster environment for MPI. In John W. Ross, editor, *Proceedings of Supercomputing Symposium '94*, pages 379–386. University of Toronto, 1994.

[8] Ralph Butler and Ewing Lusk. Monitors, messages, and clusters: The p4 parallel programming system. *Parallel Computing*, 20:547–564, April 1994.

[9] Kenneth Cameron, Lyndon J. Clarke, A. Gordon Smith, and Klaas Jan Wierenga. *Using MPI on the Cray T3D*. Edinburgh Parallel Computing Centre, June 1997. http://www.epcc.ed.ac.uk/t3dmpi/Product/Docs/user/ug-plain.html.

[10] Pei Cao, Edward Felten, Anna Karlin, and Kai Li. Implementation and performance of integrated application-controlled file caching, prefetching, and disk scheduling. *ACM Transactions on Computer Systems*, 14(4):311–343, November 1996.

[11] Bryan Carpenter, Vladimir Getov, Glenn Judd, Tony Skjellum, and Geoffrey Fox. MPI for Java: Position document and draft API specification. Technical Report JGF-TR-03, Java Grande Forum, November 1998. http://www.npac.syr.edu/projects/pcrc/reports/MPIposition/position.ps.

[12] Jaeyoung Choi, Jack J. Dongarra, and David W. Walker. Parallel matrix transpose algorithms on distributed memory concurrent computers. In Anthony Skjellum and Donna S. Reese, editors, *Proceedings of the Scalable Parallel Libraries Conference*, pages 245–252. IEEE Computer Society Press, October 1993.

[13] Alok Choudhary, Rajesh Bordawekar, Michael Harry, Rakesh Krishnaiyer, Ravi Ponnusamy, Tarvinder Singh, and Rajeev Thakur. PASSION: Parallel and scalable software for input-output. Technical Report SCCS–636, NPAC, Syracuse University, September 1994. Also available as CRPC Technical Report CRPC–TR94483–S.

[14] IMPI Steering Committee. IMPI - interoperable message-passing interface, 1998. http://impi.nist.gov/IMPI/.

[15] Peter Corbett, Dror Feitelson, Yarson Hsu, Jean-Pierre Prost, Marc Snir, Sam Fineberg, Bill Nitzberg, Bernard Traversat, and Parkson Wong. MPI-IO: A parallel I/O interface for MPI, version 0.2. Technical Report IBM Research Report RC 19841(87784), IBM T. J. Watson Research Center, November 1994.

[16] Peter F. Corbett and Dror G. Feitelson. The Vesta parallel file system. *ACM Transactions on Computer Systems*, 14(3):225–264, August 1996.

[17] Phyllis E. Crandall, Ruth A. Aydt, Andrew A. Chien, and Daniel A. Reed. Input-output characteristics of scalable parallel applications. In *Proceedings of Supercomputing '95*. ACM Press, December 1995.

[18] Cray Research. *Application Programmer's Library Reference Manual*, 2nd edition, November 1995. Publication SR-2165.

[19] Juan Miguel del Rosario, Rajesh Bordawekar, and Alok Choudhary. Improved parallel I/O via a two-phase run-time access strategy. In *Proceedings of the Workshop on I/O in Parallel Computer Systems at IPPS '93*, pages 56–70, April 1993. Also published in *Computer Architecture News*, 21(5):31–38, December 1993.

[20] Juan Miguel del Rosario and Alok Choudhary. High performance I/O for parallel computers: Problems and prospects. *Computer*, 27(3):59–68, March 1994.

[21] Dror G. Feitelson, Peter F. Corbett, Sandra Johnson Baylor, and Yarson Hsu. Parallel I/O subsystems in massively parallel supercomputers. *IEEE Parallel and Distributed Technology*, 3(3):33–47, Fall 1995.

[22] Samuel A. Fineberg, Parkson Wong, Bill Nitzberg, and Chris Kuszmaul. PMPIO—a portable implementation of MPI-IO. In *Proceedings of the Sixth Symposium on the Frontiers of Massively Parallel Computation*, pages 188–195. IEEE Computer Society Press, October 1996.

[23] Open Software Foundation. *Introduction to OSF/DCE*. Prentice Hall, Englewood Cliffs, NJ, 1992.

[24] Al Geist, Adam Beguelin, Jack Dongarra, Weicheng Jiang, Bob Manchek, and Vaidy Sunderam. *PVM: Parallel Virtual Machine—A User's Guide and Tutorial for Network Parallel Computing*. MIT Press, Cambridge, MA, 1994.

[25] Kourosh Gharachorloo, Daniel Lenoski, James Laudon, Phillip Gibbons, Anoop Gupta, and John Hennessy. Memory consistency and event ordering in scalable shared-memory multiprocessors. *Proceedings of the 17th Annual International Symposium on Computer Architecture, published in ACM SIGARCH*, 18(2):15–26, May 1990.

[26] Garth A. Gibson, Daniel Stodolsky, Pay W. Chang, William V. Courtright II, Chris G. Demetriou, Eka Ginting, Mark Holland, Qingming Ma, LeAnn Neal, R. Hugo Patterson, Jiawen Su, Rachad Youssef, and Jim Zelenka. The Scotch parallel storage systems. In *Proceedings of 40th IEEE Computer Society International Conference (COMPCON 95)*, pages 403–410. IEEE Computer Society Press, Spring 1995.

[27] William Gropp, Steven Huss-Lederman, Andrew Lumsdaine, Ewing Lusk, Bill Nitzberg, William Saphir, and Marc Snir. *MPI—The Complete Reference: Volume 2, The MPI-2 Extensions*. MIT Press, Cambridge, MA, 1998.

[28] William Gropp and Ewing Lusk. Scalable Unix tools on parallel processors. In *Proceedings of the Scalable High-Performance Computing Conference*, pages 56–62. IEEE Computer Society Press, 1994.

[29] William Gropp and Ewing Lusk. Dynamic process management in an MPI setting. In *Proceedings of the Seventh IEEE Symposium on Parallel and Distributed Processing, October 25–28, 1995, San Antonio, Texas*, pages 530–534. IEEE Computer Society Press, 1995.

[30] William Gropp, Ewing Lusk, Nathan Doss, and Anthony Skjellum. A high-performance, portable implementation of the MPI Message-Passing Interface standard. *Parallel Computing*, 22(6):789–828, 1996.

[31] William Gropp, Ewing Lusk, and Anthony Skjellum. *Using MPI: Portable Parallel Programming with the Message Passing Interface*. MIT Press, Cambridge, MA, 1994.

[32] William Gropp, Ewing Lusk, and Anthony Skjellum. *Using MPI: Portable Parallel Programming with the Message Passing Interface,* 2nd edition. MIT Press, Cambridge, MA, 1999.

[33] William Gropp, Ewing Lusk, and Debbie Swider. Improving the performance of MPI derived datatypes. In Anthony Skjellum, Purushotham V. Bangalore, and Yoginder S. Dandass, editors, *Proceedings of the Third MPI Developer's and User's Conference*, pages 25–30. MPI Software Technology Press, 1999.

[34] William D. Gropp. *Users Manual for bfort: Producing Fortran Interfaces to C Source Code*. Mathematics and Computer Science Division, Argonne National Laboratory, March 1995. Technical report ANL/MCS-TM 208.

[35] R. J. Harrison. Portable tools and applications for parallel computers. *Intern. J. Quantum Chem.*, 40(847), 1991.

[36] Rolf Hempel and David W. Walker. The emergence of the MPI message passing standard for parallel computing. *Computer Standards and Interfaces*, 21:51–62, 1999.

[37] Maurice P. Herlihy. Wait-free synchronization. *ACM Transactions on Programming Languages and Systems*, 13(1):124–149, January 1991.

[38] Virginia Herrarte and Ewing Lusk. Studying parallel program behavior with upshot. Technical Report ANL–91/15, Argonne National Laboratory, 1991.

[39] J. M. D. Hill, B. McColl, D. C. Stefanescu, M. W. Goudreau, K. Lang, S. B. Rao, T. Suel, T. Tsantilas, and R. H. Bisseling. BSPlib: The BSP programming library. *Parallel Computing*, 24(14):1947–1980, December 1998.

[40] C. A. R. Hoare. Monitors: An operating system structuring concept. *Comunications of the ACM*, pages 549–557, October 1974.

[41] Jay Huber, Christopher L. Elford, Daniel A. Reed, Andrew A. Chien, and David S. Blumenthal. PPFS: A high performance portable parallel file system. In *Proceedings of the 9th ACM International Conference on Supercomputing*, pages 385–394. ACM Press, July 1995.

[42] IEEE/ANSI Std. 1003.1. Portable operating system interface (POSIX)–part 1: System application program interface (API) [C language], 1996 edition.

[43] Ravi Jain, John Werth, and James C. Browne, editors. *Input/Output in Parallel and Distributed Computer Systems*, volume 362 of *The Kluwer International Series in Engineering and Computer Science*. Kluwer Academic Publishers, 1996.

[44] Jave Grande Forum. http://www.javagrande.org.

[45] Terry Jones, Richard Mark, Jeanne Martin, John May, Elsie Pierce, and Linda Stanberry. An MPI-IO interface to HPSS. In *Proceedings of the Fifth NASA Goddard Conference on Mass Storage Systems*, pages I:37–50, September 1996. Also available from http://esdis-it.gsfc.nasa.gov/MSST/conf1998.html.

[46] Edward Karrels and Ewing Lusk. Performance analysis of MPI programs. In Jack Dongarra and Bernard Tourancheau, editors, *Proceedings of the Workshop on Environments and Tools For Parallel Scientific Computing*, pages 195–200. SIAM Publications, 1994.

[47] Charles H. Koelbel, David B. Loveman, Robert S. Schreiber, Guy L. Steele Jr., and Mary E. Zosel. *The High Performance Fortran Handbook*. MIT Press, Cambridge, MA, 1993.

[48] David Kotz. Disk-directed I/O for MIMD multiprocessors. *ACM Transactions on Computer Systems*, 15(1):41–74, February 1997.

[49] David Kotz and Ravi Jain. I/O in parallel and distributed systems. In Allen Kent and James G. Williams, editors, *Encyclopedia of Computer Science and Technology*, volume 40. Marcel Dekker, Inc., 1999.

[50] Leslie Lamport. How to make a multiprocessor computer that correctly executes multiprocess programs. *IEEE Transactions on Computers*, C-28(9):690–691, September 1979.

[51] David MacKenzie and Ben Elliston. *Autoconf: Creating Automatic Configuration Scripts*. GNU, 2.1.3 edition, December 1998. `http://sourceware.cygnus.com/autoconf/autoconf-toc.html`.

[52] Tara M. Madhyastha and Daniel A. Reed. Exploiting global input/output access pattern classification. In *Proceedings of SC97: High Performance Networking and Computing*. ACM Press, November 1997.

[53] Andrea Malagoli. Personal communication, 1996.

[54] H. Massalin and C. Pu. A lock-free multiprocessor OS kernel. Technical Report CUCS–005–91, Columbia University, 1991.

[55] John May. Parallel Print Function. `http://www.llnl.gov/sccd/lc/ptcprint`.

[56] Message Passing Interface Forum. MPI: A message-passing interface standard. `http://www.mpi-forum.org`.

[57] Message Passing Interface Forum. MPI-2 Journal of Development, 1997. `http://www.mpi-forum.org/docs/mpi-20-jod.ps.Z`.

[58] Message Passing Interface Forum. MPI2: A message passing interface standard. *International Journal of High Performance Computing Applications*, 12(1–2):1–299, 1998.

[59] Message Passing Interface Forum. MPI-2: Extensions to the message-passing interface, July 1997. `http://www.mpi-forum.org/docs/mpi2-report.html`.

[60] Maged M. Michael and Michael L. Scott. Simple, fast, and practical non-blocking and blocking concurrent queue algorithms. In *Proceedings of the 15th Annual ACM Symposium on Principles of Distributed Computing (PODC '96)*, pages 267–275. ACM, May 1996.

[61] MPI/RT Forum. `http://www.mpirt.org`.

[62] J. Nieplocha and R. J. Harrison. Shared memory programming in metacomputing environments: The Global Array approach. *The Journal of Supercomputing*, 11(2):119–136, October 1997.

[63] J. Nieplocha, R. J. Harrison, and R. J. Littlefield. Global Arrays: A portable "shared-memory" programming model for distributed memory computers. In *Proceedings, Supercomputing '94: Washington, DC, November 14–18, 1994*, Supercomputing, pages 340–349. IEEE Computer Society Press, 1994.

[64] Nils Nieuwejaar and David Kotz. The Galley parallel file system. *Parallel Computing*, 23(4):447–476, June 1997.

[65] Nils Nieuwejaar, David Kotz, Apratim Purakayastha, Carla Schlatter Ellis, and Michael Best. File-access characteristics of parallel scientific workloads. *IEEE Transactions on Parallel and Distributed Systems*, 7(10):1075–1089, October 1996.

[66] MPI-2 C++ bindings, 1999. http://www.mpi.nd.edu/research/mpi2c++.

[67] OpenMP Fortran Application Program Interface, Version 1.0. http://www.openmp.org, October 1997.

[68] OpenMP C and C++ Application Program Interface, Version 1.0. http://www.openmp.org, October 1998.

[69] R. Hugo Patterson, Garth A. Gibson, Eka Ginting, Daniel Stodolsky, and Jim Zelenka. Informed prefetching and caching. In *Proceedings of the 15th Symposium on Operating System Principles*, pages 79–95. ACM Press, December 1995.

[70] POV-RAY home page. http://www.povray.org.

[71] Jean-Pierre Prost, Marc Snir, Peter Corbett, and Dror Feitelson. MPI-IO, a message-passing interface for concurrent I/O. Technical Report RC 19712 (87394), IBM T.J. Watson Research Center, August 1994.

[72] Real-Time Message Passing Interface (MPI/RT) Forum. Document for the real-time Message Passing Interface (MPI/RT-1.0) draft standard. http://www.mpirt.org/drafts.html, June 1999.

[73] K. Seamons, Y. Chen, P. Jones, J. Jozwiak, and M. Winslett. Server-directed collective I/O in Panda. In *Proceedings of Supercomputing '95*. ACM Press, December 1995.

[74] Kent E. Seamons. *Panda: Fast Access to Persistent Arrays Using High Level Interfaces and Server Directed Input/Output*. PhD thesis, University of Illinois at Urbana-Champaign, May 1996.

[75] Gautam Shah, Jarek Nieplocha, Jamshed Mirza, Chulho Kim, Robert Harrison, Rama K. Govindaraju, Kevin Gildea, Paul DiNicola, and Carl Bender. Performance and experience with LAPI—a new high-performance communication library for the IBM RS/6000 SP. In *Proceedings of the 1st Merged International Parallel Processing Symposium and Symposium on Parallel and Distributed Processing (IPPS/SPDP-98)*, pages 260–266. IEEE Computer Society, March 30–April 3 1998.

[76] D. B. Skillicorn, Jonathan M. D. Hill, and W. F. McColl. Questions and answers about BSP. Technical Report PRG-TR-15-96, Oxford University Computing Laboratory, 1996.

[77] E. Smirni and D. A. Reed. Lessons from characterizing the input/output behavior of parallel scientific applications. *Performance Evaluation: An International Journal*, 33(1):27–44, June 1998.

[78] Evgenia Smirni, Ruth A. Aydt, Andrew A. Chien, and Daniel A. Reed. I/O requirements of scientific applications: An evolutionary view. In *Proceedings of the Fifth IEEE International Symposium on High Performance Distributed Computing*, pages 49–59. IEEE Computer Society Press, 1996.

[79] Marc Snir, Steve W. Otto, Steven Huss-Lederman, David W. Walker, and Jack Dongarra. *MPI—The Complete Reference: Volume 1, The MPI Core,* 2nd edition. MIT Press, Cambridge, MA, 1998.

[80] Jeffrey M. Squyres, Brian C. McCandless, and Andrew Lumsdaine. Object oriented MPI: A class library for the message passing interface. In *Parallel Object-Oriented Methods and Applications (POOMA '96)*, Santa Fe, 1996.

[81] W. Richard Stevens. *Unix Network Programming: Networking APIs: Sockets and XTI,* volume 1. Prentice Hall, Englewood Cliffs, NJ, 2nd edition, 1998.

[82] Rajeev Thakur and Alok Choudhary. An extended two-phase method for accessing sections of out-of-core arrays. *Scientific Programming*, 5(4):301–317, Winter 1996.

[83] Rajeev Thakur, Alok Choudhary, Rajesh Bordawekar, Sachin More, and Sivaramakrishna Kuditipudi. Passion: Optimized I/O for parallel applications. *Computer*, 29(6):70–78, June 1996.

[84] Rajeev Thakur, William Gropp, and Ewing Lusk. An abstract-device interface for implementing portable parallel-I/O interfaces. In *Proceedings of the 6th Symposium on the Frontiers of Massively Parallel Computation*, pages 180–187. IEEE Computer Society Press, October 1996.

[85] Rajeev Thakur, William Gropp, and Ewing Lusk. An experimental evaluation of the parallel I/O systems of the IBM SP and Intel Paragon using a production application. In *Proceedings of the 3rd International Conference of the Austrian Center for Parallel Computation (ACPC) with Special Emphasis on Parallel Databases and Parallel I/O*, pages 24–35. Lecture Notes in Computer Science 1127. Springer-Verlag, September 1996.

[86] Rajeev Thakur, William Gropp, and Ewing Lusk. A case for using MPI's derived datatypes to improve I/O performance. In *Proceedings of SC98: High Performance Networking and Computing*, November 1998.

[87] Rajeev Thakur, William Gropp, and Ewing Lusk. Data sieving and collective I/O in ROMIO. In *Proceedings of the 7th Symposium on the Frontiers of Massively Parallel Computation*, pages 182–189. IEEE Computer Society Press, February 1999.

[88] Rajeev Thakur, William Gropp, and Ewing Lusk. On implementing MPI-IO portably and with high performance. In *Proceedings of the 6th Workshop on I/O in Parallel and Distributed Systems*, pages 23–32. ACM Press, May 1999.

[89] Rajeev Thakur, Ewing Lusk, and William Gropp. Users guide for ROMIO: A high-performance, portable MPI-IO implementation. Technical Report ANL/MCS-TM-234, Mathematics and Computer Science Division, Argonne National Laboratory, Revised July 1998.

[90] The MPI-IO Committee. MPI-IO: A parallel file I/O interface for MPI, version 0.5, April 1996. http://parallel.nas.nasa.gov/MPI-IO.

[91] Richard Treumann. Experiences in the implementation of a thread safe, threads based MPI for the IBM RS/6000 SP, 1998. http://www.research.ibm.com/actc/Tools/MPI_Threads.htm.

[92] L. G. Valiant. A bridging model for parallel computations. *Communications of the ACM*, 33(8):103–111, August 1990.

[93] John D. Valois. Lock-free linked lists using compare-and-swap. In *Proceedings of the Four-teenth Annual ACM Symposium on Principles of Distributed Computing*, pages 214–222, Ottawa, Ontario, Canada, August 1995.

[94] Robert A. van de Geijn. *Using PLAPACK: Parallel Linear Algebra Package*. MIT Press, Cambridge, MA, 1997.

[95] VI Architecture. http://www.viarch.org.

[96] Thorsten von Eicken, Anindya Basu, Vineet Buch, and Werner Vogels and. U-Net: A user-level network interface for parallel and distributed computing. In *Proceedings of the 15th ACM Symposium on Operating Systems Principles (SOSP)*, pages 40–53. ACM Press, December 1995.

Subject Index

Function and Term Index